YOU AND YOUR Nonprofit

Practical Advice and Tips from the CharityChannel Professional Community

Edited by:

Norman Olshansky

Linda Lysakowski, ACFRE

YOU AND YOUR Nonprofit

Practical Advice and Tips from the CharityChannel Professional Community

You and Your Nonprofit: Practical Advice and Tips from the CharityChannel Professional Community
One of the **In the Trenches**™ series
Published by
CharityChannel Press, an imprint of CharityChannel LLC
30021 Tomas, Suite 300
Rancho Santa Margarita, CA 92688-2128 USA
http://charitychannel.com

ISBN: 978-0-9841580-4-1
Library of Congress Control Number: 2011929675

13 12 11 10 9 8 7 6 5 4 3 2 1

Printed in the United States of America

This and most CharityChannel Press books are available at special quantity discounts for bulk purchases for sales promotions, premiums, fundraising, or educational use. For information, contact CharityChannel Press, 30021 Tomas, Suite 300, Rancho Santa Margarita, CA 92688-2128 USA. +1 949-589-5938

About the Editors

Linda Lysakowski, ACFRE

Linda is President/CEO of Capital Venture, a full service consulting firm. She is one of fewer than 100 professionals worldwide to hold the Advanced Certified Fund Raising Executive designation. In her eighteen years as a philanthropic consultant, Linda has managed capital campaigns; helped hundreds of nonprofit organizations achieve their development goals, and has trained more than 20,000 professionals in all aspects of development in Canada, Mexico, Egypt and most of the fifty United States.

Linda has received the Outstanding Fundraising Executive award from both the Eastern PA and the Las Vegas chapters of AFP (Association of Fundraising Professionals) and in 2006 was recognized internationally with the Barbara Marion Award for Outstanding Service to AFP.

Linda is a graduate of AFP's Faculty Training Academy and has served in numerous leadership roles for AFP. She is a frequent presenter at regional and international conferences and has received two AFP research grants. Linda is the author of *Recruiting and Training Fundraising Volunteers*, *The Development Plan*, contributing author to *The Fundraising Feasibility Study—It's Not About the Money*, and co-author of *The Essential Nonprofit Fundraising Handbook*. She has three books published by CharityChannel Press, *Fundraising as a Career: What, Are You Crazy?*, *Capital Campaigns: Everything You Need to Know*, and *The Genius's Guide to Fundraising*. She is currently working on a book on corporate philanthropy.

 Connect with Linda at http://charitychannel.com/cc/linda-lysakowski

Norman Olshansky

Norman serves as president and CEO of the Van Wezel Foundation, based in Sarasota, Florida. Previously he was president of NFP Consulting Resources. His consulting practice focused on planning and onsite counsel/direction for multi organization collaborative capital campaigns for nonprofit organizations. He has over thirty years of professional and executive level leadership and consulting experience within both the nonprofit and for-profit sectors. His clients have included both large and small service, health, cultural and faith-based organizations ranging from local and national health care companies, to military and law enforcement agencies. He has consulted for nonprofit entities throughout the U.S., Canada and Israel.

Norman has a master's degree in social work, and has received national recognition for his work in human service and executive leadership. For many years he served in executive level positions with Jewish communal organizations. He is an active member of the Association of Fundraising Professionals and was named Social Worker of the Year by the Oakland County, Michigan Chapter of the National Association of Social Workers. A frequent lecturer at universities, he has also published a syndicated column, is a national book reviewer and leader for CharityChannel, and is active as a volunteer in several civic, religious and professional organizations.

 Connect with Norman at http://charitychannel.com/cc/norman-olshansky

Dedication

This book is dedicated to all of the special volunteers and staff who give of their time, resources and expertise towards helping others through their work within the nonprofit sector. We especially want to thank the many people who have personally impacted our lives and who helped us learn the art and science of nonprofit management, leadership and fundraising.

Getting the Most Out of this Book!

The articles you are about to read cover a variety of subjects. Our book is more than just an anthology. It is not organized into chapters or by specific subjects. You will learn about planning issues in articles about governance, fundraising, administration and marketing. You will learn about leadership and other topics in many of the articles. Our goal is for you to enjoy reading about nonprofit management, leadership and fundraising and in the process learn ways to add value to your own work as someone who is, or will be, engaged in the nonprofit sector. So relax, scan, read, take notes, underline or challenge what you are about to read. We encourage you to give feedback to the contributors. If you have questions or find their articles to be especially helpful, do let them know. To help you connect with the contributors, at the end of each article we provide the URL to the contributor's CharityChannel page. This book has been written for YOU!

Contents

Foreword

It has been my privilege to spend many decades in the business of charitable fundraising, nonprofit management, governance and just about all related topical areas. It has been an incredible journey.

I am compelled today to tell you that I have just read the book I needed when I made the decision to try the business of fundraising decades ago.

Those decades have consisted of vast accumulated experiences with some good and of course, some otherwise. Overall, I have gained a wealth of knowledge from colleagues and friends and of course by trial and error. I could never repay my teachers' kindnesses in making available their stories, experiences and wise counsel to me as a beginner. So my friends are helping me to repay those favors by publishing this practical collection titled *You and Your Nonprofit* which is largely focused to serve the novice, such as I was years ago.

I have known the co-editors and major contributors to this collection for many years. I have observed their work from a distance at times and at times from very close up and always found each to be the consummate professional insistently pushing for the best in themselves as well as pushing the rest of us to improve and help our charities/clients even more. Linda Lysakowski and Norm Olshansky are two professional fundraisers now making their expertise available not only to their clients and employers, but to the rest of the world. And they are joined by more than forty-one others who likewise are willing to share freely their skills, experiences and wisdom. It is a remarkable collection.

From the opening of this collection with a very in-depth review of governance/leadership related topics, including titles such as "Who Owns You?," "Won't Someone Please Be Our President?," and the like, to essays and descriptions like, "The Importance of Branding for Your Nonprofit," "Managing Your Development Office," "Major and Planned Gifts" and all kinds of tips and advice for better grant writing success; this book is loaded with excellent advice and counsel as to "why & why not" and "what" and "how to." It is perhaps that last phrase that sets this apart from other texts which many of us accept as Holy Grail of fundraising such as Sy Seymour's treatise, "Designs for Fundraising" and Hank Russo's amazing third edition treatment of the profession in "Achieving Excellence in Fundraising." These are great books yet very different in approach with both using more singularly focused and academically authored approaches.

A large part of the attraction of *You and Your Nonprofit* is the somewhat eclectic collection of authors with two seasoned fundraising editors, each adding content and a guiding hand in the selection of the included articles. That selection is significant because of its high relevance to current needs in fundraising and nonprofit management and governance. They have pointedly included the authors' challenges to what have been the norms or standards for many years. This combination makes this piece usable today as well as for planning tomorrow.

In fact, this is the work that a relative unseasoned professional can take home and apply to some portion of their work the next day, week or month. It is just that practical and relevant. One need not read through these pages from start to end, but rather one can select those areas of interest and immediately focus on the solutions most suitable to that day's dilemmas and ponderings.

As we emerge from perhaps the greatest global recession since the great depression, the demand for highly motivated and skilled professional fundraisers is great. Nonprofit organizations of every kind and size are searching for the best structures and staffing to assure revenue flows are available to support the increased needs of their agencies and institutions. The education and training of good professional fundraisers will be of continuing importance if we are to meet the demands before us in this growing sector.

Fundraisers, volunteers, CEOs, and all who care about this sector's capacity to meet the needs and seize opportunities to benefit our communities, nation and world should have this collection on their desks for handy reference and guidance.

This is surely the book I wish I had decades ago.

Bob Carter, CFRE
Board Chair Elect, Association of Fundraising Professionals
Board Member, The Center for Philanthropy at Indiana University
Principal, Of Counsel Philanthropy

 Connect with Bob at http://charitychannel.com/cc/bob-carter

Preface

For almost two decades CharityChannel has been a pioneer within the nonprofit sector, using online technology, networking, articles, conferences, and forums to connect professionals and volunteers alike from around the globe. We got involved with CharityChannel early in its development.

Both of us have learned, shared and grown professionally as a result of our involvement with CharityChannel. So, when Stephen Nill, founder of CharityChannel, approached us to edit a book that would serve the nonprofit community, we felt that it was our turn to give back.

Our goal was to focus on readers who are relatively new to the nonprofit sector. We asked our authors to write for readers (professionals, leaders and volunteers) who have been in the field for less than ten years. We wanted readers to find the articles not only informative and interesting, but also practical examples of best practices.

We wanted our readers to be able to take ideas and suggestions from the articles and be able to implement them within their own organizations.

We wanted to create a book that would be more than just an anthology of essays, but, rather, a series of articles written by professionals who have real life experience and have been in the trenches of nonprofit work.

This is not an all-inclusive book on nonprofit leadership, management and fundraising, but rather a small sample. The articles are not presented in a particular sequence. Each stands alone as an expression of the experiences, views and expertise of the authors. These articles should not be used as a source for legal or tax advice. As always, consult with a legal or tax professional for more definitive responses to your questions.

We are most grateful to those who have generously given of their time and talents. They have responded in a very positive way to our invitation to submit articles for consideration. Our colleagues have demonstrated again to us how generous, passionate and giving they are to each other and to the profession. Check out their short biographies in Appendix B, and, if you are so moved, visit their CharityChannel pages and drop them a note—we provide their CharityChannel URLs along with their bios. We also were thrilled to have the involvement of our expert advisory panel, listed in Appendix A. They gave invaluable input to us as part of our review of each article that was submitted and the content that ultimately found its way into our book.

We also want to extend our appreciation to the many professionals who contributed articles which were not selected for inclusion. We received many more articles than we could include in this book. We hope that those articles will find their way into other publications.

We believe that all of the articles have content that will be helpful to readers. There are a few authors who have expressed opinions or suggestions about which you might not fully agree. In a few cases, neither did we. However, we believe that the business of nonprofit management, leadership and fundraising is constantly improving because people like our authors (and hopefully you) are willing to challenge conventional wisdom and think outside of the box. Read these articles with an open mind. Feel free to accept or reject the suggestions made. We are confident that within these pages you will find ideas, examples, tips and suggestions that you will find helpful. We want this book to add value to your work in the nonprofit sector. You will not find every article to be helpful to you but we hope you will find special gems that will assist you in the work you do in serving your organization, your community and the overall nonprofit sector.

We especially want to thank Stephen Nill, CharityChannel Press, and our expert editorial advisory panel who assisted us throughout the process of producing this book.

Most of all, we thank you, our readers for the contributions you have and will make in your own communities.

     Norm Olshansky   **Linda Lysakowski, ACFRE**

Section I—Getting Your Act Together

Who Owns You?

By Caroline Oliver

In setting out the "Policy Governance" approach in *Boards That Make a Difference* (currently in its third edition), John Carver introduced the concept of ownership to the nonprofit sector. In my experience, the significance of this concept is often not fully appreciated for what it is—the fundamental starting point for good governance under any model. It is also my belief that lack of an appreciation of the importance of ownership is at the root of many nonprofits' board governance problems, and certainly, without such an appreciation, the full value of Policy Governance can never be grasped. Nonprofits that do not embrace the concept of "ownership" often think instead of "stakeholders." Let us uncover what lies behind these two concepts.

Typically, the term "stakeholders" is used to include anyone and everyone that has a "stake" in how well the organization does. In most cases this includes clients, employees, suppliers and funders. The Policy Governance definition of "ownership" does not automatically include any of these groups. Clients are the beneficiaries of the work of the organization—and, except in the case of membership associations, not necessarily the same people as the owners of the organization. Employees, suppliers and funders are contractors with the organization and, unlike owners, except in the case of cooperatives, have no automatic legal or moral hold over the organization beyond the terms of their contract.

The entire Policy Governance approach starts from the principle that a board's authority to govern an organization comes exclusively from the organization's owners (subject only to the legal framework established by the state on behalf of the public at large) and the board's accountability for the use of that authority is back to owners. This is why the board's job is unique—no one else, including the CEO, has this

> "Ownership" is not a concept that nonprofits embrace easily—sounds much too "corporate," "not us," and "doesn't help anyway." I ask you to reconsider.

 practical tip

direct link to owners. It follows that a board cannot even begin to govern until it knows who its owners are. It is impossible to act on behalf of others if you have no idea what their interests and concerns are.

A local branch of the United Way, for example, would be an entirely different organization if it considered itself to be owned by donors, by beneficiaries, by the local nonprofit community, or by "everyone concerned with the development of local philanthropy." Donors might want an organization that focused on giving donors the widest possible range of choices for allocating their money together with assurance that their money was being well-spent and reasonable acknowledgement of their generosity. Beneficiaries might want an organization that focused on identifying need and stimulating as much giving as possible from as many donors as possible. The nonprofit community might want an organization that focused on raising money with as few strings attached as possible to cover their common "difficult to fund" needs such as those for training, economic office space and administration. "Everyone concerned with the development of local philanthropy" might want the organization to focus on establishing a culture of giving through school- and community-wide programs. Different owners create different organizations.

So who owns your organization? Clearly, your legal owners are those who have the right to vote the board in or out, but subject only to these people's agreement, the board is free to interpret "ownership" more broadly. Discovering your moral ownership requires uncovering those whose interest in the organization goes beyond their own immediate personal self-interest and towards the longer-term interests of your organization as a vehicle for providing benefit for themselves and others for the foreseeable future. Some or all of these owners might also be customers or funders or employees or suppliers, but the board's job is to respond to their ownership interest rather any other interest they might have.

It might sound heretical to say it, but although customer/client/user focus is a vital thing for staff, it is highly dangerous for boards. Witness the sad spectacle of boards at the mercy of "customers." School board trustees and counselors know what it is like to be constantly besieged by conflicting individual interests. Good governance comes not from board members individually reacting to the demands of customers and trying to commandeer the board to fulfill those demands, but from board members together, on the basis of their collective knowledge, considering the best interests of all. In another example of the folly arising from an inadequate grasp of the board's ownership obligation, witness the nonprofits who drift away from their founding principles as they follow the lure of funding.

The notion of ownership thus:

> ◆ legitimizes a board's authority;

> ◆ clarifies a board's accountability;

◆ unifies board members in common cause;

◆ provides a touchstone for making difficult board choices;

◆ helps distinguish the board's role from the CEO/staff's role; and

◆ enables a board to insulate itself from pressures that could divert it from achieving its goals on behalf of all those to whom they are properly accountable.

So, how can you as a member of the board or executive staff help your board to understand and use the concept of ownership to establish its unique role as owner-representative?

Help Your Board See the Importance of Ownership

This exercise or a variation of it will help to distinguish the difference between customers/ clients and owners. Ask board members to put themselves in the shoes of a customer of your organization and to write down five things that they would like to say to your organization from their personal interests as a customer. Then tell them that they no longer qualify as customers but, by some strange quirk of fate, they have become owners of the organization. Now ask them, bearing in mind that they will never directly benefit from the organization, to write down five things they would like to talk to the organization about. Compile a list of everyone's customer issues and a separate list of everyone's owner issues. Now ask everyone to contrast and compare the lists and consider what would happen if the board tried to run things from the customer list versus the owner list.

This exercise or a variation of it will help to illustrate the fundamental importance of knowing who your owners are. Identify a few alternative options for who your owners might be. Now divide your board into small sub-groups, one sub-group to represent each option. Now ask each sub-group to come up with a proposition as to whose lives your organization should seek to impact and what that impact should be. Give each sub-group thirty minutes or so to come up with their proposition and then ask each sub-group to present their proposition to the full group.

Help Your Board Identify its Owners

Determining your board's ownership is very often a matter of the board's judgment with no one "right answer." Your legal owners will generally be clear for they are the people who have the right to hire and fire your board (i.e. these persons are usually those who have the right to vote at your annual meeting which might mean just your board members or some form of wider membership). However, whatever the legal position, your board can still determine its moral ownership more widely.

Here are some questions that could help your board identify its owners. Answering the first question will tell you who your legal owners are. Answering the next five questions might cause you to consider the possibility of holding yourselves accountable to a wider moral ownership.

◆ Who has the legal right to hire and fire us as a board?

◆ What was the motivation of our founders and where does that motivation live on today?

◆ Who cares for our organization's value beyond their own personal use of it?

◆ If our organization were to fail, who would recreate it?

◆ Who do we believe has the moral right to determine our overall purpose?

Help Your Board Think and Act as Owner-Representative

Once your board has identified its owners, it needs to work out how it is going to connect with them. It can do this "attitudinally," i.e. by deliberately trying to think in their shoes; or "statistically," i.e. by surveying them; or, "personally," i.e. by meeting with them. But whichever method, or methods, your board chooses; the important thing is that the board genuinely attempts to understand its owners' wishes sufficiently to be able to translate them into a clear and wise mandate for your organization. A clear mandate is one that is written and regularly monitored in order to provide accountability back to owners. A wise mandate is one that has the organization producing what owners want it to produce in a prudent, ethical and therefore sustainable manner.

To summarize, in order to do its job properly, it is vital that a board knows to whose tune it should rightfully dance. A board that is not clear about the source of its mandate will flounder and when the board flounders, the whole organization usually flounders too (or unduly relies upon its CEO for its overall direction). To be successful, an organization needs to know where it is going and why, and it all starts with the board and its grasp of the concept of ownership.

Note: Policy Governance® is an internationally registered service mark of John Carver. Registration is only to ensure accurate description of the model rather than for financial gain. The model is available free to all with no royalties or license fees for its use. The authoritative website for Policy Governance is www.carvergovernance.com.

 Connect with Caroline at http://charitychannel.com/cc/caroline-oliver

All "A-Board!"

By Heather Burton

Executive directors, staff members, and volunteers want it. You and I want it. Everybody wants it.

The dream board.

And oh, the places we'd go with that dream board! We'd have the most beautiful vision and a clear strategy for achieving it. We'd raise all the money we need, serve all the clients in need, and make the world a beautiful, safe place.

If only the world was that perfect! Alas, it's not.

But, there are ways to move closer to that utopia. In my experience, it's about understanding not only the long-term vision, but also the current reality and the gaps between the two, and then setting the right priorities at the right time to begin closing those gaps.

I'm hoping this article provides insight into how you can re-energize and transform your board in a way that brings your organization into the next phase of its evolution.

Organizational Life Cycles and the Board

Like people, organizations experience life cycles. From start-up to adolescence, mature to decline, it's important to understand where your organization is and, therefore, where the board should be.

Understanding your stage in the life cycle is a critical step in setting the right expectations, aiding in recruitment, engagement, and priority setting. If the gap between *expectation* and *reality* is too large, then board members will disengage as the goals seem unachievable.

Use this table to see where you might fall, both as an organization and as a board. Are you expecting a mature board, yet you are more in start-up mode?

Mode	Organization	Board
Start-Up	Establish programs, secure funding, and prove viability	Hands-on, operational, focused on mission/program delivery
Adolescence	Additional paid staff, grow community awareness	Less day-to-day, various committees formed to fill staffing gaps
Mature	Strategic growth, improved operations, diverse funding	Shift to governance/strategy focus. Fundraising and board recruitment become priority
Decline	Shift in community needs, loss of funding, lack of strategy/vision	Disengaged board or disagreement on organizational future, high-turn over

An organization might go through this cycle repeatedly as it evolves. Additionally, the age of the organization does not dictate where it will fall in the life cycle. For example, when organizations merge to form a new nonprofit, the new organization will sometimes move back into start-up mode.

If your board is in decline, don't think that it's over! Perhaps your organization simply needs to enter a new phase or strategy, with a new board, to begin the cycle again.

Creating Sustainable Change Starts with the Right Leadership

No matter at what stage you are in your life cycle, you can be sure that your board dynamics will be constantly evolving. How do you ensure that the board is making forward progress and has momentum? It starts with the right board leadership.

Think back to a time where you were inspired by a former boss, or even your boss's boss. Did you work a little harder? Trust the decisions a little more? Feel comfortable with tension? Understand your priorities and where you stood with the organization? Feel valued and important?

This is exactly what leaders do. They lead. They inspire and create momentum. They build trust. They build relationships, and play to people's strengths and interests rather than their weaknesses.

Leading a board is no different. Board members need leadership, both in their executive team and in their executive director. Prospective board members are first attracted to the organization because of its mission, but agree to serve in part because of their confidence in the leadership.

What actions can you take to help ensure the board has the right leadership?

First, start cultivating the next set of officers as soon as the new officers are voted into office. This activity is often referred to as succession planning, and it both ensures smooth transitions and helps sustain momentum.

Second, identify people whom you believe can manage to the life stage of your organization. Do you need leaders who can role model "rolling up the sleeves," or do you need leaders who can facilitate discussion around strategic direction?

Third, look for these characteristics (or the potential for these characteristics) as you build your board and your leadership team.

◆ *Inspirational:* They can set the tone and set an example.

◆ *Balanced: They can balance the short-term vs. long-term needs and decisions.*

◆ *Focused:* They can establish priority, shifting directions only when necessary. I call this "appropriate reactiveness."

◆ *Facilitative:* They are comfortable with tension, willing to challenge and be challenged, and bring the board to common decisions.

◆ *Accountable:* They do what they say they will do, and serve as a positive spokesperson for the organization.

I know that this is easier said than done. Trust me, I've been there. Keep in mind that every incremental positive change you and the board makes in bringing the right leadership teams together can bring about massive transformation within the organization.

Growing Pains

It can be very difficult for a board to move from one stage to another. Why? Because, people are recruited to help meet an organization's needs at a particular time. In start-up mode, you need a board willing to be part of the day-to-day execution. Often, it's hard for these same people to step away from the operations and into a governance role. This is why board terms and rotation are an important component of a board's health.

Leadership

What is usually referred to as board leadership, or the board executive team, is the officers of the board. This team typically includes the president (or chair), vice-president (or president-elect, or vice-chair), treasurer, secretary, and often a past board president. While all members have influence over the culture of the board, the elected officers are responsible for leading the board through transition, growth, and sometimes, decline.

On-boarding Board Members

Developing the right leadership culture starts with the right recruitment. I hear time and time again that board recruitment, engagement, and continuity is a challenge. There is one thing you can do *this year* to improve these three areas: establish an official on-boarding process.

Often, board members are willing to move prospective members to voting members relatively quickly. Members raise their hand and are passionate about the cause, so we vote them in. But, in doing this, we often do a great disservice to both the new board member and the organization.

We expect board members to dive right in—and some do—but it often takes time for a person to understand where they can add value and meld with the existing board. A proper on-boarding process extends the courtship and solidifies the commitment of the incoming board member.

The chart "Sample On-Boarding Process" provides an example on-boarding process. Most organizations have a prospect fill out an application and attend only one or two board meetings. Extending the process to include visiting programs, aligning with a board committee, making a financial pledge, and even aligning with a board "buddy" or mentor allows the prospect to really start to assimilate with the organization.

It is not until the prospect completes all the criteria that they can be voted in for the board.

Sample On-Boarding Process

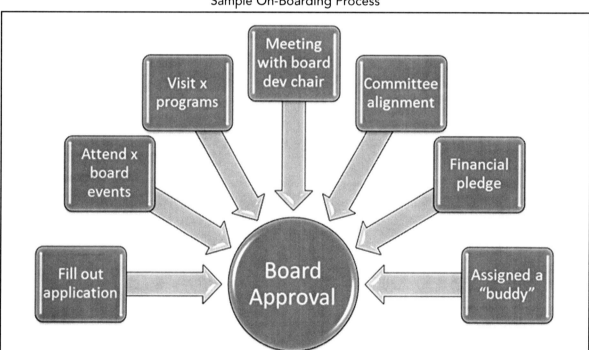

What if a prospect doesn't make it through the on-boarding process? Well, that is not a bad outcome. If a prospect is not willing to go through the process to become a board member, then what is the chance they will fully engage once they are a board member? It's probably not good.

An official on-boarding process can also bring credibility to the organization. It shows prospects that you are serious about finding the right board members, not just anyone with a pulse. It attracts professionals who understand the value of the "get to know me, get to know you" period before entering into an official engagement.

It also allows board members to get to know the newer members; therefore, giving them the ability to vote with knowledge, rather than just because "Tammy said she'd make a good member."

You wouldn't jump into a marriage without a courtship. Why would you expect a new board member to be a contributing asset without understanding the relationship dynamics? Establish an on-boarding process, and then follow it for the next twelve months and see what a difference it brings to your board.

The Right Roles for the Right People

I would be remiss if I didn't mention that board engagement truly comes when you have the right roles for the right people. No matter how passionate your members are, they are still *volunteers*.

Volunteers want a chance to network and use their skills for good. However, sometimes what I do for my "day job" is not at all what I want to do for an organization with which I volunteer. This causes an interesting tension, and it is very important to recognize it.

By allowing board members to choose areas in which to participate, rather than assigning them to roles where they have the most expertise, you are actually creating greater engagement. These are often growth areas for members, as they look to build additional skills and experience they might not be able to build through their employers. Likewise, the organization benefits from an eager, energetic, "fresh" member who will put in the extra effort.

For any role, maximum output comes from having a defined job, clear outcomes, and a timeframe to work within. Members need guidance in order to get the job done well, and also need to be reassured that their role doesn't carry on into infinity.

Finally, one of the most difficult situations is when a board member is not performing to expectations, as in this example.

Re-Aligning Roles

Carol and Janice have been working together on the board of Great Leaps for more than two years. Janice has offered to lead a new board committee focused on offering free day trips to local museums to the families they serve. This is a pilot project to determine both program and financial feasibility.

Janice's first task is to set committee meetings and to recruit a team of volunteers and board members to help. It's been three months, and no forward progress has been made.

Whenever Janice is asked about the program, she apologizes, professes her commitment, and promises to get started right away. Other board members and the executive director are starting to get frustrated, as this project has been identified as important for the coming year. Carol, as board president, is asked to have a conversation with Janice.

Carol sets up a lunch meeting with Janice and prepares for the conversation. Rather than start in with the business at hand, Carol asks how Janice and her family are doing. To Carol's surprise, Janice confides in Carol that her sister-in-law has cancer, and that all the family is chipping in to help with the care of her brother's young children.

The time and attention devoted to her brother's family, plus her full-time job and her own children, have left Janice with little time for Great Leaps.

Janice wants to help, but is coming to the realization that leading the team is not feasible right now. She also mentions that she really didn't want to lead the team in the first place; she only wanted to help identify the activities and contact the groups to see about free passes.

Carol learned two very important things at this lunch meeting. First, some major family issues are understandably shifting Janice's focus away from Great Leaps. Second, because Carol was able to frame the conversation as one of concern rather than judgment, she was able to learn that Janice never wanted to lead the committee in the first place.

It's important to not only be aware of your board members' desires, but also to be empathetic when situations arise that take priority over the organization. Setting proper expectations from the start can help when a difficult conversation needs to happen, or when another member needs to step in and take over. Just remember to be willing and ready to make changes based on your volunteers/board members' readiness levels, not just your own desires!

Recognize, Reward, and Facilitate

To all nonprofit staff out there, please make it easy for the board to do their jobs. The value you get from the board should not be in administrative tasks, such as taking notes at board meetings (have a staff person attend who can take the raw notes), but in the doors they can open, talent they can contribute, and leadership they can bring.

Recognition and reward go a long way—after all, it's human dynamics 101. Most everyone wants to feel valued and to do good work. The more you and other board members can reward and recognize each other, the more each member will continue to rise to the occasion.

Remember, transformation takes time. Trying to fix everything at once is a recipe for failure. Focus on one or two areas that will improve your board in the next twelve months, and keep those goals front and center. It can be time-consuming and frustrating, but every small step forward can result in great transformation, and that dream board of which everyone wants to be part!

Tough Conversations

This is a critical conversation, and one that is not easy for everyone to have. When you look at board leaders, identify people who can deal objectively, as well as compassionately, with board members who are not meeting expectations. This is no different than a performance conversation you would have with an employee. It just feels different, because board members are volunteers with lives, families, and jobs that often take priority over any volunteer duties.

If done correctly, as in Carol's and Janice's case, the results can be very positive for everyone involved.

 Connect with Heather at http://charitychannel.com/cc/heather-burton

Are Your Board Members N.I.C.E.?

By Lynne T. Dean, CFRE

How can I get my board more involved in fundraising? When I ask nonprofit leaders to share their most daunting challenges, they frequently regale me with sagas of boards with amazing passion for the organization but yet an unexplainable inability or even lack of will to transform that passion into fundraising.

Because I've heard that same answer so often, I've developed an array of suggestions, strategies and techniques to help organizations and board members overcome what many refer to as the "fear of fundraising." While the idea of fundraising can send shivers up the spine of some of the most experienced board members and a few executive directors as well, I contend that the real dilemma for many of those most fearful is that they don't understand that fundraising is much, much more than asking for the gift. And that yes, they can succeed at fundraising.

Board Members as Community Connectors

Prior to delving further into various aspects of fundraising, let's explore briefly the important role of board members as the connection between the nonprofit organization and the community. That role works both ways—the board represents the organization in the community and represents the community's interest in ensuring the organization is meeting the community's needs. If board members take this role seriously, the community is always aware of the importance of the nonprofit to the community and of the need to support it with volunteers and funds.

So, let's say that you have board members who understand their role as community connectors, but they still tremble at the thought of fundraising. At this point, we suggest to nonprofit organizations that they ask board members to be N.I.C.E. I developed this acronym to pinpoint a few areas in which board members can provide valuable assistance and to illustrate some of the various facets of fundraising which don't involve face-to-face solicitation. N.I.C.E. stands for Naming, Identifying, Cultivating and Engaging. Note, I did not say asking or soliciting.

Naming

When board members begin getting serious about learning more about fundraising or perhaps tackling a significant annual giving or major gifts initiative, the logical place to start is to compile prospect lists. Most organizations ask board members to complete an individual profile that includes their professional and community associations and activities in addition to personal and business contact information. By ensuring that you have obtained similar information from your board members, you'll have valuable information for developing lists of prospective donors and identifying connections between your organization and prospects.

Next, encourage them to think about who might be interested in your organization. To start that activity, we provide a one-page potential donor chart for each board member to fill out and return. The chart is divided into categories such as accountant, banker, attorney, insurance agent, doctor, fellow worshippers, realtor and several more. The chart includes columns for contact information (name, address, city, state, zip, phone and email), a place to check if the individual named has major gift potential and another column in which the board member is asked to indicate whether he or she would be willing to contact that person on behalf of the organization.

Identifying

Yes, naming and identifying potential donors represent two distinct areas in which board members can be particularly helpful. You are ready to begin the identification process when board members have assembled a list of prospects and contact information. Identification, sometimes referred to as rating and screening, involves evaluating potential donors in three areas: capacity, inclination and linkage and can be done in groups or by individuals with a trustworthy representative of the organization responsible for compiling the results.

As you determine the capacity of a prospect, ask yourself these questions: what do you think this donor can give; what is their income, what investments do they have and what assets do they hold; and what are their financial obligations such as a commitment to a large gift to another organization or perhaps a business debt.

In evaluating inclination, you will consider the generosity of the donor and how involved he or she is in civic activities. Questions to answer include whether or not the donors give to charitable organizations and are they involved with organizations which have a similar mission to yours; do they have interests and hobbies in line with your mission and programs; and have they been volunteers or served on the boards of organizations similar to yours.

In the area of linkage, a current donor who already has a relationship with your organization is the best major gifts prospect. Answer these questions: are there any ways they have already been involved with your organization; do they volunteer, attend events or know someone who does?

Cultivating

Now that you have identified a list of prospects that score high on capacity, inclination and linkage, your board members are ready to reach out to these individuals and/or organizations to build relationships and generate interest in the organization. Your "ambassadors" will show and tell what the organization is about, explain the mission and talk about programs and services.

In addition to talking about the work and accomplishment of the nonprofit or inviting prospects for a personally guided tour or to a special event, board members can also choose from an array of cultivation activities that might be appropriate for different prospects.

Looking for additional cultivation activities? Try inviting prospects to media events and sending copies of published coverage; sending copies of official news releases; sending your newsletter via first class mail and attaching a personal note; sending notes to congratulate the prospective donor on the publication of books, a promotion, special accomplishment or appointment; or sending copies of any newly published book written by your organization's staff member.

Engaging

When board members take the time to identify prospective donors, cultivate a relationship with them, learn their areas of interest and allow them to get acquainted and comfortable with the organization, they are ready for the next important part of this process—engaging. Engaging prospective donors is about building the relationship and winning the confidence of the donor.

Inviting donors to see the work of the organization and the impact that they can have with a contribution helps to involve the prospect more closely with your nonprofit and its mission. Depending on the interest of prospective donors, invite them to join a committee or task force, network with other donors or have lunch with board members. During this time, board members should seek to instill a feeling of partnership by providing opportunities for prospects to share experience and expertise.

Another strategy for engaging prospects in your organization is to have an "advice visit." This strategy is often touted as the perfect way to further promote your cause in a direct, personal visit. Board members like these visits because the other person does most of the talking. There is a fundraising adage that says if you "ask for money and you get advice; ask for advice and you get money." Board members should share their personal passion and excitement for the cause and why they are personally involved. Questions to ask include the following:

◆ What do you think about our organization/the project?

◆ What about the need in the community?

◆ What interests you personally about the problem we are addressing?

◆ Who else would you be interested in hearing about this?

It's More About Friend-raising

Building relationships is the key to successful fundraising and board members can play a major role in "friend raising" for your organization. Yes, you might have some board members eager to ask friends, neighbors and associates to support your nonprofit. And there will be others who love the idea of picking up the phone to call a donor to thank them for a gift or writing a handwritten thank-you note expressing gratitude for a recent contribution.

Every board member can support your organization's fundraising—without asking for even a penny. You should have fundraising roles for each person on your board. And, the easiest way to get started is to ask your board members to be N.I.C.E.

 Connect with Lynne at http://charitychannel.com/cc/lynne-dean

Founder Fever as Strategic Risk: How Do I Know When It Is Time to Step Up or Leave?

By Steven Bowman

The term "Founder's Syndrome" has been used extensively in literature (mainly in the USA), however we have found it is not really a syndrome, but more like a fever that infects people all around the founder, as well as the founder. Hence I propose the term "Founder Fever." Founder Fever occurs when the founder or someone in a similar position is oblivious to what is really happening around them, where they become protective and sensitive, and are unwilling to change their point of view on just about anything. Often plans are not implemented unless they were devised by that person. Money keeps running out. The organization lurches from one crisis to another. No one really seems to know what's going on, and people become afraid of the founder. There is usually a toxic, stressful environment where board and staff members quickly come and just as quickly go. Everyone has caught the Founder Fever, and it is not particularly healthy or enjoyable.

It could be the original founder of the organization. It could be the person who took over from the founder. It could be the person who took over in time of crisis and led the organization out of difficulty. It could just be someone who has been there a very, very long time. These people were at one stage a great gift to their organization, but might have passed their "use by date" for that organization. How do we recognize when this has occurred, and what can we do about it?

I will relate two stories, each at the opposite end of the spectrum, that illustrate some of the issues related to "Founder Fever."

The first story concerns the founding member of a major charitable institution, established to honor the work of a family member. This person, while not the chair of the board, was seen by all as the true founder. He asked to spend time with me discussing an issue that was increasingly keeping him up at night with worry. He stated that he was very concerned that he might be suffering from Founder Fever, and was concerned about how he would know if that was occurring. His greatest fear was that he would hold the organization back and not even be aware of it. He was unsure what to do to ensure that the organization would be true to its original vision, and stated that only when the organization truly "got" his vision, would he truly be willing to let go and step back. At the same time, he also recognized that he could be one of the greatest strategic risks of the organization without even realizing it.

The founder has instigated a board evaluation process and ongoing board education, with the recognition that it is the board's responsibility to assess each board member individually, and provide feedback to any non-performing board member. The expectation is that board members would either step up, or leave.

The second story concerns a CEO who discussed with us the various options available to assist the founding chairman of the CEO's organization to make different choices. The founding chair of this regional organization had been honored at governmental and professional levels for the work she had done fifteen years previously. She had, on numerous occasions, stated that she might be willing to eventually step down from the chair position. Her actions, however, belied that statement. She would take every opportunity to shore up support from her community connections, which in a regional center were very powerful. She would make a statement that indicated a transfer of position might occur, and then construct a "crisis" that only she could handle and renege on any handover arrangements. You were either with her or against her (and that was never a pleasant experience). This had been going on for five years! The staff was demoralized, the board members were at their wits end, and the CEO got to the stage where it was either her or him (usually not a good career move). The founder was unable to even consider that she might be a major strategic risk to the organization.

The founding chair stepped down after the board consolidated its position on whether she should stay or not. The board chose a new chair (who was not cowed by the possibility of a social backlash), and offered the founder both recognition and honor for the work she had done. She accepted.

These two stories illustrate the extremes of "Founder Fever." In one case awareness is evident but there is a level of uncertainty about how to deal with the situation. In the other there was total unawareness and the systematic creation of a toxic environment existed within the organization.

Here are some strategies that can be implemented, either from the inception of a new organization (so "Founder Fever" doesn't take hold and become pandemic) or to alleviate an existing bout of "Founder Fever." Look very closely at your situation, and choose a few strategies that will work for your organization. It is a good idea to choose some strategies from each of the four categories listed below: Performance Management, Strategy and Risk Management, Structural Management, and Perception Management. Personally, I would choose all of them.

Performance Management Strategies

Develop high expectations from the beginning

The high expectations of the board should be presented and discussed with every board member, and made clear to any potential board member before they are appointed or elected.

This can be done through a board charter, or standards of behavior document. If the board member is then not meeting these expectations, they are counseled and invited to change or resign.

Create a governance committee

Develop a governance (or CEO/board evaluation) committee of the board. It is common for the chair to be on this committee, but it is not appropriate for the founder to chair this committee. This committee is responsible for both the board and CEO succession planning, performance management, and evaluation. These responsibilities should not be vested in the chair alone. This is the forum for asking a director to resign because of non-performance issues.

Annual board evaluation

Conduct board evaluations, whereby directors rate themselves, the board and the other directors. This helps hugely in identifying non-performing directors, and presents the opportunity to provide peer advice to that director. You can also ask directors the question "Should this director be encouraged to seek another term on the board?" These individual results can then be discussed with the concerned director by the chair or the governance committee. It is not unknown for non-performing directors to resign rather than be subject to a board evaluation process.

Personal goal setting

Ask each director to write down their two or three personal goals for the upcoming year, and how they will enhance the work of the board. The chair or the governance committee can then review these personal goals every six months with the director concerned.

Strategic Planning and Risk Management Strategies

Strategic planning

Ensure that the organization develops a robust strategic plan, and then embed that into the work of the organization. Restructure the board agenda so it reflects the key elements of the strategic plan. This keeps the board focused on those key areas that the board has responsibility for, and assists in strategic decision making. Recast all reports from CEO, staff and committees so they directly relate back to the strategic plan, identify the key strategic issues and discussion points, and make recommendations or provide ranges of options.

Risk management scenarios

Develop risk management scenarios to explore what would happen if the founder suddenly left the organization. Who will/can quickly step in? What stakeholders must be contacted? Where are the files/records? Involve the founder in these scenario plans.

Succession planning

Create a succession plan that proactively deals with all the things the founder (or the board) is concerned might happen when the founder and other key leaders leave. The whole point behind a succession plan is that you plan for succession, before it is required. The best time to develop a succession plan is when it is not needed!

Structural Management

Term limits

Many organizations have specified term limits for board directors with the aim to diminish the concentration of power in a small number of individuals and to weed out inactive or difficult board members. These term limits are usually 2x2x2 (total of 6 years) or 3x3x3 (total of nine years). Some have separate term limits for officer positions (chair, treasurer etc) which effectively extends the possible terms. Be very clear, however, that term limits don't automatically guarantee that board members, including founders, will get to serve each and every term possible under term limit rules. It's not an entitlement. Therefore, if the governance committee doesn't feel that someone who is coming up for re-appointment to a second or third term is the right "fit," they can recommend that the board member be thanked for their service and be encouraged to not nominate for re-election. Some organizations include a clause that specifies time limits, with an extra sentence that states something like "or as otherwise decided by the board," to allow high performing board members to remain.

Constitution

Most constitutions have a clause that specifies the conditions under which a director is deemed to have resigned or is required to resign. These include provisions such as:

◆ being absent from three board meetings consecutively without the approval of the board;

◆ becoming of unsound mind;

◆ failing to declare an interest in a contract with the company;

◆ holding any other office through which the director might profit under the company (except that of managing director) without the consent of the company in general meeting;

◆ being automatically disqualified from managing a corporation due to, for example, being convicted of an offence relating to the business or financial standing of the company;

◆ being disqualified by the regulator or being disqualified via a court order;

◆ becoming bankrupt;

◆ removal by resolution in a general meeting; or

◆ death.

In the USA, for example, it is possible to have clauses that specify the conditions under which the board can remove directors. In Australia, members can remove a director by resolution but the board or other directors cannot remove a director. It is slightly different in each country or even within your state or province, and you need to study the specific legislative details for your location.

Executive session of board meeting

Develop executive sessions of the board, where the executive committee meets without the entire board. Performance management of a particular director, including the founder, can be discussed without the entire board being present. These are often held every two or three board meetings, usually before or at the end of the regular board meeting.

Perception Management

Codify the vision and values

Founders often have a vision for the organization, which they are concerned will be lost if they are not around to "keep an eye on things." One of the most powerful strategic focusing tools that your organization can create is a formal vision statement. A vision statement is an expression of what your organization would like to see as a possibility and a future for the community and stakeholders you serve. Having created the vision statement, then all decisions, projects and services can be filtered through the vision statement to assess whether they are truly "vision-driven" and hence creating the future and the impact that your organization desires. This should provide some comfort to the founder that the agreed vision for the organization is actually embedded into all functions of the organization, and will outlast the tenure of the founder.

Board education on the role of the board

Conduct regular board education sessions where the board explores the contemporary role of the board. Align this with the board evaluation process. Encourage robust discussion on the role of the founder. Use this article as a thought starter!

Create advisory committee/council (e.g. historian, policy advisory group)

This possibility is offered to a founder who has done a great job in the past, but no longer has the skills to provide what the organization needs today. They are still part of the loop of relevant information, and are treated as "special," because they are. The key here is that once they voluntarily step down from the board, they are given a meaningful role.

Develop a patron position

This is often used to recognize a founder, or someone who has been influential in the formation and direction of the organization, but who is no longer suitable for a board position. Some organizations have created the position of "Life Ambassador" or similar title, in recognition of the outstanding contribution that person has made.

Skills analysis for re-election

This strategy is good practice whether you have a non-performing board member or not. Identify the skills that the board requires over the next three years, ask each director coming up for election or re-election to provide a short summary of how they meet these skills, and provide these summaries to those who vote for the director positions, with details on what skills the board requires.

Celebrate the gifts and successes of the founder who is leaving

Honor "the legacy" whether so named or not. This is a vital part of caring for the founder and smoothing the way for transition. One nonprofit created a farewell function that celebrated the history of the organization and the founder in images as seen through the eyes of the founder and colleagues, music that captured the excitement of the various stages of the organization, and video testimonials from service recipients and colleagues thanking the founder for her visionary leadership in the early years. The focus of the farewell function was on celebrating the impact the organization had on the communities it served, how the original vision of the founder had been translated into true community change, and the gratitude that key stakeholders had for the vision and the influence of the founder. It proved both a historical record of the organization and a powerful, emotive acknowledgment of the founder. A copy of the presentation was then formally gifted to the founder, not a dry eye in the audience...and the transition was complete.

 Connect with Steven at http://charitychannel.com/cc/steven-bowman

Is Creation of a Governance Committee Now Considered a Best Practice in the U.S.?

By Stephen C. Nill, J.D., GPC

In the last decade, several widely-publicized scandals within the charitable sector have brought heightened public scrutiny and media attention to how nonprofit boards conduct themselves. These scandals, especially those growing out of the missteps of several high-profile charities following the 9/11 attacks, sowed the seeds that, today, bring us to a question increasingly being asked by nonprofit directors: Is Creation of a Governance Committee Now Considered a Best Practice in the U.S.?

I have had the opportunity to comment in the media on many of these national scandals in a number of appearances on news programs such as Fox News and CNN, and a variety of newspapers and magazines. (Two of the more well-known scandals were the American Red Cross scandal following 9/11 and The September 11th Fund.) As I often said in those interviews, charitable boards operate on behalf of the public trust, unlike boards of for-profit corporations. That trust had been severely breached with major missteps by these and other high-profile agencies.

I recall wondering as I prepared for these interviews what more we could and should be doing in our sector to ensure that the boards of nonprofit organizations and institutions govern with integrity. These highly-visible failures were hurting the public image of all nonprofits, and we simply had to get a grip on it if we in the nonprofit world were to continue to enjoy the public trust.

The problem was not a lack of resources available to nonprofit boards. There was a veritable industry focused on helping nonprofit boards to govern with integrity. Books and articles on governance were everywhere. There was a vibrant consultant community that specialized in governance. There were lawyers who specialized in exempt organizations. There were professional online discussion forums dedicated to nonprofit boards and governance. There were college and university courses and online courses on governance. I could go on.

So why were these highly public scandals breaking out? What was missing?

And it wasn't just a problem with nonprofit boards. The for-profit sector was also rocked with a series of corporate and accounting scandals costing investors billions of dollars (remember Enron, Tyco International, Adelphia, Peregrine Systems and WorldCom?).

Not unexpectedly, in 2002 the government stepped in to address the abuses both on the for-profit side and on the nonprofit side.

On the for-profit side, it enacted Sarbanes-Oxley. For the most part, Sarbanes-Oxley does not directly pertain to nonprofit boards. Nevertheless, it has been highly influential in spurring nonprofit board leaders to consider how to prevent failures of governance by nonprofit boards.

On the nonprofit side, the Internal Revenue Service issued final regulations for Internal Revenue Code §4958 (aka the "intermediate sanctions" regulations). The regulations were designed to address conflicts of interest, excess financial benefit transactions, and public disclosure issues specific to nonprofits. For the first time, the IRS could levy penalties against individual board directors who acted in a manner that did not comply with the code.

As more directors became informed about the legal requirements—and risks—associated with board service, directors themselves started to recognize the benefits of appointing a board committee charged with the responsibility of educating the board about its fiduciary obligations and regulatory limitations, and with monitoring directors' compliance on an ongoing basis.

In my work as legal counsel to California nonprofit organizations and educational institutions, I have increasingly been asked by clients whether or not I recommend the formation of a governance committee. Inevitably, the board wants to know whether the emerging trend toward formation of governance committees has become an actual "best practice."

Part of what makes it tempting to label formation of a governance committee as a "best practice" is that, beginning in 2003, a confluence of three factors—the Sarbanes-Oxley Act introduced the prior year, the outbreak of high-profile charity scandals, and the introduction of intermediate sanctions—led to an unmistakable trend toward the formation of governance committees, either as separate committees or, as is more common, combined with nominating (or membership) committees.

I have never been comfortable trying to define whether something is or is not a so-called best practice. Setting aside the difficulty of defining just what exactly we mean by "best practice," my discomfort stems from the fact that applying these buzzwords tends to remove the question at hand from the realm of reasoned consideration. It implies that reasonable minds may not differ on the proposition, and that failing to do the thing is falling beneath the standard of practice.

Yet, there is ample indication that reasonable minds do differ on whether or not to implement a governance committee:

◆ A 2007 BoardSource survey, referenced below, reports on a trend toward creation of governance committees. It cautions that "common practices, however, are not necessarily best practices, nor should they be interpreted as ideal examples to be adopted by every board."

◆ The Council for Advancement and Support of Education (CASE), despite having a natural interest and stake in higher-education supporting foundation management and governance issues, has not made a recommendation regarding the establishment of a governance committee. In fact, its widely-followed Management and Governance Checklist for Institutionally Related Foundations does not directly address governance committees.

◆ Many of the books on Sarbanes-Oxley and nonprofits, though discussing at length the governance challenges implied, if not mandated, by Sarbanes-Oxley and listing the usual board committees—executive, finance, audit, nominating, and development/fundraising—and their respective roles, omit any reference to a governance committee as a vehicle for implementing their many governance recommendations.

On the other hand, many leading associations and authorities seem to assume, and in some cases advocate for, the creation of a governance committee. Some notable examples:

> *Governance and Nominating Committees: Organizations should have one or more committees, composed solely of independent directors, that focus on core governance and board composition issues, including: the governing documents of the organization and the board; the criteria, evaluation, and nomination of directors; the appropriateness of board size, leadership, composition, and committee structure; and codes of ethical conduct.*

> —ABA (The American Bar Association) Coordinating Committee on Nonprofit Governance, Guide to Nonprofit Corporate Governance in the Wake of Sarbanes-Oxley, 2005—Part II: Sarbanes-Oxley Act and Related Reforms, D. Key Corporate Governance Principles of the Sarbanes-Oxley Reforms for Consideration by Nonprofit Corporations, Principle 4, p. 17.

> *Increasingly, nonprofits have turned to governance committees to expand on—and even replace—traditional nominating committees. While nominating committees have long*

been used to identify and recommend new board members, governance committees can assist with ongoing board development.

> —BoardSource (formerly The National Center for Nonprofit Boards), July/ August 1998 edition of Board Member, Volume 7, Issue 7.

Every nonprofit corporation should have a nominating/governance committee composed entirely of directors who are independent in the sense that they are not part of the management team and they are not compensated by the corporation for services rendered to it, although they may receive reasonable fees as a director. The committee is responsible for nominating qualified candidates to stand for election to the board, monitoring all matters involving corporate governance, overseeing compliance with ethical standards, and making recommendations to the full board for action in governance matters.

> —The International Center for Not-for-Profit Law, "Ten Emerging Principles of Governance of Nonprofit Corporations and Guides to a Safe Harbor" by Thomas Silk, The International Journal of Not-for-Profit Law, Volume 7, Issue 1, November 2004.

Since 2008, governance committees have further multiplied in number as a result of the Internal Revenue Service's heightened investigation of nonprofit governance practices via the newly re-designed Form 990—the informational tax return that most nonprofits are required to file annually.

The above-referenced 2007 BoardSource survey found that 68 percent of responding nonprofits have a governance committee—outranked in prevalence by only executive and finance committees. But, there is a caveat: References to percentages refer only to survey respondents, not to all nonprofits. Note the context of the survey, as stated in the report:

> *This snapshot of board practices is based on responses from 1,126 chief executives and 1,026 board members who completed two different surveys.... Participants were selected from the BoardSource membership, and they serve a broad spectrum of organizations that are well distributed geographically and across IRS classifications, budget size, and mission areas. They are not, however, a statistically weighted, representative sample of the nonprofit sector.*

Although nonprofit corporations were required to comply with only two of the many provisions of the Sarbanes-Oxley Act (i.e., limited "whistleblower" protections and the prohibition against document destruction), leadership associations in the nonprofit sector began advocating for the establishment of governance committees with the expectation that Sarbanes-like regulations would soon be developed for and imposed upon nonprofit corporations.

According to the Society of Corporate Secretaries and Governance Professionals:

> *The not-for-profit community considered Sarbanes-Oxley and developed 'best practices' based, in part, upon its precepts. Certain of these best practices have been high profile because they can be directly tied to the dictates of Sarbanes-Oxley. The effect of Sarbanes-Oxley on nonprofit governance was documented in a number of studies and surveys including:*
>
> *ABA Coordinating Committee on Nonprofit Governance. 2005. Guide to Nonprofit Corporate Governance in the Wake of Sarbanes-Oxley. Chicago, IL: American Bar Association.*
>
> *BoardSource and Independent Sector. 2003. The Sarbanes-Oxley Act and Implications for Nonprofit Organizations.*
>
> *The Urban Institute. 2004. Submission in Response to June 2004 Discussion Draft of the Senate Finance Committee Staff Regarding Proposed Reforms Affecting Tax-Exempt Organizations.*
>
> —National Association of College and University Business Officers. 2003. "The Sarbanes-Oxley Act of 2002: Recommendations for Higher Education." Advisory Report 2003. Washington, DC: NACUBO.

Governance committees would shoulder the anticipated policy-making, oversight and compliance responsibilities triggered by a regulatory expansion.

So, whether or not it is appropriate to label this or any board process a "best practice," there is no doubt that the clear trend is toward creation of such committees for U.S. nonprofits.

As mentioned, the IRS is now focusing a spotlight on the role any given board assumes with respect to self-monitoring, accountability, and ethical conduct. This new initiative, dubbed "regulation by disclosure" in Minutes of the Nonprofit Governance Subcommittee of the American Bar Association, August 10, 2008, p. 5. is reflected in the addition of an entire section to the Form 990 focusing exclusively on governance policies and procedures. The twenty-eight questions cover issues ranging from director independence to whistleblower and joint venture policies, and narrative explanations are required for a number of the responses.

Further, whether or not additional legislation is enacted that would effectively mandate the establishment of governance committees, nonprofit community customs and practices are changing. That is, more and more nonprofits are embracing a committee-based governance oversight function.

Given this focus on board policies and conduct, it seemed natural to extend the responsibilities of existing board nominating committees to include oversight of regulatory compliance. The combined responsibilities suggested that the appropriate nomenclature for such a body would be the "governance committee."

> *Some boards may presently have a nominating committee, or have had one in the past. This committee should be considered the ancestor of the governance committee. 'Nominating committees' were primarily responsible for recruiting new members to the board. Over time, boards have discovered that such a task is more important … than they expected. Further, effective boards realized that a committee should take the new members it has recruited and educate them about the work of the board, both in orientation sessions and throughout their tenure as board members. Discovering that it is not just new members who benefit from education about good governance—that everyone on the board finds this useful—good boards further developed a job description of this particular committee. Many boards called this new expanded nominating committee the 'board development committee.' The message of its expanded role was translated, but the name of the committee still remained somewhat confusing. It became too difficult to differentiate between the board development committee and the development committee, which is responsible for involving the full board in fundraising. Thus, the original nominating committee has morphed into the 'governance committee' which provides general oversight for the health, well-being, and perpetuation of the board.*

> —Berit M. Lakey, Outi Flynn, and Sandra R. Hughes, *Governance Committee: Book One of the BoardSource Committee Series* (Washington, DC: BoardSource, 2004), 2.

I have been using the term "governance committee," but I should point out that it is also referred to as a "Committee on Trustees" or "Committee on Directors." In some very rare cases, boards have elected to split the board director recruitment, training, and assessment function from the regulatory and policy oversight function and to have two committees. In that case, the Committee on Trustees or Committee on Directors has taken on the board development function (i.e., the work of a traditional Nominating Committee). A separate governance committee takes on the oversight of statutory compliance on matters such as conflict of interest, bylaws, IRC 4958, etc.

 Setting aside the question of whether or not creation of a governance committee, per se, is a best practice, there is a clear trend toward, if not an outright consensus in, the necessity that governing boards exercise certain governance oversight responsibilities that have increasingly crystallized since 2003. This following list of responsibilities is derived from the general concepts delineated in *The Source: Twelve Principles of Governance That Power Exceptional Boards*, Washington, DC: BoardSource 2005. "The Source" incorporates observations, academic knowledge and the proven practice of exceptional boards into a comprehensive reference on governance to guide nonprofits in reaching exceptional levels of performance. They are:

◆ developing conflict of interest, ethics, whistleblower, document preservation and confidentiality policies, and procedures for monitoring each;

◆ reviewing all disclosures of conflicts and dualities of interest on an ongoing and annual basis;

◆ making recommendations to the board when special action is required related to the above, especially when violations occur;

◆ reviewing all documentation relating to IRC 4958 transactions, and overseeing compliance with activities necessary to availing the board of "safe harbor" provisions;

◆ annually reviewing corporate bylaws and governance-related procedural policies for sufficiency and consistency, and developing recommendations for modifications as needed;

◆ reviewing of the effectiveness of structural relationships with affiliated entities with respect to independent and shared responsibilities, and the use of reserved powers;

◆ reviewing of all due diligence reports affecting or evaluating board effectiveness; and

◆ handling of other governance-related projects as assigned by the board.

Who Selects the Members of the Governance Committee?

The touchstone legal principle of corporate governance, including nonprofit corporate governance, is that the activities and affairs of a corporation shall be conducted and all corporate powers shall be exercised by or under the direction of the board. The board, however, may delegate the management of the activities of the corporation to any person or persons, management company, or committee however composed, provided that the activities and affairs of the corporation shall be managed and all corporate powers shall be exercised under the ultimate direction of the board.

More specifically, the board may create committees, either via the bylaws or board resolutions. In creating a committee, it may, if it so desires, choose to delegate the power to exercise the authority of the board—making it a so-called "board committee." If it does so, certain limits on what powers can be delegated are typically imposed by the state. In California, for example, a committee is prohibited from filling vacancies on any committee; fixing compensation of the directors for serving on any committee; amending or repealing the bylaws or adopting new bylaws; and the appointment of committees of the board or the members thereof. If the board does not delegate the power to exercise the authority of the board to the governance committee—making it a so-called advisory committee—these restrictions do not apply.

Recommendations

From a policy and legal perspective, governance boards, at a minimum, are advised to expressly undertake certain governance oversight responsibilities itemized above. The recommended method of doing so is the establishment of a standing governance committee, either as a stand-alone committee or, as is more common, in combination with the membership committee, for the following reasons:

◆ A governance committee focuses attention on a sustained basis on governance policies, practices and procedures. This can be particularly important at a time when governance practices are evolving, as they have been in the last few years.

◆ Its creation would be consistent with a clear trend in the nonprofit sector.

◆ Its creation would demonstrate and underscore, at a time of increasing media and government scrutiny, the organization or institution's continuing commitment to sound governance policies, practices and procedures.

Even so, establishment of a governance committee is not the only method available to an organization or institution. Rather than create a governance committee, it could divide up the specific governance oversight responsibilities and delegate them to other committees. This method, while minimally satisfying the board legal obligation to ensure sound governance policies, practices and procedures, has drawbacks, in that:

◆ It could dilute the focus of other committees on their primary responsibilities.

◆ Governance issues would not receive the focused and sustained attention they deserve.

◆ It would be more difficult to achieve a consistency in governance policies, practices and procedures.

◆ It would make it more difficult for the board to monitor and evaluate the effectiveness governance oversight by the committees.

◆ Compared with establishing a governance committee, it would be more difficult for the Foundation to demonstrate to the public and to regulators its commitment to sound governance policies, practices and procedures.

So, whether or not a governance committee is a so-called "best practice," it is certainly the best means of ensuring that a board continues to govern in a manner consistent with its duties and responsibilities.

 Connect with Steve at http://charitychannel.com/cc/stephen-nill

Get Rid of Your Nominating Committee!

By Linda Lysakowski, ACFRE

O ne of the best pieces of advice for any nonprofit organization might be to get rid of your nominating committee. For most organizations, the nominating committee has two primary functions: to fill vacant board seats and to elect officers of the board. In most cases, this committee is an ad hoc committee appointed by the president or chair a few months before terms are due to expire. Sometimes there isn't even a nominating committee in place. In fact, one of the worst examples I've seen about how *not* to recruit board members was at a December board meeting where the executive director announced, "A few of you have terms expiring this month so we need a few more board members. Anyone have any ideas?" "What's wrong with this picture," I asked myself? Several things:

◆ It was December.

◆ The executive director raised the subject.

◆ No one had any ideas (of course that might have been the good news!)

Even when an organization has a nominating committee to handle this job, it is usually done wrong. Often by the time the board chair appoints a nominating committee, most of the board members are busy with other committees and the nominating task seems to fall to someone who has not been tremendously involved in other board work. As a result, those selected for the nominating committee might not be the best and brightest of the board members. The attitude is sometimes, "Well, how much harm can they do on a nominating committee?" The answer is, "A lot!"

So What is the Best Option?

Instead of a nominating committee, I recommend a year round board resource committee. This committee can also be called the governance committee or the committee on directorship. Whatever the title, the important things to remember about this committee are:

◆ It must meet year round.

◆ It needs to be chaired by one of the strongest individuals on the board.

◆ Its duties include doing an assessment of board performance, both the board as a whole and as individual board members.

◆ It is responsible for developing or refining board position descriptions.

◆ It evaluates the needs of the board and develops a profile of the kinds of people that are needed to fill vacancies on the board.

◆ It works with the board members to help find the right people to fill board positions.

◆ It assures diversity on the board.

◆ It implements, along with senior staff members of the organization, board orientation.

◆ It is responsible for ongoing education of the board.

Duties of the Committee

The board resource committee, governance committee or committee on directorship is perhaps the most important committee of the board, *not an afterthought.* This committee, once in place, should first complete a grid analyzing current strengths and weaknesses of the board. Board members should be listed, according to the years their terms expire, and diversity indicators listed—ethnicity, gender, geographic location etc. Skills, talents and areas of special expertise should also be listed, along with giving ability and contacts with various groups such as media, funders, and government agencies. Once this grid is complete, the committee can then determine where there are gaps in board diversity, skills and abilities. A profile can then be developed for recruitment of new board members.

The committee then takes the results of their assessment to the full board and asks for names to be considered for nomination to the board. Individual board members should *never* haphazardly, or on their own, recruit new board members. Names and resumes are given to the board resource committee, governance committee or committee on directorship for *consideration*. No one should ever be approached with an automatic assumption that they will be invited to serve on the board, but rather that their name is being considered by the committee.

The committee then arranges a meeting with the prospective board member, and the executive director should be included in this meeting. Board position descriptions are shared with the prospective board member and expectations of both the organization and the prospective board member discussed. Once the committee feels it has a slate of candidates to present, names are then brought to the full board for approval. Once the new candidates are elected by the board, the committee contacts the new board members, inviting them to join the board and attend their first board meeting. The committee is also responsible for providing orientation for new board members and might implement a "Board Buddy," or mentoring program for new board members. This committee also makes recommendations for board officers to be presented to the full board for election. And, the same thoughtful process that goes into recruiting new board members should go into the board officer selection.

It is important, however, that this committee meets on a year round basis and evaluates any problem issues that might arise with the board as a whole or with individual board members. Ongoing board education is also a responsibility of this committee and can greatly improve the effectiveness of the board. As an example, this committee might arrange for case workers to make presentations at a board meeting of a human service agency. Or the curator of fine arts might provide education for museum board members. The committee should evaluate the needs for board education and work with the executive director to provide the appropriate educational segments at board meetings and/or retreats.

A board resource committee, governance committee or committee on directorship working thoughtfully, diligently and on an ongoing basis can make all the difference in the world between an effective, enthused, and inspired board and a lackadaisical board that does not understand its role in advancing the organization's mission.

 Connect with Linda at http://charitychannel.com/cc/linda-lysakowski

Won't Someone *Please* Be Our Next President?

By Ernie Ginsler

Finding quality leadership volunteers has never been easy, but over the last five years or so, it has become noticeably harder. Among leadership volunteers, convincing the best of the board to be the president of an organization has become the hardest of all. Research into volunteering in Canada has confirmed the obvious—volunteers in all organizations are becoming much more discerning and demanding in their volunteer activity. Increasing numbers of potential volunteers are letting organizations know what days, what hours, and for how long they are available to volunteer. If you can't meet their expectations, look for someone else who can.

I had intended to write this article about a year ago, but at the time I was in an ongoing search to find someone who would be willing to be the next president of an organization for which I was the current president. Now that I am happily ensconced as past-president, with a new president in place, and the next two in line identified and confirmed, I can write from practice as well as theory.

"Who Has the Time?"

The problem with the presidency, it seems, is that so many community-based nonprofits have faced funding cuts, growing demand, expectations for increased accountability, additional government regulations, and more, that many potential presidents simply can't see themselves devoting the time necessary to effectively guide the board through the process of dealing with it all.

What we did, and what the theory suggests we should do, can be boiled down into two main areas: clearly define the job, and spread the load so that the job is doable.

The first task the organization should undertake is to develop a clear and concise job description for the president. I looked at what I was doing and wrote out the entire list. It turned out that it consisted of three parts. First, the things that as president I had to do; second, there was a list of things that I wanted to do because I felt they were important and I was good at them; and third, there was a list of things that I had picked up along the way because I didn't have time to find anyone else to do them. The members of the board who I had hoped would step into the presidency had seen me doing all of them, and thought they would have to do the same. It was just too much for them to jump into. This leads to the second main area—spreading the load.

Spreading the Workload: Our Solution

The way we convinced one person to become president, and two more to be the next presidents is to make the presidency a three-person job. In our case (and tasks will differ from organization to organization), we divided the territory this way.

The president now focuses on the core job of what our president has to do:

◆ chair the board and members meetings;

◆ serve as liaison to committee chairs, ensuring that the committees stay on target and on time;

◆ lead the CEO performance review process; and

◆ take the lead with major donors.

As past-president, I took on a list of jobs that have to be done, and which the past-president can legitimately do:

◆ making presentations to funders; and

◆ maintaining and initiating external relations with other agencies, the media, government, etc.

These are usually the responsibility of the president, however simply explaining that you are splitting the workload to use board members' skills and time more effectively satisfies those you are speaking to.

The vice-president, who is incoming president, is responsible for:

◆ chairing or serving on the nominating committee (this person has a vested interest in the best possible incoming board);

◆ organizing and leading the board orientation process (for the same reason);

◆ either doing or delegating necessary board tasks and responsibilities that have not already been assigned; and

◆ chairing the strategic planning for the organization.

In many organizations, the positions of past president and vice president have the fewest real responsibilities. Past presidents "provide continuity." Vice presidents "chair the meeting of the board in the absence of the president." In other words, the board member with the most experience does the least, and the person soon to assume the position of board leader does second least. This simply isn't making good use of two presumably highly talented and experienced board members. By cutting the presidency down to size, and making good use of the past-president and vice-president, the task of finding a president should be much less onerous.

 Connect with Ernie at http://charitychannel.com/cc/ernie-ginsler

Reviewing Governance in Your Organization

By Jane Garthson

How do you know if your organization's governance is good enough? If you haven't reviewed it in the last few years, you do not know. More and more organizations are conducting governance reviews about every five years. External pressures and significantly revised strategic plans might spur a review sooner. Organizations generally find such reviews worthwhile even if they decide against major change. The discussions about why you lead as you do will still be worthwhile and you are certain to find some change, however small, that really makes a difference.

In some jurisdictions, governments have passed or introduced new laws governing community benefit organizations, and those new laws require an overhaul of bylaws. No sensible leadership group would significantly rewrite their bylaws before reviewing governance.

Warning Signs

It might be time to review your governance if:

- ◆ Feedback from community and staff indicates a growing dissatisfaction with the board's decisions and/or composition.

- ◆ The bylaws no longer reflect how your organization operates, but there is no consensus on whether to fix the bylaws or bring operations into line with the bylaws.

- ◆ Board members have ongoing conflicts of interest.

- ◆ You see checklists of good nonprofit governance practices but can say yes to fewer than half the items.

◆ Timely decisions are so difficult at the board that a smaller group makes most of the decisions for the board.

◆ Candidates for an executive director or board vacancy inquire about the governance style and are clearly unhappy with what they hear.

◆ Board members resign or refuse second terms, citing issues such as poor use of their time or skills.

◆ Board recruitment is difficult or board attendance is poor; meetings are cancelled for lack of quorum.

◆ Committees and senior staff either exceed their authority or fill up the board meetings with administrative trivia and operational matters.

◆ Executive director evaluation is problematical since committees reporting to the board have responsibilities that overlap the ED's responsibilities.

◆ Your auditor, lawyer or major funders expresses concern about the lack of oversight.

This list should give you a good idea of what improvements you might expect to achieve from enhancing your governance. But let's continue with when to do a governance review.

Is There a Wrong Time to do a Governance Review?

The best reason for delaying a governance review is a lack of up-to-date vision, mission and values statements. What criteria then would drive your primary governance choices or any other important choice in your organization, for that matter? The discussions about the kind of community you want to create, your role in creating it, and your priorities might significantly affect governance decisions such as board composition.

I used to think that organizations lacking a strategic plan *and* dissatisfied with their governance could address those issues in either order. Whichever was done first would lead to the other, and that in fact happened many times. However, I now firmly believe that approach was wrong. It is essential to at least have vision (externally focused), mission and values statements in place before conducting a governance review. And anyway, how do you know the review is a top priority if you haven't set strategic priorities?

It is not appropriate to start a governance review during a financial crisis or major project that is already preoccupying the board and staff. A governance review requires considerable time on the part of the board, the governance/board development committee (or task force if there is no regular committee supporting board operations) and executive director. If there are other senior staff members, they will get involved too, along with whoever provides the primary administrative support to the board and executive director. Often other key volunteers such as task force chairs are involved too, especially in all-volunteer organizations. Over several months, you will need to make board and committee time available for research, discussions and decisions.

Also, if you have new board members starting soon, or have just hired a new executive director, you might wait until they have a least a couple of months experience with you to receive their orientation, settle in and see what "normal" is at your organization. Governance choices that seem quite weird to an outsider might have a sound basis in the special needs of an organization, and should not lightly be tossed aside in favor of some generic wise practice.

Most organizations involve a specialist in nonprofit governance in the review, so resources might also be an issue. If your budget is really tight, you might not be able to start until you arrange for one-time funding for the review from one of your funders or another grant-maker. Use pro bono help only if the person is a specialist in the governance of community benefit organizations, and keeps current with governance thinking.

Why Do Governance Review?

That's easy. The governance review will help ensure your leaders are working together effectively to govern the organization so it can create a better community and a better world. It might identify barriers you can remove and small changes that can make a big difference. It should help you attract the kind of leaders you want and need for the future, and retain them through using their time, passion, knowledge and skills well. It should help you assure funders, stakeholders and partners that you have the right governance structure.

Best of all, it might be able to do all of that without major change, depending on how well your current structure fits your needs. If you decide to retain the existing governance structure, the governance review discussions will help you explain why your existing governance structure works well for you. Being able to articulate the reasons can be invaluable when seeking supporters and recruiting leaders.

How Does Governance Get Reviewed?

The usual first step would be to set up a governance task force or assign oversight to the existing governance committee. That group then selects and manages the relationship with a consultant who is very knowledgeable about governance in community, public and mutual benefit organizations. That person should review your governance documents, including confidential ones, and interview key people to gain an understanding how your governance works now. The reviewer will interview selected stakeholders about their perception of your governance. In the past, the external interviewees were primarily organizational stakeholders such as funders, regulators and partners. The emerging practice in some organizations is to also include, or even primarily focus on, members of the community you serve.

The review of governance is not limited to the legal framework, although issues such as who can vote for directors, board size and terms of office are very important. The review should also look at how the board functions, such as use of group time, use of committees to support the board, how decision support is provided, and the partnership with senior staff. The review should also address "softer" leadership items such as the level of decision-making, the quality of strategic thinking, the range of relevant knowledge at the board table, the accountability for results achieved for the community and the willingness (or not) of others to partner with you. It should also consider the existence and quality of important governance processes such as board and executive director assessments and succession plans, codes of ethics or conduct (including conflict of interest), and orientation programs.

Optionally, the review's initial stage can include research into governance of comparable organizations, particularly if you know of some that seem to function well. Knowing how they are different or similar can help generate options later in the review.

Who Should Conduct a Governance Review?

It is extremely difficult to conduct such a review without fresh eyes and a lack of personal stake in the outcome. I have seen governance reviews simply confirm the current system, sometimes without even describing it, because the reviewer was an insider and against change. Or the person who commissioned the review was quite explicit up-front that the review was a formality that was not to lead to major change, and so the review was unethical, a sham. Such reviews waste everyone's time, and so do reviews done by those who only know how for-profit businesses work. Volunteer boards are, and should be, different from corporate ones.

You need someone who keeps current with governance thinking in community, public and mutual benefit organizations through professional development in the form of extensive reading, conferences, workshops and discussions with colleagues. I would ignore anyone whose professional development is not being maintained. None of the books on my current list of recommended resources in nonprofit governance are more than ten years old and most are less than three.

Many executive directors take this field seriously so they can properly support their boards. You might be able to find a recently retired one who will do the work pro bono if you cannot afford a governance consultant, or your community might have a nonprofit support organization that can make a knowledgeable consultant available to you.

Although a fully independent review is preferable, a few boards manage to recruit someone trained in nonprofit governance to their board or governance committee. If you are in that position, make sure the individual leads the governance review before they get too comfortable in the way things have always been done. And remember that passion for the cause is more important in your recruitment for your board than this or any other skill set.

How Do We Develop Options?

Let's start with what doesn't work. You *cannot* just choose a few models and find out which one works for you. That's because there aren't a few models out there in any sort of common use or general acceptance. There is only one, published in 1990, by John Carver. His ground-breaking ideas tremendously improved governance in the nonprofit sector and thankfully many of those ideas are in common use today. But the model itself had flaws that have caused almost all governance consultants, academics and writers to move away from it. It still has passionate advocates, but most of us learned from hard experience that one size did *not* fit all.

Countless publications attempt to tell you that you can choose to be a 'working' board, a 'policy' board or some kind of hybrid, but such choices will be of little help to you in figuring out specifics such as how many directors you need. 'Working' boards have become associated with micromanaging, but a great many nonprofits have no staff, so that is not meaningful. And the term 'policy board' has become a pejorative in its own way, as some boards spend years writing complex policies and very little else—akin to fiddling while your community burns.

So What Do We Use to Help Us Decide?

First, since there is no overall model I can recommend, look at each aspect of governance separately. List each with options. For example, what choices do you have for an executive committee? The main choices are none (now a very common choice), one with very restricted authority, or a broad-scope one that can act for the board (becoming rare).

Then analyze the options in terms of the criteria you use for any important organizational decision. The first one could be: Does it help achieve our vision and mission? You can split this out into sub-questions such as: Will it help us make timely decisions for our community? Will it help us make high quality decisions for our community? Will it support sustainability (at least until we achieve our vision and are no longer needed)? Is there another option that would help create better or more lasting improvements in our community?

The second question should be some variation of: Is it consistent with our principles and ethical values? For example, if you highly value democracy and civil society, how will a closed membership, closed meetings and a self-perpetuating board fit?

You would also ask questions about risk management. For example the risk of frequent meetings if you have a large geographic scope is harming your ability to deliver programs due to overspending on board travel and per diems. The board has to add more value than it costs. But meeting too seldom might add a risk of missing compliance deadlines or failing to respond to opportunities in time. Remember that your biggest risk area is usually reputation.

Also ask questions about relationships. Of your stakeholders, who will care? Who might gain too much power? Who might feel disenfranchised by changes in board composition, and need another way to have their views heard at the board table? Will the changes increase staff workload, even temporarily, and how can this be offset?

The review will take into account current wise practice thinking in nonprofit governance, and the reviewer's extensive experience of what has and has not worked in other organizations.

Where Does the Governance Review Go from Here?

The reviewer should make recommendations to address each aspect of governance, and ensure some level of consistency and coherence among the recommendations. The recommendations can then be discussed in detail at the governance committee and then brought to the board for discussion and decisions. Keep these discussions high level. Each agreed-upon change will be an action item for the governance or board development committee to flesh out later.

An action plan is then needed to set out responsibilities, timing and resources to implement any changes that are chosen. A new style of board agenda, for example, can be in place next month; major bylaw revisions might take more than a year.

As with any review, it will need to be monitored, adapted over time and reviewed again. Governance thinking will continue to change, likely increasingly towards bringing the community in. Your community will change. Your organization might change its scope or direction, and need different leadership. With one well-conducted governance review in hand, subsequent ones should be easier to conduct, but the decisions arising will never be easy.

Separately, there is research showing that one-time intervention by governance consultants is far less effective than longer-term involvement. Consider at least an annual refresher with your consultant, to remind the board why it decided to change, orient new board members to your governance approach, build awareness of the newest thinking in the field, and address unforeseen barriers to completing the action plan.

 Connect with Jane at http://charitychannel.com/cc/jane-garthson

The Problem with Board Evaluations

By Steven Bowman

Board evaluations are becoming more commonplace as directors seek ways to become more strategic, make better decisions and be seen to be undertaking best practice governance. Most boards who undertake an evaluation process do so from a place of wanting to be even better at what they do, although some individual directors are less than enthusiastic about being part of an evaluation process. In our experience of facilitating many board evaluations, the main instigators of board evaluation processes are the chair (usually if there is an issue the chair wants to bring out), the CEO (usually when it is part of a general governance update process) and sometimes funding agencies or key stakeholders (usually in response to a perception of underlying governance problems). While the reasons for undertaking board evaluations vary from board to board, there is one major underlying problem with most of the board evaluations that we have reviewed.

Board evaluations are typically based around directors rating themselves, or the board as a collective, or rating both themselves and the collective board. This rating is done on a series of questions related to their responsibilities and functions as a board. The results of this self rating are then compiled and analyzed, usually by an experienced external governance facilitator, and a report delivered to the board. The major problem with this type of board evaluation is that board directors are rating themselves. This often leads to directors rating their skills as high (sometimes low), with no evidence to support that rating!

How It Goes Wrong

We have seen numerous examples where directors have rated themselves highly in most evaluation areas, yet evidence suggested that they were, in fact, not functioning well in these areas. Some of the more common situations (and we have seen these many times) include:

◆ *Evaluation Question:* How effectively did the board deal with statutory reporting, compliance and legal matters such as constitutional review and compliance with relevant legislation and/or regulatory requirements?

Rating by Directors (5 point scale): average 4.8/5, range 4-5

Yet, there was no evidence of formal statutory reporting framework, there was no compliance schedule, no constitutional review was conducted in past five years, and the constitution was full of antiquated articles that excluded electronic meetings or notices.

◆ *Evaluation Question:* How effectively did the board contribute to development of and review the implementation of strategy?

Rating by Directors (5 point scale)*:* average 4.6/5, range 4-5

Yet, there was no evidence of a strategic plan being approved by directors: It was not embedded into the agenda of the board; board minutes did not reflect discussion and decisions around agreed strategies; reports of staff did not reflect the strategic plan; key performance indicators of the CEO did not reflect elements of the strategic plan; the annual report did not use the strategic plan as a means of reporting accountability; and there was no formal or informal process for the board to regularly review assumptions behind the strategic plan.

So, What Can You Do?

We recommend three strategies to overcome this problem.

Strategy 1: Conduct a strategic governance and operations audit

One of the most powerful techniques we have developed is what we term a strategic governance and operations audit, which is conducted in conjunction with the board evaluation. An independent person (usually the evaluation facilitator) spends some time in the appropriate offices, usually with the CEO and/or executive director, investigating the key areas that are the focus of the board evaluation, looking for evidence of board processes, board compliance and operational issues that directly affect the governance of that organization. For example, you would seek evidence of processes and best practice in at least the following areas:

◆ *legal:* constitutional review, compliance schedule;

◆ *strategy:* strategic plan exists, signed off by board, board agenda reflects key strategies, board minutes reflect strategic discussion, performance management system for staff reflect impact of strategic plan, stakeholder communications reflect elements of strategic plan, annual report utilizes strategic plan, risk management plan in place, board risk policy in place;

◆ *accountability:* board succession planning protocols in place including formal skills analysis, board induction program in place, formal board charter, formal charters for board committees, CEO key performance indicators in place, relevant board policies signed off and regularly reviewed, board evaluation protocols, annual board work plan; and

♦ *culture:* performance management system in place for staff, culture and team processes, financial benchmarks and controls, CEO and chair/board relationships.

When looking at these areas, we have found it useful to identify whether the policies or procedures actually exist and address the key issues, whether they are documented and communicated, and whether they are in operation and applied consistently. This information is then used to cross check with board members' evaluation ratings.

Strategy 2: Construct the board evaluation so it asks for evidence that supports the ratings

The typical board evaluation only asks directors to rate themselves and/or the board according to agreed questions, usually in an electronic survey. These surveys almost invariably never ask for evidence that supports their rating. Even evaluations that consist of face-to-face interviews often only investigate directors' perceptions, without digging into evidence that might support those perceptions. We have developed board evaluations that ask directors to provide both evidence for their rating, and also what remedial action they perceive might be expansive for them and the board to consider. The responses to these questions are fascinating, especially when they are matched to the strategic governance and operations audit results.

The format of a board evaluation might look like the following:

Board Evaluation			
Note: These questions are intended to assess the effectiveness of the board collectively and directors individually, not management.			
The board collectively 1=poor 5=very effective	My input as individual Director 1=poor 5=very effective	Short description of processes or behaviors that provide evidence to support your rating of the board collectively (bullet points)	Recommended remedial action (how we can do it better)
Q1			
Q2			

Some of the responses we have had from directors regarding their view of evidence include:

Question: How effectively did the board provide external accountability to its stakeholders?

Rating by directors (5 point scale): average 4/5, range 2-5

Evidence provided to support rating: Financial reporting by accountants provides all the accountability we need.

Evidence from audit: There was no formal mechanism for monitoring stakeholder perceptions, and a stakeholder survey conducted as part of the board evaluation showed that stakeholders viewed the board as being operational with no strategic vision or accountability. Stakeholders rated this as 1.5/5.

Question: How effectively did the board identify and monitor key risks that could impact on its ability to achieve its strategic plan?

Rating by directors (5 point scale): average 4.3/5, range 3-5.

Evidence provided to support rating: "We are all very conscious of risk issues."

Evidence from audit: There was no risk management plan, no agreement on key risks, no risk management policy, no risk analysis for any project, and no evidence of any risk related discussion from board minutes.

Strategy 3: Develop a board work program based on the board evaluation results

One of the most common complaints about board evaluations is that they did not result in any, or many, changes. One of the key strategies we use that helps keep the board focused is to develop a board work program that specifies which recommendations are to be undertaken, who is responsible for ensuring that it occurs, and when that recommendation should be implemented. This provides a formal accountability and project plan for the board, which is more likely to result in the recommendations being actioned.

If you choose to undertake a board evaluation, first conduct a governance audit, ask for evidence of ratings as part of the evaluation, and implement a board work program based on the recommendations. These three strategies will assist in your board extracting the most value from the evaluation process.

 Connect with Steven at http://charitychannel.com/cc/steven-bowman

Board Member Absenteeism: Four Causes and Five Things You Can Do About it

By Nathan Garber

While no one would find fault with a director or trustee who misses an occasional meeting due to unforeseen circumstances, the morale and the work of the board can be compromised by persistent absenteeism by one or more board members. In this article, I'll list four causes of persistent absenteeism and five recommendations for how to deal with them.

Causes of Persistent Absenteeism

Why would someone voluntarily accept the responsibilities and duties of a director of a nonprofit or charitable corporation and then miss a third or a half of the sessions at which the board's work is conducted? It seems to me that there are four possible causes: unclear expectations on the part of the board; compelling personal reasons that lower the director's commitment to the board; dissatisfaction with the work of the board; or it might simply be a bad match.

Unclear expectations

In many organizations, board recruitment process is haphazard, often being left until the weeks before the annual general meeting. In an effort to cajole or entice a colleague or friend to join the board, potential directors might be told "It's not much work—just one meeting a month." Recruiters don't want to scare away a prospect so provide no information about the fiduciary duties of directors. After joining the board, new members receive minimal or no orientation to their responsibilities.

If the organization has a bylaw or policies on attendance, they are usually ineffectual. A typical example is a bylaw that says if directors miss three consecutive meetings without prior notice the board might choose to do something about it. Such a by-law would permit a director to attend no meetings at all, provided the board was notified in advance.

Another way directors come to misunderstand the importance of full attendance is through observing the behavior of other board members. When they see that there are no consequences or follow-up on absenteeism or lateness, they quickly learn that consistent attendance is not an expectation of the board.

You cannot hold people accountable for failing to meet the attendance expectations if they are not made clear from the outset and through follow-up.

Compelling personal reasons

Even the most loyal board member might be confronted with a personal, work, or family situation that takes precedence over voluntary activities. Because of the nature of most board meetings (we arrive; we do our board business; we leave), board members might not get to know each other well, and might have no idea that their colleague's priorities have changed.

When they become aware of such situations, some boards offer a leave of absence to the affected board member. While offering compassion and support, this approach can leave the board short of workers, giving the impression that a full complement of directors is not necessary for the board to do its work. In addition, if not addressed in by-laws, leaves of absence might cause problems with obtaining quorum for board meetings.

Lack of satisfying and useful work

As volunteers, directors need to feel that they are doing something useful, and that they can see a clear link between their activities as board members and the mission of the organization. Unfortunately, the items that make up too many meeting agendas have little or no link to the reasons for the organization's existence. Meeting time is taken up approving reports and decisions that have already been made by staff or an executive committee, engaging in lengthy discussions about trivia, or otherwise wasting members' valuable time and knowledge.

If you have little reason to believe that your participation will make a difference, why waste your time? For boards to function effectively, directors need to be able to solve problems and make decisions collaboratively. When a director feels that his or her contribution is not needed, unwelcome, unappreciated, or minimized by other board members, the director will stop coming to meetings.

A bad match

Sometimes, in spite of your best efforts at recruitment and orientation, a new board member turns out to be not that interested or does not share the core values of the organization. Neither the board nor the director wants to cause a fuss and if there is no easy way to separate, so the director just stops coming to meetings until the director's term expires, leaving the board with a de facto vacancy.

What Happens When There is Absenteeism?

When several directors are absent or when a director is frequently absent, the work of the board and the organization can be severely compromised. Decisions take longer or cannot be made at all; tasks cannot be assigned; decisions get challenged at subsequent meetings by those who were not present when the decision was made; executive directors are left uncertain about the extent of board support for their plans and actions; meetings are cancelled for lack of quorum, leaving the more dedicated members frustrated and resentful.

The overall message conveyed by failure to address absenteeism is that the work of the board cannot be very important and that your participation is unnecessary.

Board members need to know that the work of the board requires participation from all members. This message is communicated through clear bylaws and/or policies on attendance; attention to board recruitment, orientation, training and evaluation practices; careful planning of meeting agendas; and follow-up on absenteeism.

Five Things You Can Do to Reduce Absenteeism

1. Update and clarify bylaws and policies on attendance

It goes without saying that you cannot hold people accountable for meeting expectations that have not been made clear to them. Every workplace has policies and procedures for dealing with circumstances when an employee is not present during their scheduled hours. The board meeting is the workplace of the board and the organization needs bylaws and policies expressing, in writing, why attendance is required and how absenteeism will be addressed. The bylaws need to give the board the authority to deal with changes in individual director circumstances, director-initiated resignations, and performance deficiencies. Policies need to define the procedures to be followed in each type of case and specify the responsibilities of the chair, vice-chair, and secretary for following up on absent members.

2. Make attendance as easy as possible

Many board activities and decisions occur on an annual cycle. In most organizations you know months ahead when you must hold your Annual General Meeting and fundraising events, when grant proposals must be submitted, and when budgets must be approved. You can use this knowledge to plan your meeting agendas, committee meetings, and reporting dates months in advance. At least twice a year, the chair and CEO or executive committee (if you have one) should review upcoming decision dates and prepare an annual agenda and meeting schedule.

Directors should check the agenda against their personal calendars to identify any foreseeable conflicts and reschedule meetings if necessary to ensure full attendance.

Boards should ensure their meeting rooms have at least a multi-line speaker phone to enable remote participation by directors unable to be present in person. (You might need to include authority for this in your bylaws.) Developments in Internet technology like Skype make it possible to video conference without the expense of past methods of video conferencing.

3. Carefully plan meeting agendas

Garber's First Law of Board Meetings states "The purpose of a board meeting is to make decisions that require the whole board." You should not have any discussion items on the agenda that can be decided by an officer or a committee. If the board is making decisions that don't require the whole board, they should be delegating those decisions, not wasting the time of other directors.

Two tools can be used to ensure that board members' time is not wasted on matters that do not require their participation: a consent agenda and a priority-based order of business.

◆ The consent agenda enables all items on which there have been consensus to be approved without discussion. Use your Internet search engine to learn how it works.

◆ The priority-based order of business is based on a time management tool which classifies all tasks on a matrix of urgency and importance. An item is "urgent" if the decision cannot be made at a future meeting. It is "important" to the extent that the decision impacts on the achievement of the organization's vision and mission. Instead of using the standard order of business (which places new business at the end of the meeting, after reports and unfinished business), the board meeting begins with discussion of items that are both urgent *and* important. Next on the agenda are items that are urgent but less important. Third are the items that are important but for which a decision is not essential at this meeting. Items that are neither urgent nor important are placed on the consent agenda and are only discussed if someone requests it.

To use these tools, meetings must be planned in advance. If you have an executive committee, this would be a good job for them. If not, the chair and secretary, assisted by the executive director, should form the meeting planning committee. Part of the task of planning each meeting is to review and evaluate the previous meeting. How did it go? Did it start and end on time? Did everyone participate? What can we do to ensure that everyone is able to participate in the discussion?

4. Attend to board recruitment, orientation, training and evaluation

When successful performance in a job is important, the employer conducts a systematic recruitment and careful selection process. The employer provides a thorough orientation and opportunities for development, and regularly evaluates the incumbent's performance.

Too many boards recruit anyone with a pulse, provide no orientation or training opportunities, and let them keep their seats on the board whether they contribute anything or not. This sends a powerful message to everyone that the board doesn't matter, so why bother coming to meetings.

If you don't treat board members like their performance matters, you'll be lucky to get any performance at all.

The board's recruitment and orientation process should make two things clear about attendance:

◆ Excused or unexcused absences make no difference to the board. If you need board members to contribute their knowledge and experience to the decision making, they need to be there or you cannot make the best decisions.

◆ Directors who do not attend meetings might be held liable for decisions made in their absence if the board's decisions (or lack of them) result in legal action against the board. Some legal experts argue that by not attending the meeting and participating in the decision, they are in breach of their fiduciary duties and have even greater liability.

5. Pay attention to attendance

As with poor recruitment and training, failure to follow up on absenteeism sends a clear message that directors' participation is not valued. To commit to full attendance, board members must know that their participation is essential for the board to make the best possible decisions. The board must have a standard practice for contacting board members whenever they have missed a meeting without explanation and before meetings when their special knowledge or experience is important to the items on the agenda.

It seems logical that this should be the job of the chair but the chair is (or should be) a big enough job. Many boards have a vice chair whose only responsibility is to chair meetings when the chair is absent. Personally, my first choice is to give the job to the vice chair but it really doesn't matter who gets it as long as it is a specific duty and assigned to someone. If it's not built in to a job description, it won't get done. But please, don't give this job to the executive director. This is a board responsibility.

After a missed meeting, the "attendance counselor" should confirm that the director received the meeting package and find out if there is any likelihood the director will miss the next meeting. If there are issues for the board to address, these should be brought to the attention of the chair or executive committee. If there has been a history of absenteeism, the "attendance counselor" should contact the director after the board package has been sent and let the director know of any upcoming decisions that would benefit from the director's expertise or individual point of view.

Final Comments

Many boards create attendance policies that are at best, unenforceable, and at worst, make board decision making impossible. Creating and enforcing attendance policies must include discussion of the possible causes for absenteeism and an honest self-evaluation of board practices for your own organization's unique circumstances.

Board meetings of nonprofit organizations are not like workplace meetings or like legislatures. No one is paid or forced to attend. There is no hierarchy. Boards are created and maintained by people with shared values and a common vision. Their discussions are not debates but exercises in collaborative decision-making. Ensuring full attendance requires all directors to feel welcome and appreciated and to feel certain that they are contributing to the fulfillment of the organization's mission.

 Connect with Nathan at http://charitychannel.com/cc/nathan-garber

Planning a Board Retreat

By Marion Conway

A board retreat is the prime opportunity to discuss a matter of importance in-depth and without the normal board business that gobbles up almost all meetings. Another essential part of board retreats is having the time and structure for building relationships. Boards are teams and people on teams must have respectful and trustful relationships with each other in order to work well together and make effective decisions.

The only thing worse for a board member than a board meeting that wastes their time is a board retreat that is a waste of time. It is important for a board retreat to be well planned for it to be successful. It is best to form the retreat planning team a few months in advance. You'll need to confirm a location, lock in a date with a facilitator and have a mix of meetings, conference calls, and detailed agenda reviews to finalize the program. There might be pre-retreat activities like filling out a questionnaire or completing a board assessment. Whatever is the main focus of your retreat it will be a better one if you allow enough planning time. I usually say the summer is a perfect time to plan for the fall retreat.

This article provides planning tips so that your retreat will be a success.

Choosing the Retreat Theme

What will be the theme for your board retreat? Each board has different needs and each year brings new issues that should be addressed. Decide what is most important for your board to take the extra time for each year and then design your retreat around that theme. Some popular themes include:

- ◆ board development including orientation, training, self-assessment, or developing fundraising expertise;

◆ strategic planning;

◆ planning for a major/critical issue (i.e., succession planning, building plan);

◆ leadership;

◆ team development;

◆ planning for major anniversaries or other milestones; or

◆ developing the board/staff relationship.

Planning the Retreat Program

Start the planning for your retreat by asking these questions. What do you hope to *accomplish* by having the retreat and what will *success* look like? Below are two examples for very different retreats, but both examples share things in common:

◆ detailed planning;

◆ retreat built on advance work;

◆ specific goals and definition of success; and

◆ designed to have a follow-up action.

The program should be designed to keep the group's interest and focus for an extended period of time. Make the most of a variety of techniques and keep them all tied to the theme of your retreat. Recommended techniques include:

◆ *Pre-retreat materials* —These can spark interest in participating in the retreat but they can also create a bunch of "regrets." Think this through before you send a hundred pages of pre-retreat reading to board members.

◆ *Icebreakers*—The best ones will have a relationship to the theme or the mission of the organization.

◆ *Group activities*—Activities designed to build teamwork work well.

◆ *Breakout groups*—This is the time for thoughtful discussion.

◆ *Presentations*—This provides opportunity for learning and knowledge building about the organization, serving on boards, or the "industry" in which the organization is involved.

◆ *Facilitation*—Facilitated discussion and activities can help your retreat go smoothly.

◆ *Appreciative Inquiry*—Appreciative inquiry is a change management model that provides a positive approach to addressing change and has a variety of techniques that can be used.

When designing the activities keep these ideas in mind:

◆ Focus on your retreat goals.

◆ Seek consensus.

◆ Develop recommendations that will turn into action.

◆ Wrap up should include your "next steps" action plan.

How Long Should the Retreat Be Anyway?

It used to be common for nonprofit board retreats to be on Friday night and all day Saturday. But on every retreat I have been at in the last several years with this design the feedback always says make it one day. More retreat facilitation requests I get today are for a one day retreat. But I truly discourage half day events as they seem to take on the aura of a "regular" board meeting and don't allow for the crucial team building which make board retreats effective.

The informal aspects of the board retreat are as important as the formal parts and need to be taken seriously in the planning stage. Allowing time for the board to socialize informally before the program, at meals and breaks and a team-building exercise are important features in a board retreat.

Appreciative Inquiry (AI)—AI is an alternative to the traditional strengths, weaknesses, opportunities and threats (SWOT) exercise. AI builds on an organization's strengths only and rather than assume there are "problems to be solved" it assumes the organization holds "solutions" already and the process is intended to draw them out and enhance them. There are many books on this subject but a good practical primer is *Appreciative Inquiry—A Positive Revolution in Change* by David L. Cooperrider and Diana Wiley. For some organizations AI might be more effective than a traditional SWOT exercise but it requires thoughtful preparation and facilitation.

practical tip

A board is a team and team members need to develop trust, respect and camaraderie to work together well and the board retreat is a prime opportunity for this to develop.

Planning for food is also important. It should not leave participants "overstuffed and sleepy." As a facilitator I always suggest it is something that allows for flexibility in timing. Both of these thoughts equate to "Stay away from hot meals with gravy at midday. Save dessert for the break. If you are planning a "festive, celebratory" meal as part of the retreat, plan it at the *end* of the retreat—not in the middle.

The Retreat Leadership Team Checklist

The board president or board retreat chair, the executive director, the retreat facilitator, and perhaps one or two others usually form the core leadership team for the retreat. Responsibilities that need to be completed include:

- ◆ Select a comfortable retreat location (e.g. community center, corporate training center, spiritual retreat center, local college).

- ◆ Decide on the room layout and size requirements.

- ◆ Develop detailed retreat schedule with timeframes for all segments.

- ◆ Assign responsibility for each segment.

- ◆ Develop presentation materials.

- ◆ Develop/select group exercises.

- ◆ Develop questions and assign facilitators for breakout groups.

Planning Your Board Retreat with a Facilitator

The services provided by a facilitator will vary. Think about which services you are interested in before interviewing facilitators. Here are some services that many facilitators will provide:

- ◆ retreat program design;

- ◆ retreat facilitation;

- ◆ pre-retreat planning;

- ◆ choice of presentation topics;

- ◆ board self assessment;

- ◆ strategic planning exercises;

- ◆ customized retreat feedback questionnaire;

- ◆ suggested follow-up approaches for action;

- ◆ board materials; and

- ◆ specialized expertise, i.e. fundraising, leadership development, program evaluation.

practical tip

◆ Arrange for materials needed (e.g. flipcharts, markers, projector).

◆ Develop list of action items for follow up.

◆ Create a summary document of all the flip charts. (This is the permanent record of ideas and follow-up items.)

◆ Engage the board in committees and projects based on the action items.

The key is to define success up front and then make sure that your program is geared toward inspiring action and results once the retreat is long over.

Two Examples of Retreat Plans

Example #1: The purpose of the retreat is board development and recruitment. It will be a successful retreat if two invitees join the board and the board members take action to increase their effectiveness.

The retreat might include:

◆ highlights of recent accomplishments—a short video works well;

◆ presentation of board roles and responsibilities;

◆ a group activity in which board members describe their experience with the mission and prospective members describe what they hope it might be;

◆ refreshment or meal break;

◆ board self-assessment feedback;

◆ executive director presentation of goals; and

◆ next steps—action based on board assessment feedback and goals.

Example #2: The purpose of the retreat is to complete the strategic plan. The strategic planning committee will present the findings and recommendations of their work over the last nine months. The retreat will be successful if the board adopts/ updates vision and mission statements, develops goals for the next three years, is energized, adopts strategic thinking as a way of doing business and if working committees are formed to accomplish the goals.

This retreat could include:

◆ a teamwork icebreaker;

◆ presentation of the strategic planning committee report—summary of pre-retreat materials;

◆ facilitated segments with whole group activities to develop mission and vision statements and develop values;

◆ breakout groups to develop major goals—committee members lead groups; and

◆ next steps—create working committees for each goal.

 Connect with Marion at http://charitychannel.com/cc/marion-conway

Advice to Business People Joining Nonprofit Boards

By Gayle L. Gifford, ACFRE

Congratulations! You've just joined the board of directors of a charitable nonprofit. If this is a new experience for you, you are in good company. Many businesses today encourage their employees to serve on nonprofit boards.

You'll share the experience of board service with individuals from all walks of life. A few might already be old hands at nonprofit governance. A rarer few have attended workshops or studied some of the literature on nonprofit board governance.

Many, however, are learning on-the-job, just like you.

Maybe your organization provided you with a comprehensive orientation to help you start your work on the board. Maybe you were teamed with a more experienced director who is serving as your mentor. With luck, you joined a superb board that's filled with great role models.

It's not unusual to feel a little unsure of yourself at first. You should find the reception welcoming, as most nonprofit staff and directors relish the opportunity to benefit from the business savvy, strategic mindset, professional connections, and access to resources that directors from corporate backgrounds can contribute.

Yet, I frequently hear complaints that all of those desired qualities seem to evaporate as soon as a business person is elected to a board. And I often hear business people describe their frustration with their board service.

So here are a few insights about nonprofits that I've realized over the last thirty years—and a few tips to help make your board service more rewarding.

Let me start with the insights.

Nonprofits Have a Different Bottom Line

In business, the bottom line is easy to understand—it's all about *profit*. Even if your business advocates a dual bottom line (social responsibility and profit), profit doesn't take second place.

In a nonprofit, there is no private inurement. The bottom line is the delivery of a public benefit—for example, an artistic contribution, environmental protection, or health promotion. Determining what that public benefit is, how to deliver it and how to evaluate performance isn't always easy.

Imagine you are on the board of an organization dedicated to the promotion of practices for good mental health. Can you concretely define what success looks like? What evidence would you point to? What changes would your small agency claim responsibility for? These are the challenges that will face you as a director of a nonprofit board.

Nonprofits are valued for their prudence, commitment to service and fiscal restraint, yet are expected to produce significant community benefits

In the for-profit world, business owners are rewarded for taking risks—usually with other people's money (venture capital). Under-capitalization is warned against. And a personality like Donald Trump is lionized for his opulent lifestyle and forgiven for past business failures.

Not so in the nonprofit world. Here, individuals are expected to make sacrifices for the common good in the name of service. Making do with less is a familiar mantra. Pick up a business publication, and the virtuous charities are the ones with the lowest overhead.

Meanwhile, nonprofits are being admonished to "act more like businesses." In reality, most nonprofits are extraordinarily small, much more comparable to "micro-enterprises." According to January 2010 data available through the National Center for Charitable Statistics, over 78 percent of registered US public charities reported annual revenues below $250,000. At these smallest of nonprofits, nominally-paid staff or their volunteer leadership often have limited experience in nonprofit management and resource development—yet they are expected to operate as efficiently and effectively as multimillion dollar, professionally staffed organizations.

It's surprising that these tiny organizations get anything accomplished at all. But they do! From the neighborhood soup kitchen feeding the hungry to the volunteer land trust preserving hundreds of acres of open space to the volunteer ethnic organization staging an annual cultural festival for 20,000 participants, many tiny nonprofits are making significant and valuable contributions to their communities.

Nonprofits are expected to consult with their stakeholders and to collaborate with their colleagues

It's not unusual for business people to comment on the pace of decision-making that occurs at many nonprofits. Change might happen more slowly than they are used to.

Because nonprofits are accountable to their community for doing well, stakeholders (like consumers, funders, politicians) expect to have some say in their functioning. If your nonprofit depends on public generosity for a sizeable portion of its revenue base, you need to ensure that your constituents understand and support the actions you take, or you put at risk their goodwill and continued financial support.

Decisions and actions both big and small often rely on volunteers

If a nonprofit has no staff or limited staff, volunteers are performing much of the work. The biggest decisions of all—where to dedicate resources, what community needs to focus on, and what strategies to deploy, are made by volunteers, *you, the board.*

Imagine your business-self managing a motley crew of unpaid staff with varied levels of expertise, skills and experience. Family and work demands always take priority over their volunteer commitments. Managing volunteers requires all of the skills and tools you would use with your paid staff, absent one obvious and highly motivating reward—money. Get the idea of the challenges you face?

Despite these differences, there are many experiences that nonprofits and businesses have in common

Whether for-profit or nonprofit, all enterprises need to be responsive to their marketplace. All enterprises need business acumen and effective operations to be successful. Quality research and information are essential for good decision-making. Ethical behavior and accountability maintain public goodwill. And every enterprise needs the structures, systems, people, skills, strategy and self-reflection that are essential elements of success.

So, as a nonprofit director, how can you best put your business experience to work?

Here are a few tips to get you started.

Focus on the bottom line—the mission

As I said earlier, in a nonprofit, the mission is the bottom line. If you think of your community as your shareholders, achievement of your mission is the shareholder value that you've promised to deliver. Your nonprofit has committed to making the world a better place—by filling an un-met need, solving an important problem, creating new knowledge, or by increasing the level of joy or beauty for the people who live here. Everything your nonprofit does should be measured against how well it is fulfilling that mission.

Don't undercapitalize

Successful nonprofits also need the financial and other resources to get the job done. So while you focus on the mission, don't forget to ensure that your organization has a well-developed capacity to obtain the resources it needs to keep moving forward. The fewer staff you have, the more likely that you, a leadership volunteer, will play a critical role in obtaining those vital resources.

Do your homework

You wouldn't think of starting a new company or making a major business decision without quality research to inform your decision. Yet, many nonprofit board members are tempted to make decisions based on their personal feelings or individual experiences. Do your research. Don't conjecture. Seek out best practices and benchmarks. Keep up-to-date on issues affecting both nonprofits and your charitable mission. Ask for time at board meetings for education as well as action.

Share what you know

Just like your business, your nonprofit needs your skills as an entrepreneur, a resource-getter, a strategic thinker, a people-motivator, or an organization builder. That's why they recruited you. Apply those talents to your work on the board.

Ask board leadership for your job plan and annual performance measures

Just as you provide your employees with job descriptions and clear expectations for performance, you should expect the same of your board. What is it that you have committed to? What will you achieve during your term of office? What are your personal priorities? What resources do you have to work with? What relationships are critical? What are the limits of your position? How will you be evaluated?

Be serious about legal matters

It's tempting for volunteers, especially in all of those tiny organizations, to think—"those rules don't apply to our little local agency." Whether you are a $100,000 or $100 million nonprofit, you are similarly bound by federal or state statutes.

Do you know your legal responsibilities as a director? Do you understand the federal, state and local regulations governing your nonprofit? Be vigilant about these matters. You might expose yourself to personal liability if you are negligent or willfully violate the rules.

Hold core values of stewardship and ethical behavior

The nonprofit sector depends on the trust and confidence of the public for its existence. When a nonprofit violates that trust, it places the whole sector in danger of losing the unique privileges afforded to tax-exempt organizations. Nonprofits survive because they have promised the public that they will use their resources wisely for the community good and not for personal gain—the essence of stewardship. It's easier to be ethical when you're committed to wise stewardship.

Combine an entrepreneurial attitude with patience

In its study of high performing boards, the international consulting firm of McKinsey & Company report that nonprofit leaders tell us that *"when boards…devote time to providing expertise, helping managers get access to people and resources, and building managerial capacity, their organizations benefit the most."*

At the same time, McKinsey and Company stated in a report on nonprofit capacity building that *"almost everything about building capacity in nonprofits (and in for-profit companies) takes longer and is more complicated that one would expect."* Entrepreneurship and patience are important virtues.

Last, but definitely not least, be courageous

It is not easy to be a good board member. It's hard to rock the boat or risk offending business colleagues by asking questions that everyone else seems to be dodging, or by insisting on right but difficult courses of action. Even setting goals takes tremendous courage. But nonprofits need, no, they *require* the courage of board members. As Dr. Martin Luther King Jr. said, *"the time is always right to do what is right."* It's just not always easy.

Good luck. Enjoy your board service!

 Connect with Gayle at http://charitychannel.com/cc/gayle-gifford

Envisioning Community Change:
The Real Beginning to the Journey

By Jane Garthson

How often have I heard, or even said, that statement? It is meant to encourage people to take some small action towards their dream. A thousand miles can seem impossible, but surely anyone can take one step.

> The journey of a thousand miles begins with one step.
>
> —Lao Tzu

But no true journey begins with a single step. From any given point, we can move in many directions. We make choices about our destination, our route and our means of travel. Then we know what direction to step. So we have a vision of what success looks like—reaching our intended destination, or in the case of community benefit organizations, our ideal world.

Why then do people in organizations take many steps in different, almost random, directions? Without a vision of what overall success looks like, their decisions about which way to step are made in isolation. Often no progress is made towards a better community. With an inspiring destination in mind, we might chose better options that work in harmony towards that destination, and leverage resources much more effectively. The destination will inspire others to walk with us, and provide support along the way. And if we harness our efforts and enthusiasm towards creating strength, we are much less likely to choose programs that maintain dependency.

There are proven, practical, realistic methodologies to align your efforts towards a common dream, and make faster progress than you had dreamt possible. They can be used by the community as a whole, by some subset of the community, by a single organization, by an informal group, or even by one individual. Or go bigger—the steps can be used by international organizations and by groups of countries, or by related organizations or professionals around the world. A community can be whatever you define it to be: a geographic area of any size, people with shared interests, a membership group, a faith or simply those affected by each other's actions. You need to define community to make this process work, but any definition is acceptable.

These steps can work for all sizes and types of nonprofit organizations (associations, charities, corporations, community groups and more). They can be used to get new organizations off to an optimal start, or help existing organizations achieve their highest potential.

1. Create a dream for the community, using the present tense and outlining its highest potential, not some stop along the road.

Since the dream is about the community, the best initial discussions are done with the whole community. Bring as much of your community as you can, or are willing to, together for informal dialogue in a safe, casual environment. Have the session led by a facilitator neutral about the outcome, knowledgeable about strategic thinking and planning for nonprofits, and skilled in group processes.

Some organizations are only comfortable with board, staff and key volunteers at the initial session, and that's just fine. However, the wider the initial involvement, the less time you need to spend later consulting stakeholders and gaining their commitment. Those present at the start of an exciting idea will be more enthusiastic than those talked into it later.

Break the room into small groups, and ask each to consider possible futures and describe their ideal future in relation to your sector, or the sector of those you have brought together, such as health. Give no timelines other than to assume that today's personalities and resources are not relevant; we have no idea at this stage how long the journey will be. Avoid putting the current organization into the picture for now, as you do not yet know whether your organization will exist in the ideal future. Be firm on this; if you hear a group talking

---

A Six Step Process That Works

1. Create a dream for the community, using the present tense and outlining its highest potential, not some stop along the road.

2. Recognize the ethical values implicit in the dream that has been described, and know that you cannot create a community based on those values using methods inconsistent with those values.

3. Identify what needs to change in your community for the dream to become real.

4. Choose your role in changing one or more of those conditions towards the ideal.

5. Set your priorities for carrying out that role starting today, guided by the ethical values and leveraging today's resources.

6. Take the first step—then another and another.

practical tip

about the organization, bring them back to talking about the community instead. Remind them that resources limit how fast you achieve the ideal, not what the ideal is.

Often, people who never could agree on anything before find that they really do agree on the world they are trying to create—the disagreements had been about methods or speed. Sometimes, they find out who is holding them back—like a young professional employee who told us her ideal world was one in which the organization was still struggling to build awareness of the problem! No wonder no real progress was being made in her area; she was carefully ensuring lifelong employment for herself. This was not intentional; she had just been taught to limit her dreams to what was "realistic."

What is not realistic is to think there will ever be enough resources to serve a community or a world defined by weaknesses and growing needs. Deciding on the right small steps to build on strengths, to not only decrease need but increase abundance, is the only realistic route to a better future. The community might not be a lot better at first, but it will be somewhat better, and the steps are at least in the right direction.

> ### Creative Communicating
>
> I prefer to use crayons and flip charts and ask for pictures. It creates a new power dynamic, as the leader with the big ego and loud voice might not feel confident in his or her drawing ability, and the new intern or shy client might. Besides, in Western culture, we all drew as children but most of us stopped by the time we were teenagers. We seem to need our inner child back to dream of what is possible. Be flexible about how the creative process unfolds—if a group prefers to sing or dance their ideas, why not? At this stage, words hold us back, but there are many ways to communicate without words.
>
> Pictures reveal values faster than any dialogue ever could. For the health sector, for example, is the ideal future focused on the latest and best health care, or on helping people lead healthy lives with minimal dependency on health care? The pictures will show how different people in the room are really thinking, and whether there are similarities, small differences or chasms to discuss.

So if the drawings are in conflict, talk it through. An hour of guided discussion might save hundreds of hours in future decision-making. Perhaps the table that drew a picture of dependency will be inspired by other visions in the room, and willing to put theirs aside. Perhaps they realize the values depicted are not really what they want for their community. Or perhaps their vision is so incompatible that it makes no sense to remain involved with that organization. Now they know to move on, and will no longer being there holding your organization back.

Once there is consensus, or a clear parting of the ways, a small working group can take away the ideas and create an elegant vision statement. To keep the vision short enough to remember, there might also be a list of goals that elaborate on the ideal community.

Think about history. If some people once felt that it was okay for others to be slaves so some could have a life of ease and comfort, and others felt that all humanity deserved freedom and a chance for a better life, those ideas could not peacefully co-exist indefinitely. Was some dissent worthwhile so the better set of ethical values could prevail?

Usually, the conflict is really between optimists and pessimists, and whoever wins control will make their prediction come true. Countries that have believed high rates of AIDS-HIV could be significantly reduced now have lower rates than those who believed it couldn't. Think about your situation. Would you rather work or volunteer with those who are focused on changing a bad situation into a better one, or with those who see themselves forever fighting a losing battle?

food for thought

Many groups find they can establish the key concepts and give a working group sufficient guidance in about an hour and half after starting the session, by the way. But if there is no history of working together, and an environment of distrust or significant lack of knowledge about each other's backgrounds and organizations, it might take several significantly longer sessions.

2. Recognize the ethical values implicit in the dream that has been described, and know that you cannot create a community based on those values by using methods that violate those values.

The pictures or descriptions will have certain words in common, or synonyms, when people talk about them. Certain words like "caring" show up over and over. In some gatherings, there will be numerous references to social justice, equitable distribution of wealth and such. In other cases, those words will never be heard but there will be numerous references to the natural environment, lifelong health, supportive families and productive lives. Another gathering will focus on the right of individuals to live to their fullest potential, including the joy of creating and enjoying art in all its forms. A whole community get-together might have all of these and many more.

Never assume a single word or short phrase has a shared meaning among the participants, because it never does. Some dialogue will be needed as people explain what they meant, and perhaps find more acceptable words for some that provoked a negative reaction. Most groups will move towards inspirational terms such as peace rather than "absence of violence" but there is no right answer.

Once there is some agreement on key values, again hive this off into a separate working group to develop sentences about each concept and bring them back for more dialogue. Never "wordsmith" in a large group.

If the group has a good current set of ethical values, well described, amending them to reflect the new vision might take very little time. If this is the first time the organization has created real values statements, not just lists of words, but everyone is in the room, a day might be needed.

In larger organizations, where different locations and teams need to be consulted, at least two sessions will be needed.

3. Identify what needs to change in your community for the dream to become real.

Brainstorm to create what will probably be a long list of areas where people are dissatisfied. Include everything, even those that are the responsibilities of higher levels of government or that seem unchangeable. The steps in the journey might include advocacy to influence government, or primary research into a disease that has always been with us. (As I write this article, my local paper reports on promising research that could eliminate malaria!)

Talk a bit about what makes sense to tackle first, as prerequisites to other changes, but remember that others might see a different critical path. The neighbors on a street might see beautifying the street and holding a party as the first step, while those in another neighborhood are focused on a new school and others are planting trees to improve air quality. At this stage there is often great enthusiasm and energy. As long as the ideas are not in conflict, and are based on informal volunteering, they can proceed concurrently.

4. Choose your role in changing one or more of those conditions towards the ideal.

Within an organization, however, wise use of limited resources must be considered.

The organizations involved need to meet on their own to discuss their own choices. They have not lost any independence by participating in the larger discussion, but they have likely committed by now to transparency about their choices to the other participants. They have likely also committed to meeting again, or regularly, to coordinate efforts.

It might be that the new choices are consistent with the current mission or purpose statements; it might not. Many mission statements are all about the organization and nothing about supporting a vision for a better world or community. Many are about serving a "forever" need and people no longer see the need as existing forever.

Do you see now why starting with the mission makes no sense? There is no purpose in having strong, financially sustainable nonprofits excellent in customer service if they are not making the community better. Nonprofits should be the means to an end, not the end in themselves.

This discussion could take an hour or it could take much longer. The mission or purpose statement will guide every subsequent decision; the ideas in it really matter and important discussions should not be cut off.

5. Set your priorities for carrying out that role starting today, guided by the ethical values and leveraging today's resources.

This step will be accomplished within each organization, but it is often good to include larger group as well. It is then easier to find synergies, partnerships, collaborations and opportunities to share resources, as well as highlighting any areas of overlap that might waste efforts.

By the way, "today's resources" might well have expanded greatly from the date of the initial gathering, even if that was last week. Enthusiastic new volunteers might have appeared. Local businesses might be realizing they have many in kind services to offer once they realize how much difference those services can make in the community where they also live. Governments, if they were not on board at the start, might be hearing from many citizens that they need to come to the table.

As a result, the group needs to keep meeting, to engage additional people and organizations, keep each other informed about efforts, and find new ways to work together for faster and more positive change.

Even if prior sessions to establish priorities were contentious and lengthy in your organization, the earlier steps in this process make priorities obvious, and agreement usually fast. Remember that unless you are stopping all current work, continuing it must be on the priorities. One hundred percent of the budget should be allocated to these priorities, along with everyone's time.

6. Take the first step—then another and another.

A good process leads to quick actions and successes, as people realize they can start changing conditions in the community within existing resources and operational authority. Encourage everyone to consider the preliminary ideas they have heard and develop ways to apply them without waiting for the working groups to do the wordsmithing and setting of key performance indicators. Don't wait for the board to approve a plan—a plan is a record of the process, developed primarily for reference, orientation and communication. The process and discussions matter much more. But you do need to get it written down so you can monitor the plan following benchmarks that have been established.

Have fun along the road. Stop to check the map, and see where others are in their journey, but keep going towards that dream. Celebrate the milestones as you pass them. Welcome those who join, and recognize the contributions of those who cannot continue the journey. Make your dream a reality.

 Connect with Jane at http://charitychannel.com/cc/jane-garthson

Forget the Strategic Plan (Build Strategic Awareness Instead)

By Steven Bowman

Strategic planning has such a bad reputation out there. Why do so many nonprofits shudder when the strategic plan cycle comes around again? Why do so many never complete or follow their strategic plan? Why do so many not have a strategic plan? In our experience of over thirty-five years in the nonprofit sector at senior leadership levels and advisory positions, over 85 percent of strategic plans we have seen are useless and the CEOs and boards readily agree these plans are useless.

Here are some of the more common reasons and justifications we've come across as to why traditional strategic planning just doesn't work. We're sure you will be able to add to the list!

- Strategic planning is a waste of time, too complex and with limited outcomes.

- Day to day issues require a lot of time and attention, leaving little time available for us to do any planning, let alone strategic planning.

- The strategic plan process is a commercial business technique which is not appropriate or suitable for our nonprofit.

- We only do strategic planning because our funding is tied to us having a strategic plan. Thank heavens it is over for this year!

- *What, you want me to do my job and this darn strategic plan as well! Not going to happen!!* (Probably not a good career move, but very common nevertheless.)

So let's start from scratch. Let's put aside the strategic plan—at least for now. Let's instead focus on creating a culture of strategic awareness at the board and senior executive level. Once we have this strategic awareness regularly occurring at the leadership level, then the strategic plan—perhaps a different version of the strategic plan—starts to make sense and actually has the possibility of truly adding value.

How Do We Create Strategic Awareness?

Strategic awareness is how non-analytic data is accessed through what is best described as awareness or inner knowing, and is incorporated into the strategic decision-making process of the board and senior executives as an integral component. Furthermore, awareness, when combined with strategy, enhances analytic thinking and provides insights as to timing, specific strategy and innovation. Strategic awareness allows us to take in a wide range of information and perceive things in a broader context, to take advantage of opportunities and to avoid problems that trap other people.

This powerful combination of awareness and business strategy creates momentum and enables us to take advantage of all the new opportunities that the hyper-change environment is creating.

Breaking this down. . .

◆ Awareness is the ability each of us has to know something directly without analytic processing. It is an intrinsic skill and a natural gift we all have. Among its many descriptions, awareness is depicted as the ability to know without the use of rational thought processes or direct cognition.

◆ Strategic awareness is the process of fusing awareness to strategy, and incorporating real world knowledge of industry, global trends and possible futures.

◆ Our view is that being strategic is less about planning ahead and more about continuous monitoring of the environment, rapid response and fast adaptation. Being strategic means being clear about the organization's vision and mission, being aware of the organization's resources, incorporating both into being consciously responsive to a dynamic environment and being strategic results in the development of strategy.

Awareness without strategy often results in being mesmerized in the potential possibility realm, bouncing from idea to idea almost at random without the need or strategy to carry it through in physical reality. Strategy without awareness leads to dangerous practices that are not fluid and do not take into account the changing environment.

So Where Do We Start? With the Board, of Course!

To create a culture of strategic awareness at the senior leadership level means we should start with the board. Here are some tips to start creating this culture.

1. Select the right people for the board. How a board member chooses to 'be' is more important than their set of technical skills. Even for those boards who are wholly elected, these are the abilities that should be encouraged from those elected.

◆ No fixed point of view—willing to look at options rather than try to make the world fit their fixed point of view of how things should be.

◆ Willing to receive information without judgment and look at it as it is—not as good or bad, right or wrong.

◆ Willing to both analyze and listen to intuition, taking note of the risk and forecasts, and also listening to their 'gut instinct.'

◆ Viewing the world from prosperity vs. scarcity, where life is seen as possibility, not the lack of.

Everyone has these abilities. It is all a matter of personal choice. A board will be more strategically aware and create greatest change where these skills are encouraged and modeled by the chair and directors, rather than a board where the individuals have high technical skills, but choose not to use the abilities mentioned above.

2. Develop a strategic induction or orientation program. One of the best ways to develop a strategic awareness culture in the board is to start at the beginning. As part of the induction program for new board members, develop an induction session that includes:

◆ relevant documents;

◆ an introduction to the culture of the board—e.g., here's how we stay strategic as a board;

◆ questions we expect you to consider and ask;

◆ high expectations—made clear from the beginning;

◆ information on how we live the vision and mission; and

◆ site visits to relevant programs.

3. Design meetings to facilitate strategic thinking and strategic awareness.

◆ Make every meeting a planning session. Structure the board agenda to reflect the key strategies, rather than sticking the strategic goals down as item forty-six on a forty-eight item agenda.

◆ Add the vision statement to the board agenda. If the board chooses to use this to inform discussions and decisions, this can focus the discussion on what is really important to the organization.

◆ Align staff reports to strategy. Ensure that staff reports or proposals indicate how they are achieving the strategic directions and where they fit in the strategic goals.

◆ Provide professional development of the board. At every second board meeting, arrange for someone to provide the board with strategic insight into the environment they are making decisions about.

◆ Schedule staff presentations at board meetings. Every second board meeting have a staff member make presentations to the board regarding the strategic issues that staff person faces in their area of responsibility, and invite the board to ask questions regarding those strategic issues.

◆ Focus on changes to strategic environment. Develop a section of the agenda where board members are encouraged to bring to the board's attention any changes they have seen, heard about or have some insight into that might affect the assumptions the organization works under through its strategic plan.

◆ Rely on dashboard reporting. Develop dashboard reports that highlight graphically the key elements of the strategic plan, finances and relevant areas such as occupational health and safety statistics.

4. Structure interactions to facilitate strategic awareness:

◆ Provide a list of strategic questions for board members as part of the standard board reports sent out prior to meetings.

◆ Ask different board members to take on the point of view of a specific stakeholder group as part of the discussion (similar to deBono's 'Six Hats' thinking method).

◆ Insist on multiple options for discussion and decision, rather than focusing too quickly on 'the answer.'

◆ Include one or two "strategic questions for consideration" as part of each proposal to the board.

Focus on creating a culture of strategic awareness, and the strategic plan will sort itself out.

 Connect with Steven at http://charitychannel.com/cc/steven-bowman

Why is Risk Really Strategic Advantage?

By Steven Bowman

M ost chief executives, when asked to define risk, describe their view of risk as:

  ◆ something negative that happens to the organization;

  ◆ the potential for loss;

  ◆ fraud; or

  ◆ negative publicity.

When asked how their staff views risk, the descriptions get even more depressing:

  ◆ a pain in the neck;

  ◆ too complicated and difficult;

  ◆ something we have to do;

  ◆ a compliance issue; and

  ◆ not much use in our day-to-day work.

If these are the prevailing points of view on risk, then how will risk be managed by the organization and staff?

What if risk was nothing like this? What if risk was something completely different? What if risk was actually strategic advantage, hidden potential opportunity and the source of amazing innovation? If the organization chose to view risk from this point of view, how would staff view risk, and how would risk be identified and managed?

The two main formal definitions of risk are from Standards Australia (Australia) and the Committee of Sponsoring Organizations of the Treadway Commission (COSO, USA.) COSO is a voluntary private-sector organization, established in the United States, dedicated to providing guidance to executive management and governance entities on critical aspects of organizational governance, business ethics, internal control, enterprise risk management, fraud, and financial reporting. COSO has established a common internal control model against which companies and organizations may assess their control systems. They are very similar in intent, and focus on the strategic potentiality of risk, rather than the negative loss point of view.

For example, the Australian/New Zealand Standard AS/NZS 4360/2004 defines risk as: *"The chance of something happening that will have an impact on goals"* and risk management as: *"The culture, processes and structures that are directed towards the effective management of potential opportunities and adverse effects."*

What would it be like if risk was viewed as just another way of looking at potential opportunity and innovation? What if risk management was viewed as innovation?

What is the Point Behind Risk Management?

The point behind risk management is to identify all the potential risks, rank them according to potential to occur and possible impact if they do occur, determine the quality of existing controls on the risks, develop new controls and strategies for the risks (called "treatment" in risk jargon), monitor these and extract strategic advantage from the whole process. A simple process which is often made very complicated and difficult by the points of view that people hold about what risk is. And most organizations do not extract strategic advantage from the risk management process.

Risk management is the conscious awareness of all the risks involved in the organization, the strategic advantage of these risks, and the ease with which these risks can be managed. Though risk is inherent within all business opportunities,

---

Questions to ask about points of view regarding risk

◆ How does our staff view risk?

◆ How does our leadership team view risk?

◆ How does the chief executive view risk?

◆ How does the board view risk?

◆ What would it take for all organizational risk stakeholders to view risk as strategic advantage?

practical tip

many leaders prefer to be risk averse. This can lead to missing opportunities. The very nature of business endeavors and success demands leaders to have a willingness to receive everything without judgment.

How risk is defined and acted upon is all a matter of choice of the leaders. Nonprofit leaders can choose to view risk as bad, complex and to be avoided, or as a strategic advantage and potential source of innovation that can enable the organization to undertake activities that others might not even consider.

Identifying risks involves the conscious leader not having a fixed point of view of what constitutes risk, and involving others who have different points of view about the organization, and therefore different points of view about risk.

"Being the Question" and Risk Management

"Being the question" means using questions (either spoken or unspoken) to bypass the limited answers that your mind provides. A question creates the possibilities of things, not the limitations. A question allows you to see beyond conventional concepts. This is particularly important in risk management because it is tempting to just minimize a risk without looking at the risk and all the strategic opportunities and innovation that are possible once the risk has been identified. Questions will assist you to view risk from this point of view.

Questions help you to facilitate the changes you desire. They help you overcome obstacles and enable you to function from your knowing. "Being the question" allows you to create your organization with awareness.

Don't worry about the answer. Focus on the questions. Learn to love the questions themselves. This is where innovation stems from. Being the question is powerful. If your questions are infinite (not looking for the one right answer, but rather the many possibilities) and you really don't know the answers, then you set the stage for previously unthinkable leaps of awareness.

When you open up to genuine wonder, then you step out of the zone of the known and into the infinite creative possibilities of the unknown. This is what we term strategic opportunity.

When you are faced with a challenging situation, cultivate an attitude of curiosity. Allow for the infinite possibilities that are available to you by asking questions.

The key questions that the CEO and the board need to be aware of regarding risk include:

> If I had an hour to solve a problem, and my life depended on the solution, I would spend the first fifty-five minutes determining the proper question to ask, for once I knew the proper question I could solve the problem in less than five minutes. Many people are looking for answers and not asking the wisest questions.
>
> —Albert Einstein

◆ What are the potential risks from the points of view of those people who know our organization?

◆ Are the risks higher or lower than in the past, what has changed and do we have to do anything about it?

◆ What would it take for our organization to reduce or avoid the occurrence of the identified risks, and how can we turn this to our strategic advantage?

◆ Are the risks being monitored on an ongoing basis from the basis of questioning everything rather than just a compliance point of view?

Here are some practical steps to create a risk management plan that actually works.

The key steps in creating such a risk management plan are:

1. Identify all the potential risks.

2. Rank them according to potential to occur and possible impact if they do occur.

3. Determine the quality of existing controls on the risks.

4. Develop new controls and strategies for the risks (called "treatment" in risk jargon).

5. Monitor these treatments.

6. Extract strategic advantage from the whole process.

1. Identifying Risk—You Have to Start Somewhere!

Identifying risks involves you not having a fixed point of view of what constitutes risk, and involving others who have different points of view about the organization, and therefore different points of view about risk. If you involve only staff in identifying risk, they will do a great job, but will only identify what they know, i.e., operational risk.

Who will have points of view about your organization that matter to you? You might want to include:

◆ board;

◆ staff that are responsible for relevant areas;

- part time staff, contractors, others who conduct programs on your behalf;

- people affected by your services: clients, volunteers, members;

- union or staff representative groups such as the Safety Committee;

- funding bodies such as donors, government agencies, grant givers;

- regulatory entities;

- politicians who might have an electoral or portfolio interest;

- suppliers; and

- media.

Also, identify the risks that are identified with your:

- classes of assets in your asset register;

- profit & loss statement line items;

- strategic and business plan; and

- health and safety reports.

You can also benchmark against other organizations (swap risk registers/plans).

After the relevant stakeholders have been identified, decide whether to send them a risk identification survey, or conduct a short telephone interview, focus group or other mechanism aimed at identifying these risks. (NB: Use a spreadsheet so you can sort, add and compile!!)

The risk survey should be short, easy to fill in and not daunting!! Point out that you are collecting their views about the risks they perceive the organization faces.

List all major activities/projects you are involved in relevant to the organization. For each activity/project, describe:

- perceived risk and how it might occur;

- your rating: potential to occur (High/Medium/Low);

◆ your rating: impact if it does occur (High-Medium-Low); and

◆ ways to turn this to strategic advantage.

Compile the returns into a spreadsheet. Don't be surprised if most of these risks are rated as high from those who submit the risks. This is because from their point of view they are high, which is why we need to have a board-approved set of definitions of levels of risk.

Agree on the definitions to be used. The level of risk is determined by the relationship between the potential (frequency or probability of the risk occurring) and the consequence (impact or magnitude of the effect) and the robustness of the existing control mechanisms for that risk.

Each risk identified in the risk library should be analyzed for its potential to occur, and simultaneously be analyzed for its impact on the organization if it does occur, and the quality of the existing controls for that risk. The best way to ensure that everyone is on the same page is to create a list of agreed definitions for each of the potential, impact and control components. An example of these definitions can be found here: http://www.conscious-governance.com/images/stories/3.2-RiskRatingDefinitions.pdf.

It is probably best if the board's risk management committee or equivalent—e.g., finance and audit—sign off on these definitions, as they form the basis of identifying the key risks, and therefore the focus of the board.

It then becomes much simpler to identify those risks that will have the greatest impact on the ability of your nonprofit to deliver against your strategic objectives. They are those risks with the highest scores—i.e., high potential to occur, high impact if they do occur, and ineffective existing controls. And, you have agreed on the definitions of all these aspects! These risks are then put into a risk system (most common is a spreadsheet) which in risk management terms is called a risk library (all the identified risks and their ratings). An example risk library can be found here: http://www.conscious-governance.com/images/stories/3.2-RiskLibrary.pdf.

From there, each key risk needs to have a "treatment" plan (terminology used in risk management to mean what you are going to do about the risk). Most treatment plans we have seen miss the point of risk management. Most plans focus on reducing the risk. However, if risk is "anything that will impact on your ability to deliver against your strategic objectives," risk management should not be about reduction, but about how we can derive strategic advantage from understanding and managing that risk.

The risk committee (or equivalent) can then develop treatment plans for each of the identified risks, starting with the highest rated risks. A risk treatment plan should follow the principles of good project management—what, who, when, success measures etc. The one thing that will make your risk management plan create true value for your nonprofit organization is if you also include a section for each risk in the plan that explores "strategic advantage." The question to ask here is, "How can we turn this risk and our treatment of it, into strategic advantage?" Each key risk is in fact something that will impact on your ability to deliver against your strategic objectives. Therefore, key risks will have key strategic impacts and major strategic advantages if managed well. Your job is to identify these advantages and leverage off them.

You can find a sample of a completed risk management plan at http://www.conscious-governance.com/images/stories/3.2-RiskManagementPlan.pdf. Take particular note of the last column titled "strategic advantage."

What is the nonprofit board's role in all of this?

1. The board's role is to agree on and monitor the three or four critical risks facing the organization.

Regular board reports that analyze these critical risks, their monitoring and treatment provide the board with strategic information regarding the key drivers of the business. The board's role in monitoring these risks is not to ensure they don't occur, but to turn these risks into strategic advantage.

2. The board is responsible for approving and monitoring the risk management policy.

This responsibility is among one of the board's most important, as it commits the board and the organization to best practice risk management. Here is an example of a board risk management policy. http://www.conscious-governance.com/images/stories/2.6-RiskManagementPolicy.pdf.

3. Establish key performance indicators (KPIs) for the chief executive officer.

One of the most effective ways to ensure that staff, especially the CEO, treats risk as the strategic advantage it can be, is to establish one or two KPI's for the CEO that reflect the risk monitoring and management responsibility of that position. This tends to focus attention.

4. Embed risk into the strategic discussions and analysis of the board.

Risk awareness can best be embedded in the organization if some simple guidelines are followed:

a. When conducting strategic planning, conduct a SWOR (not a SWOT) analysis—i.e., Strengths, Weaknesses, Opportunities and Risks. These risks can then get added to your risk library, and provide further opportunities for identifying strategic advantage.

b. Only accept project plans or action plans if a risk element has been added to the project plan. For example, an action plan might have the headings of:

- ◆ scope;

- ◆ start date;

- ◆ finish date

- ◆ project manager;

- ◆ resources;

- ◆ success measures

- ◆ ethical implications; and

- ◆ risk

Once the risk has been identified, the management of that risk is quite easy.

c. When deliberating on decisions at the board meeting, ask the risk question: "What are the risks inherent in this proposal, and how can we turn these risks into strategic advantage?"

All of these ensure that risk is an ongoing strategic process, not a compliance issue.

 Connect with Steven at http://charitychannel.com/cc/steven-bowman

Section II—Making in Happen

The Executive/Board Chair Relationship: Good to Great!

By Mary Hiland, Ph.D.

I opened my inbox; this email greeted me:

> *Can you help me deal with a completely dysfunctional board chair? 'You know who' is destroying the board and undermining my leadership. Quite a mess! But, he is not able to destroy me or the organization! We are still strong. I will fill you in when we meet.*

Can you feel this executive's frustration? This executive/board chair disaster had been going on for more than a year!

With thirty years of direct experience in the nonprofit sector, I shouldn't be surprised by comments like these. Anyone who has worked or volunteered in the nonprofit sector for very long has heard stories of how a bad executive/board chair relationship wreaked havoc. (And I have heard equally dismaying stories about executives from board chairs.) And, you don't have to look hard to find assertions that the executive/board chair relationship is critical to the success of nonprofit organizations. A lot is at stake.

I decided to learn more about what really goes on between executive directors and board chairs. How can these relationships be strengthened? Based on conversations with dozens of board chairs and executives, I learned that those with relationships that add value pay attention to two inter-related things: building trust and focusing on work that matters. Strong trust promotes a focus on more and more strategic work. This article presents some practical strategies that not only prevent toxic relationships but help an executive and board chair build a relationship that's not just good, but great.

Relationship Dynamics That Build Trust

The fact that great working relationships require trust is obvious. But wait—do we really know all the behaviors we can choose every day to build trust in working relationships? What opportunities do executives and board chairs have to build trust that they might be missing? Executives and board chairs with great relationships engage in five types of dynamics that provide varied ways to build trust. These are described below.

Sharing information

John's experience as a board chair exemplifies the first executive/board chair relationship dynamic: sharing information. John had very different experiences with two executives. With one, he had to ask for information and, even then, he felt she held things back. He got "tidbits." It was frustrating to have to dig for more and more just to get a basic picture of what was going on. He felt she never "leveled" with him about anything. With the second executive, information flow was effortless. For example, the executive copied him on all emails she thought would be *of interest to him*, not just need-to-know items. He was confident in the amount of information he was getting.

Risk-Reward Trust

There are three levels of trust in working relationships. The first is risk-reward trust. This is the lowest level of trust and is based on deciding whether the risks or rewards justify placing trust in a person you don't know at all. For example, a brand new executive director finds herself in a relationship with a board chair she hardly knows. They start with risk-reward trust.

 practical tip

It is the perception of information "being enough" that matters in these relationships and that's going to vary from person to person. Because of that, board chairs and executives need to be proactive! Figure out together how much information needs to be shared and how often. Then, consistently act on that. Sharing appropriate types and amounts of information lays a good foundation and helps build trust, but a great relationship requires more.

Sharing ideas

Jan (executive) and Ray (board chair) were having their usual meeting at Cozy's, an old-style, mom and pop coffee shop. Ray is a retired vice president of a well-known international management consulting firm. He and Jan had been working over several months on the details of the nonprofit's new strategic direction. With others, they had gathered a lot of data and now were working together to figure out what it all really meant. Ray brought his business expertise and keen strategic thinking. Jan brought the perspective of clients and the community. Together, they worked out their next board presentation on the back of the paper placemat. Their exchange was mutual, challenging, and creative.

This pair was sharing ideas—another dynamic that goes beyond information sharing to grow trust. It is important for executives and board chairs to structure time together for this type of two-way exchange—brainstorming, problem-solving, and thinking things through. This promotes learning about each other, showing that you value each other's opinions, being open to feedback, giving feedback, and respecting each other's skills and knowledge and more: all behaviors that build trust.

Sharing knowledge

Bill's board decided to buy a building. It had been a matter of discussion for some time and now the decision was made. Bill (executive director) had been with the agency for the key strategic discussions but had never led a project of this magnitude. James (board chair), on the other hand, was an engineering executive with a lot of project management experience. "There was a whole process we had to orchestrate," Bill shared. "There was a lot of due diligence, legal issues, and financing to work out." All of this was, of course, on top of managing day-to-day operations. James fulfilled the needed roles of coach and teacher—helping and supporting Bill to create, and put into place, an effective process.

Great executive/board chair partnerships include opportunities for shared learning experiences. Board chairs can serve as mentors, drawing from backgrounds and skill sets that are relevant to challenges an executive might be grappling with. Executives can teach board chairs too—about the nonprofit sector and their nonprofit's specific field of service, for example. Board chairs and executive in great relationships also take time once in a while to attend a class or workshop together.

> **Getting to Know You!**
>
> The second level of trust in working relationships is "getting to know you" trust (think of the song from the movie The King and I!). This type of trust grows the more you get to know each other and includes a variety of behaviors related to communication, agreements, and perceived competence. The levels of trust are cumulative: "Getting to know you" trust builds on risk-reward trust (see Trust Building Model, below).
>
>  practical tip

So, in addition to sharing information and exchanging ideas, seek opportunities to teach each other and learn together. This also gives you a chance to get to know and value the other person's areas of competence—another way to build trust.

Sharing feelings

Building a high level of trust requires personal risk-taking—being vulnerable and open to the other person. Sharing feelings—support, reassurance, caring, appreciation—is a powerful dynamic characteristic of the great executive/board chair relationships.

Though inexperienced as a nonprofit executive, Sarah had a powerful presence and reputation in the community as an advocate. Her board chair, Carol, was a seasoned philanthropist and board leader. Sarah's initial experience was that Carol did not have confidence in her abilities as an executive. Carol acted like a supervisor and often questioned how Sarah was spending her time. Then something happened that shifted the relationship.

A local foundation had verbally committed a large grant to the agency. Before it was finalized, the program officer called Carol and told her they were not going to give the grant because of Sarah: "We don't think she can do it . . . she's too political . . . she's laid out unrealistic goals." They attacked her personally. Carol responded: "I'm sorry you feel that way. We believe in her." Sarah felt she lost the agency a lot of money, yet Carol stood by her; not only that, she wrote a personal check to help mitigate the loss. This demonstration of support and reassurance when Sarah was feeling particularly vulnerable was a real boost for Sarah and put their relationship on a new level. Sarah gained confidence she needed to work through her experiences of being micromanaged directly with Carol. Carol was responsive and changed to a positive mentoring role. They moved forward as a powerful team.

Give and take

Another executive/board chair relationship dynamic I call "give and take." Executives and board chairs in great relationships adapt to each other's styles, personalities, and preferences. They have ways of working out their differences. One executive described it well: "We need to be students of one another . . . I need to understand how you are wired and how I need to accommodate myself to function with you." Even adapting to each other in small ways makes a difference. For example, after being frustrated with the executive director's lack of timely response to her emails, one board chair learned that "He's not that great with email. Conversations—the telephone works better." So she called him instead.

Identification Trust

The third type of trust in working relationships is rarer than the others: identification trust. It is the highest level of trust. Identification trust happens when we don't just know each other but we identify with each other. This requires us to get personal and, yes, with appropriate boundaries, that is a good thing for executives and board chairs to do! When you share and learn about what you have in common on a personal level, you can build even stronger trust.

 practical tip

---

What do you know about the other person's preferences? How have you accommodated each other's styles? Have you had a conversation about what works and what the other person would like to be different? Asking and answering these kinds of questions leads to the clarity and understanding that can move a relationship from good to great.

As trust builds, using all five dynamics described above, there is a parallel change: the type of work that executives and board chairs do together gets more and more strategic. High trust promotes a focus on board and community engagement with the mission and that yields real value for the nonprofit.

Trust Building Model

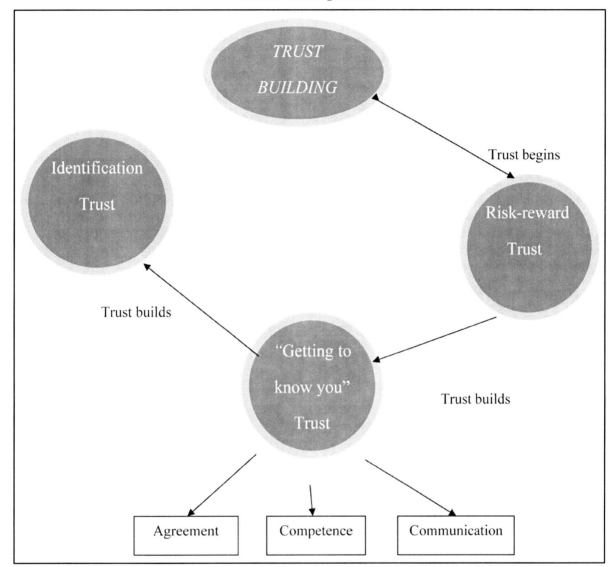

Focus of Work: Creating Impact

When there is low trust, the board chair's attention is on overseeing the executive and wanting a lot more information and input about operations. Micromanaging is happening! On the other hand, when the executive doesn't trust the board chair there is simply avoidance. The executive withdraws from the relationship as much as possible. Energy and time (valuable resources) are directed to getting by. The entire board is affected too. No value creation can happen when this is going on!

As trust builds, this changes. Executives and board chairs spend time on the organization. They share information and think things through together about operations: finances, personnel, facilities, or the logistics of the board itself (e.g., agendas, meeting locations, committee structure). Engagement with the board is minimal. The relationship is cordial but there is not a lot of synergy or excitement. Things are OK.

When trust is higher still, in addition to dealing with budgets or personnel, executives and board chairs engage board members on strategic priorities. And, they tap into board members' expertise. Board members are fully utilized and the organization is benefiting.

Executives and board chairs with the highest level of trust (identification trust) do all of the above *and* focus on leveraging board members' networks, building external relationships, and connecting with the community. These executive/board chair relationships are great and result in more energy, resources, networks, productivity, confidence, and better decisions for the nonprofit.

A True Life Example of Poor Executive/Board Chair Relations

Ann had successfully avoided a one-on-one meeting with her relatively new board chair for several months. Until he became board chair she had not experienced his intense and abrupt style. Once he became chair, he began to cut her off in conversations and she felt intimidated and patronized. Issues that she had considered discussing with him (and ultimately the board) got tabled. Whatever she could put aside got put on hold. Strategic planning and a new fundraising event were some of the casualties of this relationship.

practical tip

Wrapping It Up

Executives and board chairs build great relationships by:

♦ sharing information according to each other's needs

♦ sharing ideas: brainstorming, problem-solving, thinking things through together;

♦ sharing knowledge: learning together and helping each other learn;

♦ sharing feelings: opening up, sharing appreciation, support, concern, and caring; and

♦ give and take: being students of each other and adapting.

By doing these things together, you will build trust from the lowest risk-reward level to trust that comes for getting to know each other and, finally, to the strongest trust that comes from personal sharing and identifying with each other.

As you build trust, pay attention to what you are working on together. Notice that as trust grows, you tackle operational issues as a matter of accountability and consultation not micromanagement. Higher trust will help you partner to tap board members' talents and resources. Ultimately, together you can become a powerful influence for board and community engagement. Working *on* the relationship is as important as working in it! Make it a priority!

A True Life Example of an Effective Executive/Board Chair Relationship

When Sue (executive) and Jack (board chair) first met in their respective roles with the Community Resource Center they discussed how they wanted to work together and with the board. The next month, Sue brought a challenging personnel issue to Jack for advice and, as a result of his support and coaching, she sought his advice frequently on operational challenges. Jack began to share information about his family and how the mission mattered to them. They learned about each other's personal interests. After a few months, they began working on engaging the board in planning to increase visibility and impact. Jack and Sue attended a series of fundraising classes and brought what they learned back to the board. They partnered on strategies to connect each board member with a key community partner of influence. They created synergy and excitement among board members leveraging each person's talents and resources. Within a year, the Community Resource Center (formerly focused on providing emergency food and shelter) convened a widely attended community summit to end poverty, significantly broadening its reach and impact.

 Connect with Mary at http://charitychannel.com/cc/mary-hiland

Inside Out: A Fresh Perspective on Finding Volunteers

By Lisa Kay Schweyer

You need to find a way to replace retiring volunteers. Fewer & fewer people are calling and offering to volunteer. Increased program needs require a whole new set of volunteer skills.

Sound familiar?

Sometimes in trying to keep up with the various projects, impending deadlines and continually recruiting new volunteers, we get so close to our work, mission, etc. that we might be missing the bigger picture. Taking the time to step outside and look in, can help bring a fresh perspective. Once you have that new point of view, marketing your program and recruiting new volunteers becomes much easier.

This article will provide you with some ideas on how to take a quick assessment of your volunteer program and connect what you learn, to recruiting new volunteers.

First, I want you to imagine a time when you went to a new restaurant for the first time. What did you do?

◆ You looked at the outside of the building (what it looked like, decided whether the colors looked nice, whether the parking availability was adequate/close enough to the restaurant's front door?)

◆ Then you went inside (you noticed the decor, what it smelled like, whether there were lots of people waiting?)

◆ Then you met your server (did they greet you in a pleasant manner, return when they said they would?)

◆ And when the food arrived (did it look appetizing, was it hot/cold, prepared the way you requested?)

And the assessments go on and on. Since it was your first visit, your perspective was still fresh. You had very few preconceived notions.

In order for you to take a fresh perspective about your own organization, I encourage each of you to try to look at your organization and program as if you were visiting it for the first time. Taking a good hard look at your organization, your volunteer program and what you actually offer volunteers.

Okay, remember how you assessed the restaurant—ask yourself the following questions about your organization and volunteer program and make note of your responses. We will refer to your answers later when we review some different ways to look at marketing.

◆ Does your organization's mission appear on any of the volunteer recruitment materials? Newsletters?

◆ Do you provide volunteer training? Computer skills development? Other skills volunteers might need when applying for a job?

◆ Do you allow volunteers access to your professional journals, listings of new jobs?

◆ Are you willing to send volunteers to advanced training or conferences?

◆ Do you provide volunteers with mentors or buddies?

◆ Are you willing to write letters of reference for your volunteers?

◆ Do you ask clients to write thank you letters to the volunteers?

Now that you have your list, let's take a look at how you can use this information to market your program to potential volunteers. We know people volunteer for a variety of reasons. When I question volunteers, the reason most people tell me they want to volunteer fall into one of three categories:

1. Commitment to the mission,

2. Building career skills, or

3. Wanting social interaction.

Let's look at how you can use what your organization and program offers to match them to potential volunteers.

Commitment to the Mission

Many people just believe so much in what your organization does, or have been personally touched by the organization's services, that they want to be involved themselves. Often they will mention wanting to "give back." For this type of volunteer, they usually just need to know your organization is in need of help. Providing an updated list of volunteer opportunities as well as an explanation of how the activity is a benefit will usually be your best recruitment tool. This group of volunteers can also be your best ambassadors within the community and great "recruiters" of new volunteers.

Now refer back to the checklist you answered when assessing your program. Do you include the organization's mission on your volunteer recruitment materials? This is one way to help connect with those volunteers who are motivated by your program's mission. Do you ask clients to write thank you letters to volunteers? This is a great way for volunteers to learn how their efforts have made a difference.

Building Career Skills

Some individuals become involved in a volunteer activity because they want to gain certain skills, so they can transfer those skills into a paid position. For these individuals, offering free training or taking the time to provide advanced training can be the reason why they decide to give you their time. I have trained several volunteers on how to use the computer (from turning the computer on, to creating files). This not only provided the volunteers the benefit of learning the computer, but also helped our program by having several new volunteers who could assist us with the ever-growing amount of computer work.

If possible, look for ways to include some training for volunteers who are interested. It might just be thirty minutes a week helping them learn a computer program or how to read a financial statement. Or,

---

Recruitment Ideas for Volunteers Committed to Your Mission:

◆ Use your own organization's newsletter. Include a "learn more about volunteering" coupon for your readers to pass on to someone they think might be interested (or they can even use it for themselves).

◆ Check your own organization's client list. If appropriate, send a special mailing to your organization's current and past clients. Who better to give back then someone who had received your services?

◆ Create materials that specifically include a description of how the job promotes the mission.

 practical tip

Recruitment Ideas for Volunteers Looking to Gain Job Skills

◆ Post recruitment materials in the local unemployment or job skills training location. Be sure the posters include a prominent message that training and letters of reference will be provided.

◆ Partner with local schools to provide service learning/internship opportunities for students.

◆ Provide volunteers access to any job listings sent to your organization and the job opportunities that might come up at your organization.

you might be able to pay for a volunteer's attendance at a training or industry conference.

Wanting Social Interaction

Wanting to get out of the house or have more social interaction is the third category. Find activities for these individuals where they could be paired with a partner or work in a group setting. The work will get done and the volunteers will enjoy their "visit."

If your program provides volunteers with mentors or buddies, you are already addressing the volunteer's need for social interaction. If you don't have this currently, you could ask staff to help "adopt" a volunteer—someone they will check in with on a regular basis or to call periodically to see how they are doing.

Obviously not every volunteer falls neatly into one category. There can be several reasons why someone wants to volunteer and several ways to successfully recruit new volunteers.

Your program has benefits to offer potential volunteers. The truth is your program probably lots to offer; it is just a matter of how you view it and how you match what you have to offer with the type of volunteer. Please remember to take account of all you do offer, and to look for creative ways to match that with the needs of the volunteers.

Good luck as you learn to view your organization with a fresh perspective.

 Connect with Lisa Kay at http://charitychannel.com/cc/lisa-kay-schweyer

Recruitment Ideas for Volunteers Wanting Social Interaction

◆ Contact the local senior centers. Many times, senior centers are looking for projects for their clients to perform. Compiling direct mail or stuffing brochures can easily be an activity done by a group of seniors while enjoying coffee and conversation.

◆ Design a special promotion—"It takes two." Mention how the volunteer can turn their weekly get-together with a friend into a chance to visit and give back. Volunteers can work together to make meal deliveries to your clients for example.

Hang Up Your Cape and Empower Leaders: Utilizing Volunteer Team Leaders to Build Program Capacity

By Tammy Holland

Volunteer managers are often thought to have super-human strength and stamina, and the ability to single-handedly coordinate large teams of people. Yet, even the best of us can quickly burn out and become disillusioned. It's time to hang up your red cape and retire from your *Super Coordinator* role!

Believe it or not, your program will actually prosper when you step back and empower key volunteers to take on leadership positions within your organization. This might require a large amount of trust and patience on your part—and you will have to relinquish control over some aspects of your program. But you'll thank me for it in the end!

The team leadership concept is often discussed at volunteer administration conferences and workshops, but it is a mindset that must become ingrained into your everyday thinking. You must accept the fact you cannot effectively do everything yourself. You must admit you don't have all the answers. And more importantly, you must lose the excuses!

Over the course of my career, I have seen dramatic improvements in organizational capacity when volunteers are permitted to take ownership of projects and teams of people. Highly skilled volunteers have organized teams of first-responders at a rape crisis center. Neighbors have transformed their community by assuming greater responsibility for the success of their home owners association. Passionate animal-rights activists have stepped up to the plate when staffing limitations prevented a humane society from achieving its mission. In all of these real-life scenarios, volunteers were given the liberty to make important decisions, the opportunity to determine the strategic direction of the organization, and the recognition they deserved for their contributions.

The traditional concept of organizational leadership is usually depicted by a pyramid and defined by hierarchical relationships. The pyramid might be very simple in small nonprofit organizations; nevertheless, direct-care staff generally report to department managers, who report to administrators or directors, who ultimately report to a chief executive officer and board of directors. In short, your attention centers on the needs and desires of your supervisor. This chain-of-command style of leadership often results in volunteers and their contributions being minimized.

The idea of promoting volunteers into leadership positions is based upon the concept of "servant leadership." The term was first coined by Robert Greenleaf and has been promoted by many others, including Ken Blanchard, James Laub, and William George. In this model, your attention centers on the needs and desires of *those you serve.* Dr. Kent Keith, author of *The Case for Servant Leadership*, lists seven key practices of a servant leader: self-awareness, listening, developing your colleagues, coaching not controlling, unleashing the energy and intelligence of others, foresight, and *Changing the Pyramid*! Changing the pyramid turns everything we've traditionally thought to be true upside down! The chain of command is tossed aside for the "chain of service." One could argue the CEO now serves the administrators and directors, who focus their attention on the department managers, who then empower the direct-care staff. And guess who you serve? That's right—your energies are focused on equipping your volunteers to serve your customers.

The case for servant leadership is strengthened by the work of James Laub, who assures that organizations can increase their influence and impact by sharing the power with others so they too can make important decisions and exercise their own initiative. The vision of an organization does not belong to the person who gets the biggest paycheck. When the vision is shared by all of the stakeholders, our potential, skills, and abilities are maximized. The organizational capacity becomes expanded.

Step 1: Decide to Promote Volunteers into Leadership Positions.

"Hello, my name is Tammy and I am a control freak!" Isn't that the first step of many recovery groups? It works for volunteer managers too! Expanding your organization's capacity begins by changing how you perceive volunteers and your own role as a program manager. It's true that you'll be taking risks by putting volunteers in charge, but it's a risk worth taking. When you give the volunteers ownership of the program, they will take responsibility for its success, or failure.

How do you know when you are doing a good job at work? You get praise, letters of commendation, recognition at work, a pay raise, and maybe even greater responsibility with a new job title. What makes volunteers any different? Many of today's volunteers have high-level skills and knowledge. Promoting them into leadership positions recognizes their assets and value to the organization. This might be the best way to retain and recognize exceptional volunteers.

Step 2: Create Meaningful Leadership Opportunities.

These four questions will help you identify the most critical tasks that could be assigned to a volunteer team leader.

What gets pushed to the back burner in your organization?

My challenge while managing a mentoring program was maintaining close contact with my mentors, supporting them as they establish rapport with a troubled teen, and providing ongoing training as the relationship grows.

How would the mission/purpose of your organization be accomplished if this need were fully met?

I knew that if our mentor relationships could be sustained for the optimal length of time; youth could realize their potential and become successful in school, family, and community.

What is currently keeping you from getting this task done?

Unfortunately, there were only twenty-four hours in a day!

If a volunteer is asked to do this job, what are the risks? And can these risks be mitigated?

My solution was promoting one of my mentors to a team leader position; there were no more risks involved in promoting him into a leadership position than for his original mentoring assignment.

Now that you have one or more tasks identified, it's time to develop a team leader job description. This type of description goes far beyond the typical volunteer job description, and should include the following elements:

- ◆ Identify the task/project, and give the team leader a title. The ideal leadership ratio for large projects and teams of volunteers is one team leader to every fifteen to twenty volunteers.

- ◆ Decide who will supervise your team leader and briefly describe any supervisory protocol to follow. The degree of supervision depends on the difficulty of the assignment. The supervision you give to your team leader should never stifle their ability to direct their team. Effective supervision results in empowered, confident leaders.

◆ Describe the primary responsibilities of the team leader.

◆ Define the duration of the job—don't leave it open-ended. I would suggest no more than a twelve-month commitment, with a three-month "probationary period" after which you and the team leader reassess the assignment and do any trouble-shooting.

◆ Specify the limits of the team leader's authority with the project and the volunteers. Consider how your team leader should handle performance problems of a volunteer on the team. Define how far the team leader can go in modifying the project.

◆ Team leaders can provide that much-needed individual contact with your volunteers. Team leaders may facilitate the team meetings, including training sessions. Their job descriptions should outline the frequency and mode of contact with team members. You might ask leaders to provide you with monthly or quarterly reports summarizing their contacts with volunteers.

◆ Include the work schedule that is desired and the resources to be provided.

◆ *Most Importantly!* Define your expectations of the team leader and communicate them clearly and in writing on the job description. This will enable you to hold the leader accountable for the outcomes. Just be sure your expectations are realistic and achievable.

Step 3: Select and Recruit a Team Leader

Recruit a team leader from within your existing pool of volunteers. This promotes a positive morale among the volunteers. You could even go as far as posting the team leader position and interviewing the volunteers who are interested and qualified. This promotes a sense of fairness. Leadership abilities are among the skill sets to be screened during the initial interview and orientation phase of volunteer recruitment. Create a tickler system that will help you track potential leaders' involvement throughout their first several months as a team *member*. As the potential leader becomes more involved and invested in their team, begin nurturing that individual and assessing their inclination to assume a leadership role with the team.

Give careful consideration to the qualifications required for your team leader. Keep in mind that you are looking for a supervisor, someone to manage a task/project and oversee the performance of other volunteers. I would recommend screening for someone who is skilled at developing relationships, problem-solving, effective communication, and exceptional organization.

An additional interview is necessary when considering a current volunteer for a leadership position. Delve deeply into the volunteer's motivations to assume a leadership role at your organization. Look for red flags regarding power/control, inappropriate access and relationships with the clients served by your organization, and the volunteer's personal support systems.

Step 4: Train Your Team Leaders

Team leaders' level of commitment is entirely dependent upon the time and energy you invest in properly training, clearly outlining expectations, allowing leaders to make decisions, and encouraging their autonomy. In other words, you have the responsibility to adequately prepare them to lead—and then let them do it!

Team leaders need a higher level of organizational understanding, so spend sufficient time reviewing the mission and strategic plan of your organization. Provide management training. Invite your team leader to join you at volunteer management conferences and help them achieve certifications, as appropriate.

Step 5: Develop Your Team Leader through Support and Coaching

You should meet with your team leader regularly. Don't neglect to communicate frequently with your leader, and troubleshoot any problems that arise. Your team leaders will naturally have his/her own unique ways of developing

Take Care of Your Team Leaders

The first time I promoted a volunteer to a team leader position was soon after I established a mentoring program at the agency where I worked. It didn't take long to realize I simply could not stay in close contact with my new mentors. As they struggled with building rapport with their new mentee, they would quickly become discouraged and fall away from the program. I needed someone to help me encourage the mentors, provide needed resources to them, and follow up on concerns and requests.

Bobby was one mentor who was particularly interested in the program development aspects of mentoring services. He also had a special knack for connecting with people—that nurturing, encouraging type of personality. Bobby was eager to take on more responsibility in the program. I soon came to understand that if I just took care of Bobby, he would take care of all the mentors on his team. Taking care of my new team leader meant providing him with adequate work space, a computer, and custom-designed simple stationary on which he could communicate with his team members, allowing him to determine many of the logistics of the services, and recognizing his accomplishments. The program exploded with success!

their project and leading their team of volunteers. Team leaders will learn the intricacies of your organization by trial and error. Encourage them to learn from their mistakes; that's how new leaders become great leaders! They can be successful if given the proper amount of support.

Expect your team leaders to be creative and encourage them to pursue new ideas and program initiatives. Allow them to own their programs. Resist holding team leaders back from the decision-making process. Permit direct communication between team leaders and paid staff. In one very successful program I've come across, team leaders gained significant credibility and developed lasting rapport after they were permitted to have meetings with paid staff to discuss common issues. The volunteer manager simply attended the meetings as a silent observer and allowed her team leader to guide the discussions and speak freely. The once-resistant staff now sings the praises of the volunteers because they understand how passionate they are about the organizational mission.

Step 6: Recognize Your Team Leaders

There's nothing wrong with using the traditional means of recognizing volunteers with your team leader, including certificates, cards, gifts, and special meals. But there are creative ways in which you can recognize your leader. Recognize the extra work that goes into such leadership positions by awarding merit hours to team leaders. For example, you might credit team leaders with two hours for every one hour worked. This is a way to acknowledge time spent away from the program in promoting volunteer opportunities.

Recognize the role leaders have within your organization by inviting them to management team meetings and asking them to report on their team and project. Ask them to contribute to organizational annual reports and strategic plans. Let them decide how they wish to recognize the volunteers on their team and then let them speak during formal recognition programs. Recognize the communication skills of your leaders by inviting them to plan and teach volunteer training sessions. Enable them to recruit volunteers in the community and encourage them to speak to civic groups. And permit your leaders to evaluate the success of their team's efforts and the performance of individual volunteers.

You might be thinking that these tips sound less like ways to recognize, and more like additional responsibilities. But keep in mind that exceptional performers in any organization are often recognized through greater levels of responsibilities. This is how you share the power! You will have to modulate the amount of responsibilities given to your team leader according to their availability.

Final Considerations

I don't deny there might be special challenges to utilizing volunteer team leaders. It seems there are some meek and mild volunteers who morph into dictators when you put them in charge! Some veteran volunteers can become jealous of a peer who is promoted to a leadership position. But this can be relieved when you use the formalized job posting process. As with any supervisor and subordinate, interpersonal conflicts might arise. When this occurs, evaluate your team leaders' performance and hold them accountable for outcomes that were identified at the beginning of the assignment.

The benefits, however, far outweigh the challenges! Volunteer team leaders will expand your organization's reach and provide a higher level of support to the individual volunteers on your roster. As a result, you'll be able to retain your volunteers for longer periods of time because they are better supported. You might see an increase in fundraising dollars, greater community visibility, improved staff and volunteer morale, and less burnout among staff.

Team leaders are only as good as you allow them to be. Don't be afraid of retiring your red cape. You'll find you enjoy those free moments you'll soon have.

 Connect with Tammy at http://charitychannel.com/cc/tammy-holland

Six Secrets to Volunteer Recruitment

By Lisa Kay Schweyer

Tonight is the agency's biggest fundraising event of the year; you needed forty volunteers and were only able to find thirty to say yes. Finding enough volunteers to help support your organization's mission and programs can be a daunting task. No one wants to be in the position of not having enough volunteers to help with an important event. Read on to learn six "secrets" to volunteer recruitment. The secrets can help you think through your volunteer needs and some ways to find volunteers to fill them.

1. Know what positions you need to fill

Late on a Friday afternoon, many volunteer managers have found themselves being asked to "find me three people to help us on Monday." As we know such a request usually ends up frustrating you, the volunteer and the person who asked for the help—why? Because no one really knew what was expected and or needed.

Ideally for a volunteer program to work well, the volunteer manager knows the recurring volunteer opportunities that are available and is given ample time to plan for special requests. Being involved in the organization's planning can help the volunteer manager have a better handle on current needs and what will be needed in the future. But if you aren't involved directly in the planning, you can still get prepared. *How?*

2. Create position descriptions

Whether a recurring position or a one-time special assignment—position descriptions allow you and the volunteer to gain a better understanding of the assignment. The description does not have to be terribly formal, but should be written down and include the following components:

◆ volunteer position title;

◆ volunteer supervisor;

◆ minimum and preferred requirements;

◆ special skill requirements;

◆ general responsibilities;

◆ specific position tasks; and

◆ time commitments (recurring/one time, hours/days per week and length of commitment to position).

Once the volunteer position descriptions are drafted, ask current volunteers and staff to look them over and give you feedback. It can be really helpful to get the second opinion.

You might also want to develop a position description template which can be shared with senior management so when they become aware of a volunteer need, they will know the information you will need to find a volunteer to help with the task.

3. Develop a Recruitment Plan

Now that you have a better idea of the volunteer positions you are looking to fill, you can create a recruitment plan.

◆ Do you have a budget for recruitment efforts?

◆ Where have you found volunteers in the past? What has been successful?

◆ Can you utilize your current volunteers, staff and clients to help you recruit new volunteers?

Use the position descriptions you've developed to create a recruitment calendar. Recruitment plans are highly customizable based on budget, resources, etc. The important thing is to have one. Many organizations recruit new volunteers year round. Others might target specific time periods based on the organization's need. Know the volunteer and organizational needs—you'll want to start your recruitment efforts about three months before you want the new volunteers to start. That will give you time to perform interviews/screenings and to provide the new volunteers with orientation/training.

Depending on your resources, you might also be able to recruit volunteers by:

- ◆ requesting help in your organization's newsletter;

- ◆ advertising in the local paper;

- ◆ placing notices in church bulletins;

- ◆ post notices at the unemployment office; or

- ◆ contacting local service groups (i.e. Girl Scouts, Rotary Clubs).

One of the most effective volunteer recruitment tools I have ever seen is "Refer a Friend." Ask your current volunteers to ask people they know to consider volunteering. Who can be a better recruiter than your current volunteers? The key is to ask.

4. Interview/Screen Potential Applicants

Hopefully you have a lot of potential volunteers to choose from, but even if you don't, you want to be sure to interview and screen potential volunteers. You can do this in a group setting where you provide a general orientation and encourage volunteers to ask questions or individually. Either way, it is imperative to get to know the people who want to volunteer for your organization *before* they get started.

Most nonprofit organizations have more than one volunteer role and not every volunteer would be good in all of them. By getting to know your applicants you are going to be able to better match them with the available positions and help them to have a better experience.

It is critical to keep in mind, that screening and interviewing volunteers should follow the same non-discrimination policies you use when screening employees. This includes not asking about ethnicity, marital status, etc. Please check with a human resources professional for the current guidelines in your state.

During the interview process you want to be sure to ask about:

- ◆ previous volunteer experience—positive and negative;

- ◆ previous work experience and how it relates to the volunteer position;

- ◆ special skills the volunteer is willing to share (i.e. can do calligraphy, has a catering business); and

- ◆ how much time the volunteer has available to give.

Also, keep in mind that even though the applicants might really want to volunteer, they might not be appropriate volunteers for your organization. Maybe their ideological beliefs are not in alignment with your programs, or maybe their personality would not be a good match with your clientele. It is okay to say no to volunteers. However, it is much easier to have a range of volunteer position options to which you can help direct volunteers. If the position descriptions are specific enough, volunteers will probably understand why their skills are not the best match at the time.

5. ACT!

Through personal experience, I have noticed that the longer it took from the first time volunteers showed interest to when they would start volunteering, the greater the chance they would never begin. Volunteers who are engaged quickly and are put into positions that match their interests and skills were more likely to stay involved.

Some ways to get volunteers started quickly is to have a monthly orientation/volunteer "get to know you" meetings. This will allow a new volunteer a chance to meet some staff, other volunteers and maybe some clients. Assure them that they will be assigned a volunteer position within at least four weeks. Another way to encourage quick integration of volunteers is to run a contest between your organization's departments to see who can get the new volunteers placed on the schedule the quickest.

I have also seen experienced volunteers assigned to newer volunteers as mentors and it works very well. More experienced volunteers are able to "elevate" their role by becoming more of leaders and newer volunteers are able to learn from peers. Often volunteers will not ask a staff person a question if they think it will sound silly—but they are comfortable asking another volunteer. This can create a strong bond among your volunteer corps while creating ways for the newer volunteers to follow in the more experienced volunteers' footsteps once the experienced volunteers "retire."

6. Follow-up

So now you have a good idea of the organization's needs, you have position descriptions for all of the volunteers, you have successfully recruited, interviewed/screened potential volunteers and gotten them started in their roles—now you can rest. *Wrong!* This is actually the most critical part of the process.

Follow-up, Follow-up, Follow-up

Make sure the new volunteers you have spent so much time finding are actually enjoying their volunteer work and that they have the resources to be successful. Check in with the volunteers. If you have the time, call each of your new volunteers within one month (or call as many as your time allows). Ask how their volunteer experience is going and if there is something that needs to be corrected, correct it. Also, check with the staff members who are working with the new volunteers and ask how things are going. It is amazing how many times we make incorrect assumptions.

So, we have not solved the dilemma of finding volunteers for your event tonight, but we have outlined a basic system by which you can recruit new volunteers for the longer term. The plan you develop will be unique to your program; the *Six Secrets to Volunteer Recruitment* can serve as building blocks or a checklist for your plan. Find what works for you, develop a plan and get started; as you know, no one is going to volunteer until *you* ask.

 Connect with Lisa Kay at http://charitychannel.com/cc/lisa-kay-schweyer

Developing Effective Volunteer Training

By Jesse Bowen

Volunteers need training! We all know that, but how do we do it with a minimum amount of resources and with a maximum amount of impact?

We're going to look at three components of training: Developing Materials, Preparation, and Delivery.

Developing Material

Ask yourself (and perhaps other staff or current volunteers) these questions:

◆ What do new volunteers need to know in order to do the best job possible?

◆ What policies and procedures do they need to be aware of?

◆ What tasks do they need to learn?

◆ What skills must they have to be effective?

◆ Of the topics and material gathered, what falls into the 'need to know' category and what falls into the 'nice to know' category.

The answers to these questions will help you figure out what material to include in your training. Some things are nice to know but not necessary for the job; I suggest putting those items into a talk or workshop for current volunteers. Short info sessions, talks or additional training can be provided as ongoing education and is a perk for both the agency and the volunteers.

The right amount of detail

Trying to cram ten years of experience and knowledge into three hours of training is impossible and overwhelming. On the other hand, just touching on broad topics without much detail can leave volunteers with many unanswered questions. Striking the balance between the two extremes is important. If you are not certain if you've hit the mark, ask a friend or colleague who is not knowledgeable about the subject to read it over and provide feedback.

> Sometimes we know the material so well we forget to include important information because it is so obvious to us.
>
> **warning!**

Make Learning Interactive

The least effective method of teaching others is through lecture and yet it is still one of the most common forms of instruction. Even when you include a PowerPoint presentation, visuals on the wall and manuals to follow along with, the default is often you standing at the front of the room and providing information. Over and over studies have shown a more effective way to ensure learning is to have the student experiment, practice, and/or teach someone else. Take every opportunity you can to create exercises where the volunteers puzzle out the answers for themselves, practice the skills you are teaching them and share with each other what they

---

Building Communication Skills for Drop-In Volunteers

Let's say your agency runs a drop-in center and you need to ensure your drop-in volunteers have good communication skills. Before launching into a lesson on communication, have the class break into two groups. Ask one group to identify the things people do and say that shut down a conversation and ask the other to identify the things people do and say that open up or encourage a conversation. Give them five to ten minutes, have them record their answers on white board or flip chart paper, and then they can each present to the rest of the class. Now you can build on what they already know and present new information. Then have them practice. Break them into groups of three and ask one person to be the volunteer, one to be the client and one to be an observer. Have them switch roles until each person has played all three parts. As the facilitator you can move about the room and listen in, help those who are stuck, and get a sense of who is doing well and who needs more assistance. Then debrief the entire process with the class as a whole. The time that it takes to go through this whole process this is well worth the effort.

practical tip

already know. Creating an interactive environment that engages as many senses as possible is crucial to great learning.

Look for ways to have the class break into small groups and work on an assignment together. Create assignments for them to mine their own knowledge and then have them present their findings to the rest of the class. You can fill in any missing pieces and correct misinformation afterward. It takes a little longer and requires more effort to create learning scenarios, however, when you do participants will be more likely to remember what they learned and remain engaged.

When teaching a new manual skill (from answering a multi-line phone to handling baby animals), arrange for volunteers to practice it in class or at least before they start their first shift. When teaching 'soft skills' such as assertive communication, boundary setting, enforcing policies, or handling complaints make liberal use of role plays. It's true that many people dislike role playing, however this is the most effective way for you to know whether or not your volunteer is ready. It also gives the volunteer time to develop some confidence before having to interact with your clientele or the public.

Successful Role Playing

◆ Set expectations: let volunteers know that this is an artificial situation, it will be awkward and uncomfortable and that's okay.

◆ Make it safe: start them working in groups of two or three before moving to role plays in front of the class. Give permission for those who are really anxious to skip the role plays in front of the class. Before or after, demonstrate one of your harder role plays to give volunteers an idea of what it can look like.

◆ Give permission: let them know it's okay to get stuck, to start over, and to make mistakes. This is a learning situation and they don't need to get it right every time.

◆ Build confidence: tell volunteers that if they can work through a role play, they will likely do well in a real situation. For many people, artificial scenarios are much harder than the real thing.

◆ Debrief: discuss what worked and didn't work. Give examples of responses for the places where class participants got stuck.

Timing

Once you have decided what needs to be included in the training, assign a timeframe for each topic and exercise. Add time in for introductions and housekeeping issues, questions, and, if needed, breaks, an icebreaker, and evaluations. As a general rule when assigning time for individual or group exercises, time yourself completing the exercise, and then triple the time. If it takes you three minutes to complete the exercise, allow ten minutes in class. Then add a few minutes for discussion afterward.

Visual aids

Keep handouts, flip charts, and PowerPoint slides neat, clean and uncluttered. Use fonts that are easy to read in a size that does not need a magnifying glass to see it (24 points or higher). Include color when you can but don't overdo it. I have asked clerical volunteers to retype old handouts that had been photocopied for years and were overcrowded and difficult to read. One page might become two in the retyping, but I'd rather have two pages the volunteer will read than one page that gets ignored or thrown out. Break up large blocks of writing with bullet points, borders, and boxes to highlight important points, just as this book does. Keep wording on your PowerPoint slides to a minimum. You should be speaking to the points on the slide, not reading all the information from the slide.

Well run training sessions require good materials. The time you invest in developing your material will pay off with happy, informed and prepared volunteers.

Preparation

Different strokes for different folks

Some people need to take notes, others need to follow along in the manual; still others need to doodle or draw pictures. Ensure there is note paper and pens available. Some people have physical ailments or injuries that make it difficult to sit for any length of time. I always give permission for anyone who needs to move, to stand up at the back of the room and move about as required. For training that lasts three hours or longer, I scatter about the tables quiet hand toys such as stress balls, miniature Slinkies, silly putty, and squishy rubber animals. There are usually one or two people who use them throughout training, but after lunch I find most of the toys are in use. Keeping the hands active helps to keep the mind engaged and focused at a time when it would be easy to "zone out."

Deal with irritants

Flickering lights, noisy fans, blocked visual lines from participant to you, uncomfortable room temperature, construction outside your window and other bothersome things will take the participants focus away from your message. Check out your training room ahead of time and correct as many issues as possible before your training starts. Acknowledge to the group that you are aware of any remaining detractors. When a distraction is acknowledged, participants are often able to find a way to tune it out or deal with it. Give permission to have windows and doors opened or closed if temperature/noise/etc becomes an issue.

Keep track of time

Ensure there is a working clock where you can see it, *not* on your wrist. Have a clock in your line of sight so you can keep track of time without taking your attention from the group. If you get caught up in the training, you are more likely to see the clock in front of you than you are to see the watch on your wrist. When a clock is not available, take your watch off and put it on the desk or table that holds your notes.

Delivery

Group guidelines and housekeeping

This should be covered first. Include how the session is going to operate, when breaks are, where to smoke, expectations about food and drinks, when questions are appropriate, evacuation or emergency plan, and give permission to get up and use the washroom, access snacks, stand and stretch, etc. Cover the various learning needs mentioned above. While most people will do whatever they need to take care of themselves, rules-bound people might not unless express permission has been given at the beginning of the session.

Be yourself

The most important feature of effective training is you. Know your strengths, your weaknesses and your preferences. Be yourself and tailor your delivery to best suit your style. *Following someone else's guideline or attempting to deliver training the way your predecessor did will likely be disastrous.* Ask yourself the following questions:

◆ Do I like structure?

◆ Am I flexible? Can I change things on the fly?

◆ Am I funny?

◆ Am I forgetful?

◆ Do I like lots of detail or am I a bottom-line kind of person?

◆ What are my habits that drive my colleagues mad?

◆ What are my strengths that others compliment or count on me for?

◆ Is there anything about me that could get in the way of being a good instructor?

Identify your strengths and use them in your training. Identify your weaknesses and develop a plan to compensate for them.

Know your material

There is nothing worse than coming to training and having the presenter read from the manual. It wastes participants' valuable time and creates an environment where they are likely to tune out. Quite frankly, many of your volunteers could just read the material themselves. If you are asking busy adults to sit in a room for a few hours, you need to give them something of value for that time. They want to know they are learning from someone who is knowledgeable. They want to hear about stories and details they aren't going to get from reading the manual. Weave true stories from your agency into your delivery. It highlights points you are making, gives context to the material, and demonstrates why things are done the way they are.

Delivering training can be a fun and exciting part of your job. Careful planning and preparation will make training easier and help ensure the material is relevant and useful. Remember to continue honing your skills and materials over time. Well planned training lets your volunteers know that you value their time. Your volunteers will have realistic expectations of what their job is and what it involves. They will have confidence that they made the right choice for donating their time and energy.

I frequently do or say things unintentionally that are funny, but when I try to be funny, 98 percent of the time it falls flat. Comedy is not my strong suit so intentional jokes of any kind are not included in my training. Organization is a struggle for me and I'm forgetful. I tend to be a bottom-line kind of person which means I can sometimes shortcut instructions. I compensate for these traits in a number of ways. I had a highly organized person develop a checklist for me so I don't forget anything when setting up. I have bulleted notes for reference to ensure that I provide all important information and instructions. When I post an agenda it is simple and without timeframes. I have been known to change the focus or spend extra time on a topic to best accommodate the group's needs. Therefore, detailing the activities for the day and posting times for them only sets me up for failure and erodes the confidence of the participants. A methodical, rules bound, organized person might have a detailed lesson plan rather than a bulleted note, and might have clear timeframes for each topic and will likely have decided in advance exactly where and how a topic could be expanded or shortened and would only do so if absolutely necessary.

 practical tip

Summary Checklist:

◆ Balance the amount of detail.

◆ Keep training interactive.

◆ Use well designed visual aids with color.

◆ Address different learning styles.

◆ Deal with irritants.

◆ Keep track of time.

◆ Include stories.

◆ Maximize your strengths.

◆ Compensate for your weaknesses.

◆ Be yourself.

◆ Have fun!

 Connect with Jesse at http://charitychannel.com/cc/jesse-bowen

Tips on Volunteer Leadership Succession for Nonprofits

By Norman Olshansky

Leadership succession planning in nonprofit organizations is a critical and high stakes endeavor. Too often nonprofit organizations struggle to fill vacant top leadership positions. The consequences of poor succession planning can be devastating.

Every organization has a unique culture and history. When there is a lack of succession planning, organizations find it difficult to fill positions and often recruit individuals to serve in key roles who have minimal experience, few leadership skills, and no history with the organization. Problems often develop when new leaders are asked to take on major leadership roles without significant prior involvement within the organization. Relationships can become problematic between new leaders, key staff and past leaders.

This article focuses on the volunteer president/chair of the board position (chair). Even the most extraordinary nonprofit president/CEO/executive director (ED) cannot achieve the organization's fullest potential without a good board chair. All major leadership positions (officers, committee chairs such as development, planning, marketing, finance, program, etc.) are similarly impacted. The following are recommendations I often make as a consultant to nonprofit organizations related to succession planning.

1. Bylaws

The bylaws of the nonprofit should be clear regarding the organization's leadership structure, process for nominations, elections, and responsibilities of leadership.

2. Job Descriptions

Nonprofits should have a clear and realistic job description for each leadership position that outlines the duties, responsibilities and expectations for each position.

3. Governance/Nominating Committee

A governance/nominating committee should be tasked with the responsibility to identify potential candidates for leadership positions, interview those candidates, review roles and responsibilities with the candidates and obtain their permission to submit their names for consideration for leadership positions within the nonprofit. This committee should obtain input from leadership and staff in order to determine the type of skills, experience and leadership that is most needed to address the current and future needs of the organization. Determining where the current gaps are and how to develop existing leadership in addition to determining who to recruit, should also be part of the charge of the governance/nominating committee. While being considered, the candidates should be provided with an opportunity to meet with existing leadership and key staff to learn more about the expectations of the position.

4. Performance Tracking

The ability of the governance/nominating committee to be successful will be greatly enhanced if the nonprofit has a system in place to track the involvement, relationships and performance of volunteers and supporters. The more information made available to the committee, the better they can identify and recruit the best potential candidates.

5. Orientation

Once the positions are filled, there should be a formal orientation process and where possible, the assignment of a seasoned veteran leader to act as a mentor for each new leader.

6. Chair/Executive Director Consultation Input

Both the current board chair and the executive director should be consulted for input throughout the process and play a major role in the orientation of new leadership.

7. Chair/Executive Director Working Relationship

After the election and preferably before the new term begins the new chair and executive director should meet privately and discuss how they can best work together. This is a time to review in more depth any special needs or suggestions either has related to their working relationship, style, frequency of meetings, best ways to communicate, immediate priorities, etc. This meeting is an important start to the development of the lay/professional partnership between the new chair and executive director.

8. Vice Chair/Chair Elect

I often recommend that when each new board chair is identified, a vice chair be identified as the individual to be groomed to be the next board chair. Often the bylaws identify one position on the executive committee as president elect which accomplishes the same goal. During the course of the board chair's term of office, the individual being groomed (the chair elect), becomes a key player on the executive committee and board, acts in the absence of the board chair and is encouraged to attend as many key meetings as possible related to planning, problem solving, community affairs, etc. The time they serve next to the board chair provides an opportunity for in-depth mentoring, education and hopefully, a smoother and easier transition upon moving up to the chair position. During the mentoring period a determination can be made of the strengths of the next chair and what areas of knowledge or leadership will be needed to further develop prior to beginning the term as chair.

9. Past Chair

The outgoing board chair is often overlooked as part of succession planning. Many organizations keep the outgoing chair on the executive committee and board for one additional term in an official "past chair" position. Past chairs who so desire, can be a tremendous asset to the organization following their time in the leadership position. However, there can be problems if the transition is not handled well. The extent of involvement of the past chair is usually determined by the new chair. Often the new chair wants to establish their own identity and will want the past chair to play more of a behind the scenes role. Other new chairs seek out and encourage past chairs to play a more active role.

10. Past Chair Transition

The transition out of the chair position can be a difficult time for the individual. In most cases they have been heavily involved with the organization for many years and it has become a major part of their lives. I have seen outgoing chairs struggle with the sudden loss of intimate involvement with the organization. They miss the frequent contact and counsel with the staff and other leadership. They miss being the "go to" person or visible leader for the organization. How an organization handles those leaving a key position is just as critical as how new leaders are handled. It's an important aspect of an organization's overall volunteer human resource and stewardship process. Often the executive director is the person who has the closest relationship with the outgoing chair and needs to be actively involved in the transition and stewardship process.

11. Recognition and Stewardship

All outgoing as well as incoming leaders need to be recognized for their contributions to the organization and be part of an ongoing stewardship program.

When a nonprofit utilizes a well planned and implemented leadership succession process it sets the course toward future success.

 Connect with Norman at http://charitychannel.com/cc/norman-olshansky

Reengineering Volunteer Engagement

By Jill Friedman Fixler and Beth Steinhorn

Imagine a world in which your nonprofit has a pool of talented and passionate individuals who are actively partnering with you to deliver more programs, serve more clients, lead new projects, spread your message more widely, increase financial stability, and nurture community partnerships.

Picture yourself with your own skilled assistant, mentor, or partner dedicated to helping you personally achieve more in your work and enabling you to focus on the work you have always dreamt about. Envision each of your colleagues having a skilled individual to serve as a consultant, mentor, project manager, or personal coach. If you could implement a business strategy to ensure these visions become a reality, would you?

That business strategy is not out of reach. Neither are the talented, passionate individuals or the skilled assistants, mentors, and partners. They are all within your reach. In fact, they are likely already in your world. These valuable teammates are your current and potential volunteers, and the business strategy that can make this all possible is strategic volunteer engagement. Volunteer engagement is a capacity-building strategy that builds organizational capacity beyond what staff alone can accomplish. It moves volunteer engagement past the traditional scope of programs, services, and administrative assistance to accessing the talents and professional skills of volunteers for all areas of the organization.

In the competitive philanthropic landscape and with the fallout from the recent recession, the world of volunteerism has evolved significantly over the past few years. For example, as

Baby Boomers enter their sixties, as *Generation X-ers* (born between 1965 and 1979) approach their mid-career marks, and as Millennials (born between 1980 and 2000) enter the workforce, these generations have markedly different views on work, family, and service than previous Greatest and Silent Generations. Their interest in volunteering is high—yet their approach to volunteerism demands more flexibility, short-term opportunities, and clear impact than previous generations of volunteers have done. With all these and other changes in the expectations and motivations of potential volunteers, traditional volunteer management methods that focus on "recruitment, retention, and recognition" are not as effective as they once were. To be successful, organizations must embrace a new volunteer engagement model, one that strategically engages and deploys volunteers toward filling your organization's most critical needs. It's more than simply creating a few new position descriptions; it's about being willing to reinvent how your organization views the volunteer resource and to re-engineer how your organization engages and supports volunteers as true partners with your staff. In this strategy, volunteers serve in a wide range of roles such as pro-bono consultants, planned giving fundraisers, community ambassadors, social media coaches, technology mentors, and project managers, to name a few.

Common Threads

In our consulting work over the years with many kinds of organizations—large and small, new and established, and multi-leveled—we have observed the common threads uniting organizations that are successful in their efforts to thrive through a changing external environment, demographic shifts, and unpredictable economic challenges. What unites them are both the ability to see a future in which volunteers are strategically partnering with staff at all levels to build organizational capacity and the willingness to make the investment today (in terms of time, training, and tools) in order to sustain those partnerships for the long term.

If you can see a future in which volunteers are collaborating with your organization in more robust and meaningful ways than they are today, then you are already on your way to implementing one of the most far-reaching impactful business strategies in your nonprofit's history. The rest is simply figuring out how to get started. This article presents the first key steps towards embracing a culture of volunteer engagement, by starting with discrete, achievable changes that will reap big rewards for you and for your nonprofit.

The steps are:

1. Don't try to re-engineer your volunteer program alone—convene a team of staff and volunteer leaders.

2. Understand your starting point by completing an organizational assessment.

3. Identify your best opportunities by assessing your needs.

4. Start small by piloting change in a few critical areas.

5. Build momentum that will sustain the culture of volunteer engagement.

Steps Towards a Culture of Volunteer Engagement

Convening a team

As your first step toward embracing a culture of volunteer engagement, engage both staff and volunteers to collaborate on a task force charged with shepherding this exciting initiative. Brainstorm first what skills you think you would need on such a team. Include individuals who are experienced in starting new things, who are skilled in project management, who know a lot of people and would be able to leverage their extensive networks on your organization's behalf, and who have expertise in the areas in which your organization has strategic needs (e.g. finance, marketing, development, programming, etc.). Be strategic about composing your team of complementary skill sets and styles. And, most importantly, identify individuals who just simply "get it." Whom do you know who will be excited about the prospect of engaging volunteers in truly high-impact ways?

Then, invite a group of five to eight individuals to not only help you bring that vision into practice, but also to be among the first to model such a collaboration by joining you on this staff/volunteer task force charged with identifying a pilot project of volunteer engagement and shepherding it to success.

Getting started: assess where you are

Any organization—no matter its size, age, or stage of organizational development— can benefit from strategic volunteer engagement. But, success depends on starting from where you are. Complete an assessment of your organization's current volunteer engagement practices in order to identify areas of strength and opportunities for change. We recommend assessing current practices in each of the following areas:

◆ organizational support for
  volunteers;

As you and your colleagues debrief on the organizational assessment, consider these questions:

◆ What are your strengths?

◆ What surprised you most about the results?

◆ What will you have to do differently to raise your scores to all 3's?

◆ How is your volunteer landscape changing?

◆ Can you project how your organization will score on this assessment if you change nothing as Boomers, Gen Xers, and Millennials begin to dominate the volunteer workplace?

◆ Are you positioned to meet volunteers' evolving needs for flexible schedules, high-impact volunteer roles, and collaborative relationships?

◆ What are the biggest challenges for you in making changes for quality improvement?

◆ What are you willing to invest (time, money, people, etc.) in this process?

practical
tip

◆ program planning;

◆ recruitment and cultivation;

◆ interviewing and placement;

◆ orientation and planning;

◆ supervision and support; and

◆ sustainability and retention.

A comprehensive assessment tool is downloadable and available free at www. BoomerVolunteerEngagement.org, including questions on each of these areas and a scoring rubric. Start by convening a task force of staff and volunteers to conduct this assessment as a group, working first individually then gathering to compare and discuss answers.

Making a plan: prioritize your needs

While the organizational assessment defines where you are, the next important step is figuring out where you need to go. You can do this by completing a needs assessment. This is a simple, straightforward process that helps your task force members see what is possible when volunteers are engaged in building the nonprofit's capacity to address the dreams and challenges it faces. A comprehensive needs assessment is also downloadable free at www. BoomerVolunteerEngagement.org, or you can get started by reviewing and discussing these questions. Compare your answers to the results of the organizational assessment and identify two or three ways that you can engage a skilled volunteer in a high-impact role to help fulfill one of your needs. This is the first step toward letting go of the past and establishing a vision of a more expansive, sustainable future.

Needs Assessment

◆ What are the *dreams* for your organization that require more people, expertise, money, or tools to accomplish?

◆ Where are the *opportunities to engage* volunteers to build your personal capacity?

◆ Of which projects, processes, and/or deliverables can you *let go*?

◆ List three *high-impact* volunteer opportunities to engage volunteers with their skills.

practical tip

Starting small: the power of pilot programs

We are all too familiar with the big initiative rollout. These are usually slickly marketed and capture our attention for the moment, but in the long run they are rarely sustainable. Our advice is simple: start small. We remember well how a volunteer management colleague advised implementing volunteer programs with the organization's internal champions. She said, "Where is it written that you as the volunteer manager have to work with everyone? Pick your internal champions and grow the program from there." It was sound advice and served her well in developing several volunteer programs and continues to do so for both of us in our ongoing volunteer engagement work.

Based on the results of your organizational assessment and needs assessment, you can select one or two projects to be used to demonstrate the power and potential of high-impact volunteer engagement. When identifying new, high-impact roles for volunteers, the possibilities are limitless. A few examples from real case studies might help inspire the task force in its brainstorming. One social service agency engaged a professional writer/journalist as a volunteer to write an annual report. Not only did the agency get an innovative, new annual report, but the piece won an award from a public relations association, garnering the agency additional recognition. At one library, volunteers responded to an increased demand for services from unemployed patrons who needed computer skills and job search assistance. Tech-savvy volunteers and those with human resources background developed and offered computer classes and job-hunting workshops. In another example, volunteers with human resources expertise stepped up to help screen hundreds of potential volunteers in preparation for the opening of a new healthcare facility.

When piloting new ways of doing things, clarity is very important. Define the project concisely. Work plans are crucial. They are a critical tool to establish the vision for success, define the scope of the project, identify the necessary resources, and determine the desired impacts and outcomes for benchmarking and evaluation. Whenever possible, include the volunteer in the development of the work plan so you can negotiate the deliverables with your volunteer and ensure that you share the same expectations. Using a work plan, you also have a built-in instrument for tracking progress, measuring success, and, holding the volunteer—and yourself—accountable. When creating the work plan, negotiate communication methods and checkpoints to track progress, as well as the reporting plan (i.e. who else should receive your progress reports). When you are just

> ### Work Plan
>
> A work plan is your itinerary to success. It clearly defines where you want the project to take you and lays out the route to get you there. An effective work plan should include:
>
> ◆ vision statement;
>
> ◆ resources;
>
> ◆ actions;
>
> ◆ yield;
>
> ◆ initial impact; and
>
> ◆ sustained outcome.
>
>  practical tip

Cultivating Skilled Volunteers: How do we Find Them?

◆ Use online search engines, such as VolunteerMatch.org and Idealist.com; they are free and highly effective.

◆ Cultivate from your organizational sponsors, corporate partners, and professional organizations. Create a compelling invitation to volunteer with desired skills and anticipated impacts, then broadcast that message to those who likely have the skills you seek.

◆ Take a skills inventory of your current volunteers, donors, and other constituents. You might be surprised what resources are already in your world. These individuals already care about your mission. If asked, they would gladly share their skills with you.

starting the project, it's often better to meet (either in person or virtually) more frequently to track progress, to adjust the plan to emerging issues, and to develop mutual trust and true collaboration. As the collaboration matures, check-ins might be less frequent. As you track progress, it is crucial to intentionally share stories of success widely. Celebrating the successes is the only way that others will learn about the power and potential of strategic volunteer engagement.

Building momentum: creating a sustainable culture

Change begets change. By tracking the progress on pilot projects and measuring impact against the anticipated outcomes, these new initiatives can be assessed. They should be assessed for scalability (can they be repeated in a bigger—or smaller—way in other areas of the organization?). Also check for replicability (how can this be repeated to build capacity in other areas of the nonprofit?). As the pilot is wrapping up, the task force should look ahead to new opportunities to apply the learning from this pilot endeavor. If the pilot project was designed around engaging an online marketing expert to consult and help improve the social networking tactics around one program, for example, then where else can those tactics be applied? Think even bigger. If a marketing expert partnered with your marketing department, are there other departments that could use the model of volunteer consultant to help in their work areas? Finance? Education? Program evaluation?

Creating a sustainable culture of volunteer engagement means embracing innovation and leveraging the success of those pilots by creating champions for change. These individuals' excitement will inspire others to imagine a future in which their nonprofit, as described at the beginning of this article, "has a pool of talented and passionate individuals who are actively partnering with them to deliver more programs, serve more clients, lead new projects, spread the message widely, increase financial stability, and nurture community partnerships..."

What Does it Take?

By investing in volunteers as capacity builders, you and your organization will reap big rewards. Starting small will lead to tangible results and, yet, even starting small takes some investment of time, talent, energy, and possibly budget allocation. What does it take to revitalize your organization through strategic volunteer engagement?

◆ *Volunteer and staff champions*—individuals who see the potential and are passionate about volunteer engagement as a business strategy;

◆ *Professional development*—training for staff and volunteer leaders, focusing on building volunteer engagement competencies and providing field-proven tools to use in their work;

◆ *Commitment*—from senior management and board leadership to change the culture and follow through with what it takes to make this change;

◆ *Accountability*—the recognition that engaging volunteers is everyone's responsibility and all will be held accountable for success; and

◆ *Patience*—starting small is the key to sustainable change, but once the momentum builds, change can come quickly and broadly!

There is a human and financial cost to change, but the return on investment is high and long-lasting. We have seen organizations of all sizes make strategic investments in volunteer engagement by embracing a collaborative partnership between staff and volunteers. These organizations—small, local agencies to multi-level national organizations—report:

◆ Innovation works well by starting with a discrete pilot project.

◆ Successful pilot projects breed champions for change, and champions, in turn, help build momentum for embracing new ways of engaging volunteers.

◆ New models of volunteer engagement not only attract new volunteers, but also revitalize an existing volunteer corps. Plus, working with skilled volunteers revitalizes staff!

◆ Volunteer engagement builds passionate advocates in the community as well as organizational capacity.

Case Study

We would like to share a story about our work with the California state libraries. Over a two-year period, our team worked with thirty-seven libraries to pilot initiatives using volunteers to build their libraries' capacity to meet the growing needs of their communities. On the surface, the results are impressive: volunteers worked with library staff to develop new programs, deliver services to new audiences, improve their technologies, and create volunteer leaders who are self-directed and who build their own teams of new volunteers. On a deeper level, the impacts are nothing short of extraordinary. Their work has successfully repositioned the library as a community asset in tough economic times. As the State of California was facing unprecedented budget crises, libraries that participated in these pilot programs not only have proven models for successfully utilizing broad generations of volunteers, they also have cultivated a powerful corps of passionate advocates in the community, fighting for their libraries' future. By welcoming innovation, they increased event and program participation, significantly deepened community partnerships, and are called upon as resources and experts by their municipalities and neighboring organizations. In short, by focusing their volunteers' efforts in high-impact, strategic ways, they are now key players in the landscape of their communities.

Making the Vision of a Bigger Future a Reality

Shifting from a traditional practice of volunteer management to an innovative culture of volunteer engagement has far-reaching benefits. Your organization will gain access to the abundant skills of multiple generations of volunteers. By strategically accessing this human capital, your team will be nimble and better positioned to respond to any future circumstance. Your staff will have the capacity to do critical work that plays to their strengths while volunteers partner to achieve other mission-based work. As an added bonus: your staff and volunteers will enjoy their work more because they will have teammates with complementary talents, partners and allies to meet the challenges, and friends and colleagues with whom to celebrate the successes.

Through an investment in reinventing and re-engineering your volunteer engagement strategies, you will see immediate results while building long-term impact. You will build a future in which your nonprofit has a pool of talented and passionate individuals actively partnering, not in your imagination, but rather as a part of your everyday life. And you will achieve the opportunity to live out so many more dreams for yourself, your nonprofit, and the people it serves.

 Connect with Jill at http://charitychannel.com/cc/jill-friedman-fixler

 Connect with Beth at http://charitychannel.com/cc/beth-steinhorn

Vision Quest—Finding a New Executive Director

By Patricia Smith

One of the most important responsibilities that any board will undertake is the quest for a new executive director. There are many choices along the way, roadblocks to avoid and maybe a detour or two. It is not a journey for the faint-hearted. However, even novice travelers can be successful if they follow a few simple rules of the road.

Having served as interim director for organizations that found themselves "director-less" as a result of retirement, termination or resignation, I have been on the journey for a new executive several times. Think of what follows as "roadside assistance" for your expedition and remember it takes planning and persistence to recruit just the right director for your organization.

What Do You Need?

It takes quite a unique and varied skill set to succeed as an executive director. Successful directors need experience in finance, budget preparation, fund development, program planning and evaluation, human resources, facilities

---

Key Attributes to Look For in an Executive Director

Finding the right person isn't easy and if Brian O'Connell is correct in his book *Recruiting, Encouraging and Evaluating the Chief Staff Officer,* you are looking for someone who:

◆ is committed to public service;

◆ likes people and gets along with them well;

◆ is flexible, patient, tolerant and mature; and

◆ is willing to work hard.

 practical tip

management, technology, community relations, working effectively with a voluntary board, and it helps if they have a sprinkling of charm, charisma and staying power.

Where Do We Want to Go?

The departure of the executive presents a unique opportunity to assess or re-assess the strategic direction of your agency. If this were being written as a top ten list, the first thing on the list would be to take the time to plan.

◆ What is your board's vision for the future?

◆ Where does your organization want to go?

◆ Have you been coasting along providing the same services?

◆ Are there emerging needs that your agency is well positioned to address but the former executive didn't really want to?

> Don't focus on where your organization has been but on where you want the organization to go.
>
> Don't be so focused on the former executive's shortcomings that they become the exclusive criteria for hiring.
>
>

Who/What Do We Need to Get Us There?

Once the board has clarity about where it wants the organization to go, then the next step is to assess the skill set, attributes, characteristics and experiences that will help you achieve that vision or direction. What does your agency need right now?

◆ a skilled fund developer;

◆ someone who has experience in developing new programs;

◆ someone who can take your organization to the next level in terms of systems or technology or community relations;

◆ a good collaborator or fence mender;

◆ a visionary leader; or

◆ all of the above?

Don't limit yourself to the characteristics of the departing executive. To further refine the skills and abilities and experience levels think about the job requirements and the "must haves" and the "it would be nice ifs."

What's It Going to Cost?

Determine a competitive salary and benefit package for the position. This is an opportunity for honest reflection. *The Non Profit Times* conducts an annual salary survey for nonprofit directors that can give you some idea of ranges. Often United Ways have this type of information. While they are not going to reveal specific agency executive salaries, if you give them a salary range, they can probably tell you if you are in the ballpark or not for your locality.

While most how-to's start with the creation of a search committee, I truly believe that consensus on agency direction, executive characteristics and credentials and compensation package must come first; and are the responsibility of the entire board and should not be delegated. I'd also expect the board to develop a budget for the process, but some might delegate that responsibility to the search committee.

Do We Need a Designated Driver for the Trip?

Determine if you need outside help in facilitating the process. There are HR firms and nonprofit consultants in most communities who can assist with the process. *Just remember it is your organization and your future so if you do use outside help remember their job is to facilitate not dictate.* One of the benefits of an outside facilitator is they can do much of the busy work - finalize the job description, place the ads, make the initial screening of the resumes based on your criteria, set up the interview schedule, etc.

Who Is Searching and How Far are We Going?

At this point a search committee is formed and, with or without an outside facilitator, they finalize the job description and determine if it is going to be a national, regional or local search. Where and how will you advertise and in general spread the word about the search—internal posting, letters to other non-profits, advertise in national publications, post on your agency web-site, newspapers, etc? All of these choices will be contingent on your budget.

Other things to think about:

◆ How do you want to receive resumes—mail, fax, e-mail?

◆ Who will receive them?

◆ How long will the search remain open?

◆ What is the time line for the search including target dates for reviewing applications and a date for recommendation to the full board?

◆ Will the committee screen each resume, or will one or two people make the initial review?

◆ What information do you want from applicants?

Let's Recap

The job description and credentials have been determined, a deadline for accepting resumes has been decided, the word is out, and the ads are placed. Now the resumes start to trickle or flood in. Congratulations! You have completed the first phase of the quest!

Yes, no and maybe

Once resumes start coming in, it is important to acknowledge their receipt via e-mail or letter. If you have resumes going to a separate e-mail account, you can set up an auto reply and save the committee some time.

Each applicant has a different set of experiences and skills and connecting those to the responsibilities and requirements of the position can be challenging. Many search committees put together a check list or assessment grid which includes the criteria outlined in the job description in priority order.

This helps to systematically screen resumes so that you can select the best candidates to interview. Determine who on the search committee will be responsible for the initial review of resumes and try to have at least two members assigned to do this. Generally, this process will result in three stacks of resumes, the *yes resumes* of those who best meet your criteria, the *no resumes* of those who do not and the *maybe resumes* of those who meet some but not all of your criteria.

> You might be surprised that applicants with an engineering or manufacturing background will apply, as will recent college graduates with no real world experience so you could have to sift through a lot of resumes!
>
>

When the committee meets and determines who will be interviewed, they also set up an interview schedule and identify questions that will be asked. Questions should be open ended and probe for behavioral competencies and results. At this point, some organizations will conduct brief telephone interviews especially if the candidates are from out of the area. One of the side benefits of this is that it takes away the snap judgments we make about people in the first thirty seconds of meeting them.

Selected candidates are then invited in for an interview. The interview information can be confirmed in writing and sent along with an information packet about your organization to each interviewee.

Interviewing 101

It's difficult to interview more than two candidates in one morning or afternoon. Also, be sure that there is sufficient time for and in between interviews. Remember that candidates always come early. It can be awkward if departing and arriving candidates bump into one another, especially in a small community where everyone knows everyone else.

Expect that candidates will have been to your web site, or read your annual report or talked to friends about your organization. They might know some of the search committee members or know friends of the search committee members—the six degrees of separation rule is usually in play here.

The interview format includes a welcome and introductions, questions to and from the candidates and a closing. I know you know that it is important to create as comfortable an atmosphere as possible, but I wouldn't want anyone to think I intentionally left that out.

Be sure each member of the search committee knows the questions that they can't ask. Don't assume everyone is up on the legalities or has been involved in interviewing and hiring.

I always find the questions the candidates ask, or fail to ask instructive and as important as their responses to questions posed by the search committee. It bothers me when candidates do not ask to see the audit or ask any substantive questions about the financial condition of the organization.

Some interviewers like to have an interview rating sheet, while others are more comfortable with taking their own notes and sharing impressions.

What happens next?

At the close of the interview, tell each candidate what will happen next. It is very disconcerting to applicants to be interviewed and then feel as if they are in limbo wondering what, if anything is happening. Be specific—"We expect to make a decision within the next two weeks and we will be back in touch with you."

Should we check references?

If a resume is a balance sheet with only assets listed, aren't references much the same thing? Who is going to give you the names of someone who will say negative things about them? Sometimes search committees are so attracted to a candidate that they don't think reference checks are necessary but they are.

When checking references you are looking for hard data that confirms the candidate's track record, skills and competencies. You are also looking for qualitative data—tangible examples that allow you to better understand the candidate's management and communications style.

With candidate's written permission you can also check educational degrees received and criminal and civil records. When checking references all search committee members should be asking the same questions, so a standard form for this is also necessary.

How do we make the final selection?

For this executive position you are probably going to want to bring your top two or three candidates back for a second interview. Some organizations ask them to make a specific presentation outlining how they would improve community visibility or implement new programs. If this is the route your organization takes, staff and other non-search committee board members can be invited to the presentations. Let's face it, staff members want to be in on hiring their new boss.

Staff Input: What Fits Your Organization?

Some organizations have a non-voting staff representative on the search committee, some ask for staff reaction to the candidates in an informal setting and in other instances staff have no interaction with the new director until they show up for their first day of work. There is no right or wrong here, only what fits your organizational culture.

After the interviews, the reference checks, the feedback, comes the moment of truth when the committee makes a selection for recommendation to the board. This can be difficult if you have two strong candidates, or no candidate that is a stand-out.

Once the successful candidate is identified a verbal offer is made. If the candidate accepts you are almost home free. If the individual declines then you can go to the next candidate in line or you can consider it a failed search and start all over again. You might be asking, why someone would go through two or three interviews and then decline the position. Strange but true I have seen it happen on more than one occasion. It is very disheartening. But for the sake of this article, let's assume the candidate accepts the position at the salary offered. What's next? You will need board approval, a contract, goals for the first thirty days, three months, six months and a year. Also, there needs to be a plan to announce the appointment and to introduce the new executive to the staff, clients, funders, community.

And that, my friends in the nonprofit world, is the short version of how a group of volunteer board members finds a new executive for their organization. It is a challenging process and if statistics are correct and you are a board member, you will probably find yourself on this journey at least once during your board service.

 Connect with Patricia at http://charitychannel.com/cc/patricia-smith

Ten Terrible Reasons for Hiring Your Director of Development—and Five Great Ones

By Gayle L. Gifford, ACFRE

It seems one of the hardest assignments in any organization is hiring the right person for the job. Many nonprofits report that finding a great director of development seems a daunting challenge.

Executive directors or board members often confide to me that their last development director didn't work out as well as they hoped. When I probe a little deeper into how they came to select that individual, I'm not surprised. Predictably, the decisions to hire the unsuccessful individuals were based on reasons that had little to do with the competencies for successful fundraisers.

So here's my list of don'ts and do's for choosing a director of development.

The Top Ten Terrible Reasons

Terrible reason # 10: He wore a really nice suit

Yes, a well-pulled together physical appearance is usually an indication that the candidate took the interview and the job seriously. But just because he dressed nice and sounded great, don't rely on appearances. It is essential both in your interviewing and your reference checking that you verify he can do what he said he could.

Terrible reason # 9: She showed up

Don't hire the best of the worst. If you haven't found the right candidate yet, keep looking. Like any other industry, the job market for fundraising professionals expands and contracts. Sometimes it's just a matter of timing. Try recruiting again. If you continue to have trouble attracting good candidates, do some investigating to find out why. Is the job underpaid? Does your nonprofit have a poor reputation for the way it treats staff? Does the job description sound really boring? Word gets around. If you are repelling good candidates, you've got to fix the problems before you'll ever find the best person.

Terrible reason # 8: He was referred by your cousin Selma

While I would certainly give cousin Selma the courtesy of interviewing her referral, I wouldn't base my hiring decisions on Selma's say so. I wouldn't use Selma as my only reference either— *even if Selma is a big donor*. It is absolutely essential that you put the needs of the nonprofit first in your recruiting effort. Can this person do the job? Take the time to find good candidates, interview well, and check many references.

Terrible reason # 7: She worked at a bank

I don't know how this started, but there seems to be a belief in the nonprofit world that people who work *around* money, automatically know how to *raise* money. *(See also Reason #3)*.While your development director certainly needs to be financially savvy, that doesn't necessarily mean a good financial manager is a good fundraiser. Often, it's just the opposite—while we want our money managers to be on the conservative side, we want our fundraisers to be people-centered individuals who will take some risks (within reason) in their drive to turn straw into gold.

Terrible reason # 6: He used to sell real estate ... or boats, or insurance or whatever

Yes, one of the earmarks of a good director of development is the love of the "sale." You should be looking for someone who isn't afraid of cold calls, meeting new people, building relationships, closing gifts and keeping donors connected. But, don't expect that someone with good sales skills can just walk into the job of a development director without technical training and support. There is a lot to know about fund development in the nonprofit world—the legal and tax laws of fundraising, proven fund development techniques, managing volunteers, budgeting and planning, and negotiating the complex relationships between program and fund development, to name a few.

Terrible reason # 5: She is related to the board president

(See Reason # 8) If you think Selma is tough, hiring the boss's son or daughter is sure to muck up the distinctions between governance and management—no matter what side of that fence you sit on. To prevent this problem, many organizations have conflict of interest policies that prohibit family of board members from seeking employment with them. Only you can decide if that's the right decision for your organization. If you are considering hiring a board member's relative, I can't overemphasize the importance of hiring for the competencies needed in the job and verifying past performance. Plus, I'd certainly want to lay out some ground rules for behavior and confidentiality with both my candidate and her board relative.

Terrible reason # 4: He is the board president

The board president might be a great fundraiser. But there are lots of land mines here—not the least of which is the complete supervisory flip flop which will take place between the staff and this person. While it might be tempting to think you won't have to spend all of that time and money recruiting someone new, you might be missing out on a better candidate who doesn't come with all of the added baggage. And, according to Jane Garthson, an ethics consultant for nonprofits, the executive director should have full authority to hire the best candidate for the job, without the worry of repercussions for not hiring one of their bosses. Imagine continuing to report to a chair you rejected!

Board members who are interested in applying for a job should resign from the board before they throw their hat in the ring—with no guarantees of employment and no return to board service. This should be a board policy. If after reviewing other candidates the *former* board president is still looking good, make sure that you check references and that you have clearly outlined your executive director's authority before you hire.

Terrible reason #3: She knows people with money

Wow, this one is really tempting. Keep reminding yourself that just because someone has access to individuals of wealth, that still doesn't mean she has the skills and competencies to do the job successfully. If she's worked in another development job and tells you that she will bring their donor list with them—drop that candidate as fast as you can. Donor lists are confidential property—they are not transportable from one organization to another. In any case, even if there are no ethical problems, a good thing to know would be if she's leveraged her personal contacts in other circumstances. Chances are if she hasn't been a rainmaker before, she is unlikely to start now.

Terrible reason #2: He writes well

I wish I had a $1000 for every time I've heard this given as the number one reason for selecting a certain candidate. Unless your development director will do nothing other than write mail appeals or grant proposals, this shouldn't be among your top three hiring qualifications. Even grant seeking and direct mail require many other skills—like creative thinking, problem solving, a knack for research and analysis, and, in the case of the grant writer, a talent for program development and relationship-building. The lack of good verbal and writing skills is a reason to screen out candidates—but not the top criteria for hiring someone.

Terrible reason # 1: She is alive and she isn't you

Some people hate the idea of fundraising so much, that just about anyone will do. I've said it throughout this article—you won't find the best person until you know exactly what it takes to do the job that you've developed. Interview your nonprofit colleagues about their experiences, examine your past mistakes and successes, seek out advice from seasoned professionals, and talk to individuals within fundraising professional associations to learn more about the core competencies and essential skills for all aspects of fundraising.

And when you do hire someone, don't expect to never worry about fundraising again. Whether you are a board member, executive director or even program staff, raising money is a collaborative effort that requires the support, creativity and commitment of an entire organization.

By now you are wondering what the right reasons are. Here's the short list.

The Top Five Right Reasons for Hiring Your Development Director

Right reason #5: She is guided by a strong moral and ethical compass

Your development director must be someone that you and your donors can always trust to do the right and ethical thing. There are too many tempting opportunities in fundraising to go ethically astray in pursuit of a gift, like accepting donations with unreasonable strings, taking advantage of naïve or vulnerable donors, misallocating restricted funds, personally benefiting from donor giving, or soliciting a gift that could risk your organization's reputation. Ask your prospective candidate what code of ethics they subscribe to. And don't be shy about asking the candidate to share an ethical dilemma she encountered and how she handled it.

Right reason #4: He loves people and has great people skills

At its root, philanthropy is the "love of humankind." Fund development, in service to philanthropy, is about creating and nurturing lasting relationships. Good development directors thrive on relationships. They enjoy meeting new people, they listen, they connect donors to their dreams, and they truly appreciate donors for their act of giving and not just for the size of their check. Development directors worth their pay know how to enable volunteers to act, how to motivate their own staff and how to develop valuable partnerships throughout your organization and among other parts of your community. Find out what other people have to say about your prospective candidate, and dig deep to learn what kind of relationships he has built with all types of constituents in the past.

Right reason #3: She really believes in what you do

Not every organization puts this near the top of their list. But I happen to think that it is a lot easier to go to work every day and do your best when you are really passionate about the cause you are working for. Not to mention that sincere enthusiasm for the mission is noticed by your donors and volunteers. And if your candidate really believes in what you do, my guess is that she is likely to stay around much longer than those individuals who hop from job to job whenever the title, pay and benefits look a little better. Ask why this job? Why this organization? Listen to what she says about your mission and the issues or clients you serve.

Right reason #2: He is smart, creative, self-managing, professional, and a great strategist

Okay, I cheated and put almost everything else into this reason. You want someone who understands how all the pieces fit together. Someone who can intuitively solve problems, who rises to challenges, who doesn't need a lot of hand-holding, and who considers fund development a noble profession and takes their own learning seriously.

And, finally:

Right reason #1: She is really good at raising money

This is the point after all. Your candidate can talk a great game, write great plans, be a lovely person and team player. But you absolutely want to hire someone who has a proven track record of meeting *and beating* her goals. Your director of development can never take her eyes off the ultimate objective, which is to raise the resources your organization needs. Past history is a good predictor of future behavior. Find out what exactly she has done and how she accomplished it. Beware of the "royal we"—what did she do specifically?

And before you make that offer of employment, please verify everything you were told by rigorously checking references.

 Connect with Gayle at http://charitychannel.com/cc/gayle-gifford

Are you a Board-Savvy CEO?

By Steven Bowman

What does being a board-savvy CEO mean to you? Does it mean understanding what the board requires from you and your staff? Is it about providing information to the board in a manner you know they can receive? Is it about how to keep the board strategic and out of your back pocket? Is it about navigating the unknown personal agendas of board members so you keep your job? Is it all of these and many more?

Below are the six attributes of a board-savvy CEO. How do you measure up?

Solid understanding of the roles and responsibilities of the board

A board-savvy CEO will steer the board to ensure that all responsibilities of the board are carried out. You need to be up to date with the latest governance and strategic thinking techniques, constantly review the work of the board to ensure that the board is truly adding value, and work very closely with the chair and the board members to keep focused on all the responsibilities of the board. Subscribing to relevant professional governance organizations, reading extensively and participating in governance forums all contribute to a board-savvy CEO.

Awareness of the skills and aspirations of each board member

A board-savvy CEO will be aware of the personal skills of each of the board members, both formal (education, work related etc.) and informal. Often board members have untapped skill sets, and the board-savvy CEO will understand and make use of these. Each board member will have different aspirations regarding their term as a board member, and the board-savvy CEO will have discussions with each board member regarding these aspirations and work with the chair to meet or to manage these aspirations.

Strong working relationship with the chair

A board-savvy CEO will forge a strong, robust relationship with each chair of the board. Before the chair formally accepts the position, have a discussion about how it would best work for both of you. The board-savvy CEO will help the chair understand the responsibilities and possibilities of the chair position, and will create a clear set of expectations between the CEO and chair position. The board-savvy CEO will brief the chair on any potential surprises and issues in the board agenda of each board meeting, prior to the meeting, and work with the chair to develop processes for board and CEO succession planning, performance management, and evaluation.

A diligent working relationship with the board

A board-savvy CEO will develop a strong working relationship with the board as a collective entity. This means have robust performance evaluation measures in place, both for the CEO (with agreed key performance indicators and contract review mechanisms in place on a regular basis) and the board (an annual board review process as well as regular meeting review processes), continually refining the information that the board receives and monitoring if that information is providing what the board needs, and developing relevant mechanisms to show that the board can trust the CEO, as that trust is constantly tested and independently verified.

Ensuring that the board's professional development meets the needs of the board

A board-savvy CEO will develop a regular board professional development program that meets the aspirations and needs of the board members individually and collectively. Develop guest speaker sessions to support the board. This might include presentations from other CEO's of like organizations, funding bodies, academics etc.

Focusing the board strategically, while keeping them aware of the operational components

A board-savvy CEO will focus the board strategically whilst keeping them informed of the key operational aspects of the organization. Reports to the board will provide strategic options, not the answer. The CEO will pose strategic questions, rather than trying to ramrod a decision through the board. The board-savvy CEO will create a culture of strategic awareness within the board, not rubber-stamping.

 Connect with Steven at http://charitychannel.com/cc/steven-bowman

Breaking Down the Silos

By Michael J. Nizankiewicz, PhD, CAE

You've probably heard the word "silo" used in organization-speak referring to isolated departments or isolated functional areas where information sharing is rare and even discouraged. In an organization like this, protecting one's turf (department) is foremost and colleagues working toward the same mission rarely have an exchange except in social settings at work. These organizations considered professional development a "luxury" expense so employees often go without enhancing their professional skills. Webster is succinct in defining a silo as "a trench, pit, usually sealed to exclude air."

In organizations, the exclusion of "air," or lack of ongoing and disciplined communication, lack of integrated work plans to achieve common objectives, and lack of capitalizing on synergies is far too common today. The downsides far outweigh any possible advantage to fostering silos. They include confusion, lack of mission focus, duplication of efforts from one department to the next, ignorance, persons within the same organization looking at their colleagues as competitors rather than teammates. Ultimately the deterioration of morale results in high turnover and low productivity.

Many, if not most of those reading this article, have experienced these symptoms. People in one department of an organization who express jealousy at staff fundraisers, staff lobbyists,

> **Silo**
>
> Webster's defines "Silo" as a "trench, pit or especially, a tall cylinder usually sealed to exclude air and used for making and storing silage."

or community service staff (just to name a very few) who accomplish their jobs meeting with donors, legislators, or community volunteers. Their jobs are best accomplished meeting their constituents face-to-face and not at their office desks. Those whose jobs are done at their desk neither understand the key results areas of those working outside the office and, more importantly, do not understand how those "outside" jobs directly or indirectly impact the work of those working at their desks (and vice versa). Silos like these exist in all sectors: nonprofit, for-profit, and government organizations all are guilty of fostering silos including hospitals and medical centers, hotels and resorts, the airline industry, philanthropic, trade and professional membership associations, and others.

So why would any organization tolerate having silos? Misguided egos are typically the root cause whether it's a department head who feels that communicating important information somehow reduces "power" a manager who is overly protective of his or her "turf" or even a CEO who encourages silos thinking that only the strong will survive, and that departments and staff competing with each other is somehow a good thing. Another reason is the absence of mutually agreed objectives towards a common goal. Associations and other organizations themselves can be mega-silos by refusing or resisting collaboration with similar organizations to more effectively reach mutual goals and advance missions. In this latter example, both staff leaders and boards of directors are guilty of enabling mega-silos.

While he never used the term "silos" in the bestselling book, *The Fifth Discipline*, Peter Senge cuts to the very heart of the antithesis of "silos"—the learning organization. Senge, an engineering professor at the Massachusetts Institute of Technology and now an author and international speaker, seemed to have found the meaning of life. In defining the "learning organization," Senge emphasizes the need for intercommunication within organizations to clearly understand the interdependency between departments and functional areas. To Senge, virtually everything is systemic. A problem or malfunction in one area of an organization can adversely affect one or several other areas resulting in dysfunction. Of course, no one would say they support silos. Virtually every manager believes that what they are doing is right or somehow justified, but ego too often gets in the way.

One event that has an uncanny way of eliminating silos is a crisis that directly impacts the entire organization. A crisis typically puts an organization in survival mode where teamwork is absolutely critical. Departments and the individuals within them realize that if the entire organization does not work together, then the organization, and their very jobs, are doomed—which is often the case for organizations entrenched in their short-sighted and isolated visions and actions. A good professional sports example is the Pittsburgh Steelers who were on the verge of elimination during the 2005 regular season. Bill Cower, their coach, instilled in them a "do-or-die" crisis mentality meaning that if they did not click into full throttle as a team, they would be eliminated for the season. Not only did they get a "wild card" berth in the playoffs, but they were the *only* 6th seed wildcard team in NFL history to win every post-season playoff game and go on to win a Super Bowl (XL). A more current example is the oil spill disaster of BP in the Gulf Coast. Even if that corporation were guilty of supporting silos in the past, the oil spill created a global crisis for this petroleum giant that had every employee concerned about their company's future and that of its employees.

So, how can an organization reduce or eliminate silos without creating a crisis? The most obvious solution is to stop it before it starts. A new CEO should make it explicitly clear that silos will not be tolerated. This begins with the CEO's leadership team and must be *explicitly* communicated throughout the entire organization. Ongoing meetings of the leadership team and general staff meetings can be used as an opportunity to snuff out the beginnings of silos and to reinforce the interdependency of all departments to ensure organizational success.

Four-Part Approach

Patrick Lencioni, in his book *Silos, Politics and Turf Wars,* offers a four-part approach that includes a thematic goal, a set of defining objectives, a set of ongoing standard operating objectives, and metrics:

◆ *Thematic Goal.* He defines a thematic goal, or "rallying cry" as a "single, qualitative focus that is shared by the entire leadership team—and ultimately, by the entire organization—and that applies for only a specified time period." Lencioni is quick to point out that a thematic goal is not to be confused with a long-term vision, which is also important in any organization. Also, the thematic goal should be somewhat short-term—no more than six months in scope.

◆ *Defining Objectives.* The second step is "defining objectives" which are four to six defining targets directly linked to the thematic goal. Naturally, these objectives should be qualitative and shared with the entire leadership team and to the staff reporting to them.

◆ *Standard Operating Objectives.* The third component is "standard operating objectives." These are nothing more than the day-to-day performance targets of the organization for which a leadership team member is directly responsible. This can include (but is not limited to) revenue targets, membership goals or even "maintenance objectives" which are necessary for keeping the organization, or a department, running efficiently.

◆ *Metrics.* The final component is "metrics" which is a measurement device directly linked to the defining objective. Lencioni strongly encourages weekly leadership team meetings in which each member of the leadership team gives a very brief (thirty second) report on their top three priorities for the coming week. Then each member of the team uses a scorecard with a simple scoring mechanism to determine which priorities need the most attention (Lencioni suggests a "green, yellow, red" system with the reds and yellows demanding the most immediate attention).

practical tip

Hearing words like "my department," or "my people/staff" is a clear warning sign that silos exist. So the next question is: "How do you address and breakdown silos once they are entrenched in an organizations culture?"

Consistency in the leadership team meetings and addressing weekly priorities as they feed up to the thematic goal is critical in keeping silos out of an organization. Of course, once the thematic goal is achieved then the leadership team must challenge itself for the next "rallying cry" or thematic goal and keep the same four-part process in place to ensure a cohesive and interdependent organization.

While this can all be achieved by a very strong and dedicated CEO, an organization and the leadership team might find it more palatable to engage an outside consultant familiar with the ability to identify and address silos, including the four part process defined herein. This does not mean the consultant should be at every weekly meeting of the leadership team, but rather be used to identify the thematic goal, defining objectives, standard operating objectives and metrics, then be a part of the first few leadership team meetings to ensure that metrics are being used and the right priorities are being addressed each week.

To recap, here are strategies for the CEO

◆ Make it clear from the very beginning that silos will not be tolerated.

◆ Educate members of the management team of the importance of integrated components. Senge's *The Fifth Discipline* should be required reading for any management team and they should discuss the opportunities in collaborative work units.

◆ Create the "thematic goal" that Lencioni describes and use management meetings to discuss integrated progress toward the objectives that support that goal and what will be further done in the week ahead.

◆ Use performance evaluations to discuss individual commitment to an integrated workforce. Reward or discipline accordingly.

◆ Above all else, be sure the right people are on board as department heads who share the same commitment towards unity and against silos.

Regardless of the process engaged, a CEO should be vigilant of the warning signs of silos and do everything within her or his power to keep the leadership team, staff and the entire organization on point with its thematic goals, defining objectives and standard operating objectives.

 Connect with Michael at http://charitychannel.com/cc/mike-nizankiewicz

Purchasing Insurance: Don't Do It Again Until You've Read This

By Pamela Davis

Observing the decision making process some organizations use to purchase insurance is like watching a train wreck. I am convinced that there is something about the insurance purchase that causes many otherwise smart decision makers to go off the rails. My particular experience is observing the purchase of property/casualty insurance. But, I suspect that these observations can translate to the purchase of just about any type of insurance.

You Buy a Promise to Pay

I suspect that the problems start because, with insurance, what you buy is a promise to pay if something goes wrong. What else do we purchase that is really of no value unless something goes wrong in our lives? And, with insurance, you can't just "return" it if you don't like what you get. Too late for that once that bad thing has happened.

Furthermore, insurance policies are so arcane and boring that just about the only thing that would motivate most people to read them is to cure a serious case of insomnia. Insurance policies contain all kinds of legal terminology and huge differences in coverage can result with the clever insertion of the word, "or" rather than the word, "and."

Like other financial products, consumers want to believe that there is some "regulator" somewhere out there that is going to protect the consumer. We want to believe that "they" won't allow insurance companies to sell policies that are illegal. Well, to some extent that is true. However, as we found out with the financial crisis and recession caused by the housing bubble, products don't have to be illegal to be misleading or deficient, even dangerous. Products that technically meet the letter of the law can, nonetheless, be very bad for the consumer.

Insurance Responsibility is an "Orphan" at Most Organizations

What does this have to do with the nonprofit executive? A lot. Often at nonprofit organizations, the responsibility for the purchase of insurance is relegated to the most junior clerical staff that doesn't have the clout to turn down the assignment or else it becomes a big political fight at the board level. Either scenario is not healthy. So what are some of the common pitfalls of the insurance purchasing experience?

Recognize That You Have an Expertise Problem

There are precious few nonprofit organizations that have anyone on staff or the board qualified to advise the organization about all of the types of insurance and which policies from which company or companies makes the best sense. And, if that person does exist, he or she is probably an insurance broker on the board or maybe a friend of a board member or the executive director.

Insurance is a relationship business, no doubt about it. But just because a broker has a good personality and is a friend of a board or staff member is not a good reason to have that broker advise you on the insurance purchase. More times than I like to admit I have taken calls from exasperated executive directors asking what they can do about a board member who has inserted a friend of his into the broker relationship with the nonprofit. The executive director is convinced that the service and coverage options from this broker are not the best, but does not want to challenge the well-liked and influential board member about his broker friend.

Policies and procedures at the nonprofit should prevent this situation from happening. Consultants, including insurance brokers, should be selected for their quality of work in service to the nonprofit organization. Period.

Rule #1

Your broker should not be one of your board members, nor should friendships or donations drive the broker selection decision.

So, is there a match.com to find a great insurance broker?

As with personal relationships, there is no sure fire way of finding the right broker for you. But, whether the selection is done by a committee of the board or by a single executive or team, using a thoughtful process can go a long way towards getting to the right result. First, make sure that the selection process is not political or a "beauty contest." You are hiring a consultant to provide a very important service to your organization. Even though the fee the broker gets is imbedded in your insurance premium doesn't mean the broker works for free or that who you hire doesn't much matter. Start by asking nonprofit colleagues and associations whom you respect who they use for their insurance broker and why they like them. Throw out the recommendations that simply focus on personality, "he's a great guy," and pay close attention to the ones that focus on the expertise of the broker and her focus on prompt service. Be wary of associations who refer brokers who pay them an "endorsement fee." Don't be afraid to ask for examples of broker conduct that has impressed the person making the referral.

Once you have collected a couple of names, call these brokers and speak with them on the phone. Interview them like you would interview perspective new employees. Ask for references and call them. Once you think you have the right one, have one more person you respect give the broker a call and see if their impressions match yours. Ideally, you will then meet with the broker in person. In reality, if you are a very small nonprofit, you might need to work with the broker over the phone most of the time. However, if you are a nonprofit with staff and operations, you should generally expect to have the insurance broker visit your facility periodically. As with every rule, there are exceptions.

Rule #2

It's not how much "face time" you get from a broker that matters, it's whether the broker is skilled in the profession and is committed to doing what is best for your organization, first and foremost.

But isn't the best broker the one that takes me to lunch or gives the biggest donation

There is nothing wrong with having lunch with your insurance broker, but if you take an honest look at the situation and determine that this is the broker's greatest value, you have a problem. Nonprofits have special insurance needs and there are certain insurance carriers that have developed policies that address those special needs. Good brokers are incredibly knowledgeable about their profession and are in a good position to be extremely helpful to your organization. Your broker should be able to discuss with you your various options and be versed in coverage that matches your organization's particular risks. You want your broker to be an expert and a professional that gives you great advice that you can turn into actionable decisions. You want a broker who will return your calls and emails and who will answer your questions in ways you can understand and trust. You need donations, but please do not base your decision on your insurance broker on whether or not or how much the broker or the company donates to your cause. That is short-sighted and could cost you a lot of money in overpaid insurance premiums or coverage inadequacies.

Rule #3

You should not have to be the insurance expert. (You have a nonprofit organization to run!) Make sure your broker is an insurance expert with a good understanding of nonprofits' special insurance needs.

You Have to be "Into" the Details

I just said you don't have to be an insurance expert. But, that doesn't get you off the hook. The person responsible for purchasing the insurance for the organization, should have an intimate knowledge of the nonprofit's operations and have access to information required on the insurance application. Make no mistake. A broker who encourages you to leave a bunch of blanks on the insurance application and doesn't take the time to get the information requested by the insurance company is not doing you any favors. You wouldn't turn in a half-completed application to a foundation from which you are requesting a grant, would you? But, you can't be bothered to give some basic detail about your organization to an insurance company who is putting out at least a $1 million promise to pay? If the insurance company is going to "fill in the blanks" for you, it is going to estimate high. You won't get the best offer.

Rule #4

Take the insurance application process as seriously as you would a grant application.

Your Website is Your "Facebook" to the World

Prospective employers now check out social media sites to see what future employees are telling the world about them. Insurance companies use websites in much the same way to learn about prospective insureds. You might want the world to be amazed by all the wonderful things you are doing by embellishing the truth a bit on your website (230 clients served rounds to 700, right?), but be aware that insurance companies use this information for rating purposes. If you say on your website that you have six programs, but three of them are kinda, sorta, in the works, a good insurance underwriter will wonder why you list three on your applications and six on your website. By extension, the underwriter will then question the truth of the rest of your insurance application.

Turn into the Inquisitor When Your Broker Presents the Options

One of the most common and surprising questions I get is, "Can I ask my broker how much he is being compensated?" My response is, "What other professional consultant would you hire without asking about compensation?" The fact that brokers are paid by insurance companies, makes the question even more important. When reviewing your options with the broker, ask how much compensation he or she is receiving from each insurance company for which a quote is presented. You should

---

Rule #5

Make sure your insurance application and website reflect the same organization.

---

also ask whether the broker is receiving any "contingent commissions" or any other compensation from any of these insurance carriers. If the broker refuses to disclose this, find another broker.

> **Rule #6**
>
> There are no "dumb" insurance questions.

When the insurance broker is going over the quotes for the different coverage, remember that it is the broker's job to translate what you have told the broker about your nonprofit to get you the right insurance coverage for your exposures. If you are concerned that the broker might have failed to understand something about your operation now is the time to ask questions about coverage. Insurance is an arcane and complex subject.

Insurance Isn't a Substitute for Good Management

Insurance is a necessary cost of doing business. It is the safety net you are glad you have when, despite your best efforts, something goes wrong and someone is hurt or property is damaged. Risk management isn't a mystery. Risk management is simply good management.

> **Rule #7**
>
> Good leaders recognize that risk management is not something you have to do to keep your insurance company happy; it is a discipline to help you do whatever you do the best you possibly can.

Many of the books published on the topic make risk management about as appealing as trigonometry to most high schoolers. Good risk management doesn't have to be daunting. It is a state of mind. It is a keen awareness of the workings of your organization and how you interact with your clients, your staff, your volunteers and members of the public. Good managers and leaders of nonprofits put policies and procedures into place to anticipate what might go wrong with these interactions. They train staff and volunteers how to conduct themselves so that injury will be avoided whenever possible and properly handled when it does occur. This brings us to our final rule.

In summary, next time the responsibility for purchasing insurance falls on your lap, see it as an opportunity to work with an engaged professional to protect your organization if something goes wrong, as well as a resource who will work with you to make sure the odds of accidents and injuries are low. Expect this person to have a broad and deep understanding of insurance and to learn enough about your operations to help you purchase just the right coverage. Ideally, that person should be someone with whom you would enjoy having lunch, but that should be really low on your list of selection criteria. With insurance, it's best to go for expertise and great service, even if you have to buy your own lunch!

A simple guide:

◆ Remove even the appearance of a conflict of interest from your insurance purchase.

◆ Hire a broker for insurance expertise, market access and service, period.

◆ As with any consultant, ask about compensation.

◆ Take your broker's request for information as seriously as you would a funder's.

◆ Expect your broker to be able to translate "insuranceze" in a way that works for you.

◆ Expect your broker and insurer to assist with risk management needs.

 Connect with Pamela at http://charitychannel.com/cc/pamela-davis

Purchasing Technology: Return on Mission

By Andrew Urban

Small and large organizations alike are running the critical day-to-day aspects of their mission with technology products more and more. Volunteers sign in with touch screen systems. Applying and ongoing reporting for grants involves communicating and integrating with a funder's website or database. Donors come online to see what the history of their pledge is and register for events and so forth. An increasing number of people inside your organization are involved in the financial accounting processes through web access portals and executive dashboards. There is also, most likely, a software package tracking the intake of your clientele, tracking the billing/allocation of their treatment. The examples are seemingly endless today as to how technology is touching every aspect of your daily work and the delivery of your mission itself.

While technology has made incredible improvements over the years to help our sector do the most good what is difficult for so many organizations is to know how to find the right product and make a purchase that solves the right needs they have for their unique mission. As a nonprofit executive there are many books, workshops, and materials for nonprofit management of all kinds (volunteer, board members, donor relations, etc.). What has been missing is a methodology to ensure that the applications purchased to support the mission in all of its respects is the right fit to deliver the most direct impact to the mission. This decision-making model, the nonprofit buyer model of control, focuses on more than a return on investment, but rather on the return on mission.

Return on mission is the ability to calculate and map tangible impact and value back to your unique mission. Sorting through the dizzying array of choices available today can be very difficult not to mention the ability to gain agreement for the desired solution across all of the stakeholders at your organization. By keeping the return on mission always at the forefront it makes sure that both vendor and staff have the same ultimate goal in mind as each stage of the buying process happens (discovery discussions, demonstration sessions, and pricing negotiations).

The Vendor Dance

Before we can get to how we calculate what is the return on mission it is helpful to first understand that the process to get to a decision for your organization is, and I'm being slightly tongue in cheek here, fraught with danger, peril, and potential missteps at every turn. Danger rears its ugly head in that you could go through a whole painful process of buying a new critical system for your mission only to end up with something that only feels marginally better than what was there before. The peril is that you could do the whole search only to be shot down by an executive or board member who doesn't understand the justification. Potential missteps are always around where I see nonprofit staff utilize the same inefficient and ineffective buying techniques to make decisions based on what they know today and not based out of where they wish to be in the future.

What we as sales reps get used to, since we do this job over and over again, client by client, and year after year, is what I call "The Vendor Dance." This is my name for the back and forth that happens during a potential sale. It is different for every transaction you might have in your life. It could be personal, like haggling at a market, or impersonal, like buying a computer online. There is another arena of sales that is very personal. Meetings, demonstrations, tradeshows, webinars, personal phone calls and relationships are all hallmarks of the buying process for a business critical application whether you are a nonprofit or not. The vendor dance is done every day. You are probably involved in it right now in ways you aren't even aware. "So what is it then and how am I involved in it already," you ask?

Let's think of it as being asked to a high school prom. Does she like me? I heard she does. Sally told Jimmy that Johnny thought she might sort of like me, but doesn't want to say anything in case I didn't like her first. She likes me? Great! "Would you go to the dance with me?" "Yes!" "I'll pick you up at 7 p.m. in my dad's car." Translated to a sales process..."What software do you think we should buy?" "I don't know. Let's call a few vendors." "Do you think we can afford them?" "Tell them we're a nonprofit." "Would you like a demo of our software? Do you like what you see?" Maybe they want to buy our stuff. "Do you think they want to buy? What signals did they give you? Did it seem positive? What else can we do?" "They'll buy if we do this, this, and this." "Really? We can't do that. We can only do this." "Their legal team wants what?" Now the board has to look at it. "You can sign a contract? Great! I'll pick you up at 7 p.m. in my rental car to celebrate."

That same back and forth communication happens over and over again. We all end up in the same awkward dance together unless I, as a sales rep, can begin to guide them through what I know they will need to see and do in order to make an intelligent buying decision. Some organizations I have dealt with over the years were definitely better dance partners than others—that's for sure. However, it is clear that this is one dance in which many in our sector do need a few more lessons. The fact that these lessons might be necessary is understandable. So much focus has been put on the needed areas of board, donor, volunteer management, etc., and for good reason. This has been a neglected arena compared to the other well-studied and detailed procedures we have in so many other areas of nonprofit management. It's time we get better at this dance together.

The "Nonprofit Buyer Model of Control" is a model that will make your next vendor dance one that feels like a dance done just right, one that feels like you are on the dance floor at your senior prom with that perfect guy or girl.

Return on Mission

I'll detail here a core point of the nonprofit buyer model of control: Return on mission (ROM). ROM is the ability to look beyond the standard return on investment (ROI) formula in order to make sure your investments have the maximum impact on not just the bottom line, but to the maximum impact on the mission itself. This is not necessarily a standard scientific equation, is to be thought of much as a standard ROI is, but with the extra component of understanding the impact of the purchase on the mission of the organization. I've represented this in the formula below:

The "Impact to Mission" is to be based upon the particular mission of your organization, of course. If you serve meals to the homeless, for example, then every purchase made should be seen not just for the productivity gains it could give your organization's employees, but in the light of how it can help your organization serve more meals, advocate for your cause, or purchase more supplies. The goal of an exercise like this is to make tangible the reality of a new business application purchase to all of the stakeholders at your organization and for the vendor to always keep in mind that every decision is rationalized and justified by how it affects the mission of the organization.

> ### The Nonprofit Buyer Model of Control
>
> The Nonprofit Buyer Model of Control consists of these four points:
>
> ◆ critical business issues (CBIs);
> ◆ organization outline;
> ◆ return on mission (ROM; and
> ◆ doable logistics.
>
> $$ROM = \frac{(\text{Gain from Investment - Cost of Investment})}{\text{Cost of Investment / Impact on Mission}}$$
>
>  practical tip

As a nonprofit executive what are you told over and over again by board members, consultants, and your resident helpful know-it-alls? They say, in the nicest of intentions of course, "You need to act more like a business." The implication being that, as a nonprofit, there is little resemblance to being a real business. They miss the fact that, just like any other work out there, a nonprofit relies on marketing, sound accounting, a core vision and principles, human resources, rent, and so much more. The only difference is in outcome. The corporation lives to make a profit whereas the nonprofit, many would seem to think, lives solely to not make a profit. They don't realize a nonprofit can make a profit. The money just has to be, at the end of the day, given towards the philanthropic mission instead of, for example, as dividends to shareholders.

Thus, you need to be concerned about return on mission. It bridges the divide between the business and the mission to create a metric that all sides can agree to work towards. It makes tangible the reality of a new business application purchase to all of the stakeholders at your organization and for the vendor to always keep in mind that every decision is rationalized and justified by how it affects the mission of the organization.

ROM Analysis Example

A quick and easy ROM analysis example for a new large printer/copier solution:

Assume:

- ◆ print 10,000 pages per month on current printer/copier;
- ◆ current printer/copier costs $0.02 per printed page; and
- ◆ new printer/copier costs $800.

If new printer/copier costs $0.01 per printed page:

- ◆ new copier/printer has half the cost per printed page;
- ◆ monthly printing costs from $200 to $100; therefore
- ◆ a gain of $200 in trade-in on old printer/copier.

Then:

- ◆ ($100 printing savings per month x 12) – ($1000 for new copier/printer - $200 for trade-in) = $400 savings over 1 year;
- ◆ the initial investment of $600 ($800 for the new printer/copier minus the $200 trade-in for the older printer/copier) produced a return of $400 in the first year of production; then
- ◆ Standard Return on Investment = 33 percent.

Return on Mission calculation for this scenario:

$400 savings in first year of production/$400 (a sample amount of one month of electricity cost at a children's shelter building) = 100 percent return on identified mission costs.

practical tip

Your Nonprofit Buyer Model of Control Checklist

❑ Recognize the vendor dances that you are involved in.

◆ List the contacts that you have had with vendors and start to recognize those within the context of their sales cycles. Have a conversation with vendors you are interested in about how their sales cycles work to see if their unique business processes could be of help to your nonprofit.

❑ Know thyself first—define your internal critical business issues.

◆ Do the internal soul-searching to map out your own critical business issues that are the true needs for the project for which you are about to embark on a buying process.

◆ These must be done apart from any consideration of a vendor, what solutions you might have been considering as you have been informally polling the marketplace prior to your formal buying process, or your own personal biases towards specific products because of prior experience with that product.

❑ Organization outline

◆ This is your dating profile, so to speak, in the context of your vendor dance. It is the profile document that outlines why this project is important to your mission, what specifically it will support for your mission, and what goals you hope to have achieved by success with this project.

◆ This document can also be a good internal guideline for your team to understand the agreed upon mechanics about how the buying process is going to work. It can define particular feature or product advocates who work specifically with certain vendors to champion one product or another internally.

◆ It can define the communications and process schedule for vendors so they understand who is and who is not okay to contact within the process in order to avoid back-channel communications that can interrupt an open and transparent process.

❑ Return On Mission

◆ This formula would be relayed to your vendors within the organization outline.

◆ It should be an expectation that every vendor be able to detail their product to your mission in terms of how they expect to match the return on mission criteria. If they are unable or unwilling to do so then that is an easy disqualifier to doing business with them for your organization.

❑ Doable Logistics

◆ Doable logistics refers to the pieces of the process you can nail down as milestones for your discussion with your vendors. I am referring to the ability to set guidelines to manage your communications most effectively. The pieces that definitely should be included within these guidelines are items such as timeframe, your potential budget, communications' process and demonstration schedule.

- ◆ Timeframe—not a "when you want to purchase by" date, but rather a "when you need the solution to be ready to use" date.

- ◆ Budget—obtaining pricing early from vendors is important as it can sometimes be used as a sales tactic for them. Remember, don't buy based upon price alone. The defined CBI's drive must drive your decision.

- ◆ Communication process—defining this for your vendors insures that they:

❑ Demo to your CBI's

❑ Demo to your processes

❑ Demo to their unique product points

❑ Maintain brevity to insure clarity in proposal responses

❑ Detail ROM for their product solution

Conclusion

As we go further and further down the path that has technology managing ever-increasing sections of our missions it is critically important that we have an understanding as to how we can make the decisions for that technology in the best manner possible. By understanding the vendor dance, insisting that your vendors be wonderful dance partners, and instilling your own model of control into your process your organization will be able to make decisions that will have the most impact on the mission. The goal of the buying process becomes an understanding of how to utilize each solution not as a patchwork of functionality to solve a particular pain, but rather as an organization's choice that can directly trace benefit to the mission in a way that is understood by all stakeholders (staff, board, funders, etc). The buying process won't be one fraught with danger and peril, but rather it will be one that you can look forward to because of how it will enable innovation with your mission and provide greater utilization of the donor dollar.

The Nonprofit Buyer Model of Control, if followed, will put you in control of your buying processes. It will remove the mystery from these situations, save everyone a good deal of time and effort, and produce a final outcome—the actual purchase—more in line with the needs of the organization. A relationship that starts off on the right foot will, more often than not, lead to a long-term relationship built on trust and understanding. The end of the vendor dance is the actual marriage between the now customer and the vendor. What the nonprofit buyer model of control has brought together let no one put asunder.

 Connect with Andrew at http://charitychannel.com/cc/andrew-urban

How Well Are You Handling "Risk" in Your Nonprofit Organization?

By Norman Olshansky

Over the past few years, increasing attention has been given to potential liability, mismanagement and ethical practices within the nonprofit sector. Whether as a result of the Sarbanes-Oxley Act of 2002 or more recent high profile Ponzi schemes and fraud cases, boards and executives of nonprofit organizations have begun to put more focus on risk management.

By "risk management" I mean the identification, assessment, and prioritization of risks followed by coordinated and economical application of resources to minimize, monitor, and control the probability and/or impact of unfortunate events or to maximize the realization of opportunities.

When was the last time your organization conducted a serious risk management process?

While many of the prime areas of risk are related to finances, personal injury liability, and unforeseen disasters, there are many other areas of nonprofit operations and governance which can create risk for an organization.

The following are a few of the more common areas of risk which can be assessed and addressed:

1. Availability of information for decision making
2. Billing and collections
3. Business expenses
4. Business interruption
5. Cash management
6. Continuity/disaster
7. Contract compliance

8. Copyright infringement
9. Corporate governance
10. Data security
11. Donor/member records
12. Donor/member recognition and benefits
13. Emergency preparedness
14. Facility management
15. Financial reporting
16. Fraud & ethical behavior
17. Fundraising
18. Gift acceptance
19. Harm to clients
20. Human resources
21. Insurance/risk
22. Investment policies
23. IT infrastructure
24. Litigation risk
25. Misfeasance/malfeasance
26. Malpractice
27. Operational quality performance
28. Personnel/volunteer behavior
29. Regulatory compliance
30. Related party transactions
31. Special events
32. Storm damage
33. Subcontractor utilization
34. Succession planning
35. Tax exempt status
36. Transportation
37. Unrelated business income
38. Use of intellectual property

As you can see from the partial list above, there are many areas of potential concern. In most cases, it would be cost prohibitive and next to impossible to attempt to eliminate all risks in a nonprofit. However, depending on the type of organization and its operating issues, there are usually several high priority potential problem areas which should be addressed. The cost of prevention is usually a fraction of the cost of correction after the fact. Typically, discussions related to risk management are first initiated by financial advisors and/or auditors. However, the scope of their concern is often limited to financial issues.

There are risk management tools that can be used as part of a nonprofit organization's annual audit process. The assessment is typically a comprehensive problem solving process that starts with an analysis of needs, prioritization of areas of concern, a recommendation on how to address those concerns and measurement of progress. Progress is only possible if the starting point is identified correctly and candidly. Nonprofits are asked to provide data for the baseline assessment—the more accurate the data, the greater the prospect of substantial improvement.

The assessment is administered again annually in order to assess impact. The assessment should be conducted by an external assessor which is why doing so, as part of an annual audit, is advantageous. By comparing year to year results, nonprofits can observe their progress and continually reduce the extent of risk in their organization.

Most auditors will address issues such as separation of duties related to bookkeeping and accounting, or documentation which is required in personnel files. However, a more thorough risk assessment will also include a review of many other potential areas of concern.

Consider Some of the Following Questions

◆ When was the last time you looked at your facilities to determine if they are safe and secure, if data is protected, how to minimize damage in a storm or to determine if computers or other electronics are located under sprinkler systems?

◆ Does your organization have a published plan that is reviewed annually with staff and volunteers related to procedures should there be a natural disaster, bomb threat, or fire? Who is responsible for what when an emergency occurs?

◆ What type of reporting takes place when someone incurs a work-related injury or has an accident on your property?

◆ What have you done to minimize risk associated with activities which could result in litigation against your organization?

◆ Is there clutter or areas of storage that are potential fire hazards?

◆ What have you done to educate the individuals in your organization regarding ways to avoid potential ethical or conflict of interest concerns?

◆ Have you addressed the potential "Mack Truck" problem? This is when you have a key employee, volunteer or vendor who you rely on so much that if they were hit by a truck and were unable to continue their involvement, your operations could be significantly impacted. Do you cross train staff? Are you prepared for the "Mack Truck" incident that takes away the one person who knows everything about your accounting, computer systems or service delivery?

◆ What insurance do you need (liability, business interruption, property, automobile, travel, health, equipment or other potential losses, etc.)?

These are but a few of the issues that should be evaluated as part of your risk management assessment.

The time to be concerned and take action around risk management is *before* you have the problem. As the saying goes, "An ounce of prevention . . . ."

 Connect with Norman at http://charitychannel.com/cc/norman-olshansky

Is it Time for Your Organization to Go International?

By Bonnie Koenig

Have you ever felt that your organization could benefit from a more global perspective? Perhaps you'd like to exchange experiences with colleagues from other countries. Or maybe you'd like to attract some overseas participants to your annual meeting—or even hold your meeting overseas. Or you might just want to explore a more global focus for your programs.

What are some of the reasons local and national organizations have decided to engage internationally and why might your organization want to do the same? Some of these include:

◆ finding ideas from other cultures or countries that might be beneficial to your organization's national or local programs;

◆ better understanding and supporting multicultural diversity among your organization's leadership, members or colleague staff members;

◆ expanding your program's reach by increasing the understanding of how to reach critical immigrant and ethnic target groups within the U.S. with your program services; or

◆ increasing your credibility with members, clients, donors and others who think internationally (a growing group).

Multiculturalism vs. Multinationalism

Multiculturalism and multinationalism are not quite the same thing—see more below—but understanding different national cultures can certainly help you understand how differences in cultures play out within the U.S.

definition

For member organizations this international engagement can also become a member benefit, expanding their own networks and opportunities overseas.

So, let's say this sounds like something your organization might like to pursue: where do you begin? Here are suggestions to help you move your organization into today's global environment.

What Would You Like to Accomplish?

First, clarify your options. You don't need to plunge right in and form a full-scale international program. There are many other ways to add an international dimension to your organization. From the simple, to the more complex, here are a few of a spectrum of possibilities.

Exchange information with colleagues in other countries

This option is helpful if you want to increase your organization's knowledge base. It's also useful for keeping up to date on technology in your field. This increase in information, in addition to helping your organization, might also be considered a member benefit that members in their professional careers.

Invite colleagues in other countries to attend your organization's conference or seminar

If you believe you have expertise worth sharing, if your work has brought you in contact with the work of colleagues in other countries, or if you'd like to expand or add a new "twist" to your organization's conference, this might be an option to consider. You can target potential attendees in different ways - through professional networks, personal contacts, sister organizations in other countries, and so on. (Be aware that if your meeting does attract attendees from other countries, you'll want to do some extra planning to be sure your overseas guests will have a positive experience. Ideas to consider include creating a special information sheet explaining U.S. protocols for your venue; hosts who wear nametags showing the different languages they speak; or a special reception for international attendees).

Develop a joint project with a sister organization

If you're interested in holding a seminar or meeting in another country, a local partner can help to insure its success. Or you might know an organization in another country with which you want to share information and a joint seminar would be the best way to do so. Other joint projects might include developing a professional exchange program or exchanging publications. Affiliate with a sister organization in another country. This option is worth considering if you feel that there might be benefits to a sustained relationship with a sister organization in another country for joint meetings, cooperative publication exchanges, joint lobbying on international issues of concern to your organization and so on.

If you're a membership organization, you can offer international membership

This is one of the most difficult stages of an international program. While your international activity might lead you in this direction, you would be well advised to think through the implications. Overseas members need "servicing" just as local members do, but their needs will most likely be different. You might quickly lose your overseas members if you don't put some effort into understanding their expectations.

Hire an international staff member, or create an international department

This obviously takes additional resources to accomplish. But if you know you're ready to add a sustained international component, dedicating the resources to see that it happens might provide the best chance of success. Integrate a commitment to global perspectives into your organization's goals. This stage can be the most difficult to reach, but in the long run it might be the most effective.

Hiring a staff member or creating a department might appear to be a more significant commitment, but if "international" is just tacked on as an unrelated program, its life might be short and ineffective. You might find it more productive to integrate a global perspective into your daily operations. Begin by assessing your existing resources. For instance, do you have board or staff members who have traveled or lived overseas or have international connections? Tap these resources to build global thinking into your plans.

Where to Begin?

Choose geographic locations strategically

Don't connect with a country simply because someone in your organization has a tie to it. Instead, set criteria at the very start of your international engagement process. Then search out regions that match your goals. Do some preliminary research before settling on specific countries. There are many good sources of information, including:

- ◆ colleagues who travel in other countries;

- ◆ foreign embassies (in Washington, D.C.) and consulates located throughout the country;

- ◆ online sources, where many foreign government now have home pages with valuable introductory information; and

- ◆ international association directories and websites.

Intensify your research

Once you've decided on a region, find out as much as possible about it. With so much information readily available in today's technology age, international partners have higher expectations that you know all about their country, culture and concerns.

Identify potential partners

Ask yourself not only what these international partners can offer you but what you can offer them. If you see opportunities for joint benefit, there is a good chance that the collaboration will work.

Make your initial connection with a potential partner

If possible, make it a contact between two people who know each other. Ask your board, staff, and other stakeholders if they belong to international societies or have attended international conferences. If so, they might be able to make the first contact. Remember that first impressions are important. Many countries have formal cultures. It's best, therefore, to make your contacts formally. It's always easy to become less formal but it's had to reverse a negative impression if your start too informally.

How to Increase the Chance of Success

Set specific, tangible goals

You won't know if you're successful if you don't know what you're trying to accomplish. Conversely, pointing to targets effectively met will help persuade skeptical board members and justify additional resources if necessary.

Don't try to do too much at once

Starting slowly will let you show achievements along the way. It will also lessen setbacks that might sour the organization on continued international activity.

Build in successes

Set some "easy" targets along with tougher ones. Success with the easy ones will help you achieve the greater challenges. For example, if your goal is to hold your annual meeting overseas, start with a board or committee meeting to test your "systems" for organizing such an event.

Assess your organization's strong and weak points

Then choose your goals to match your strengths. If you're struggling for members in the U.S., think twice about expanding membership overseas. However, if you have successful conferences and strong programs, a joint conference might be a good option for you.

Set a budget

It needn't be large (there are ways to economize, even when dealing with global expenses) but it does need to be realistic. Itemize all costs. International activity is an area ripe for charges of "boondoggles" and "waste of money" from critics, so you want to be meticulous.

Identify "champions" and skeptics

Who supports the move to international engagement, and who is skeptical? As in initiating any new program, you will need allies to help persuade the skeptics.

Keep key players vested

Since international engagement can seem to some as an "exotic exercise" waste of money, it's vital that your leaders, members, and staff feel they have a stake in the idea of going global.

Orient your staff and members to an international environment

You can do so in many simple ways. Include the country as part of your address on all outgoing correspondence. Publish internationally oriented articles in your organization's newsletters or other forms of communication. Identify foreign language speakers on your staff who can be utilized as the need arises.

Develop a strategic plan before going international

Ask yourself: What resources can the organization allocate to an international program? Can current staff be reassigned or is new staff needed? How can we best achieve our global goals?

Periodically assess and reevaluate your goals

Is this still the direction the organization wants to go? Have you learned lessons that should be applied to the process or your goals? Surveys are a good tool to keep in touch with members or partners. Don't be complacent!

Understand the difference between multiculturalism and multinationalism

Multiculturalism exists within one country. Although people have different cultural perspectives, these views are modified by receiving the same political messages, reading the same newspapers and blogs, and watching the same television programs. The context in which decisions are made thus has similarities. In multinationalism, this common context does not exist. Hence, cultural differences are more pronounced.

Anticipate the consequences of meeting your goals

For example, overseas attendees at your meetings will call for a different type of meeting planning. International members might look for different membership benefits than your domestic members. To keep the benefits you gain from reaching your international goals, you must adapt to new expectations.

Recognize when not to go international

Not all organizations will benefit from starting an international program. Or the timing might not be right. If an international orientation does not flow logically from your organization's mission statement, or strategic plan, it might be a mistake to force it. Part of your initial analysis should include the option of not developing an international program.

This article was published in Nonprofit World *in the May/June 1998 issue and is reprinted by permission.* Nonprofit World *is published by the Society for Nonprofit Organizations, PO Box 510354, Livonia, MI 48151, Ph: (734) 451-3582.*

 Connect with Bonnie at http://charitychannel.com/cc/bonnie-koenig

Program Evaluation Made Easy

By Jana Braswell, M.S.

A ll funders want to see the impact of their support. When applying for a grant, you will inevitably be asked to complete a section that requires you to "Describe how you plan to measure the effectiveness of X." Funders are increasingly interested in outcomes which leads many applicants to submit the following: *"Effectiveness will be measured by administering an assessment at the start of the program and again at the end of the program to determine the extent to which 'X' was achieved."* This is a great strategy overall but all too often we propose to measure things we can't really measure and find ourselves struggling to make sense of data that, frankly, makes no sense. As a result we fall short of our targets, threaten future funding opportunities, and wonder what in the heck went wrong. The goal of this article is to provide you with a basic understanding of program evaluation and a step-by-step plan for collecting and reporting meaningful data.

> Don't let perfection get in the way of good enough.
>
> —Author Unknown

Step 1: Draft a 'Straw Man' Proposal

Before you submit your proposal, it's important to determine if what you are proposing is realistic. One way to do this is to develop a straw man proposal for discussion. A straw man is a draft document that can be used as a starting point for discussions about the feasibility of your project. Using a straw man helps to illuminate challenges and/or barriers that you might not have otherwise seen. Consider the following questions when crafting your straw man for discussion:

◆ What are the goals of our program? What kind of impact are we trying to make?

◆ Do I have enough time to get the information I need? (Most grants have a start/end date and if you plan to follow up with participants after the program ends, you need to account for this time.)

◆ Where will the information come from? Can I get what I need directly from the person/people participating in my program or do I have to go to another source?

◆ If I need to go to another source to get my information, what does that process look like? Do I need special permissions? Are there limits to what I can/can't access? Who do I need to talk to?

◆ Who will be responsible for collecting the information?

◆ After everything is collected, how much time do I need to put it all together and write a report?

> **Outcome Evaluations**
>
> Evaluation design matters. Outcome evaluations typically follow one of three designs: randomized controlled trial, comparison group, or pre/post comparison. In this article, I present some basic steps to get you started on a pre/post comparison evaluation. Although this design is the least scientifically rigorous, it's a great place to start when resources are limited. For a more complete overview of Outcome Evaluations, check out the following on-line publication at http://www.unodc.org/docs/treatment//outcome_evaluation.pdf.
>
>  practical tip

Your straw man can look like anything you want it to be. You can structure it to look like a formal action plan complete with tentative goals, objectives, activities, dates, etc.; it can be a series of questions to discuss, or a simple document that says something like this: "We are requesting funds to run our program. In order to get funding, we have to tell our funder how we plan to measure the impact our program had on our participants. Got any ideas for how to do that?'

Your straw man can evolve into a finalized proposal, but the purpose of developing a straw man is so you have something tangible to discuss with your evaluation team, which we discuss next.

Step 2: Identify Your Evaluation Team

Once you have your straw man, select a small group of individuals that you expect will be involved in the evaluation and can serve in an advisory capacity. Include individuals who will be responsible for collecting surveys, following up with participants, entering and managing the data, establishing relationships with community partners, administering the programs, etc. These individuals can be volunteers, administrative support, caseworkers, staff members, or just about anyone you can think of that will have a hand in making your evaluation a success. Be realistic about who will be involved and invite them to a meeting.

In your meeting invitation, explain why you are asking this group to come together. Explain that you are seeking their feedback on an evaluation you are considering for a grant. Prior to your first meeting, send a copy of your straw man and ask that everyone review it and come prepared to discuss their thoughts with the group. During the meeting be sure to take plenty of notes (it doesn't hurt to assign a minute taker), provide food and drink when possible, and do your best to create an atmosphere where people can speak honestly about their work load and what they think is doable. Give your team an opportunity to tell you what they think is doable and what is not. This will create buy-in and avoid the pitfall of expecting outcomes that cannot be achieved. Poor or incomplete evaluations can usually be attributed to skipping this step.

Step 3: Brainstorm with Your Evaluation Team What Is Possible And What Is Not!

Consider the services you provide and the impact you are trying to make on your program participants. The types of outcomes you can measure largely depend on how long you can track your participants. For example, if you only have participants for a short amount of time and cannot do any follow up after the intervention has ended, consider measuring short term outcomes such as change in knowledge before and after the program (change in confidence is also a good one to measure). If you can follow up with program participants over time, you might want to consider intermediate outcome measures such as changes in behavior. Long-term outcomes can be more difficult to collect, but feel free to brainstorm these as well. Did your program have a long lasting impact on participants such as on their health or economic status? Again, consider what your program does when you brainstorm possible outcomes.

Step 4: Create Your Survey

Once you've decided on the kind of outcome measures you want to collect (with the help of your team), start drafting your survey. There is a wealth of information available to you on line regarding survey design, but here are some basic tips to get you started:

Tip #1:

If you want to measure change, you must ask the same questions on the pre survey as you do on the post survey. The only exceptions to this rule are for questions that are static, or do not change and if there are supplemental questions you want to ask on the post survey about their experience of the program. Examples of static questions are 'What is your gender?' and 'What is your birth date?' and historical information such as 'Have you ever been arrested for a crime?' or 'Who raised you as a child?' A supplemental question might be, 'If you could change anything about the program, what would it be?' and 'What did you like the most/least about the X program?'

Tip #2:

Be sure to capture the following information:

◆ participant name or ID (be sure participants use the same name or ID on both the pre and post survey);

◆ date the survey was taken;

◆ pre/post identification (you can ask respondents to circle one); and

◆ basic demographic information to describe your program participants; consider including age, gender, race or ethnic group, and any other information relevant to your program that might experience change (e.g., employment status, marital status, income level, education level, etc.).

Only include information that will be useful to you. When possible, try to keep your survey two pages or less.

Tip #3:

Use Likert Scales, True/False, and Yes/No questions as often as possible. These are the easiest to compare from pre to post. Here are a few example formats:

How confident are you that you can do the following?

	Very Confident	Somewhat Confident	Confident	Not at All Confident
Eat healthy foods				
Exercise on a regular basis				
Drink water instead of soda				

Now, for the questions below please tell us which statements are true and which statements are false:

1. A small banana has the same amount of calories as a Twinkie.

♦ True
♦ False

2. It is better to eat a fast food hamburger when you are hungry than to skip a meal if there are no other options.

♦ True
♦ False

3. If obesity runs in my family, I have a higher chance of becoming obese.

♦ True
♦ False

Be creative with your survey, but try to keep the questions short and simple. Limit the number of open-ended questions (e.g., Tell us what you think about X: _____) and keep your audience in mind when deciding the kinds of questions to ask. Before you administer your survey be sure to have a few of your colleagues or your team members complete the survey to see if it flows easily, if there are any typos, or if any of the questions are leading or double-barreled. A leading question is one that prompts a specific response and a double-barreled question is a question that can have two answers. You will want to avoid these kinds of questions.

> **Avoid Leading and Double-Barreled Questions**
>
> Example of Leading Question:
>
> *Don't you agree that kids who are obese will have health problems later in life?*
>
> Example double-barreled question:
>
> *Do you think schools should have salad bars and snack machines?*
>
>  practical tip

Step 5 Collect, Analyze and Report

This is where the evaluation comes together.

Collecting Your Data

Be sure to administer your pre-survey during the first session, or at the very start of any initiative that has regular attendance. Explain that the survey is meant to help you improve your program and participation is very important. Depending on the population you are working with, you might even want to offer some token of appreciation if they agree to complete both the pre and post survey. Explain that every question should be answered, and you encourage truthful and honest responses. You can decide if you want the surveys to be confidential and not require participants to give their name, but remember that you will need some method for connecting the pre survey to the post survey so be sure to assign a unique identifier if you make providing their name optional. The post survey should be collected at the very last session, or at the end of the initiative you are trying to evaluate.

Analyze

Fortunately, there are a ton of options out there when it comes to managing and analyzing data. I strongly recommend Survey Monkey, which is a free on-line resource for small data projects and relatively inexpensive if you want to take advantage of their analysis package for larger projects. For the full package, the monthly rate is less than $25 a month and worth every penny. With Survey Monkey you can design your survey forms online and print them out, as well as enter them directly into the program and have your data analyzed on the spot (for more information check out: www.surveymonkey.com). A quick Internet search will give you a host of other options to explore such as Zoomerang (www.zoomerang.com), StatPac (www.statpac. com), Surveygizmo (http://www.surveygizmo.com), Keysurvey (www.keysurvey.com) and many others you can try.

You can also choose design your own Microsoft Excel or Microsoft Access database to enter survey information and calculate your results. If you are not using an analysis package, try the most basic analysis first: count the total number of responses on the pre survey, then compare them to the total number of responses on the post survey and note where you see a change. This works well with a Likert scale questions where you might see a significant number of 'Strongly Disagree' responses on the pre survey change to 'Strongly Agree' responses on the post survey, or 'False' responses change to 'True' responses, etc. Again, solicit the help of your team when setting up your database and analyzing your results. Often you will find someone in your office, or someone in your office that knows someone who enjoys analyzing data and calculating numbers. Make use of these people.

Report

When reporting your findings, be sure to describe the steps you took to collect your data and highlight the major findings. Below is a sample of what you can include:

◆ title page, table of contents, executive summary (optional);

◆ introduction;

◆ description of the program/intervention being evaluated;

◆ purpose of the evaluation;

◆ approach and methodology;

◆ findings, conclusions, and limitations;

◆ recommendations;

◆ lessons learned; and

◆ appendix (here you can provide samples of your survey instrument, materials, and any other program documentation you'd like to include).

Charts and visuals are nice to include (usually under the 'Findings' section) and should be used when possible. Choose from the categories above, but be sure you are meeting the requirements as stated in your grant. You should also feel comfortable contacting the grant administrator to find out exactly what is expected in the grant report. You can rest assured that the quality and type of reports your funders have seen are all over the map, so be confident that what you are submitting will be among best they've seen.

Summary

Trust in your expertise. Performing an evaluation might seem daunting at first but the more often you do it, the easier it will become. There is an enormous amount of information available on-line regarding program evaluation, but try not to get overwhelmed. Evaluation is integral to successful interventions and even when evaluation isn't a requirement of your grant, you should still consider evaluating your efforts and adopting strategies that can help you to strengthen your program. Consult with others, use the resources most readily available to you, and above all else don't let perfection get in the way of good enough.

 Connect with Jana at http://charitychannel.com/cc/jana-braswell

Measuring Success and Making Change with Evaluation

Reid A. Zimmerman, PhD., CFRE

"Mommy, Daddy, look at me! Look at what I did!" From the earliest ages, children seek approval of their accomplishments. The same can be said of organizations. Each of us in our own way wants to demonstrate to the world, or at least our own little corner of it, the good work we are accomplishing. Often though, there seem to be many challenges and barriers that prevent nonprofits from sharing the incredible positive impact they make on people and society.

Why Evaluate?

Evaluation is everywhere. From the moment of our birth when an APGAR score (Appearance, Pulse, Grimace, Activity, and Respiration) is assigned, to report cards in school, sports statistics, consumer reports, work performance reviews and pension plan recommendations, most facets of our lives are evaluated. In the same way, whether you acknowledge it or not, your organization and your programs are already being evaluated. Public opinion is the strongest evaluator a nonprofit faces and could be the *only* one if the organization does not have and share solid evaluation data to back up its claims of providing positive change in people's lives and adding value to the community.

Addressing public opinion is only one of many reasons why your organization both needs and should want to evaluate its programs. Acquiring and continuing funding as well as informing stakeholders and the community are other strong motivators for evaluation. Cost benefit relationships and more efficiently using your resources are also worthy objectives of evaluation.

The most important reason to evaluate, however, is to learn how to provide the best service or greatest good to your clients and community. Putting an evaluation process into place is the only way your organization can ascertain what is working efficiently, what produces results and what needs to be changed to make it better.

I've heard it said that: "We don't evaluate our programs because we can't prove they have an impact. There are too many other influencing factors to say that what we do makes a difference." That implies that there is only one form of evaluation and that is the scientific method. If we followed that logic we would need to reconsider the value of most programs of the social sector because few, if any, could *prove* unilateral and single handed community impact. So if there are indeed other reasons to evaluate what we do, let's take a look at some common questions about the process, measures and methods of evaluation.

How Difficult is it to Evaluate?

Evaluation can be as complex as the procedures required to get a new drug approved by the Federal Drug Administration or as simple as asking clients if they learned something from participating in a particular program. It can be quite expensive or done for little discernible cost. Evaluation can look at hard facts or attempt to detect feelings. While no two evaluation protocols are identical, all evaluation attempts to describe benefits, advantages, problems, or pitfalls of a program, service, product, or organization. The type and method of evaluation used will depend on the questions your organization wishes to answer.

What Does it Take to Produce the Product or Accomplish the Service?

Most often referred to as inputs, these are the funds, staff, time, space, technology, volunteers, supplies, donations, products and other requirements to accomplish what your program or organization proposes to do. These inputs are sometimes impacted by external factors such as legal requirements, economics or restrictions placed by donors.

There is good reason to measure inputs and track them. Knowledge about the level, kind, quality, severity, cost, availability and other descriptors of the inputs to your organization might provide significant information as they are juxtaposed against program activities and accomplishments. While inputs are often just counted, they can also be analyzed for the descriptors mentioned above. For example: How experienced are our counselors, actors, clinicians, students, participants? What credentials do they bring? How big are the issues confronting our clients individually and collectively? How can I calibrate that information? How much time is reimbursed and how much is volunteered? Are some inputs provided in-kind that might otherwise need to be purchased in order to provide the same service? What is the quality of these in-kind resources? Answers to these questions can help ascertain correlations between what goes in, and what comes out of your program.

How Many Products or Services Were Provided?

In this case, your organization is simply tabulating the number of products or services delivered for the benefit of your clients. Usually referred to as output data, these relevant measures include things like the number of performances held, number of counseling sessions, pounds of food distributed, number and type of unique clients served, tickets sold, hours of broadcasting time or visits made. These are the traditional markers required on reports to government funders.

To provide additional insight and to differ from simple monitoring, these measures are usually compared to similar data from a previous time period, against a predetermined goal or another source (often a competitor). Trends in the levels of outputs should also be considered and correlations made with other measures of input or activity for your program. This type of data collection shows the capacity of a program or organization to provide a particular service or product. When coupled with solid financial information and juxtaposed against input and expense data it can be used by management to evaluate cost / benefit relationships or consider ways to increase services or decrease expenses of the program.

How Efficient is the Program or Service, and/or how well is it Delivered?

These questions assess the quality and efficiency of an activity, product or service. To measure quality and efficiency, it is necessary to know what the clients, customers, or constituents expect. Therefore, the organization might ask them questions like: How good was the performance? How timely was the delivery of the service? Did the product work appropriately? Is the cost reasonable? Often stated in percentages, these measures provide information about the quality or efficiency of the program as assessed by users; for example, "83 percent of all program participants indicated 'good' or 'very good' when asked about the seminar leader's presentation skills."

Efficiency measures can also assess the number of service units provided by the staffing or other resources needed to accomplish those activities. Reductions in time, staffing or other resources without jeopardizing quality can mean big savings to the budget. Or, better quality with the same resources can offer a big advantage to your participants and stakeholders.

How Effective is the Program at Changing Individual Lives?

This is ultimately about being a social sector enterprise. As Peter Drucker pointed out, the bottom line in the social sector is measured not in dollars, but in changed lives. Outcome evaluation determines the effect of a program or organization on the life of a participant, client, or customer. This is usually more challenging information to obtain and analyze than the other kinds of data we have discussed. Data gathering to determine outcomes looks to discern positive changes in a person's life, habits, situation, or attitude, and provide benefit to the individual or their family from your work. Outcome measures seek demonstrable changes in the person or situation shortly following use of the service or over a reasonable period of time afterward. These changes are at the heart of the mission for nonprofits and are worthy of every possible attempt to measure.

Does the Program Impact the Community?

The question of community impact considers the ability of a program, service, or organization to improve the quality of life for a community, culture, or society. This is usually measured in percentage of your group as compared to the greater community. For example, "The program created a reduction of incidence of the disease by 2.5 percent in the whole population during the last decade." This is the most difficult and yet the most meaningful type of evaluation. It is often undertaken by government and large foundations.

While, as mentioned earlier, there are many influencing factors that impact social change in addition to your program. So we are challenged to say that what we do is the sole reason for community or social improvement, the question of the involvement of your program should still be considered and credit given where there is reasonable conclusion that what you do makes some positive contribution to a better and more livable community. The difficulty and long term nature of evaluation of community impact should never be used as an excuse to not evaluate a program or service at all.

Who is Responsible for Program Evaluation?

Ultimately it is the senior leadership of the organization that needs to want and sometimes demand that evaluation be undertaken and utilized. Getting it done, however, will require a team effort. The best people to collect the data are often front line staff members who are closest to it. Accuracy is important, however and everyone needs to understand what is being collected and why. Supervisors are often appropriate for amalgamating data into usable information for management. Senior leaders should be the responsible parties for analytical analysis and dissemination and communication of the evaluation results and its meaning.

Sometimes it can be beneficial to engage an outside consultant to help formulate the evaluation plan or help establish data collection methods. Because consultants are outside observers, they might be able to ask hard questions and provide an objective viewpoint, which is critical to really understand what is happening. A good consultant can teach the organization's board and staff about the importance of evaluation, help them be proactive in gathering data, and assist them in analyzing the information. Nonprofit leaders might want to look for a consultant who can provide a broad spectrum of services from initial consultation to recommendations for improvement, not just the development of data collection processes.

How Often is Evaluation Conducted?

Evaluation is continual and ongoing. It is usually practical to gather data at periodic intervals. Often gathering small amounts of data frequently has advantages over collecting large amounts of data just once. How long people are involved in your activities, funding cycles, management and budgetary decisions as well as the initial questions addressed by the evaluation also impact frequency of data collection and analysis.

How Can You Use the Results of an Evaluation?

Evaluation is less than it can be when it is done simply to fulfill a funding requirement or to satisfy the board of directors. Evaluation is most useful when it begins and ends with your organization's clients, customers, and constituent's needs and interests. The results of a well done evaluation can challenge an organization to change its programs and services. Evaluation can inform your organization about where to invest its resources or how to improve its activities. These improvements can have significant impact on the number of people served or the total resources expended to provide a particular service. A small improvement resulting from evaluation can have a significantly positive impact on your organization's financial picture and might make a significant difference in the lives of your clients.

By evaluating program outcomes, your organization will also find out if it is really accomplishing what it intended to do. Is it possible that your organization is doing something unintended? Is it accomplishing positive results that are not being documented? Does your organization need to change its strategy entirely in order to really accomplish what it wants? Evaluation can answer these questions and therefore direct program enhancements.

The use of evaluation needs to be determined before you begin. All of your stakeholders, including board members, organizational and program leaders, staff members, funders, clients, patrons, customers and the public are potential users of the information gleaned through evaluation. Determining the use of evaluation and the audience for reporting will make the job of developing the data collection and analyzing much easier and more beneficial.

Other Thoughts on "Meaning Making" in Evaluation

Pay attention to the culture of the organization. Understand if there are culturally specific issues that need to be considered when collecting data or in order to really comprehend the data. Does a particular minority or diverse culture want to be asked questions in a certain way? What are the outcomes which they seek? Are those outcomes different than those of the predominant culture in the community? Make sure you have this discussion before you begin.

Change is constant in our world and the nonprofit sector. Knowing how to react to change, understanding what changes you need to make, when, and to what degree will be aided by good evaluation. Change resulting from evaluation can only improve a nonprofit organization's future. Choosing not to evaluate a program or service will ultimately serve as its demise whether from lack of funding, poor results for clients, someone else doing better work or simple indifference.

So go ahead, find out the Apgar score for your brand new program. Determine your grade: A+, B-, C, etc. Strive to improve your batting average or get a better return on your investments. Check out the consumer report score for your organization. Evaluate your programs and let the community know what you do instead of letting them evaluate you.

Evaluation "To Do" list:

◆ Make evaluation an organizational priority. Leadership must become passionate about understanding how and why something is working or if it can get better.

◆ Determine what is important to measure and start gathering data.

◆ Decide the purpose for which you will use evaluation. Who will read it or use it and for what purpose?

◆ Teamwork and agreed-upon goals make for better evaluation processes and results.

◆ Be data driven! Intuitions make bad decisions on a regular basis if the organization does not capture and interpret data.

◆ Remember that data precedes information and information precedes analysis. It is analysis that helps make good leadership decisions.

◆ Watch for trends. Don't just evaluate once.

◆ Make sure the evaluation is important. Use what you learn.

◆ Change the evaluation method if it is not getting you the information you need to manage.

◆ Culture and social norms are important to observe in data collection and analysis.

 Connect with Reid at http://charitychannel.com/cc/reid-zimmerman

Why *Outcomes,* Anyway?

By Ken Berger & Robert M. Penna, Ph.D.

With all the talk in nonprofit circles regarding *performance measurement, effectiveness, impact, outputs, outcomes,* it is not surprising that many might be confused about what it all means. All these terms relate to what we call the *outcomes movement*, a gradual change that began to sweep across the nonprofit world over two decades ago, beginning almost simultaneously in such disparate fields as health care and human services. The primary focus shifted away from what we are *doing*, and towards what we are *accomplishing* through all our efforts.

Going back easily to the New Deal, and certainly through the programs of the Great Society and following, there is no question that our country, its governments and philanthropies, have taken great (and costly) steps aimed at alleviating negative conditions in education, housing, income distribution, social equality, environmental degradation, and a host of other areas. The individual initiatives have been many; the individual successes noted. But overall, the questions remaining seventy years later are:

◆ *What has been gained on a societal level?*

◆ *What have we really accomplished; what do we have to show for all this effort and expenditure?*

◆ *How do we know which (if any) among all our efforts are actually working?*

Answering these questions requires a fundamental shift away from what we were looking at, what we were measuring, and how we were approaching our challenges in the past.

Traditionally, our field has been looked at and measured by two yardsticks that were thought to be determining factors for success: *how much?* and *how many?* concepts that were often captured in the "service units" familiar to the realm of:

◆ How much money was allocated toward an effort?

◆ How much service/information was provided?

◆ How many clients/patients/constituents were reached, treated, or served?

The principle underlying this approach would be familiar to anyone who ever saw *Field of Dreams*; except instead of that film's precept, *"If you build it, they will come"* the faith moving most of the nonprofit efforts of at least the last forty years was "If you make it available, people *will* benefit, and things *will* be better."

When it became apparent that this was not as true as thought, rather than the concept being questioned, it was decided that more control was needed over the processes by which services were made available. The result was a host of regulations and the dawning of the age of compliance. Thus, by the closing decades of the 20th century nonprofit entities were basing their notions of success on the measures of how much they were doing, and how closely they stuck to "the rules."

As a result of all of this, the traditional ways many organizations approach their work, emerged.

The Problem Approach

A natural and difficult-to-avoid perspective that focuses most of its attention on what is wrong with a given situation, how big or bad the situation is, who or what is responsible for the negative condition, how much work needs to be done to fix things, and what stands in the way of applying that fix. Because of this, the questions the problem approach triggers tend to be, *"Why do we have this problem,"* *"What or who caused it,"* and *"What obstacles exist to solving it?"* A focus on the magnitude of the problem, the insurmountable nature of obstacles standing in the way of correcting it, and the approach's tendency of keeping us focused on blame can all be depressing and demotivating. Most importantly, however, the problem approach often limits our ability to envision success in any terms other than the problem no longer existing.

The Activity Approach

This approach is characterized by an accent on *getting started*; its appeal being that it gets us moving and makes us feel productive right away. The problem, however, is that what follows an activity approach is often more about the journey than the destination. By focusing early attention on the questions of *"What* should we do?" *"Who* can do it?" and *"When* can we start?" instead of *"Where* we are going?" Beyond this, the activity approach strongly tends to equate activity with results. Asked what we are accomplishing, the activity approach prompts us to relate how busy we are, how hard we are working or trying, and how much yet remains to be done. At best it might move us to answer in terms of how many classes we have held, clients we have passed through intake, letters our advocacy group has written, or people we organized for a demonstration. But all of these measures are *outputs*, and miss the question of effectiveness and impact entirely.

The Process Approach

If the activity approach is about the journey instead of the destination, the process approach is focused on the details of that journey. Largely a product of concerns regarding compliance and inclusion, the first question the process approach urges us to answer is, *"What are the rules?"* The attraction of the process approach is that is can be extremely useful in helping programs and organizations steer clear of mistakes, regulatory violations that all organizations seek to avoid. Unfortunately, with all the checking and rechecking of procedures and specifications, often lost is the *reason* for the project or effort in the first place. But also potentially lost can be the resources and energy needed to bring the project to a successful end.

The Vision Approach

The attraction, and the trap, of the vision approach is its focus on the big picture, on ultimate ends, and on issues beyond the scope of most programs and organizations. Motivated by the vision approach, organizations do not focus upon clearly defined, well formed goals, but rather upon those aspirations better reserved for mission and vision statements. In fact, for organizations and programs mislead by the attractions of the vision approach, the mission statement and action plan are often virtually the same. The problem here is that, their reach exceeding their grasp, in attempting to solve everything about a situation, many of these organizations actually accomplish little or nothing.

The problem with all of the above, as a growing number of observers realized, was that at best these were measures of activity, of outputs, but that none of this had anything to do with whether anything of value was actually being accomplished. David Hunter has gone so far as to suggest that the paucity of evidence of actual effectiveness leaves one to wonder if any nonprofit efforts are accomplishing anything.

How is an "outcomes approach" different from all this, and how can a focus on outcomes help make nonprofits more effective?

The idea of an approach based upon "outcomes," a collective term that can refer to targets, goals, results, achievements and similar indicators of effectiveness, is grounded in the following:

◆ Outcomes are not what you *do*; they are what results *because* of what you do.

◆ An outcomes approach does not define success merely as the absence of a problem. An outcome is a value added, positive improvement in a situation.

◆ Outcomes, in the words of Steven Covey, "begin with the end in mind." Planning for outcomes begins not with the actions or activities you will undertake, but rather in a concrete definition of what you will accomplish, how it will be identified and measured, and then moves to questions of capacity for achieving those goals.

◆ Those providing the resources for an effort should be viewed not as "funders," parties primarily interested in the allocation of resources, but rather as "investors" who are due a definitive return on their investment. Moreover, these parties are not investing merely in the provision of services, but in *change*. To the extent that this change is not achieved or cannot be documented, the investment was not a success no matter how much effort was expended.

◆ The identification of, management toward, and tracking of progress toward outcomes is not primarily for purposes of reporting or investor satisfaction, but rather as a learning tool. The most useful facet of an outcomes approach is the opportunity for learning how to do what we do better, how to improve the effectiveness of our activities and to create greater benefits for those we exist to serve.

In an era of dwindling resources and greater pressures on performance, all nonprofits owe themselves, their staffs, their investors, and their constituents nothing less than concrete measures of effectiveness. Arguments to the effect of how big the challenges are, how much we care, how hard we try, how many we serve, how well we follow "the rules," or how inspiring, inclusive or encompassing our visions of a better tomorrow are no longer suffice. Only an outcomes approach can bring the sector beyond the appearance of impact, and to the documentation of effectiveness.

Here are five simple questions you should ask about your organization to see if you are in the right track:

◆ Does your organization define success in terms of what it accomplishes, or what it does and *tries* to accomplish?

◆ Does your organization have concrete targets toward which it works and against which it measures success?

◆ Does your organization track its progress toward its goals in real time, in an ongoing way during the course of its programs?

◆ Does your organization make a point of using the tracking information to make course corrections during the delivery of its programs?

◆ Does your organization use the information regarding the success in achieving goals to actively examine and refine its programs at the end of each annual or budgetary cycle?

If you answered "Yes" to most of these questions, you are well on your way. If you answered "Yes" to only some or only a few, you have a way to go. If you could not answer "Yes" to any, it is time to think about getting started. The tools and knowledge you will need are available. It is up to you to make the commitment to effectiveness, find the tools and put them into practice.

In the end, we owe those we serve nothing less than our best performance. Caring, trying, and compliance are no substitute for doing the best we possibly can. And *that* is the answer to the question, "Why *outcomes?"*

This article is excerpted from Penna, Robert M., *The Nonprofit Outcomes Toolbox: A Complete Guide to Program Effectiveness, Performance Measurement, and Results.* New Jersey: John Wiley & Sons, Inc., 2011.

 Connect with Ken at http://charitychannel.com/cc/ken-berger

 Connect with Robert at http://charitychannel.com/cc/robert-penna

Defining Your Outcomes

Ken Berger & Robert M. Penna, Ph.D.

W ell-defined outcomes are neither an accident nor a collection of good intentions. Knowing their characteristics is a key step in moving to an outcomes framework.

For many nonprofit practitioners, identifying the outcomes increasingly asked for by funders and other stakeholders can be a frustrating experience. For some, the problem is that they attempt to make this identification after the fact, looking backward and trying to figure out and articulate exactly what they accomplished. For others, the challenge is that they still confuse outputs—activity measures—with the outcomes that ought to be the evidence of their effectiveness. Finally, there are those who are stumped because they simply do not know what a good outcome looks like.

Above all else, the following should be your overall guide in identifying your outcomes:

◆ Good outcomes are best defined *before* the work, the project or the program begins. They are something you work *toward*, not something you try to identify amidst the confusion of all else that might have gone on or been done.

◆ A good outcome is *not* defined in terms of the absence of a problem.

◆ A good outcome is *not* defined merely in terms of the delivery of a service.

Beyond this, good, well-defined outcomes, no matter what the subject or the area of an organization or program's focus, tend to share certain usually interrelated and mutually reinforcing characteristics. Among these are that the targeted goals are:

◆ positive improvement;

◆ meaningful;

◆ sustainable;

◆ bound in time;

◆ bound in number;

◆ narrowly focused and doable (with a stretch!);

◆ measurable; and

◆ verifiable.

Let's take a few moments to examine what each of these characteristics actually mean.

Positive Improvement

This is a characteristic that, at first glance, confuses a number or practitioners. "*Of course* we want to see positive improvements," they say. "We're certainly not in the business of making things worse!" This much is certainly true. However, what many practitioners do not recognize in identifying their outcomes is that the mere absence of the given problem is not a really good, satisfying, or sufficient outcome.

In the case of a teen who quit school, for example, the absence of the problem would be either that she did not quit, or that he agreed to return to class. But is that enough? Wouldn't a better outcome be a student who appreciates the value of school, who wants to succeed, and who has the tools at his or her disposal to help them succeed?

Two of the central questions to be asked when establishing an outcome statement are:

◆ What is in place that wasn't there before?

◆ What has been *gained* for those we serve?

If a desired outcome is defined merely in terms of the absence of a problem, then the answer to both of these questions is "Nothing." There is nothing there that wasn't there before, and nothing new has been gained for or by the client. On both of these counts an outcome statement defined only in terms of the absence of a problem fails.

Meaningful Change

The difference between a meaningful and a cosmetic change is one of both quality and degree: The question, "*What changed*?" therefore becomes the first test.

For a change to be "meaningful," it must alter the client or situation in some fundamental way:

- a negative behavior is stopped and replaced by a positive one;

- a self-destructive attitude is altered and replaced by a self-actualizing one;

- a harmful condition is replaced by a protective or nurturing one; or

- useful knowledge is absorbed and applied, or a significant improvement in status is achieved.

> What does your program add that "wasn't there before?"
>
> **food for thought**

A meaningful change, and therefore a "meaningful" outcome, is something that makes a marked difference in a situation, something that creates essentially a new situation. This new situation admittedly might still be dogged by other problems, issues or negative characteristics, but also one in which the particular negative characteristic that was the focus of the program's efforts has been replaced by something fundamentally positive.

> How does your program define "meaningful" change?
>
> **food for thought**

But also playing into a determination of how meaningful a change might be is *how much* something changed. The person who cuts out his daily 4 p.m. milkshake, but otherwise continues to consume his usual allotment of fast food, jelly doughnuts, and midnight snacks is not really making *meaningful* progress toward the goal of a healthful eating routine. The line between meaningful and cosmetic changes is not always this clear, however.

The difference here is between an "accomplishment," any one of which can be worthy of note, and a good outcome, which is a targeted *fundamental* change. A program or an organization might "accomplish" any number of things. But the issue is whether any given accomplishment actually brings about or leads to a fundamental change, and real alteration in the underlying situation. In the end, the key insight here is that *while every achieved outcome is an accomplishment, not every accomplishment is a meaningful outcome.* We have to weigh and recognize the difference.

Sustainable

Something that is "sustainable" is something that lasts. In terms of a well-defined outcome, what this means is that the benefit outlasts the intervention. It means that the intervention continues

> What does *your* program look for in its outcomes that would suggest that they are sustainable?
>
>

to prove to be beneficial to the targeted audience for a significant period of time after the intervention is complete.

If a plot of land, for example, has been used as a dumping ground, the benefit is not sustainable if a few days after a clean-up effort has been completed, people can and do begin dumping trash at the site again. In order to be sustainable, there must be some barrier or other proviso for preventing a repeat of the abuse that dirtied the site in the first place.

A good outcome is sustainable; if the benefit evaporates, vanishes or otherwise disappears after the program or intervention is over, the targeted outcome was flawed. In setting an outcome target, our goal is to identify a target gain we are reasonably sure will last.

Bound in Time

When we say that an outcome is "bound-in-time" we mean that the proposed outcome is *designed to be and will be accomplished within a certain set period*.

The requirement that a good outcome be bound-in-time serves a number of purposes. Primarily, it focuses our attention on what can reasonably be done. Setting a goal to be reached within a certain specified time, shifts our sight away from all that we would perhaps *want* to do, and resets it on what we *can* do given finite resources.

The characteristic of being bound-in-time also provides us with a timeline. Knowing when an effort "officially" begins, and when it is scheduled to deliver its final and stated benefits,

> Does *your* program "bind" its outcomes in time?
>
> **food for thought**

lends itself to approaching and thinking about the initiative as a sequence of accomplishments that must be realized if our goal is to be met. Being bound-in-time also gives our investors a firmer understanding of when the return on their investment can be expected to begin to show. Explaining a project only in terms of activity does little to tell an investor *when* she might reasonably expect us to be able to report on the return she intended for her investment. "We will be running an after-school sports program for at-risk youth" does not tell an investor when the payoff will be. Making our outcomes bound-in time answers this question.

Bound in Number

As with the requirement that a good outcome statement be bound in time, the requirement that it be bound-in-number also focuses our attention on what can reasonably be done . . . and what doing that will take. Bound-in-number means that when we state. "*We will accomplish this within X weeks or months,*" we also say "*for/among this number of people.*"

Bound-in-number forces us to consider our capacity, the inevitable attrition the program will experience, and whether we have properly planned for the number of clients our program will need to be considered a success; it provides a firm target, which can help us track our progress during the course of a project. Similarly, at the end of the program, the bound-in-time requirement gives us and our investors a way to easily measure our success. We said that by the end of our program, we were going to have X number of our target population experiencing a fundamentally altered situation, attitude, or set of actions. Did we, in fact, accomplish that? Prior to (or as part of) any formal evaluation that might be planned for or required of our effort, this bound-in-number requirement tells us virtually at a glance whether or not we were successful.

Does *your* program define its outcomes in terms of a set number of successes?

Narrowly Focused

The best outcomes are those that are narrowly focused and specific. Not everything about a situation needs to be changed in order for an outcome to meet the standard we want to set; in fact, an outcome that envisions changing everything, or at least everything negative, about a situation, is probably *not* a good or useful target. There might be a thousand things we would *like* to do to improve the quality of life in our communities, and many of these properly *do* find their way into mission and visions statements...but they do so precisely because those statements are intended to state some totality of the ultimate condition we would like to see someday emerge.

Outcomes, however, are not the broad sweep of tomorrow's horizon, but the here and now of today; what will we accomplish with *this* portion of our population within *this* period of time?

Still, trying to include a broad sweep of related issues, or all facets of a negative situation, is a common pitfall for many organizations attempting to establish outcome targets for the first time. Many organizations have difficulty separating the concepts and breadth reflected in their mission and/or vision statements from the particular targets that belong in program or initiative's outcome statement.

The important thing to remember is that, in contrast to mission, vision, goals and objectives, which tend to be multiple and broad, outcome targets are narrow and focused. They speak to specific benefits for specific customers.

Are *your* program's outcomes broadly or narrowly defined?

Doable (with a stretch!)

The first measure of "doable," has to do with whether the aspect of a problem we propose to attack is something we have the ability to change. Some might put it in terms of whether the proposed target is something over which we can exert any meaningful level of control or influence; to the extent that the truthful and realistic answer is "No," then the target is not "doable."

But "doable" should not translate into "easy." Smart, concerned investors are not looking to invest in "slam dunk" efforts. The investor wants to know that the bar, the target, has been set sufficiently high that its achievement will make some socially meaningful difference, that it will be a "stretch" for the organization or program proposing the action, but at the same time that the targeted outcome is not unrealistic. Overly ambitious outcomes are often a recipe for disappointment. They key is in distinguishing what you can accomplish if you stretch yourself, as opposed to what can't be done with limited resources.

> How does *your* program measure whether goals are really "doable"?
>
>

Measurable

The issue of "measurement" is one that troubles many nonprofit practitioners. But "measurable" really means only three things. The targeted outcome needs to be:

♦ *Clearly defined:* Be clear in the definition of the change we seek to bring about. Notions that are too broad or too abstract often lead to trouble when we try to measure change.

♦ *Discernible:* This simply means a *readily observable difference between the before and the after*.

♦ *Quantifiable:* Have some standard against which to assess the discernible change we have brought about. In most cases, this means that we need to have a *baseline* that serves as our picture or description of the "before" situation.

> How does *your* program measure its success?
>
> **food for thought**

Verifiable

The requirement that a well-defined outcome be verifiable is closely related to the issue of its being discernible. But where the accent in the "discernible" requirement is whether or not a difference between "before" and "after" can be seen, the issues surrounding "verification" have more to do with the ability of others to ascertain for themselves that something has occurred. Verification is what clients or stake holders report they have experienced, but it is *also* what third parties report they see.

Using outcomes should not be a frustrating experience for you or your organizations. But understanding the characteristics of a good, well-defined outcome can make all the difference between success and disappointment. As Yogi Berra said, "If you don't know where you're going, you might not get there." Well-defined outcomes help us ensure that we always know where we—and our programs—are going.

How does *your* program "verify" its success?

food for thought

This article is excerpted from Penna, Robert M., *The Nonprofit Outcomes Toolbox: A Complete Guide to Program Effectiveness, Performance Measurement, and Results.* New Jersey: John Wiley & Sons, Inc., 2011.

 Connect with Ken at http://charitychannel.com/cc/ken-berger

 Connect with Robert at http://charitychannel.com/cc/robert-penna

Section III—Getting the Support You Need

Ten Basic Fundraising Axioms Simplified

By Norman Olshansky

Yes; science, technology and skill sets are necessary to be successful as a fundraiser for a nonprofit organization. However, there are also several very basic axioms which, if followed, will greatly increase your success.

You Don't Get—If You Don't Ask.

Doing a good job providing services and programs does not automatically bring in contributions. It's relatively easy to identify prospects that care about your mission, have great capacity and are knowledgeable about your organization. However, they are not going to become donors until they are asked. Asking can be in many forms. For major gifts, a personal "face-to-face" request to a prospect, to consider a suggested gift amount, provides the best return on investment. However, grants, group meetings with a general request for donations, events and direct mail, can also be utilized as a method to make "an ask."

Connect to Hearts and Minds Before You Connect to Wallets

People are not going to make significant contributions to an organization that is of no interest to them and about which they have no personal connection or feelings. The ability to secure a gift and the size of the gift will be enhanced if the donor is educated about the organization, "feels" the importance of what is being accomplished and has a relationship (directly or indirectly) with the organization, solicitor, project or program. Cultivation of those relationships provides added value to the donor and organization.

Fundraising is Both Art and Science. Success Requires Both

There are definite processes, sequential steps, ethics, legal guidelines, tax laws, accounting and other requirements that need to be followed to be successful within a nonprofit engaged in fundraising. This is the science of fundraising. Just as important, if not more so, is the art of fundraising which focuses on relationships, personality, leadership, engagement and follow through.

The 80/20 Rule is Now 90/10 and Applies to Fundraising

Eighty to 90 percent of funds raised typically come from 10 to 20 percent of donors. Most nonprofits obtain the largest share of their philanthropic income from major gift donors. Time spent on major gift solicitation provides the greatest return on investment of nonprofit resources both human and financial.

The Quality of a Gift is Directly Related to the Quality of the Relationship between the Solicitor and the Prospect

Major prospects deserve personal attention. People give to people. Your relationship to the prospect has a direct impact on the gift. The more donors know and trust the solicitor, the more comfortable they will be making major gifts. They need to know that they are getting accurate, current and reliable information about the organization and the impact of their giving. They also will be more comfortable knowing that the solicitors, with whom they have a relationship, are likely to be more familiar with their background, interests and abilities than would strangers.

Avoid the Ready, Fire, Aim Temptation

Too often the desire or need to raise funds creates a sense of urgency which translates into volunteers and staff wanting to get started and solicit as many people as they can, as broadly and quickly as possible. Fundraising without a plan, organization, and discipline is an invitation to failure. There needs to be proper organization, leadership, communications, marketing, budgeting, back office systems and a well-defined case for support. A fundraising plan is critical and should be integrated within the overall business plan of the nonprofit. Fundraising should be conducted sequentially (top down and inside out). Initially the campaign should focus on the largest potential gifts and existing leadership of the organization. Events, group meetings and mass appeals should not be utilized until major gift solicitations have been addressed.

Leadership Sets the Example

Before making their commitments, many major donors, corporations and foundations want to know that the leadership of the organization has demonstrated its fiduciary responsibilities, not only through stewardship of funds and budgets but also as donors. Early in any fundraising effort, boards and leadership within the organization should be asked to participate as donors, to the best of their abilities. Full participation is as important, if not more so, than the total dollars raised from leadership.

You Can Never Thank Donors, Volunteers or Staff Member Too Often

They are your keys to success. Whether it be stewardship, public recognition, ongoing communication, personal thank you, gifts, member benefits, etc; the more you are in touch with donors, volunteers and staff in a way that demonstrates your appreciation, the more likely they will be there for you when you need them in the future.

Donors Expect and Deserve a Good Return on Their Charitable Gifts/Investments

Treat your donors as if they were major stockholders. They deserve to know how their investments in your organization are working and if the funds they have donated have accomplished the purposes for which they were given. The more you can demonstrate a good return on their investment, the more likely they will contribute in the future, and be a positive advocate for your organization in the community you serve.

Don't Do Anything That You Wouldn't Want to Read About on the Front Page of the Newspaper

Nonprofits must conduct themselves ethically and appropriately if they are to maintain the trust and confidence of their supporters and those they serve. When faced with difficult decisions, nonprofits should take the moral high ground and work diligently to ensure that a culture is established that promotes ethical behavior at every level within the organization. Challenges will occur. Whether related to gift acceptance issues, donor requests for special treatment, financial management, reporting, disclosures, personality conflicts or other issues, every nonprofit will have to confront delicate and potentially controversial problems. How problems and challenges are addressed is a true test of an organization's strength and effectiveness.

 Connect with Norman at http://charitychannel.com/cc/norman-olshansky

Straight Talk about Fundraising

By Linda Lysakowski, ACFRE

I recently asked a group of fundraising professionals about their biggest challenge. Contrary to what I had expected, it wasn't raising money in a challenging economic climate, or finding new donors, or even getting donors to give at higher level. It was "getting the rest of my organization (board, CEO and program staff) to understand what development staff people actually *do*, and getting them to support development efforts."

This is a huge area of concern for many development officers. But, think about it, what is usually the last position filled in an emerging nonprofit organization? The program people were there first; after all, if you don't have programs, you don't need a nonprofit. Then, as the organization grows, an executive director is appointed and a finance director hired. Often a PR or marketing person comes next, and then one day the organization grows to maturity and says to itself, we need more money to expand programs, move to a larger facility, hire more program people, or whatever. So, let's hire a fundraising staff person.

The result? Most of the people in the organization have no idea what "development" actually means. A few tips to change this attitude which I've found helpful in my career as a development director:

◆ Make sure that, as the chief development person, you report directly to the CEO and that you are part of the management team.

◆ Make friends with the CFO. It is critical that these two departments understand and appreciate the needs of the other department Financial officers must understand the importance of the development office receiving incoming donations first in order to record and acknowledge gifts, while development people need to understand the importance of accurate tracking of restricted and non-restricted gifts, for example.

◆ Practice "MBWA" Management by Walking Around—get out of your office and participate in a program when possible, talk to the receptionist, the security guard, the maintenance staff; it is amazing what these people know and how helpful they can be to your development efforts.

◆ Ask for time at department staff meetings to talk about the role of development, how it helps the organization fulfill its mission, and how the rest of the staff can help development efforts.

◆ Be sure your CEO supports your attendance at board meetings and that as chief development person; you are the liaison to the development committee of the board.

Titles and Reporting

It is critical that the development office is given its rightful place in the organization. The title of the chief development officer should be similar to the heads of other departments, vice president, director or whatever is used in your organization. Development staff should not be expected to report to the chief financial officer or the public relations director. If you are, you cannot succeed because you will not have the autonomy to act on your own nor will you have a title that indicates to the public, including donors, that the organization has made philanthropy a top priority in the organization.

Development Budget

Your development office budget must include sufficient funding to operate and to provide the tools needed in order to raise money. A typical development office budget should include funding for:

◆ Staff costs including salary and benefits for support staff. You will not succeed as a development professional if you are sitting in your office entering pledges and gifts all day.

◆ Professional development, including attendance at workshops, conferences and seminars, as well as membership in AFP or another professional association: development is a rapidly changing world and as a development professional you need to educate yourself on the latest trends and techniques.

◆ Publications that are pertinent to the profession: Wall Street Journal, Chronicle of Philanthropy, and others are important tools to help you stay on top of trends.

◆ Research tool such as the Foundation Center Directory, Wealth Engine or other similar tools: development is both an art and a science; this is part of the science.

◆ Consulting costs when needed. Major capital campaigns, planned giving and specialized areas will require expert advice and counsel. Sometimes tasks such as writing grant proposals and other development materials can be more cost effective when outsourced.

◆ Entertainment expense account for donor cultivation, volunteer recognition, and similar events: this is where the art of development comes in; building relationships with donors should be your primary role.

◆ Donor software, including maintenance and training for staff who will manage the donor database: maintaining good donor records is a science that helps you work your "art."

◆ Website, annual report, brochures and other fundraising materials: savvy donors will look at the quality of materials produced; these materials don't have to be expensive, but they must be professional.

◆ Communication tools such as a smart phone, GPS system and other electronic tools. Another example of how science can foster the art of building relationships.

◆ Membership in community associations that serve as sources to identify and cultivate potential donors, i.e. Chamber of Commerce, country club: this is where your donors are!

It is also critical that your organization not only understand development, but make a commitment to it in every way. You might want to use the following tool to assess your organization's commitment to philanthropy and development.

Assessing Your Organization's Philanthropic Profile

1. Does the organization have a development office?

2. Do experienced professionals staff the development office?

3. Does the development budget include money for professional development (membership in professional organizations, conferences and workshops, books and periodicals, etc. for the development staff?

4. Has the organization allocated a budget for a donor software system to manage fundraising activities?

5. Do the organization's staff members understand the importance of the development function? Do staff members support the development office's efforts?

6. Does the organization seek to hire development professionals that are certified (CFRE or ACFRE, FAHP, etc.) or assist current staff in obtaining credentials?

7. Does the chief development officer attend board meetings?

8. Is the board committed to development (do they give *and* get money for the organization)?

9. Is there a development committee on the board?

10. Does a development officer staff this committee?

11. Is there clerical support for the chief development officer?

12. Does the development staff act and look professional?

13. Is the development office in a prominent location and does it have a professional appearance?

14. Does the organization support the Donor Bill of Rights?

15. Is the organization aware of and supportive of the AFP Code of Ethical Standards?

16. Does the organization understand the importance of donor centered fundraising?

17. Does the organization understand that it takes time to establish a development program, and that building relationships with donors is the key role of the development office?

18. Is the organization committed to work with consultants when it is appropriate to do so, and not expect staff to manage major efforts such as a capital campaign?

19. Is the CEO involved in fundraising?

20. Are there volunteers involved in fundraising?

Calculate your "score"

Give your organization 5 points for each "Yes" answer! If you have a score of 80 or higher your organization is philanthropically savvy. If not you might need some help to educate your organization's leaders. Some ideas are:

◆ Hold a time, talent and treasure hunt within your organization.

◆ Invite a board member and/or executive director of an organization in your community that has a high philanthropic profile to come talk with your leadership about the importance of development.

◆ Engage a consultant to come in and work with your board and executive director to help them understand the importance of philanthropy and the function of a development office.

◆ Have your leadership attend a workshop or conference on development.

The Time, Talent and Treasure Hunt

One organization, for which I consulted, had a unique way to welcome the new development officer and help the rest of its staff understand the concept of development. We realized that because the organization was new to the world of development, its more than 250 employees did not understand the importance of fundraising. We found a cardboard treasure chest, filled it with trinkets such as cheap beads, gold foil-wrapped chocolate coins and a number of envelopes containing prizes that the new development director was able to obtain from local businesses—gift certificates to spas, restaurants, movies, etc.

The development officer and the chair of the newly-formed development committee asked to speak at each of the organization's three divisional staff meetings. The director of development made a ten minute presentation on what development meant and what her work would involve, including the fact that many unfunded programs would benefit from new development efforts. The chair of the development committee then asked for the help of the rest of the staff. Cards were distributed asking if they might be willing to offer a gift of their "time, talent or treasure." All employees who filled out a card had their name entered in a drawing for the prizes in the treasure chest.

Both the development officer and the chair of the development committee were amazed at the number of offers they received from staff members who volunteered to provide calligraphy of all their event invitations to those who had contacts with prospective major donors. The most important aspect of this event was that the entire staff understood what development was all about, how it helped the organization and how they could help the development office succeed.

practical tip

Connect with Linda at http://charitychannel.com/cc/linda-lysakowski

It All Begins with the Donor

By George Colabella

O ver the course of the past thirty years, I have developed a fondness for community-based organizations which might be broadly defined as public service organizations. That is, they provided a direct service and programs to a targeted population of individuals. These have been organizations that have responded to such issues as illness, poverty, homelessness, and a range of "social services." As such, they have not been multi-million-dollar organizations with large development budgets nor with board members of great wealth or connections. As a result, I've been in a position to establish, implement, and put into place many fundraising programs. I have always found this exciting, for it provides the opportunity to meet a host of people and requires thoughtful and innovative fundraising strategies.

I am pleased to state that over the years these ventures have been quite successful. In working with directors and staff, I've been able to develop fundraising plans that have resulted in considerable, extensive, and ongoing funding. I have often been asked how this has been possible without the usual budgets and connected leadership. The answer is surprisingly simple. *I think in terms of the funders and not in terms of the organization.*

Start at the Beginning—What is Fundraising All About?

It all starts with a very simple premise. I wholeheartedly believe that nearly all people wish to help others. Whether it is a neighbor facing a crisis, a community struggling to provide services, or even a national issue, nearly everyone has a driving force within themselves to reach out to others in times of need. Although this might be a simple concept, it is truly a powerful one for it influences our thinking and our fundraising strategy.

For those (hopefully few) who believe the job of the development professional is to persuade and convince the reluctant to part with their finances, there tends to be an innate and often unspoken adversarial relationship with donors. Far too often I have heard colleagues speak about the onerous task this presents. Of course, if you consider the donor a challenge and mountain to be climbed then it is indeed a task. It is a task that bears little fruit and does not recognize the true meaning of philanthropy. If you will excuse my being pedantic, let's remember the actual derivation of the word. Philanthropy: from the Greek *philos* (the love of) and *anthropy* (humankind). Thus we need to start right at the beginning. Philanthropy is generated by the innate drive within all of us to reach out to those in need.

However, it is important to remember who this describes. It does not describe the organization, it does not describe the development professional—it describes the donor. This, then, must be the starting point of all fundraising.

Organization-Focused or Donor-Focused?

I have seen the leaders of an organization develop a list of their funding priorities—what they need. Although this might be good managerial planning for such things as allocating resources and personnel, it is not how fundraising works. This vantage point of "what do we need/want" creates the very situation is which the donor "has to be convinced" and is often contrary to their views and areas of concern.

I have seen this in action. It takes the form of approaching a donor (individual, foundation, or corporation) with an organizational predetermined focus and then trying to steer the donor into that mode of thinking. It just doesn't work. It doesn't work for a variety of reasons. First and foremost this approach is oblivious to the donor's innate beliefs and interests, and tends to discount them. The underlying message is that the donor's interests are not as important as the organization's interests. Hence we have a scenario in which the donor and the organization are at odds. The result is that the donor is lost to the organization. Even more disturbing is the fact that the donor is left with a negative impression of fundraising and might become disillusioned in the entire process.

Knowing and Respecting the Donor

There is another approach—it is the approach that I have used for many years and have found to be one which first and foremost builds a positive, respectful, and sustained relationship between the donor and the organization. I spend the time to learn what the donor's interests entail and why they are of unique importance to them. In so doing, the donor is sharing with me their view of the world and their willingness to help. It is interesting that so many colleagues ask me how I learn of their interests. The answer couldn't be simpler—I ask.

I spend time getting to know donors. I not only share with them the workings and focus of the organization, I ask them what causes interest them and why. One can never over-estimate the value of listening. From this feedback and through regular contacts with donors I develop a feel for their "heart," understand their motivations, and appreciate their interests.

This is the point at which thoughtful and truly professional fundraising comes into play. Since nearly all organizations are multi-faceted, I seek to match that specific part of the organization with the interests of the donor. For example, you might be in the midst of a capital campaign, yet your donor states she has no interest in buildings, but has a strong commitment to your programs. Take the hint. Do not speak about the capital campaign—speak about the programs of the organization. In so doing, further refine the relationship to learn if there is a specific program which is of great interest to the donor. From this point on, all focus should be on this program. This could still lead to a gift that can be counted towards the endowment of program portion of your capital campaign.

Make it Real

Introduce the donor to the folks running the program, have the donor visit to see the program in action, provide an opportunity to see the clients who comprise the program. Also, ask the donor's specific thoughts about the program. In short, help the donor invest. Once this has been established, it is now possible to explain to the donor that you need help in moving forward with the shared vision of the organization and the donor. The goal is to form a true partnership.

Remember, the process does not end with a gift. Invite the donor back and explain what their gift has made possible. Keep them informed of all activities and successes. Most importantly, translate their gift to a real individual. Explain to them how their gift has truly changed the life of this individual or family. Again, remember that philanthropy refers to people and it is critical that the donor has a direct link to those who benefit.

The end result? Everyone wins. Your donors are pleased with their support, your organization is provided with funding, and most importantly clients benefit. In short, this is a true partnership.

If you take the time to remember that your donor gains much from providing support, and that you as the development professional can help make this happen, the results can be extraordinary. I, like nearly all fundraisers, have stories of how a donor became an integral part of the organization and have made significant and ongoing gifts. Many times, beyond our expectations.

A Few Rules of Thumb

Over the years I have had the good fortune to establish strong and meaningful relationships with donors. Like any relationship, it is built over time and takes a commitment to making it happen. A few thoughts to keep in mind will keep you on track:

◆ How did you first come into contact with the donor? Was it via an introduction, a letter, or perhaps meeting at a conference? Whatever the source, it is the first thing you have in common.

◆ Have you taken the time to talk in general terms without overwhelming them with the organization? No one wants to be showered with either problems or achievements on a "first date." Remember, you are building a relationship.

◆ Have you taken the time to remember a few personal things about the donor? Do they have a family, are they involved in other organizations, where do they live? All of these can be great reference points.

◆ Have you provided them with information about the organization that they might find interesting? This is not a request, an "ask," and does not include a donor response card. It is informational.

◆ Did you invite them to visit the organization and meet some of the folks that "make it happen?" There is no greater connection than seeing operations first hand and even meeting clients.

◆ Did you take the time to ask them what they thought? This must be done in a candid manner, setting a stage for them to share both their positive and negative feedback. Be attentive! Do not be defensive! Value their thoughts!

◆ Did you write or call them thanking for taking the time to visit? Make it personal—take out your pen and write a note—it says you believe they are worth the time. For some donors email can be an effective marketing or cultivation tool. For others a personal handwritten note is more effective.

◆ Have you asked them what in particular interests them the most about the organization? Once they answer, keep your mouth shut and let them tell you why and what. From this point on, this is the exclusive focus.

◆ When it comes time for a request, do you do it correctly? By this time, I have a relationship with the donor and an understanding about their commitment. Quite often, I will say, "I would like to ask you for your help." No fancy words—the straight truth—we are indeed asking for help. At this point the dollar amount and how the gift is structured becomes a function of the donor and logistics. You have asked for help and once they agree, the rest is only formality.

◆ Do you contact the donor on a regular basis to provide an update? How about just calling or writing to see how they are doing, how about a birthday card, how about inviting them to join you at a conference or reception?

◆ Have you learned when it is time to move on if the donor has no interest in your organization? There might be an occasion when it is in the donor's best interest to suggest that the donor contribute to another organization that better matches the donor's interest.

In short, the gift is not the end point of the relationship. Good fund raising and respect for donors comes from a true belief in philanthropy and sustaining friendships.

 Connect with George at http://charitychannel.com/cc/george-colabella

Gift Acceptance: Why Does Your Nonprofit Organization Need a Gift Acceptance Policy?

By Norman Olshansky

Decisions related to acceptance of out of the ordinary donations and pledges can be among the most challenging issues nonprofit professionals and leaders have to address, related to fundraising.

Some of the areas these policies need to address include:

◆ How do you deal with a donation from someone who is well known and of "ill repute" in the community who has made their fortune from being a slumlord and now is offering you a lead gift to your capital campaign with the proviso that the building be named after him?

◆ How do you avoid accepting a gift of real property that might cost you more in the long run than it is worth due to zoning, structural concerns, carrying expenses, legal or tax issues?

◆ What "strings" attached to gifts related to its use, recognition, investment, etc. are you willing to accept?

◆ What type of assets are you willing to accept? (Collectibles, art, autos, boats, jewelry, privately held stock, real estate, etc.)

◆ Are you willing to accept life insurance policies which might require future premiums?

◆ Are you willing to accept "split interest" gifts? These are gifts which allow the donor to make the gift today, while retaining an interest in the property and receiving both immediate and longer-term tax benefits.

◆ Do you sell all stock donations immediately, hold them as investments or make decisions on a case by case basis? What guidance is given to those making day to day decisions?

◆ Who in your organization can make a decision not to accept a gift?

◆ How do you recognize testamentary gifts, especially those that might not materialize due to the terms of the gift? What about a testamentary gift where the donor or his/her family is able to change the beneficiary or amounts at a future date?

◆ When there is a need to make an "exception," what process is used to authorize a decision which might not be covered clearly by established policy or practice?

These and similar issues occur more frequently than one might expect as part of the ongoing fundraising and development efforts of nonprofits. The type and frequency of these issues might vary from one nonprofit to another, but all nonprofits engaged in fundraising need to address gift acceptance.

If you do not have a policy in place to establish guidelines, practices and procedures for your staff and volunteers, you are leaving yourself vulnerable to problems, potential conflict with donors and liability to your organization.

Where to Start
There are many sample policies online which can be of assistance to you if you do not already have an established policy. If you do have one, it should be reviewed to make sure it covers conditions that could impact your organization. Review of policies and input from legal counsel can be most helpful.

The CEO/executive director should also seek input from fundraising staff and volunteers. The CEO/executive director should then engage the board chair for input so that a policy, or revisions to the existing policy, can be taken to the board of directors for review and approval.

For Consideration

Should your organization accept the following gifts and, if so, under what conditions? What are the questions you would need to answer?

1. A residential property that still has a mortgage?
2. A stamp collection?

3. A valuable piano or violin?
4. A gift from a truly anonymous source?
5. A portion of a limited partnership?
6. Stock which can't be sold for four years?
7. An apartment building?
8. Interest in a commercial business
9. Undeveloped property?
10. Art?
11. Jewelry?

Do not wait until you have to deal with issues related to a specific gift before you develop gift acceptance policies! Make sure you have an established gift acceptance policy and committee to which staff and/or volunteers can bring unique concerns which need to be addressed. By planning, thinking and acting smart, you can minimize, if not avoid, many of the problems other nonprofits have faced in the past.

 Connect with Norman at http://charitychannel.com/cc/norman-olshansky

Why You Need a Development Plan

By Linda Lysakowski, ACFRE

How many times has a well meaning board member or volunteer come to one of your board meetings and offered this sage advice: "We should do a (golf tournament, gala dinner dance, art auction, walkathon, etc., etc.,) because (Girl Scouts, Boy Scouts, the Hospital, etc., etc.) did one and raised $100,000"?

Before the meetings ends, the whole board or committee is caught up in "event fever' and has the invitations designed, the flowers ordered, and the T-shirt sponsors listed. And there you are, the new development officer, trying to meet grant deadlines, straighten out the donor database that is a mess, and organize the other events that your organization is currently conducting. So what do you do when the board is bitten by the "event bug?"

Another fatal mistake that organizations make is relying solely on a grant writer to raise all the money it needs for programs and operations. Given the fact that foundation grants only account for approximately 14 percent of all philanthropic giving in the United States, this approach seems equally as foolhardy as depending mainly on events to raise money for the organization. While both grants and events are important parts of a well rounded development program, they should not be the *only* methods of fundraising used by nonprofits. So how does one handle these board suggestions, or (in some cases) mandates?

Often boards and volunteers do not realize that events and grant research can be costly, not only in terms of hard costs, but in "opportunity costs." In other words, what activities must you give up in order to focus your limited time on this proposed new activity? Your first reaction to the board or development committee that suggests either of these approaches should be, "Well, let's pull out our development plan and see if this event/activity is part of our plan; if not, what other activities must be dropped in order to concentrate on this event/activity?" However, many organizations do not have a development plan to reference. If your organization is one of those, this is one good reason why you should have a development plan.

Organizations that have a development plan complete with timelines, areas of responsibility and budgets, will be more successful at keeping the staff, board and volunteers focused on the activities that are most cost effective and produce the best results.

What Should the Development Plan Include?

The development plan should start with an analysis of current development activities. Some questions to ask:

◆ What has been the history of this activity; have results increased or decreased over the years?

◆ What are the costs of this event, both hard costs, staff time, and opportunity costs?

◆ Do we have the human resources to manage this activity?

◆ Do we have the technology needed to manage this activity?

◆ What are the ancillary benefits of this activity, i.e., if the activity is a cultivation or awareness raising events, should we continue the activity even if it does not raise money?

◆ How do current trends affect this activity?

◆ Are there ways we can increase the effectiveness of this activity?

Once the current activities have been analyzed, a decision should be made to keep them status quo, focus more time and energy on them, or drop them.

A solid development plan lists detailed goals for each activity. Goals do not always have to be monetary ones. For example, a goal might be to raise constituent participation by five percent this year, increase the size of the development committee by four people, to personally visit three major donors each month. Without specific goals, it will impossible to measure success of the plan next year.

The development plan provides:

◆ a way to measure success of your development activities;

◆ assurance that your development activities provide a balanced approach—in other words, "Don't put all your eggs in one basket;"

◆ a way to determine the appropriate budget for the development office;

◆ assurance that you have the human resources to implement the development activities that are planned; and

◆ timelines that allow the development office to best utilize staff and volunteer time.

practical tip

A development plan also helps the development office justify its budget, provides measurement tools to be used in performance appraisals and provides donors with a sense of confidence in the organization. So, is there any reason your organization does not need a development plan?

Who Develops and Implements the Plan?

Now, how does the busy development office find time for planning and who will implement the plan once it's done? By involving the right people in developing the plan and then implementing it, the development office can move forward in a timely manner and provide a framework for evaluating all their programs.

Typically these are the people involved in the development planning process and implementing the plan:

Chief development officer

This CDO, in most cases, has the chief responsibility for the development plan. The CDO establishes goals for the department including creating the development office budget. This person also develops the objectives and strategies to reach these goals, and usually assigns responsibilities to those who will implement the plan. The CDO is the person who will be held responsible for implementing the plan, evaluating the plan's success, and adapting the plan as needed. The CDO will want to have a development plan in order to facilitate running the development program and to use in the CDO's own performance evaluation.

Other development staff

In an office where there are additional development team members, they should be involved with the planning process, and will implement the various segments of the plan that pertain to their duties. Large development offices will often have different staff people responsible for areas such as planned giving, major gifts, annual fund, alumni relations, etc. It is important that these people are involved with establishing goals for their areas of the plan. It is also important to include support staff in the planning process. The development plan goals can suffer serious delays if there is not enough support staff and technology available to implement the strategies to meet these goals.

Non-development staff

The CEO of the organization should be involved in setting the goals of the development office. The CEO's role in implementing the plan, particularly the identification, cultivation and solicitation of major gift prospects, will be critical in the plan's success. Therefore the CEO must be willing to support the plan and to fulfill his or her involvement in the process. The CFO might also be involved in the plan, particularly the budget for additional staff, technology or other resources that will be needed to implement the plan. For some organizations, there might be other staff members' involvement such as program people who might be consulted regarding their funding requests, facility managers that might have capital needs that will require funding.

Board

While the board is instrumental in developing a strategic plan for nonprofit organizations, their role in the development plan is often minimal although the board should endorse the goals and can often offer ideas for strategies to reach these goals. If there is no development staff, the board will be more involved in the development of the plan. In any size organization, however, the board's role in implementing the plan will be critical. Like the CEO, they will have a key role to play in identifying, cultivating and soliciting donors.

Development committee

The development committee will have a larger role in the planning process than the full board will have since this is its area of focus. The development committee should have some board members as committee members, and is usually chaired by a board member. However, it is important to expand the committee beyond the board and involve community members, especially those with community contracts and/or specific skills and talents that can be used on the committee, such as an estate planning attorney, financial planner or CPA that can help with planned giving. This committee, along with the CDO, will play a key role in implementing the plan.

Other volunteers

If there are other volunteers involved in the development program, such as a parent group, auxiliary, alumni association, planned giving committee, events committee, etc. They might also be invited to review and provide input into the parts of the plan that pertain to their activities.

Consultants

A consultant is often involved in the planning process, particularly in the assessment phase. Many organizations engage a consultant to conduct a development audit of their past development performance before they establish goals for the current plan. A consultant can provide an objective view of the organization's development program and help establish realistic goals as well as develop strategies for the plan.

What Does the Plan Look Like?

One thing to remember about your plan: it is more than a document! Both the *process* and the *product* are important.

We've talked about the importance of planning and who should be involved in the development planning process. However, it is equally important to have a written document to follow. The document itself will be critical to the evaluation process.

The plan should start with an analysis of prior development efforts (assuming, of course, that your organization has done development in the past.) It should also state the mission and vision of your organization, because the mission and vision should drive all development efforts.

The plan should then list the broad based goals of the plan and the objectives under each goal.

A word about goals and objectives

Many times, people confuse goals and objectives. Goals are broad based items, for example: Raise public awareness of our organization, develop a more effective board of directors, or increase alumni participation. Objectives, on the other hand are more specific, and should be S.M.A.R.T.:

◆ *S*pecific,

◆ *M*easurable,

◆ *A*ction-oriented,

◆ *R*ealistic (yet visionary), and

◆ *T*ime defined.

Objectives for the above stated goals might include:

◆ to develop a website that is frequented by one hundred potential donors each month, by December 2011;

◆ to increase the size of our board from nine to eighteen people, by 2014, adding three people each year over the next three years; or

◆ to increase the percentage of alumni who contribute through the annual phonathon from 14 percent to 25 percent over the next two years.

The Specific Steps

Each of the objectives should then have specific strategies or action steps to accomplish the stated objectives. It is critical to address these three questions for each objective in the development plan:

◆ Who is going to do it?

◆ When will it be completed?

◆ How much will it cost/how much will it raise?

All areas of development should be covered in your plan including various fundraising approaches, such as direct mail, grants, special events, telephone fundraising, personal solicitation. Your plan should also address the various constituencies that will be approached, such as foundations, corporations, individuals—which might include alumni, parents, members, community members—and organizations, such as churches, service clubs etc.

Your development plan should also focus on infrastructure that is needed to manage a development program—technology, communications, research and cultivation, stewardship, human resources, including board, staff and volunteers, policies and procedures.

A typical segment of the plan might look like this:

Goal	Objective	Strategy	Area of Responsibility	Budget	Timeline
I. Increase the board's involvement in fundraising	A. Establish a development committee	Appoint a development committee chair from the board	Director of development/ board chair	N/A	6/30/12
		Develop a position description for development committee	Director of development/ consultant/ development committee chair	$500	7/31/12
		Develop a list of twenty potential development committee members from the board and outside sources	Director of development/ consultant/ board of directors	$500	7/31/12
		Develop volunteer recruitment packet	Director of development	$100	8/31/12

Goal	Objective	Strategy	Area of Responsibility	Budget	Timeline
		Recruit at least ten development committee members	Director of development/ board members/ development committee chair	n/a	10/31/12
		Conduct orientation meeting for development committee	Director of development/ consultant/ development committee chair	$500	11/31/12

Each goal and objective must have the strategies and actions steps to accomplish them as well as the timelines, areas of responsibility and budget, which will be critical in the evaluation process.

In setting goals and objectives be sure to think about the S.M.A.R.T. objectives mentioned earlier. Each strategy must be specific enough to be able to identify exactly what the organization is going to do in order to achieve this goal and objective. It must be measurable—you can determine if you have accomplished this step. For example, did you identify twenty potential development committee members by August 31? It must be action-oriented, outlining a specific action that will be taken to achieve this objective. It must be realistic, yet visionary, not too easy to accomplish. Can you list twenty people who are logical prospective members of this committee and whom you believe would likely agree to serve on the committee? And, as shown above, each step has a timeline to measure the organization's progress.

Evaluate

The development planning document should be easy to follow, be referred to often, and be evaluated regularly.

One of the biggest problems with many development plans is that they sit on a shelf gathering dust. If the plan has all the components discussed in this article, it should be easy to implement and easily measurable. Most plans fail because the organization is really good at setting goals and objectives, but not always as diligent when it comes to establishing the action steps necessary to implement their goals.

Before your plan is complete, an evaluation process should be in place. This process will include assigning a person, usually the chief development officer, to monitor the plan on a regular basis. Your plan should also include a section which lists all the action steps in chronological order; a section that lists each step that has a budget impact, both positive and negative; and a section that outlines tasks by areas of responsibility.

If each person, committee or department that is responsible for implementing the plan has an easy tool to measure their own progress, it is much more likely that they will follow the plan. Similarly, the budget outline will be helpful when presenting the plan to the CEO, the CFO or the board that must approve expenditures needed to implement the plan. Finally, the timeline in chronological order will make it simple to measure progress on a monthly, or even weekly, basis.

At every development department staff meeting, your plan should be reviewed, especially in relation to the timeline and the areas of responsibility that relate to development department staff. You should not use the plan to point fingers at staff members who might be falling behind in carrying out their parts of the plan, but rather as a tool to celebrate progress and discuss issues that might be impeding the progress of the plan. Often there are segments of the plan that are not accomplished according to the timelines, but there might be extenuating circumstances that justify this deviation from the plan. For example, perhaps a direct mail piece did not get mailed on time because there was a major grant application due which took precedence over the mailing.

The development committee, who has a great deal of responsibility for both developing and implementing the plan, should also review it on a regular basis. A segment of each development committee meeting should be devoted to reviewing progress on the plan, and making adjustments if necessary. And the board, which also has a major responsibility for certain segments of the plan, should also review the plan periodically to assess progress and help establish goals for the next planning year. Your plan will also be helpful at performance evaluation time. As CDO, you should discuss the plan with your CEO and outline progress made on the plan and areas that might be hindering implementation of the plan, such as lack of technology, lack of board and CEO involvement, and budget constraints.

Tools to Help

One of the tools that can help set realistic goals is to review already established guidelines for each component of the plan. In my book, *The Development Plan*, there are established guidelines for various development components that can help you compare your organization's progress with acceptable standards in many areas. Remember that some non-monetary goals should also be established in the plan, particularly for organizations that are new to development. Be sure to celebrate progress made on these goals as well, it is not always just about the money!

Try not to get discouraged if not all your goals are met; looking at the plan on a regular basis will assure that some goals are not totally ignored while other areas are being perused. Staff, board and volunteers must not be led astray by delving into areas that are not in the plan. If a good idea is presented that is not in the plan, you should suggest that the idea be investigated further and possibly incorporated into the next plan. If the opportunity is immediate and your organization feels compelled to pursue it, then those involved need to examine the plan to see what area might have to be eliminated from the current plan in order to pursue this new opportunity.

One thing to remember is that the plan is not written in stone, but neither is it written in disappearing ink! It should be flexible, but not *too* flexible.

 Connect with Linda at http://charitychannel.com/cc/linda-lysakowski

How to Start a Development Program

By Amy M. Eisenstein, MPA, CFRE

Whether you are starting a new nonprofit or are at one that has functioned without a formal development office for several years, it might be time to begin a proper fundraising program. There are several key steps you should take before launching a development office or fundraising program, which are outlined below. Use what works for your organization and leave the rest.

1. Create a Development Committee

Work with your board as you begin to create a new development program. Select key volunteers (board and non-board members) who seem interested in helping with fundraising to serve on a development committee and invite one to chair the committee. Including volunteers from the beginning will be key to their continued buy-in and involvement in the process. While you are getting your development program started, this committee should meet regularly. I advise monthly meetings at the beginning until you have a solid plan in place.

Create a development committee job description with things you expect of them, including:

◆ Attendance at development committee meetings

◆ Participation in fundraising events—soliciting sponsors and selling tickets

◆ Making introductions for the executive director to potential supporters

◆ Advocating for the organization to community groups and individuals

◆ Becoming a donor or increasing their gift as an example of leadership

If you can afford to, hire a consultant to help you with an initial board training and planning process. If you cannot afford a consultant, try to identify someone at another agency who is doing well with fundraising, and might volunteer their expertise for a few hours.

Be sure to utilize committee members for their expertise and relationships in the community. Never meet for the sake of meeting. Make sure each meeting has an agenda with discussion items, tasks to delegate and next steps.

2. Planning

It is important to strategically plan out the fundraising activities you will implement throughout the year, and not just haphazardly do whatever comes onto your radar screen (or whatever the committee suggests on a whim).

Take time to think about and write down what you do now.

◆ How many grants did you write this year/last year? How do you identify those grants? Who writes them?

◆ How many events do you do? Who plans them? How much money do they raise?

◆ Do you send any appeal letters or other mailings during the year? How much do they cost? How much do they raise?

◆ Do you have any individual donors? How do you identify them? Who solicits them?

◆ Does your entire board give to your organization? Are they asked?

Once you know what you currently do (your baseline) then you can begin to plan what you will do the coming year. How many more activities can you add? Do you have the staff and resources to write more grants, plan more events, send appeal letters, and solicit individuals?

Create a calendar to determine what you will do each month. For example:

◆ January—Send out electronic newsletter and solicitation and research grants for the year

◆ February—Meet individually with each board member to solicit their annual contribution

◆ March—Send out spring appeal letter and meet with two prospective donors

◆ April—Write two grants and solicit sponsors for your event

◆ May—Send invitation for your spring event and meet with two prospective donors

◆ June—Spring fundraising event

◆ July—Write one grant and send out electronic newsletter and solicitation

I strongly suggest diversifying your funding base as much as possible, and implementing a diverse funding plan – not simply all grant writing or all events. There are many great resources available to help with your planning process.

3. Budgeting

Before launching your new fundraising office, it is important to create a budget which will cover all projected activities, needs and staff salaries. In preparing a budget, consider the following:

◆ Will you be hiring new staff members or consultants? Will you offer benefits?

◆ Will you need additional office space, desks, computers, consumable supplies, etc.?

◆ Do you plan to invest in fundraising software?

◆ Will you be sending new mailings? Remember, costs include printing, postage, reply envelopes, a mail house, etc.

◆ Do you plan to buy a subscription to a grant database?

◆ Will you send staff to fundraising training, conferences or meetings?

◆ Is your website up to date and can you accept donations on it?

◆ Will you be holding more events? With food, entertainment, invitations, etc.?

These are just a few of the questions you will need to answer when you create your budget. Be realistic and optimistic when creating your budget. Remember, it is not simply the cost of a new staff member (if you are hiring one) but all the activities that you expect that person to initiate and implement as well.

4. Staffing

Is the executive director (you, perhaps) going to be the staff member doing all of the development, or are you ready to hire your first development officer or other support staff to share the load? The executive director is ultimately responsible for fundraising, regardless of whether or not there is additional fundraising staff. The executive director's (or CEO) role is to be the face of the organization and front and center with donors. They need to share their vision and build relationships on behalf of the organization.

If you have the funds, you will want to hire your first development staff member. It is important to remember when budgeting for your first development staff member to have realistic expectations about what they can raise in their first year. You should have at least twelve months salary in the budget before they arrive, and not expect them to raise their own salary, especially in the first year. That being said, they should be able to raise some funds in the first year, but the funds might be restricted and not available for use as administrative salary.

If you are not ready to hire development staff, consider who will oversee the development functions. It is likely to be the executive director with help from a few board members, other volunteers, interns or program staff.

5. Infrastructure and technology

One of the key components of any good development office is a good database, where information about donors, prospective donors, and supporters is captured. There are many good fundraising software programs on the market. Although they can be extremely useful once your list has reached a certain size and you are receiving many donations annually, I do not believe you need to start with costly software. Microsoft Access is more than adequate if you are just getting started. The important thing, with regard to your database, will be to have someone on hand who can set up the database and build and pull reports. Key pieces of information to collect include:

- Name

- Address

- Email address

- Phone number

- Donation history

- How they became involved with the organization

- Any other information you have or want to collect

◆ Key contacts and relationships

◆ Information for acknowledgement, billings, and tax receipts, etc.

Whatever system you are using, you should be able to quickly generate thank you letters and mailing labels.

A word of caution: there are some extraordinarily expensive fundraising databases on the market that are targeted at large and small nonprofits alike. There is NO need for you to invest in an expensive database if you are just building your list. There are plenty of middle-of-the-road and cheaper versions available that will be perfectly adequate for your needs at this stage.

Wrapping Up

If you are just getting started with fundraising, I highly recommend investing in some resources and training. A great resource is CharityChannel (at http://charitychannel.com) which provides webinars, articles and books, and conferences. Another great organization is the Association of Fundraising Professionals (AFP) which provides many different types of educational opportunities and as well as regular, local chapter meetings. These meetings can be great places to find colleagues and mentors who can help and advise you.

The main secret to fundraising is not being afraid to ask. There is no right or wrong way. The important thing is to get out there and do it. Remember, you are not begging for money, you are asking people to join you in investing in an important cause.

Best wishes for your fundraising success!

 Connect with Amy at http://charitychannel.com/cc/amy-eisenstein

Creating a Development Strategy by Relationships

Dr. John R. Frank, CFRE

A nonprofit had begun its development program and decided to focus on major donors. This was successful at first because the executive director was very good with these types of relationships. The organization got off to a good start. But in year two, I received a call from the executive director in August stating, "We are in trouble. We have plenty of commitments, but no gifts are coming in right now. What do we do?" They had put all of their efforts into their major donors and they were not giving during the summer months. Because they had focused only on major donors they did not have a variety of donor types that would give during the seasons in which major donors do not give. They had put "all of their eggs in one basket."

Why Focus on Relationships First?

I have learned through the years that only focusing on "fundraising strategies" is shortsighted. Your donors are more than just a source of money; they are partners in championing your cause. They care what about you do, and they want you to care about them, what they think, and how they want to be connected to your cause.

In other words, they want a relationship with you, their favorite charity. And I have also learned that as all people are not the same, so too your donor relationships are not all the same.

The chart on the next page represents my strategy for considering relationships first, then strategies in order to create a comprehensive development strategic plan.

While there is not room to go through this entire flow chart, I will share some of the critical components in the process.

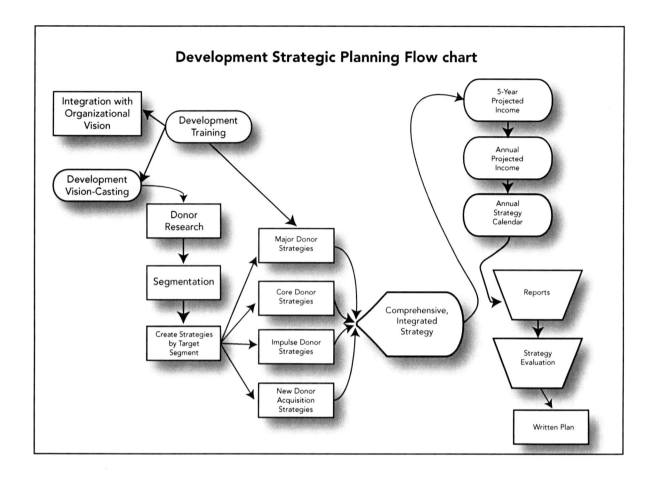

Development Strategic Planning Flow chart

Four Main Types of Donor Relationships

Major donors

For purposes of this article, I define major donors as those who give $1,000 or more during a calendar year, although each organization defines major gifts differently. Major donors make decision differently than other donors. They usually do not make decisions impulsively, but require more planning, thinking, and sometimes more time to come to their giving conclusions.

Major donors desire unique strategies to be connected their causes. It might be very personal, or part of a group of "insiders," but it is usually different for each major donor.

Core/monthly donors

Some donors prefer to give the same amount every month. They are disciplined in their personal lives and budget their giving. They require a system for giving that meets their style. Two key considerations for core donors are convenience in giving and efficient use of their gifts. They are very faithful in giving every month and do not want your nonprofit to waste their money by sending back "gifts" the costs of which they feel could be better spent on programs.

Core donors will stay with a charity a long time if they feel they are appreciated and that their gifts can make the difference in financial stability during the summer slump or other lean times.

Impulse donors

There are other donors that give randomly or impulsively. They might truly enjoy direct mail appeals, or special events. And they usually give several times throughout the year depending on the communication strategy you use.

The key in reaching impulse donors is frequency. You must stay in their mailbox or email box to keep your cause fresh. They do not plan their giving, so you must be available when they are ready to give. The idea of doing fewer mailings to save money might be true for other relationships, but not for impulse donors. You must proactively reach out to them throughout the year and especially in the fall giving season.

New donors

New donors might think good thoughts about your organization, or they might already be a volunteer for your organization. But there is a psychological and even spiritual change that takes place when someone moves from thinking about your cause, to giving to your cause. This step makes them one of your donors and changes the relationship from outsider to insider. Your organization must recognize every new or first-time donor, and welcome them immediately.

A careful cultivation strategy for new donors is critical to bring them into a more committed and giving relationship over time.

The Key: Create Strategies for Each Type of Relationship

The proverbial, "do not put all of your eggs in one basket," applies here. Just as the organization that relies on one foundation grant each year can be in trouble if they reduce or eliminate that grant, so too the organization that relies on one special event each year can run the risk of the attendance being down or less giving.

Each relationship group demands different strategies to reach each relationship. Can you send a letter to each group? Yes, but it must be a unique letter that understands what it will take to get each group to open and respond to the letter. And understand that a major donor responds to a letter much less often than impulse donors.

However, if you have designed a special letter to major donors with whom you already have a close relationship, there is a better chance they will open that unique letter.

Not all strategies work for every nonprofit. Just because one organization is successful with an auction, it does not mean that your donors will respond well to an auction. You must match your strategies to the unique relationships of your organization with its donors.

Strategies to Connect with the Donor

Strategies should be created because donors want them. How do major donors wish to communicate with your organization? Face to face, phone, personal letters?

Do you have a monthly partner program for those disciplined donors who want a systematic approach to their giving? Do you offer EFT (Electronic Funds Transfer) to them?

And what about those occasional donors? If you only mail to them once or twice a year, do you expect them to respond to your timeline? Maybe providing more opportunities for them to give will bring greater response.

These strategies must work together. A donor might start as a monthly donor and then decide to invest in a major project. You must create ways to get to know you donors so as to offer them opportunities to give in other or greater ways.

Income projections by relationship groups

Once you have identified each of your relationship strategies, you can begin to project the annual income from each strategy. This can seem daunting at first, but as you learn from each direct mail appeal, special event, major donor call, you will get more accurate at projecting each strategy's results.

Reporting and Evaluation

After you have created individual strategies for your various relationship groups you will need to report the results. This can be a simple report that shows the number of gifts that come in from a major donor strategy, and includes the total dollars given. This simple report for each strategy within a relationship group will give you a summary view of how your strategies are doing and how your donors responded.

Many stop with this report. But that is not enough. You must evaluate your results based on what you forecasted each strategy to accomplish. If you do not connect your results to your forecasts, you will continue to repeat the same strategy each year, whether you are on target or not.

A successful development strategy must connect your results to your forecasts. Then you can make the necessary adjustments as you learn from the success or failure of each strategy. When you adjust strategy you are learning about how each relationship responds. Since people always are changing, your development strategy by relationships needs to adjust and change.

Concluding Remarks

Here are a few key steps to begin your development strategic plan by relationships.

1. List all of your major donor strategies. (i.e., personal contact, phone, proposal, special event, etc.)

2. List all of your monthly giving strategies (i.e. monthly checks, EFT, credit card, website, etc.)

3. List all of your impulse donor strategies (i.e. direct mail, special events, etc.)

4. List all of your new donor strategies (i.e. direct mail acquisition, special events for new donors, etc.)

5. Project the income (goals) for each strategy within the group.

6. As you prepare your calendar year, enter each activity in the month the donor will be responding to the strategy.

7. Now you have created the outline for viewing your donors as relationships, rather than just as sources for money.

The "one size does not fit all" is always true when it comes to people. So too should your development programs not try to make different donors "fit" into your strategies. Creating a comprehensive development strategy by relationships takes time. But if you listen to your donors and respond to them, they will lead you in how they want to give. You will find yourself becoming comprehensive in your mindset and the various strategies that connect donor relationships to your nonprofit will be a part of your overall development efforts.

 Connect with John at http://charitychannel.com/cc/john-frank

Developing Your Case for Support

By Linda Lysakowski, ACFRE

Sometimes development professionals only think about the importance of having a case for support when they are preparing to launch a capital campaign. However, your organization needs a case for support for *all* of your fundraising activities. The case has been defined by some as "the reasons why an organization both needs and merits philanthropic support...," (AFP Fundraising Dictionary); ...a clear, compelling statement of all the reasons why anyone should consider making a contribution...(Harold J. Seymour); and "...an internal database...of information that will support the preparation of various documents and publications.."(Henry A. Rosso). The case is all of this and more.

Your organization needs to develop a case for support first, before designing a brochure, developing a website, preparing grant proposals, developing speeches, PowerPoint presentations, DVDs and any other material used in your fundraising activities. The reason for having the case in place first is that it is crucial to present a unified message and a consistent look and feel in all your organization's fundraising materials. Too many times someone in an organization decides that the organization needs a brochure, a website, or video and someone heads off to develop that material, while other individuals are preparing grant proposals and fundraising appeal letters, and still others might be out making presentations to groups and individuals. If these people are not all working from the same source document, the case for support, the messages they deliver will be inconsistent and sometimes even contradictory.

Steps to Developing a Case for Support:

◆ Develop the organizational case for support.

◆ Develop individual case statements for various fundraising activities.

◆ Test the preliminary case statements.

◆ Prepare final case statements.

◆ Translate final case statements into fundraising materials.

In other words, development of the materials is the last step, not the first!

Content of the Case

Your case should contain your mission and vision, both of which are important in order to motivate the donor to become involved. A history which shows success will help donors understand that your organization has a track record of successfully implementing programs. An outline of the programs and services for which funds are being solicited is important. It is also critical to show donors who the people are that are involved in your organization, both staff and board members. This will help build credibility for your organization. It will also be crucial to demonstrate a compelling need for funds; however the difference between being compelling and looking desperate is a fine line that the case cannot cross. Donors will not support an organization whose case sounds like a desperate appeal for funds to keep the organization afloat. Donors, instead, want to invest in a winning cause, an organization that has support from other sources, and one that shows it is filling a need in the *community*, not one that stress the *organization's* needs.

However, it is critical to outline the costs of the programs you are trying to fund and provide solid financial information about your sources of funding and how the donors' contributions will help you achieve the goals presented in your case. The case also needs to provide options for donors to become involved. Outright gifts, pledges, gifts-in-kind, matching gifts, group gifts, named gifts, and planned gifts are all options that should be described to for the donor. Above all, your case needs to present both emotional and rational reasons for the donor to contribute. Emotion usually draws the reader into your case, but before writing out a check, most donors will want to analyze the rational reasons to give.

Who Prepares the Case?

Generally the chief development officer will prepare the case for support, although often a consultant w be brought in to accomplish this task, particularly if the case is for a capital campaign. Sometimes public relations staff might be involved in the final product, especially in preparing the final fundraising materials from the case. Whoever is charged with developing the case, however, must be someone who understands the need for and the uses of the case, has good knowledge of the organization and its constituents, and understands basic fundraising principles.

The case should always be tested before the final materials are prepared. In the case of a capital campaign, the preliminary case for support is usually tested through the process of the planning (or feasibility) study. If the case is for more general use, other ways to test the case might be by meeting individually with donors to ask their opinions, holding a focus group of donors, or posting the case on a section of the website open only to invited guests whose opinion is valued by the organization. You might also conduct surveys of leadership and key influential people (donors, funders, government officials, community leaders, etc.) Often the case will need adjustment after it is tested in order to assure that it is compelling to potential donors.

Developing Your Case

The case should answer these questions:

- ◆ Who is your organization and what does it do? (mission statement)

- ◆ Why does your organization exist?

- ◆ What is distinctive about your organization?

- ◆ What is it the organization plans to accomplish? (vision statement)

- ◆ How will the fundraising appeal or campaign help you accomplish this vision?

- ◆ How can the donor become involved?

- ◆ What's in it for the donor?

- ◆ Who are your organization's leaders (both staff and volunteer) and what is their ability to effectively implement the mission?

- ◆ What is the project or program going to cost and (including a budget to support the goal/need)

- ◆ What is your organization's successful track record? (your points of pride)

- ◆ How will the project or program be sustainable in the future?

- ◆ How can the donor become part of your vision?

practical tip

Translating the Case into Fundraising Materials

Remember that the case serves as the source document for all fundraising materials and that although the message is consistent and uniform, the way it is translated will vary greatly for different audiences. Foundation or government grant proposals may, for example, require almost the full case be included in the proposal. Corporate foundations and business donors might expect a greatly abbreviated version of the case stated in the form of a fact sheet or a simple letter. Board, staff and other "insiders" will not expect a glitzy brochure, website readers will look for graphics and an easy way to contribute. Current donors might not need as much emphasis on current programs if they are familiar with the organization, whereas new donors might need more information.

Before translating your case into written or electronic materials, it is crucial that you do a stakeholder analysis and determine what materials will appeal to each constituency. If your budget precludes multiple print materials for different constituencies, you might need to develop a generic piece that can be supplemented with internal reports or documents to address the individual needs of target audiences. Various types of organizations will have different looks expected by their constituents. In general a small human service might turn off donors if these donors feel the materials are too "glitzy" (and are therefore perceived as too expensive). On the other hand a university, major health center, or museum might have donors who expect very sophisticated materials. In any case, the materials should be professionally done and presented in a way that is consistent with your organization's image.

You will find a case statement evaluation form to help you determine the strength of your case on my website at www.cvfundraising.com.

 Connect with Linda at http://charitychannel.com/cc/linda-lysakowski

Changing Prospects into Donors: How Change Theory Can Guide the Way

By Gayle L. Gifford, ACFRE

We have all struggled unsuccessfully to break old habits, like eating pastry with our mid-morning coffee, or tried to adopt rewarding new routines, like daily exercise workouts. But it wasn't until I stumbled onto the ideas in a book called *Changing for Good* that I made the connection between fundraising and the difficulty we adults commonly experience in changing our behaviors.

The change model in *Changing for Good* is called the *"Transtheoretical Model of Change"* developed by James O. Prochaska, a psychologist at the University of Rhode Island, and a number of colleagues.

Fortunately, I didn't let the imposing name stop me from learning more. I discovered that Prochaska's model of change was well known and respected in public health and other disciplines concerned with changing human behaviors.

The model describes the process of behavioral change. It answers questions like these:

◆ *Why are some people more likely than others to succeed in dropping bad habits or picking up positive new ones?*

◆ *Why do some programs have high success rates in helping individuals make lasting changes in their lives while others rarely work?*

As someone who views philanthropy and charitable giving as a positive social behavior, I wanted to see if this model of change could provide fundraisers with helpful insights into the work that we do.

The Five Stages of Change

According to Prochaska, successful change isn't a *single event*—for example, people don't decide out of the blue to lose weight, change their diet that very day and successfully keep that weight off for the rest of their lives.

Instead, change is a *process* that involves *five stages*, a spiral of forward and backward progress.

The five stages of behavioral change are:

1. "I'm not yet thinking about a particular behavior"—*precontemplation*

2. "I'm thinking about this new behavior and weighing how it will work for me"—*contemplation*

3. "I've made the decision to act and I'm deciding how to do it"—p*reparation*

4. "I'm doing it for the first time, or first few times"—a*ction*

5. "I've made this a continuing habit in my life"—*maintenance*

Let's look at the five stages a little more closely and see how they might apply to our work with donors.

Stage One: Precontemplation (or "I'm not yet thinking about this particular behavior.")

When we set about to recruit new donors or to ask current donors to deepen their giving, we know that we can't jump right in and ask for money the first time we meet. Why?

If our potential donor is in the *precontemplation* stage, they haven't yet given any thought to our request—really, we probably aren't even on their personal radar screen. Or, they might briefly have considered taking such an action but decided it wasn't anything they were interested in right now.

Our job then is to move our prospective donor from the precontemplation to the *contemplation* stage. Two processes, or tools, that work well at this stage are:

◆ raising awareness; and

◆ arousing their emotions about a problem or for a solution

We raise awareness by exposing our prospect to more information about our cause, our institution or the particular giving option that we are promoting. We can employ hundreds of ways to get our message noticed: radio or TV spots, newspaper articles or newsletters, a carefully tailored brochure, or even a face-to-face conversation.

But factual information alone usually isn't enough to move beyond this stage. We need to arouse the *emotions* that will help our prospect overcome their indifference, apathy or resistance. Vivid examples of need and touching personal stories of changed lives help our ideas grow deeper roots. We are successful in our efforts when prospects want to investigate more closely what this means for them.

Stage Two: Contemplation (or "I'm thinking about this new behavior and weighing how it will work for me.")

The contemplation stage most closely parallels what fundraisers call *donor cultivation*.

At this stage, our prospects are taking stock of our institution and its impact on their personal circumstances. How well do our programs and values align with their beliefs about social problems or community betterment? Can they afford a gift right now? How big? What difference will it make? What will happen in return? Are there other organizations that might be a better investment? Or are there other ways to spend the same money and receive more personal satisfaction?

Our prospects are weighing the pros and cons of action, but so far the "pros" don't have enough weight. We can help our prospects tip those scales by helping them:

◆ harness their emotional energy for change;

◆ get more relevant information; and

◆ imagine the future once the change has happened!

Because the questions at this stage are very personal, more individualized forms of communication are helpful. You can create opportunities for your prospect to experience your program in action, feel its excitement or empathize with the individuals who benefit from your services. Site visits, testimonials from clients or passionate volunteers can be very moving. Testimonials from peers, co-workers, family or trusted opinion leaders can help the individual see how becoming a donor might feel to them. Providing targeted information helps your prospects visualize how your institution can fulfill their dreams of a better world.

Stage Three: Preparation (or "I've made the decision to act and I'm deciding how to do it.")

You've done a very good job of cultivation. Your prospect is excited, confident and ready to give. Now is the time to for them to make the commitment and for you to make "the ask."

Make the final act of commitment as safe and simple as possible—don't place obstacles in the way of giving. This might be as simple as including that reply envelope or accepting a donation by credit card. If your donor is making a complicated planned gift, be sure that they have everything they need for their legal advisor to draw up the final documents.

But first, recognize that there is likely to be some ambivalence that might still get in the way of the final commitment. Be ready to respond to any last minute hesitations and to reinforce the positive consequences of a well-thought-out giving decision.

Stage Four: Action (or "I'm doing it for the first time.")

Congratulations! Your prospect has made a gift. They are feeling great and so are you.

Stage Five: Maintenance (or "I've made this a continuing habit in my life.")

So how can you make a habit of this great new feeling?

First, make sure to tell your donor how good you feel. A prompt, personalized and personal thank you is absolutely critical at this stage.

But as every fundraiser knows, one gift from a new donor does not signal a lasting commitment. Direct mail fundraisers tell us that over 50 percent of new donors never make a second gift. Even donors who have named your institution in their will can just as easily write you out again.

Think of the first gift as a test, a trial run. Your job is to help reinforce for your donor that this was a good decision and that you will fulfill the promise that was inherent in the act of giving.

You can help your donor move from action to maintenance by providing positive benefits for their action and reinforcing their relationship with your organization.

In her ground-breaking work *Donor-Centered Fundraising*, researcher Penelope Burk reports what donors want from our nonprofits. *More than anything else*, Burk tells us, *donors want to know that —*

1. *their gift was received, and you were pleased to get it;*
2. *the gift was 'set to work' as intended; and*
3. *the project or program to which the gift was directed had or is having the desired effect.*

Reinforce initial acts of giving by providing your donors with meaningful information throughout the year. *Show* your donors how their gift made a difference. Tell stories of change in your printed or online newsletters, and annual reports. Tailor your communications to your donors' needs. Invite them again to visit, and if they desire, keep them informed of important new happenings through phone calls, letters or email.

Respect your donor's wishes for public recognition—it can be reinforcing for donors who want it, and have negative implications for those who don't.

The Value of Models

Models work for me because they help bring meaning and structure to what otherwise might feel like random activities. Tested models of change like this one can help provide the conceptual underpinning to our fundraising experiences—why most individuals aren't ready to make a gift upon first contact, why it takes time to develop lasting donor relationships and why some actions are effective and others aren't.

Approaching personal philanthropy as a process, as a set of stages that we can help facilitate prospective donors through, helps us more effectively focus our activities and sustain our efforts—even on those days when it feels as if we aren't making forward progress.

Donors' Interests First!

Philanthropy is a voluntary act. As fundraisers we provide support to individuals who are searching for ways to make a difference in the world. We present our own organizations as a voluntary option for achieving our donors' quests. We shouldn't use a model of behavioral change to manipulate, coerce or trick donors into giving. As ethical fundraisers, we always place donor interests first.

principle

As we know in fundraising, "timing is everything." Prochaska's model of change helps us understand "what time it is" in the minds of our prospects and donors.

 Connect with Gayle at http://charitychannel.com/cc/gayle-gifford

Cultivating Big Gifts from First-time Donors

By Margaret Guellich, CFRE

Today's donors require cultivation. Every major gift officer lives by this directive. But cultivation starts way before the donor reaches the major gift prospect pool. In fact, sometimes the donor gets into the pool because of cultivation from the ground up.

The Annual Fund's Role in Cultivation

The annual fund, which for many organizations relies heavily on direct mail, or direct response, is frequently referred to as the workhorse of all development. We all hear the stories of the twenty-five dollar donor who leaves your organization $1 million in a bequest! Or the monthly donor who wins the lottery and shares it with your organization. The reason this happens is usually because the annual fund is doing its job: communicating, storytelling, teaching credibility and acknowledging.

How is this done? You might be mailing to thousands of people. How can you possibly cultivate *all* those donors? How can you make them feel special? As the workhorse, the annual fund can cultivate the hundreds or thousands and effectively raise their gifts to the leadership, major gift and ultimate gift level. These ideas are common sense and have been around as long as I have been in fundraising—and that's a long time. So, put on your donor hat and let's examine a few of those strategies for renewing donors.

Welcome Aboard

When a donor first comes on board, treat them with care. Remember how much it cost to acquire them and that you need to get at least three gifts before they begin to make a serious commitment to your organization.

Avoid Assuming New Donor is New!

All "new donors" are not new. The donor might already be in your database with different information such as a misspelled name. Be cautious with your welcome wording and work with your gift processing staff so duplicates are not added. Make sure they are coded properly so acknowledgments and welcome packets are appropriate.

Welcome, care for and thank but don't smother! Think back to your first gift to a group. What would you like in return? A thank you call? A prompt acknowledgement? A special acknowledgement? More information? There's nothing like saying back to a donor, "I noticed you (*special* you) and I am now communicating with just you."

Too many organizations put together an overwhelming welcome packet—brochure, pictures, book and many times a 'dear friend' acknowledgement! And too many donors are thinking, "You just spent all the money I contributed," or, "I'll never get through all this stuff!" Welcome packets should be brief but informative. Supply credibility information and facts. Tell donors how important their gifts are and what those gifts help you do. And do it promptly—within forty-eight hours of receiving the gift is a good rule of thumb.

New Donor Program

After a new donor comes on board, it is easy to roll them right into the current renewal program. After all they now need to be renewed. Right? Yes and no. These new donors really need special treatment. They need more information about your organization than what was sent in the acquisition package. Feed them that information by rolling them into a special *new donor program.* This special program is easy to monitor and can really help with getting that second and third gift so building donor commitment to your organization happens in a short period of time. Steps to take include:

1. Sending a renewal appeal with the *best* results within the last year or eighteen months;

2. Sending an appeal with more credibility information, e.g. financial statistics, numbers served; and

3. Calling the donor to renew them instead of using mail.

These steps are tried and true often increasing results by 20 percent. When using this strategy, focus on getting another gift rather than an upgraded gift. Don't forget to acknowledge. Keep the donor in the new donor mail program—Steps 1 and 2. Use Step 3 for donors who have not yet made a gift through Steps 1 and 2.

Calling donors should be simple and easy. The script should be based in acknowledging support, providing information and indicating urgency. Speaking directly with donors provides you with information about the donor and donor giving. This cultivation/solicitation call supports previous mailings and is most often welcomed by a new donor—contrary to how fundraisers themselves feel about phone calling!

Thank You Acknowledgement Calls

There's an old saying that we should thank our donors seven times before asking for the next gift. Some donors might take exception to that philosophy but most donors don't mind the attention. Besides an appropriate and timely acknowledgement through the mail that meets tax regulations, you should set criteria for thank you phone calls. These calls can be short and to the point or long and chatty. Let the donor set the pace of the call.

Who should call? (This list is *not* prioritized.)

1. Board members;

2. Chief development officer;

3. Program staff;

4. Financial development staff;

5. Volunteers;

6. Professional communicators; or

7. Clients or users of your services.

> ### Track Your Donors Carefully
>
> If a donor renews by phone be sure to be able to track that for the future. Those donors might be phone donors and not mail donors—meaning they will only renew by phone.

practical tip

Please put your donor hat on again and recall the last time you received a thank you call. Are you thinking? And thinking? Have you ever received one? I did once, about seven years ago, and I still give to that group. That's because I remember who made that call and what the executive director said to me. If you've never received a thank you, I am sooo sorry because it reflects one of our core values as fundraisers: being donor-centered.

The script is simple and requires a quick jump to the words thank you. Trust me, if you don't get to thank you quickly, the donor thinks it is a telemarketing call and hangs up. I've even had that happen to me when I've returned a call from a donor.
State your name, where you are from and that you're calling to say thank you very much for the recent gift. Tell the donor how important the gift is and how important they are to the mission of

your organization. I will frequently ask the donor how they got to know the organization. You'll be surprised what donors will share! (They might not remember exactly *how much* they gave but they will tell you *why* they give). Examples would include passion for your mission, guilt, a desire to make a change, knowledge of someone who uses your services. This information is critical for major gift planning so make sure that you put a summary in the notes section of the donor file for future reference.

> ### Welcome New Donors
>
> Ask board members and volunteers to call new donors to welcome them to the organization. This gives credibility to the organization.
>
>

Your first question is probably how to keep tabs on who's doing what calls and following up with notes for the donor's record. Although having notes from the call is important the process is not fool proof. You'll have more control over getting information from staff rather than volunteers and board members. So, don't be disappointed. Simply do the best you can. Be a cheerleader and give the callers what they need to be successful.

Your next question is having professional communicators call. Sometimes an organization is blessed with having thousands of donors giving one hundred dollars or more. Many times this size gift is the criteria for calling. Because it is important to make that call, communicators outside of the organization are hired. Frequently these calls are cheaper than solicitation calls with the added feature of copious notes from the caller. The professional call should be transparent to the donor. The only difference would be that the caller will not know many details about the organization, making it critical for development staff to read through notes and to plan follow up calls.

Handwritten Notes

First get some nice note cards with your logo. If it is appropriate, you can add pictures drawn by children served or photos of people being served on the cards. The card should also include your address, phone number and website. The card should be functional and just big enough for three or four sentences. I usually sign my first name and enclose my business card and an insert left over from one of the recent mailings.

> ### Handwritten Notes
>
> Handwritten notes can also be sent to donors who call in for any reason even to complain about too much mail. Don't underestimate their value.
>
>

Handwritten notes should definitely go to donors not reached on the phone. Remember these are not replacements for the formal tax acknowledgement but in addition to those letters. Handwritten notes might also go to donors who have given within the last year *and* have been on giving for a number of years. This strategy can precede a planned giving mailing featuring wills or charitable gift annuities. Your long term donors are prime prospects for future support through any planned instrument.

Cultivating donors is as much part of the overall annual fund strategy as the plan to obtain the first gift or the renewal gift. Creating ways to touch base and make a donor feel important and critical to your organization's mission goes much further than spending inordinate amounts of time preparing the ask!

 Connect with Margaret at http://charitychannel.com/cc/margaret-guellich

Making it Work: Managing the Development Office

By Gayle L. Gifford, ACFRE

In preparing for a workshop called "Managing the Development Office," I paused to reflect on my many years of experience as a development director, senior manager and consultant.

Using my favorite mind-mapping software to organize my thoughts, here's what my workshop outline looked like:

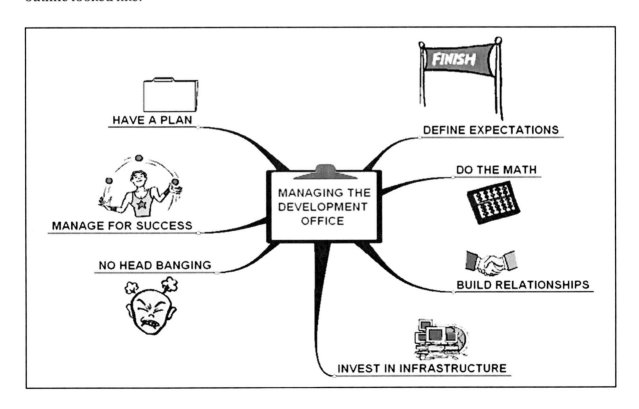

It looks like a whirlpool, doesn't it? I think it's much more reflective of what life is like in an organization than any neatly boxed flow chart.

Let me take you through each element.

Define Expectations

Every good leader keeps their eye on the prize. For such a leader, lofty goals and more achievable shorter term objectives drive all activities. Such is true of the fund development leader. So how does your department help the whole organization reach its broader objectives?

Maybe this sounds obvious—raise the money, right? Yes, but, that's not all. Here's an example.

I was once the director of development at an environmental nonprofit. While we needed to raise more money annually, we also needed to increase the numbers of our members. Now, strictly from a fundraising perspective, the $25 and $35 donors contributed a relatively small proportion of the total dollars raised but consumed a big share of the development budget. Yet, because we sometimes needed legislation passed (or stopped) at the state house, we were aware of the political clout that a large base of members brought with it. So, money and numbers were both important.

Once you've got the big picture, then you're ready to collaboratively define with the other members of your department how each person contributes to the success of the department and the organization. Ask yourself: What is success for my membership coordinator? For my major gifts officer? My database manager?

Your staff needs to know what they are expected to deliver, and *why it matters*.

Have a Plan

Your fund development plan is likely to contain three major elements:

1. The plan to get the money in the door—*the solicitation plan*;

2. The plan to keep donors well-informed, appreciated and connected to your organization for the long haul—the *stewardship plan*; and

3. The plan for how the department will run like the well-oiled machine it needs to be— *the management plan*.

I won't go into detail about the first two components of the plan, but let me say a little more about the management plan. Items to include in this plan include how you'll build the expertise and performance of your team (both staff and volunteers), what you'll need in the way of technology (e.g. donor management software), research and analysis, planning, budgeting, and any other supporting activities you can think of.

Do the Math

Good development managers inhale data and use it to make wise decisions. One of the cool aspects about fundraising is that you can count and analyze numbers and calculate results—a lot easier than, in my opinion, trying to determine the impact of your *stop smoking* education campaign.

Now, don't go too data crazy. What you are trying to understand is what works and what doesn't—both in the short term and projected into the future. Remember, to stay even financially, your organization must retain the donors it has acquired and replace the donors *and* the donations it loses. To grow, you've not only got to stay even but also raise more money, either by acquiring more donors or increasing the giving of the donors you already have.

Build Relationships

Of course you know about building relationships with donors. But have you paid attention to the other relationships that really make a difference in your work. For example, it's hard to get grants written without the support of program staff or to make purchases without the support of finance. And you depend on really good partnerships with your CEO, other members of your management team and your volunteer leadership, especially your board.

I highly recommend building relationships outside of your organization. Your fundraising colleagues can be great sources of new ideas, policy templates, referrals and a sympathetic ear when you really need it. I also found that some of the best training I got was free—from vendors who walked me around their facilities and shared their amazing technical knowledge in aspects of my job like direct mail, printing, graphic design, or postal regulations. Other community institutions have also been great partners—providing interns, research, or even background information on complex issues.

Invest in Infrastructure

It is really hard to run a growing and dynamic fundraising program when you don't have quality donor management software, access to the internet, online giving capabilities, ready access to your budget and in-house networks, among others. Enough said.

Manage for Success

All the best plans and technology are just paper and machines without the people who put them into action. It really makes a difference to have competent, enthusiastic staff, with a quest for excellence and knowledge, as part of your team. Nurture them. Give them the authority and feedback they need to do their jobs well. Remember that their personal lives are really important too—life outside the office helps all of us be happier and more informed employees. Celebrate success.

Stop the Head Banging

I've seen too many development directors spend too much of their psychic energy trying to move immovable objects (darn those board members for not doing what I think they should!!). Unless you've got some pretty significant leverage, it's really hard forcing other people to do things they don't want to do.

Instead, the best strategists figure out how to move around resistance. They identify what does work, and do more of it.

I happen to believe that people should be energized and enthused about their choice of work. After all, we spend so much of our time there. When I reached the point that I couldn't stand coming home every day angry and frustrated by a job, when it no longer satisfied me, I knew it was time to move on. Sometimes that's the best decision any manager can make.

 Connect with Gail at http://charitychannel.com/cc/gayle-gifford

Return on Investment: Getting the Most from Your Fundraising Efforts

By Norman Olshansky

You are an executive or development professional of a nonprofit who has been in your position less than a year. You know the honeymoon is over. One of the many issues you want to address is the concern that so much of your fundraising time, energy and resources are spent planning fundraising events. It seems like the mission of your agency has shifted, and staff as well as volunteers spend more time planning parties than delivering service.

Fundraising events can and do play an important role in many nonprofits. However, too many organizations do not fully understand how to maximize their fundraising efforts.

This might seem like blasphemy to some, but I believe that events should primarily be utilized to attract new donors, cultivate existing donors and volunteers, say thank you to your donors, volunteers and staff, and/or to provide community education. *For most organizations, events (with a few notable exceptions) should not be undertaken if they are expected to provide a good financial return on the organization's investment of time and resources to produce the event.*

According to *Giving USA*, published by the Giving Institute, approximately 75 percent of all charitable contributions come from individuals. It is also well known that 80 to 90 percent of all funds raised from those individuals are from the top 10 percent of donors. In other words, major giving is where it's at. This is not to preclude the importance of broad-based memberships and giving at all levels, but rather to focus your fundraising energies on the best return on investment (ROI) of time, staff, volunteers, and other resources, facilities, etc.

Fundraising Costs and Return on Investment—National Averages		
Method	*Cost*	*Return on Investment*
Direct mail to general lists (non-donors)	115%	-15%
Special Events	50%	50%
Planned Giving	25%	75%
Direct mail to prior donors	20%	80%
Foundations/Corporations	20%	80%
Major Gifts	5-10%	90-95%
National Average, all methods	**20%**	**80%**

(Based on: Greenfield, James, *Fund Raising: Evaluating and Managing the Fund Development Process.* Second Edition. The NSFRE/Wiley Fund Development Series. New York: John Wiley & Sons, Inc., 1999.

The chart indicates that you would need to spend $1.15 in order to raise $1.00 through direct mailings to general lists. To solicit major gifts, you would spend 5 to 10 cents to raise $1.00.

When calculating ROI, keep in mind the indirect costs associated with fundraising. For example staff costs are not just for those who are directly involved with fundraising. Other staff and administration typically are involved as well, albeit to a lesser extent. The costs associated with staff and volunteer time, facility usage, overhead expenses, as well as out of pocket direct costs should all be factored into determining ROI.

From an ROI perspective, it costs less and produces more income to raise major gifts than to use other methods of fundraising. While a variety of methods should be used in each organization, all too often, nonprofits tend to utilize, to a disproportionate degree, those methods which produce the lower returns, (events and direct mail) rather than those that are more effective (major gifts).

Major gift fundraising requires more relationship building and time cultivating potential donors. But the return is so much greater than what can be accomplished with other methods. A major event or gala could take four to six months or more to plan, might involve multiple committees, ten to a hundred volunteers, and most of your staff. One board member and one staff person could spend two to three months with three or four potential major donors and raise five to ten times what the fundraising event or gala raised as net income.

Work with your accounting/budgeting department/staff to allocate the cost of staff time based upon their involvement with the event or fundraising activity. Add that amount to your financial report on the fundraising program or activity. Even without adding volunteer time, you will find, in most cases, that your bottom line net gain from the event is much less of a percentage of the total gross revenues than you had expected.

Special events can build excitement, engage people, and provide enjoyable opportunities for volunteers but they typically cost too much to produce to justify the amount of money they raise, especially in smaller organizations. As a result, most organizations are reducing the number of events they hold and are putting more emphasis on major gifts and planned giving.

Using the return on investment approach to analyze fundraising performance is an excellent way to engage leadership and staff on how best to plan your future fundraising activities. You will find that board members who have for-profit business experience will likely better understand such an approach to planning and resource allocation.

 Connect with Norman at http://charitychannel.com/cc/norman-olshansky

Annual Giving: A Letter Once a Year Does Not Make an Annual Appeal!

By Linda Lysakowski, ACFRE

Many organizations say that they have an annual appeal, but upon further investigation, what the annual appeal consists of might be a letter sent to donors or prospective donors once a year. A strong annual giving appeal consists of far more than just an annual direct mail appeal. For most successful organizations, annual giving might include personal visits with individual major donors, a corporate appeal, a telephone campaign, Internet fundraising and direct mail.

The first step is to understand that annual giving is an important component of your organization's development program for several reasons:

- ◆ It is generally unrestricted money that can be used for operating expenses such as salaries.

- ◆ It helps you build relationships with new and existing donors.

- ◆ The methods and techniques used can lay the groundwork for your other fundraising efforts such as planned giving and capital campaigns.

- ◆ It is the best way to bring donors into your organization for the first time, donors which can be cultivated for major gifts in the future.

For successful development programs, the annual giving appeal is a major focus of the development plan and these organizations attempt to diversify both their constituent base and the fundraising methods they use to approach these constituents.

Diversifying Constituents

As most development professionals know, approximately 83 percent of all contributions in the United States come from individuals (including bequests); approximately 13 percent come from foundations and 4 percent from corporations and businesses (from *Giving USA* 2010's report on 2009 giving). Therefore, for your organization to be successful, focus most of your fundraising efforts on individual giving. However, don't ignore foundations and corporations as these are also good sources of funding. Foundations, in general, prefer supporting specific programs, so will not be addressed here. Corporate fundraising, however, is often unrestricted and should be considered as part of your annual giving program.

Your annual approach to individuals does not necessarily mean that you contact your donors just once a year. Some donors respond to direct mail as often as monthly, others will contribute several times a year if you have a compelling case for support. Major donors might prefer being approached just once a year. It is important that you have a plan that outlines who will be contacted, how they will be approached, how often and when.

Some other groups constituents appeals you should include are your annual board appeal, a staff appeal, and appeals to various other constituencies including vendors of your organization, groups such as alumni, parents, students, clients, members, volunteers, patrons, attendees at performances etc. Each of these groups will be part of your annual appeal strategy and you will contact each group separately with a personalized approach appropriate for each.

The most effective way to plan the annual appeal is to list your constituent groups and then plan an appeal for each. Here are some steps that can help you with the annual fund appeal.

◆ Develop the overall case for support for your annual appeal.

◆ Prepare position descriptions for all volunteers.

◆ Recruit an annual appeal chair that will be recognized by most of your constituents.

◆ Develop a list of your various constituency groups.

◆ Work with your annual fund chair to recruit a chair person for each division of the annual appeal. This should be one who represents that constituency and will be recognized and respected by their fellow constituents, i.e. alumni who are well known and respected by other alumni.

◆ Determine the number of constituents in each division, the level of gifts you will be soliciting from each group.

◆ Determine what materials need to be developed from your case for support for each division (For example the corporate appeal might use a one-page fact sheet while your alumni and parents might need a tri-fold brochure and your major gift prospects might require personalized proposals).

◆ Select the methods you will use to approach each constituency—in person calls, phone appeal, direct mail, and Internet.

◆ Plan the timeline and set goals for each division.

◆ Recruit volunteers to help in each division.

◆ Run each appeal as a separate appeal with its own goal, timeline and materials.

Diversifying Approaches

When planning how each group of prospects will be approached, one good rule of thumb is to look at the 95/5 Rule (or the 90/10 Rule), recognizing that 5 percent of your donors will generally account for 95 percent of your donations, (this may be translated as 90 percent of contributions coming from 10 percent of donors for some organizations). A little research of your organization's donor records will help establish a plan to contact the top 5-10 percent of your donors in person each year.

Other donors, falling in the majority of 90-95 percent of donors who account for 5-10 percent of contributions can be approached by mail, telephone, or the Internet. Telephone approaches work best when you contact people who already have a relationship with your organization—members, existing donors, clients, etc. Others, such as names contributed by staff or board members, names acquired through list brokers, etc, are often best approached by direct mail.

Approaching current donors or friends by phone is almost always more effective than direct mail, because this approach is more personal. Volunteers or professional telephone fundraising firms can be used effectively for phone appeals, depending on the number of individuals to be called, the purpose of the call, and the availability of volunteers.

Direct mail, likewise, can be done in-house or through a direct mail firm. Again the number of individuals to be approached, your organization's budget, the ability of your organization to prepare and mail the appeal will usually help you decide the method to use.

Internet fundraising is becoming more effective as it becomes more popular. Again, it can be done in-house if your organization has the tools to effectively set up and manage the program. Third party vendors are also available to set up programs, usually with a small percentage of the donation charged for managing the process.

You will be most successful if you can make personal visits to that top 5-10 percent of your donors. Approaching these donors in person is always the most effective way to raise money. Board members and other volunteers are often very effective in making personal calls especially when teamed up with the executive director or chief development officer.

Corporate contributors are best approached in person, unless there is a corporate foundation that handles requests through a grant proposal process. Small businesses or corporations that do not have a foundation, often make their decisions by either a committee or one individual, usually the owner or manager. For this type of approach, volunteers who represent your local business community can be very helpful in planning and implementing a corporate annual appeal.

Before starting your annual appeal make sure you have the systems in place to acknowledge, recognize and steward gifts properly. You should establish, as part of your development plan, a strategy to use the most effective methods to reach the broadest base of constituents with the greatest number of staff board and volunteers you have available.

 Connect with Linda at http://charitychannel.com/cc/linda-lysakowski

How to Develop a Strong Fundraising Board

By Norman Olshansky

How can nonprofit organizations increase revenues? This is one of the most frequent issues that I am asked to address as part of my consulting practice.

Most nonprofits depend upon private philanthropy (in addition to user fees, memberships, grants, earned income, ticket sales, etc.) to support their operation. According to the Giving Institute, 75 percent of all charitable contributions come from individuals. So if the largest portion of philanthropy comes from private, (individual) sources, what is the best way to seek out those funds?

There is a direct relationship between fundraising success and the quality of volunteer and professional organizational leadership. Better leadership equals better success.

Nonprofit boards are usually populated by individuals who are committed to the mission of the organization. Many have come up through the ranks as volunteers within the organization. Others are on the board based upon their professional expertise in the areas related to the organization's service, operations or administration. All too often, however, boards are lacking in members who have the characteristics necessary to obtain significant private philanthropic support from individuals. In addition, staff members are often ill prepared to be successful fundraisers, especially in the area of major gifts.

Staff members need to be trained, mentored and encouraged to engage in those activities that will contribute to fundraising success. New hires should be selected, in part, on their ability to provide professional leadership to the fundraising process.

If your board does not have sufficient members who have major gift fundraising experience, access to wealth in the community, and the ability themselves to be philanthropic leaders for the organization, you might need to take steps to make needed changes/additions. Your goal should be to bring onto the board and fundraising committee(s) individuals who have a positive passion for your organization's mission, are known and respected leaders in your community, have the ability to inspire others, can recruit additional leadership, are able to make a major gift to your organization and can open doors to other major donors. Your organization should be among their top philanthropic priorities during the length of their service on the board or fundraising committee.

Many organizations are at a loss on how to recruit board members with the above characteristics. If yours is one of those that does not have a strong board and needs to bring on new people, the following are a few steps you can consider.

1. Appoint a three to five member nominating committee drawn from your most prominent board members, current supporters and past chairs.

2. Have this committee, with staff input, develop a position description for leadership which includes expectations for participation, attendance, philanthropy, and committee involvement. Establish what will be the length of service. Identify your expectations of time commitment, including time needed for the review of minutes and other materials in preparation for meetings.

3. Review prospect lists you've developed, as well as other input from leadership and staff, for names of individuals who would be ideal to involve in your leadership. Think

---

Fundraising Axioms

◆ You don't get if you don't ask.

◆ Connect to passions, hearts and minds before you connect to wallets.

◆ The quality of a gift is directly related to the quality of the relationship between the solicitor and prospect.

◆ Fundraising is both an art and a science. Success requires both.

◆ Most worthwhile endeavors, including fundraising, start with a clear vision/plan and require lots of planning, preparation, hard work, engagement of leadership and strategic execution.

◆ You can never thank a donor, volunteer or staff member too often. They are the keys to your success.

practical tip

high and boldly. Look at names of philanthropists and other leadership who have been successful with other organizations. Prioritize prime candidates with whom you have or can obtain access.

4. Cultivate your top choices by inviting them to visit your organization and/or participate in small group briefings about your work. Provide a quality experience for the prospective leader when they visit/tour your operations.

5. Based upon their desire to learn about your organization and their reactions to cultivation activities, approach the key leadership prospects to obtain their willingness to have their names put into nomination for a board or key committee position. Show them the list of people who are being considered. This will demonstrate to them the quality of people with whom you will be talking. Tell them that you are interviewing many people on the list to determine if their names should be put into nomination. Ask what they know and what their feelings are, about the mission and work of your organization following their visits and involvement in the cultivation briefings. After you answer any questions they have, show them the position description for leadership and ask if they would be willing to be considered, among others, for submission to the nominating committee. Emphasize that only a few of the people submitted, will be asked if they can be nominated for a slate to be presented to the existing board/membership. Ask for their bios, list of nonprofit board and leadership experience, and professional accomplishments. The purpose of this strategy is to build status for participation.

6. Avoid presentations about existing weakness or the need to upgrade leadership. However, answer all questions honestly. If describing challenges facing the organization, also describe the opportunities that can be capitalized upon with proper leadership and vision. Make sure that the people talking to them are the select group that was recruited for the nominating committee. In addition you might want to involve your key professional from your organization (executive director, CEO, etc.) in the prospect meetings.

Recruiting the right people into leadership, who have demonstrated fundraising success in the past, in addition to training and mentoring existing leadership and staff in the art and science of fundraising will give your organization a tremendous return on investment.

 Connect with Norman at http://charitychannel.com/cc/norman-olshansky

Creating a Fundraising Board

By Linda Lysakowski, ACFRE

"We can't get our board to help with fundraising; they aren't the 'movers and shakers' in town." If this is a statement you have heard in your organization, read on!

While some organizations do not set fundraising as a priority for its board members, most nonprofits can benefit from having a board more actively using their connections to benefit the organization.

The key to getting your board to embrace fundraising lies in three simple steps—-the recruitment process, assuring that board members are committed to the organization and removing the fear of fundraising that is inherent in most people. In this article, I will address these issues. First, let's talk about the recruitment process.

Recruiting the Right Way

Often, boards are reluctant to fundraise because they have not been recruited with that purpose in mind. For many organizations, fundraising has never been a part of their culture for various reasons—perhaps in the past they relied on government funding, fees for service or foundation grants. Then suddenly, when these funding sources shift priorities and income streams dry up, the organization decides it now needs to rethink fundraising and is stymied by how to introduce this concept to the board. Even if the organization originally intended for its board to be involved in fundraising, many times, board recruiters are reluctant to use the "F" word for fear of scaring off potential board members. Many well-intentioned organizations operate under the noble idea that, "once they get on our board and see the great work we are doing, they will want to go out and ask for money." Wrong! If they have not been told up front that fundraising is a part of their role, they will not embrace it later when you decide to "slip it into" their job description.

One key concept to consider is *who* does the recruiting for new board members. Instead of a nominating committee that meets once a year to fill vacant seats, one recommended approach is to have a year round board resource committee. (This committee can also be called the governance committee or the committee on directorship or any name with which your organizations feels comfortable.) Whatever the title, the important things to remember about this committee are:

◆ It should meet year round.

◆ It needs to be chaired by the strongest person on the board.

◆ Its duties include doing an assessment of board performance, both the board as a whole and each individual board member.

◆ It is responsible for developing or refining board position descriptions.

◆ It evaluates the needs of the board and develops a profile of the kinds of people that are needed to fill vacancies on the board.

◆ It works with the board to help find the right people to fill board positions.

◆ It assures diversity on the board.

◆ It implements, along with senior staff members of the organization, board orientation.

◆ It is responsible for ongoing education of the board.

A board resource committee, working thoughtfully, diligently and on an ongoing basis can make all the difference in the world between an effective, enthused, and inspired board and a lackadaisical board that does not understand its role in advancing the organization's mission and is reluctant to become involved in the fundraising process. One of the key roles of this important committee is to develop a board position description that includes a required financial contribution from each board member as well as the expectation that each board member be involved in the organization's fundraising efforts through attendance at events, planning development activities, and helping to identify, cultivate and solicit potential donors.

This committee is also responsible for assuring that the position descriptions are not glossed over during the recruitment process and to make sure that each potential board member understands that fundraising is an important part of his or her role as a board member. They must be expected to deal with potential board members that are obviously reluctant to accept this responsibility. It is better to turn away a prospective board member who is not willing to get involved in fundraising, than to 'fill a seat with a warm body' just so the committee can say it has met its expectation to bring on a certain number of new board members each year. The reluctant fundraiser might instead be invited to serve on a committee or in some other volunteer position, other than being invited to serve as on the board.

Now that you have a board in place with the diverse skills and talents and connections you need to expand your resource development program, where do you start?

Uncovering the Spheres of Influence

Once the board is recruited and each has made their personal financial commitment, the next step is getting them involved in the process of identifying, cultivating and soliciting donors. Remember, *every board member* has a sphere of influence that can be used to help your organization. They just need to be made aware of the value of their connections and how they can use those connections to help your organization. The following steps can help turn board members into "movers and shakers" in their own sphere of influence. (The same method has also been used with staff members to yield some amazing relationships.)

First, board members need to understand the development department and its role in the organization, as well as their own role in the development process. Start by holding a briefing session at a board meeting—board orientation is a good time to introduce this to new board members. A staff member can explain how important development is to the organization and what unfunded programs need support from private donors. You should explain the function of the development office and how the board and staff work together as a team to raise money. This is a good time to introduce board members to the fact that most giving comes from individuals. (The giving charts from *Giving USA* will be helpful handouts and are available through the Giving Institute.)

Next, schedule a brainstorming session in which board members (and staff) develop a list of people they know who could be potential donors. It is important not to start them out with a "blank slate." Giving people a blank sheet of paper and telling them to list people they know will almost certainly result in getting back a bunch of blank pieces of paper. Give them instead, some lists to spark ideas. A form to start ideas rolling is available at www.cvfundraising.com. You can also provide a list of people who already contribute to your organization and ask board members to discuss each name to determine "who knows whom."

The next step is refining the list into potential major donors, potential smaller donors and people about whom there isn't enough information to proceed further. A small group of staff and development committee members who are well connected in the community can do this, based on their knowledge of the person's ability, interest and the strength of the linkage with this prospect. The smaller donor prospects will be added to your mailing list to receive newsletters and direct mail, and the "unclassified" prospect list will need further research. This research can be assigned to staff or development committee members.

The final step in the identification process is a major donor screening meeting. Starting with the list identified as potential major donors, bring together the board and development committee members who have identified those people and review each name carefully. (This can be done in a series of meetings if the list is large.) Discuss each name to determine the ability (how much *could* they give if properly motivated and approached by the right person); the interest (are they known to give to causes similar to this organization's mission, have they given to the organization in the past, do they have any connection to the organization, is there a particular program of the organization in which this person might be interested?) and the linkage (who is the best person to contact this person; how strong is the connection; if there are several people who have a connection, which relationship is the strongest; is there a "team" of people from the organization who should approach this prospect?). It is crucial to understand that screening is a very sensitive issue and participants in this process must be carefully selected. Information that is sensitive should not be openly discussed. Participants can suggest giving amounts of areas of interest without discussing the prospects private details. And, of course no information about a donor's giving history should be given out unless that information is public information (listed on your organization's annual reports with the donor's permission for example).

This process will almost always uncover connections that most board members haven't thought about involving in the organization. A good facilitator is needed to help the board work though this process. A consultant, a board member or staff member who has gone through this process is essential. An experienced facilitator will be aware of privacy issues and organizational polices about what can be discussed within this group. Once the calls are assigned the next step will be the solicitation process.

Taking the Fear Out of Fundraising

So now you are ready to get your board out there making the "asks." Understand that most board members have a fear of fundraising. It has been said that the fear of public speaking is higher on most people's list than the fear of death. But that the fear of asking someone for money is probably a close second to the fear of speaking in front of a large group. The two most sensitive areas for discussion are often said to be death and money and when asking for planned gifts, you are usually discussing both. But let's start with little less-painful approach, the "ask" for the first gift to an organization which might lead to a future major gift.

The steps to a successful "ask" are:

    ◆ Make your own gift first.

    ◆ Ask a peer.

    ◆ Know the "case."

    ◆ Know your donor's needs and interests.

◆ Ask for a specific amount.

◆ Ask for enough.

◆ Analyze what you did wrong or right.

◆ Plan the next step.

First, board members need to get rid of their fear, and realize that they are not "begging for money," but rather giving someone an opportunity to be a part of the exciting work of your organization.

Board members need to understand that giving really does feel good and that being generous even makes people live longer!

Experiencing the Joy of Giving

Board members need to experience the joy of giving themselves before asking others to give. The board appeal, addressed elsewhere in this book, should always precede any public fundraising campaign. Board commitment will have a definite influence on your board's ability to ask others for money. The key thing all "askers" must do is to make their own gift first. It is a proven fact that those who have made a gift themselves will always be more successful at asking others to give, because they can ask them to "join me in investing in a great project."

> Doug Lawson describes philanthropy as the bringing together of a "joyful giver, a grateful recipient and an artful asker."
>
>

Ask a Peer

Through the screening process already discussed, board members will have identified people with whom they have a relationship and feel comfortable asking so the next step of asking a peer is already taken care of. In most cases, the asker should be giving at a level equal to what they are asking others to give. It is usually easier for people to ask someone they know than a total stranger. Of course, some board members might not understand this and feel reluctant to ask their friends. It all goes back to the compelling case—if a person really believes in the mission of the organization and knows others who share their values and beliefs; it is very likely that their friends will also be interested in supporting this organization. Always have them start with a call that is likely to be successful. It also helps to "stack the deck" and assign calls that are sure to be successful. Nothing builds success like success and a board member who has made that first successful call will be far more motivated to continue making calls.

Make it Easy for Your Board

It is important not to ask too much of board members, especially the first time around. No board member should be asked to make more than about five calls. That is usually a manageable number for most people. Staff also needs to provide the board members any information that will be helpful in their call—the donor's past giving history to the organization, if any; other gifts that this person might have made in the community (a little research will help build the chances for a successful call); any connection this prospective donor has to your organization or interest in specific programs of the organization.

> ### It's About Relationships!
>
> Leadership must always be encouraging—remember that, especially if this is a first effort for the board, not all calls are going to be successful, but encourage solicitors to continue by stressing that they are building relationships and not just raising money. After all, the three keys to successful fundraising are Relationships, Relationships, Relationships.
>
> 👍 practical tip

Training Sessions

Bring in someone to train the board in how to make the "ask." Your training should include having them always ask for a specific amount for a specific project. And remember that people are very seldom, if ever, insulted by being asked for too much, but they can be insulted by being asked for too little. Role-playing is often a successful and fun way to help board members and other volunteers feel at ease before they have to ask for the "real thing."

A consultant or experienced development professional with experience in major gift fundraising will be needed to provide training on the techniques and the psychology of asking for money.

Evaluate and Plan

Make sure you schedule regular reporting meetings so board members can share successes and challenges they have faced. Knowing others are sharing their experiences helps build a team spirit on the board and helps solve some of the challenges that solicitors might be having. And of course everyone likes to report his or her success. Often the board has a healthy sense of competition once they get going and having an opportunity or report their success to others is a strong motivator for many people. This debriefing will help plan for the next approach to each prospective donor.

 Connect with Linda at http://charitychannel.com/cc/linda-lysakowski

The Annual Board Appeal

By Linda Lysakowski, ACFRE

Is it important, even necessary, for your board members to contribute to your organization's annual appeal?

Yes, for several reasons:

◆ It increases the level of "ownership" the board members feel towards your organization.

◆ It shows others that your board members are good stewards.

◆ It enables your organization to raise funds from foundations and other entities that ask—"How many of your board members have given?"

◆ It makes them feel good about their involvement with your organization and enables them to ask others for money!

While there might be some exceptions to this rule (a professional association that does not do fundraising, one that has a single source of funding such as a major grant, or one where board members serve on the board by virtue of their position in another organization) in most nonprofits board giving is essential. A board member who has made a financial commitment to your organization, regardless of the dollar amount, can then invite others to "join me in supporting this wonderful cause."

Okay, so now that we all agree it is important and necessary for the board to give, we are faced with several questions. How much, when, and how does this all happen?

How Much Should the Board Give?

I always discourage requiring board members to give a set dollar amount each year for several reasons—it limits you in recruiting board members who might have a lot of talent and skills but might feel hampered by the minimum level of giving. On the other hand, board members who could easily give more, tend to give at the stated minimum level because that is how they interpret the expectation for giving and assume that is what others are giving. Therefore it is better to stress in the board's position description that all board members are required to give at a meaningful level. The two key words are *all* (100 percent of the board should be giving annually) and *meaningful.* A good way for each board member to determine what is a meaningful level for them is to include in the board position description that the organization expects each board member to include it as one of the top two or three charities to which each board member will contribute each year. Board members should be rated by staff and a committee of the board individually for an appropriate "ask" amount.

When Do We Approach the Board for a Gift?

The board appeal should be completed before asking others to contribute. The best time to do the board appeal is at the very beginning of the fiscal year. For many organizations that are on a July-June fiscal year, summer is a good time to "gear up" for the fall campaign and having the board appeal out of the way during July and August put your organization in a good position to launch its annual appeal to the public. Just as with capital campaigns, annual giving should start "from the inside out" and "from the top down."

How Do You Get Started?

Start with a board appeal committee—the chair of the board, the chair of the development committee and as many other board members as are needed to personally solicit the board, keeping in mind that one solicitor should be responsible for no more than five calls. Committee members should be selected from those board members who are regular, generous givers themselves. The chief development officer should be part of the committee but, in general, should not solicit board members, except for the board chair who is often solicited by a staff person before the committee is appointed.

The committee should conduct a screening and rating session of the entire board. Treat the board appeal as you would treat any major fundraising appeal; make it personal, challenging and exciting. The committee should develop a proposed board goal after the screening and rating session and have the board approve this goal with a formal vote. This will enable the entire board to take ownership of the appeal. You will not need glitzy campaign material for the board appeal; after all, board members should know the "case," but a one page summary of the case and a graphic showing the importance of the board appeal can be very effective. This fact sheet should contain a pie chart with the annual fund broken down by categories, i.e. how much comes from grants, events, mail, board appeal, corporate, etc.). Another helpful tool a list showing board members various ways their support will be needed throughout the year. Most board members get annoyed at being "nickled and dimed" to death for every special event that comes along. A menu of options for how they can direct their support will be helpful, but should always include unrestricted board giving. It could also include things like purchasing a table at an annual dinner, sponsoring a golf tournament, etc. Board members will appreciate knowing up front what activities they will be expected to support throughout the year and that they can make their commitment as a part of the board appeal.

Training

The board appeal committee might need training in how to schedule the appointment and how to make an ask, but remember that the board appeal should be a serious effort with personal visit to the board members, not just having the board chair hand out pledge cards at meeting and say, "Okay everyone, make your commitment now." This method usually offends board members and results in a much lower gift than allowing the board member to feel special enough for a personal visit and a face-to-face opportunity for them to ask questions and share their interests.

What if Board Members Do Not Give?

Regular reporting of results at board meetings is critical and if there are board members who have not made their commitment by the end of the appeal, it might be necessary for the chief executive officer and the board chair to meet with these board members to determine if there is a problem that might require action. You should offer the board member options such as monthly giving, offering a one year pledge period, and suggesting that matching gifts from their company can help them give at a more significant level. Unless board giving has not been part of the expectations of board members, those who absolutely refuse to give should be asked to step down from the board and accept some other volunteer role within your organization. Explain to these board members that 100 percent giving from the board is essential to successful fundraising.

 Connect with Linda at http://charitychannel.com/cc/linda-lysakowski

Monthly Partners—Hidden Jewels in your Development Program

By Dr. John R. Frank, CFRE

W ho are the faithful friends of your organization? Who are the ones who are with you through thick and thin? The ones who make sure you get the gift even during the summer slump? Answer: your monthly partners. These disciplined, faithful, cause-driven donors are the ones who can keep your organization going, year after year.

Yet, they are many times overlooked because they might not appear to be "major donors." They might give small gifts, but month after month, and year after year, they truly become major contributors to your cause.

Why is a Monthly Partner Program Needed?

Here are the main reasons a monthly partner program is needed in every development strategy:

- ◆ You can increase your annual income.

- ◆ It helps build better relationship with your partners.

- ◆ Partners tend to stay with organization longer (90 percent continuity rate vs. 50 percent).

- ◆ Monthly revenue is predictable.

- ◆ It will lower fund raising costs.

- ◆ Your income will grow over time.

- ◆ Monthly giving is convenient for donors *and* for your organization.

These points all have a positive impact on an organization's overall success. While they are self-explanatory, once you begin your program, you will realize the results.

Start by creating a donor pyramid that shows how many people you have giving at various amount of money throughout a year. In the middle of this pyramid are the monthly givers. They do not usually give a large gift once or twice a year like a major donor, and they do not give like the impulse donors at the bottom of the donor pyramid who do not plan their giving. They have a giving plan and a budget and give every month to their favorite causes.

Development

I define *development* as creating opportunities to connect people to the causes they care about. This definition is at the foundation of why a monthly partner program is essential to every nonprofit development program. It is not about raising more monthly income, it is about creating a convenient way for people who care about your cause and want to give on a consistent and disciplined way.

The monthly partner is someone who gives to their favorite nonprofits on a monthly frequency. The amount does not matter, but rather their faithful giving that is their defining characteristic.

Every month after their house payment or rent, car payment, food, and whatever bills they have to pay, they *give* faithfully to your cause. That is reason to celebrate! What wonderful and generous people they are!

Essential Ingredients

Loyalty to donors brings loyalty to your cause. When you show your monthly partners that you care about them beyond just their money, you have a long-term partner.

For a successful program, you must have a strong mission and vision. Your monthly partners are prudent givers. These donors know about your mission and what you stand for. They want to know your vision for the future, and expect to be kept informed.

Effective communication strategies are critical, whether it is through email, invitations, newsletters, or traditional mail. This demands a well-managed system that will make sure every monthly gift is received, put in the proper account, receipted, and thanked. A monthly partner expects this type of system as part of good stewardship of the donor's contributions.

The monthly partner program must be part of integrated development strategy. It is to be part of a number of relationship strategies that connect various types of donors to your charity. While these donors are faithful and consistent, there are other donors who wish to give through different strategies. The monthly partner program must be a part of a well-designed relationship based development strategic plan.

Why Donors Support a Monthly Partner Program

Who are the people that give monthly? Why do they give this way? What makes them faithful? What does your organization need to do to keep them faithful?

Some of the answers are common sense. But many have to do with changing trends in giving (technology), the use of time, and generational shifts in views toward giving. It would be good to list some typical prospect groups to answer this question.

There is not enough room in this article to provide all of the research to list of the trends and issues. Suffice it to say monthly partners give monthly because it is best for *them*, not because someone wrote a book about it. The trends in society, the available technology, and other nonprofit issues have created a convenient and effective way for those who can give a little bit each month, to make a different in the cause of their heart.

It is up to us in the world of development to create convenient ways for the monthly giver to support our organizations.

Elements of the Monthly Partner Program

The key elements of a monthly partner are listed here. They are not exhaustive but give you a place to start your planning:

Marketing tools

> ◆ membership brochure;
>
> ◆ group name (yes, this is important to create an "insider" relationship);
>
> ◆ targeted segment to invite/honor;
>
> ◆ designated giving (if appropriate);
>
> ◆ marketing materials (letterhead, bookmark, membership card); and
>
> ◆ web page option to become a monthly partner.

Management

Your management system can be manual or computerized, but should include the following:

> ◆ consistent, proactive communication system;

◆ timing—calendar for invitations, newsletters, etc.;

◆ monthly update/reminder package (can also be electronic);

◆ response envelope;

◆ update letter;

◆ pledge reminder; and

◆ year-to-date report information.

Building the Relationship

Here are few ideas to keep and build the relationship with monthly partners:

> **Make Sure Your Program is Ready!**
>
> Make sure your program is ready to go before you offer it to anyone. Monthly givers are disciplined givers and expect the charities they commit to, to be able to keep them connected in a disciplined way.
>
>

◆ Draw them close—keep them informed of newsworthy events.

◆ Send invitations to special events/receptions.

◆ Hold a members-only open house (once a year, even if just to your administrative offices).

◆ Offer discounts on books, tapes, videos, etc.

Adding New Members

Every year it is important to add new members to your monthly partner program. I find that January and September are the most obvious times people start something new in their lives. This is a very good time to send an invitation to some of your more loyal donors and give them an opportunity to make a significant impact on your cause.

Another opportunity to join could be through an article in your newsletter. This could be a testimony from a current member who shares why they give monthly. People are encouraged to give by other people who endorse giving. The potential monthly giver will consider this as evidence that your monthly partner program has been proven successful.

At your special events, website, and other situations, have your monthly partner literature available. Give potential members the opportunity to consider how they can make a long-term impact on your cause.

In Summary

A well-designed and well-managed monthly partner program will find the "hidden jewels" of your faithful donors and connect them to your cause.

Here is a brief summary of steps to remember as you create your monthly partner program:

1. Create your partner club including name, benefits to membership, and letterhead/logo.

2. Create a membership brochure that includes the benefits info and options to give. (EFT, credit card, etc.)

3. Identify the faithful givers (those already giving nine to twelve times per year), and honor them by inviting them to be charter members of your new program.

4. Identify those who give four to eight times per year and invite them to join your new monthly giving program.

5. Create the management system to communicate, thank, receipt, and connect with your members.

6. Continue to grow the membership and appreciate their loyalty!

I have seen organizations start with a handful of members, and then grow to a large group that supports and sustains their organization through all seasons of giving. The monthly partner will become one of the key strategies in your overall development that builds relationships, honors the donor, and sustains your cause into the future.

I hope your hidden jewels become your loyal and faithful friends as together you will make an impact in your community and the world.

 Connect with John at http://charitychannel.com/cc/john-frank

Intro to Online Fundraising and Social Media

By Ted Hart, ACFRE

If you want to succeed online, heed this advice.

Just as it was with ePhilanthropy more than a decade ago, there are some people who suggest that social networking and web 2.0 sites are simply a fad, and will not prove helpful to fundraising. They were wrong then, and they are wrong now. Donor interactivity online and social networking are tools and techniques that have changed, and will continue to change, the way charities communicate with their supporters. The way these tools will succeed in helping most charities is through the use of people to people fundraising strategies. Just as with traditional fundraising, raising money using technology is all about relationships.

For charities looking to introduce these online social concepts to their fundraising strategy, it's important to know that they take time, attention, and good communication skills to succeed. A strong digital fundraising strategy is now a core asset of a well-run charity, and if it's not well-designed, it's going to do more damage than good.

> **Imagine the Potential!**
>
> The greater universe of potential lies in the vast number of supporters who can be inspired.

ePhilanthropy fundraising is now the fastest growing form of philanthropy around the world. In 2009, online giving in the U.S. grew to $15.48 billion (up from $10 million in 1999). As promising as those numbers are, those charities that continue to simply email their database seeking gifts from current supporters, or rely on a "donate now" button on their website, will be disappointed with the results. It takes serious strategy to succeed online. The ability to interact with supporters, and to inspire them to take action on the charity's behalf, is the most important difference between traditional offline fundraising and successful online fundraising. The possibilities online are endless! Donors are spreading the word, even faster than charities are themselves. Even start-up organizations can participate online, along with the long-established organizations in the online world.

I founded The ePhilanthropy Foundation back in 2000 to bring attention to the use of the Internet by charities around the world, and to help train charities in best practices of the web. I coined the phrase, 'ePhilanthropy,' to denote the convergence of philanthropy and the Internet. After eight years of service, the foundation concluded its work, and many have asked me, what comes next?

The answer came in this integration concept of people to people fundraising (p2pfundraising). This "next generation" of ePhilanthropy entails fundraising that is inspired by charities but is initiated by individuals. P2pfundraising techniques involve individuals using online tools, which might or might not be provided by the charity, to connect with their family, friends, and colleagues to raise money for and support the causes they care about. No longer will charities succeed only through direct solicitation of donors and prospects in their database. The greater universe of potential lies in the vast number of supporters who can be inspired and referred by current donors. A friend of a friend is much more likely to donate to a cause than a non-donor being solicited directly by the charity.

Your Website Is Now Your Front Door

Now, more than ever before, a charity's website is its front door. A well designed interactive website must be the first goal for every charity interested in both competing and succeeding. Well designed charity websites will meet six criteria for measuring effectiveness and will integrate social networking opportunities/web 2.0 tools. These tools will provide for interaction not only between the charity and the site visitors, but between site visitors and other supporters.

ePhilanthropy is More!
ePhilanthropy is much more than electronic direct mail.

If the website doesn't have something that inspires, if it doesn't have a strong "call to action," has no good original content, and is not well-designed, it's absolutely useless to try to do anything online.

Digital technology has given nonprofits new ways to pursue traditional strategies for involving more people more personally in their organizations, a critical step in raising money. There are infinitely more powerful tools available to use today—for even the smallest charities that don't have big budgets—to be able to do a better job. The core ways we raise money have not changed. It's still about people inspiring people.

Your website must provide opportunities for its supporters to contribute their own content by posting, leaving comments, uploading photos and videos, and leaving reviews of various sites and products. Strong communication and relationship building are the real drivers of fundraising success both online and offline. Charities who stick to these principles will learn that they are the road to their success. The Internet is an ideal platform from which to reach, inform, and engage current and potential donors, many of whom might be beyond the reach of traditional fundraising channels.

Email

When consumers want to share something from the Internet with their friends or family, such as a video, link or article, they are still overwhelmingly going to use email. Charities must maximize their efficient and effective use of email communication. Avoid one of the biggest errors made by any charity! Do not use email as if it were nothing more than electronic direct mail. It is more important to inspire the sharing of information than simply to send out large volumes of messages.

Website Benchmarking: Six Criteria for Measuring Effectiveness Online

1. Usability—is the site easy to use?

2. Accessibility—can everyone access the site?

3. Communication/Social Networking—can users communicate with the charity and each other?

4. Transparency—is the charity open with its information?

5. Responsiveness—Is giving, volunteering, fundraising, and corporate involvement encouraged and supported?

6. Housekeeping—does the charity put search engine optimization (SEO) into practice, and does the site support and work in harmony with social networking sites?

 practical tip

GuideStar

Nonprofits also should make it a priority to provide all the information they can about their organizations at www.guidestar.org. GuideStar is a website that features financial and programmatic information about nonprofits, and serves as an informal clearinghouse for institutional funders, individual donors, and anyone else interested in finding detailed information about nonprofits.

There's too much at stake not to optimize charity profiles on GuideStar. Many grant proposals you will write will be followed by that foundation or corporation checking the data about that charity on GuideStar. If you fail to provide the maximum updated information, you are putting the funding potential of your organization at risk.

Social Media

Only when a nonprofit has acted on the priorities of website, email and GuideStar, should it begin to think about social media tools like Facebook, Twitter and LinkedIn.

Rather than simply jump in and expect those tools to produce immediate results, you should take the time to learn how to use them, and should recognize that it takes time to build the kind of social capital that you will need to succeed using social networking.

In four to five years, having a strong social networking strategy will be as important as having a strong website today, so now is the time to build the strategy, now is the time to build the community, now is the time to build that social capital. It's not going to happen overnight. If you wait three to four years, you're going to be playing catch-up, and most likely your competition will have eclipsed you.

A Strong Social Networking Strategy

In four to five years, having a strong social networking strategy will be *as* important as having a strong website today.

 practical tip

---

Face to Facebook

To understand how to succeed using digital technology, you need only to understand fundraising at its most basic level—the right person asking for the right amount at the right time will always raise money, whether online or offline. Technology and social media are simply a set of tools that are available at the disposal of every charity. You will not go wrong if you treat a donor as a person, connecting the donor to your organization using the tools, but not substituting tools for relationship. Simply deploying a new tech tool will not in itself generate contributions.

It is not true that 'I Facebook, therefore I fundraise.' All that a connection on social media sites means is an invitation to communicate. The key is to be genuine. By allowing users to generate content themselves and create communities, it helps them to connect with people with whom they share common interests. You might never have the opportunity to meet face to face with all your donors, but you can still connect with them around causes they collectively support. By deploying these tools and techniques, your website becomes your organization's 24 hours/7 days a week advocacy, fundraising and education hub. It is the legions of supporters and the networks they represent that will make this promise a reality.

People to People Fundraising Strategy

Approach the Internet primarily as a communication tool, and secondarily as a fundraising tool. If you can build and enhance a relationship with a prospective donor, you have a much higher chance of successfully soliciting a gift.

By taking full advantage of social networking, you can utilize a whole new set of techniques and deploy a new generation of tools to inspire donors. You will learn, either now or later, that these techniques are important to your ability to remain charitable, to remain connected, and to your ability to reach out and give supporters the opportunity to connect with your cause. These techniques require you to learn to share control with your online community of supporters. This can be scary, this removal of complete control in the hands of your nonprofit. Gone are the days of word-smithing, creating and owning all content. People to people fundraising, social networking and other Web 2.0 tools involve inviting supporters and communities of people to become a part of your cause. Involvement of this sort, by supporters, will become as much a part of what it means to support your organization as is writing a check today.

For those that like to keep a tight rein over all communications, Web 2.0 can create an uncomfortable scenario. Over time, you will grow to understand the power and necessity of these tools. It is becoming more important to develop a strategy linking the digital life of donors and supporters to the charities they care about.

Social networking has become a major influence in connecting people to each other and to causes they care about. Sites such as Facebook, LinkedIn, Bebo, YouTube, and MySpace (and scores of others) have dramatically increased the awareness of charitable causes and events. These social networking sites create a buzz, and connect people to each other.

> **Courage!**
>
> It can be scary, learning to share control.
>
> **warning!**

As you begin venturing into the integration of social networking into your overall marketing and fundraising plans, here are ten easy tasks every nonprofit executive can deploy to start building social capital.

YouTube is a great way to advertise your organization or cause without paying a dime. Videos are uploaded onto the site and can be viewed perpetually. When a good video is posted on YouTube, the word spreads. Facebook users can post YouTube videos on their profiles and causes/events pages further expanding their reach. Smart charities do not post video directly to their website, but post to YouTube first, and then use that site's online technology to bring the video into their site. Similarly, sites like flickr.com and slide.com are recommended for photos.

Those who support nonprofits, and who tend to be passionate about a cause, will ultimately pass the word onto friends, family, and co-workers. Giving donors the chance to participate, and to contribute to the success of your organization beyond the gift online, is proving to be successful for nonprofits. Although using these new techniques will prove a serious area of growth, they challenge the traditional top-down, ask-give relationship that charities have traditionally had with their supporters.

Online fundraising and social networking combine into an important concept called people-to-people fundraising. Through social networking tools, online fundraising will begin to meet its true potential. Charities around the world are encouraged to let loose the reins, open their organizations, and encourage supporters to share content, get involved, post comments, and help spread the word. By learning to stop fundraising, and start inspiring, more friends will be made, more relationships will be built, and more money will be raised.

Ten Tasks to Build Social Capital

1. Join Facebook and LinkedIn Groups related to your cause.

2. "Like" pages and friend those who "friend" you.

3. Follow related Twitter hash tags (#).

4. Respond to every post on your wall.

5. Listen more than talk: social networks are not simply broadcast channels.

6. Update your "status" as often as possible.

7. Post pictures and video.

8. Post recommendations on LinkedIn, request them from others.

9. To build authenticity, cover special events before the event to build interest, and then report and include pictures afterwards.

10. Encourage people-to-people campaigning.

 Connect with Ted at http://charitychannel.com/cc/ted-hart

Integrating Individuals into Your Fundraising Plan: How to Start an Individual Giving Program

By Amy M. Eisenstein, MPA, CFRE

According to *Giving USA 2010*, individuals gave 75 percent of the donations to charity last year. That number increases to more than 80 percent when bequests are included, which leaves corporations and foundations contributing less than 20 percent. However, if your organization is like most nonprofits, you are probably highly focused on fundraising from corporations and foundations, and not concentrating nearly enough on individuals. If your fundraising revenue is dependent on grant writing, fundraising events, and perhaps an appeal or two, you will want to start incorporating individuals into your development plan.

There are a variety of reasons why organizations concentrate their fundraising efforts on corporations and foundations, and not on individuals, but I will simply say that one of the major reasons in my experience is that fundraising from individuals can be difficult and time consuming. However if you want your organization to raise big bucks, you will need to dive into this unknown territory.

Another reason that many organizations do not fundraise from individuals is because they don't know where to start. If that is you, you have come to the right place, so read on.

It is also important to understand that when you are fundraising from individuals, in a face-to-face way for the first time, it is unlikely that you will be asking for major gifts. It is a common misconception that all face-to-face asking is for enormous sums of money (major gifts). It is important to include person-to-person asking as a part of your annual campaign. This will significantly raise your annual campaign results and prepare you for any capital campaign and major gifts asking you wish to do down the road.

Where to Begin: Identifying Prospects

When trying to identify who the organization's individual prospects are for the first time, your database can be a goldmine. This is true only if you have built up a database of supporters. A good database should have all of your past donors, including those who have given through your annual fund or other appeal letters, attended or supported your events, foundation funders and anyone else who has donated to your organization. The database should contain all of your donors contact information, including name, address, email address, phone numbers, as well as their donation history. You (or someone at your organization) should be able to run reports from your database to identify your donor's largest gifts as well as their cumulative giving.

The first two things to look for when searching your data for prospects are:

    1. Highest (largest) donors.

    2. Most loyal donors.

Your highest donors might seem obvious, but be sure to identify both those who give one-time gifts as well as cumulative giving for the year. You might have some donors who give $1,000 at year-end, who appear to be your largest donors, but once you include cumulative giving, you might discover people who give more. An example is someone who gives $500 to your annual appeal at year-end, buys two tickets for $250 each to your annual event, and also supports your annual raffle by buying ten tickets. A simple search for large one-time gifts will not identify this individual because their giving is spread throughout the year, over several campaigns, appeals or events.

Your most loyal donors are those individuals who have given every year for the last several years, regardless of the amount, for five, ten or even twenty years, depending on how far back your data goes. These might not be your largest donors, but they are your most consistent and loyal donors and they are critically important to your annual fund.

As you might know, it costs more money to acquire a new donor than it does to retain an old one. Donor attrition is a major issue for many nonprofits, so it is extremely important to keep the donors you have, whenever possible. These donors, by staying loyal over a period of years are telling you loudly and clearly, that your organization is important to them. If I were you, I would want to get to know these individuals, find out what interests them about your organization, and why they are so loyal. Once they are treated like the VIP's that they are, you might find their giving skyrockets. Also, these are your most likely candidates for bequests or other types of planned gifts down the road.

If you do not already have a direct mail program, I strongly encourage you to start one. Although direct mail is expensive and might not pay for itself in the first few mailings, it is an important investment to make for your future individual giving program. Direct mail can be a wonderful way to raise unrestricted dollars and, as stated above, your data will ultimately become your portal into the world of individual prospects.

Direct mail is one way that individuals can begin giving to an organization. It is through direct mail that they identify themselves as interested in the organization and self-select as potential prospects for increased annual giving and possibly as major gift candidates.

In addition to your database, whenever possible, work with your staff and board members to identify prospects from their list of contacts and networks. If you do not have any data to start with, you will need to rely on your staff and board members to identify a list of people to meet.

Between the database reports of your largest and most loyal donors and the new names provided to you by your board and staff members, develop a list of the top twenty to thirty people that you will work with this year.

Now that you've found them, what should you do? Cultivation!

The next step in starting an individual giving program is to begin to build relationships with your donors or prospects. Cultivation can take many forms and is an ongoing process, but generally involves routine and regular contact with individual prospects to get to know them and educate them about your organization. You can invite them to your events, programs, graduations, on a tour, etc. It will also be important to meet with them in a one-on-one setting to really learn more about their needs and interests. Whenever possible, get board members involved in the process. Have board members do the initial inviting for a meeting or to an event, especially if the board member knows the prospect.

One of the common mistakes made by executive directors, development directors, and board members is that they are so eager to tell the story of the organization that they forget to listen and learn about the prospect. Listening to the prospects interests and particular needs is an important part of the process that fundraisers often miss.

One of the best ways to build relationships with potential donors is to get them involved with your organization. Find out if the person is interested in volunteering for your organization in any capacity, whether it is a one-time event or on a regular basis. They might want to get involved in a direct care capacity or on a committee of some type. Personal involvement will raise their commitment level and have an impact on increased donations like nothing else.

During the cultivation process, you should ask open ended questions to learn more about the person. For example:

1. Why is this organization important to you? Why are you interested in this charity?

2. Would you like to volunteer with the organization and how? (After you have reviewed the potential volunteer opportunities, which include a variety of choices.)

3. Which of our programs is most interesting to you and why?

4. Do you have any questions about the organization or anything we have discussed?

Before meeting with a prospect, always have a goal or outcome for the meeting and create a follow-up plan for your next contact with them. When you feel that the person is fully committed to your organization and your cause, and you know the answers to the above questions, it is time to ask for a gift (donation).

The Most Critical Step: The Ask

Everything discussed so far is leading up to the most important aspect of the fundraising process, the "ask." You will never get donations without asking, so it is critical to plan and execute this step, even if you feel uncomfortable or unsure. The more frequently you ask for donations for your organization, the easier it will become.

This article is not about asking for major gifts, but for contributions to the annual fund. That being said, there is no need to over-plan, over-research, over-think or over-stress. A reasonable amount of planning, research, thinking and stressing will certainly suffice. You are likely not asking for a million dollars, so it is more important to make the ask then to have it planned out perfectly.

1. When to ask?

When asking for an annual fund gift, there is no right or wrong time to ask. It is important to ask as soon as you think it is appropriate and not wait for the perfect moment. There is never a perfect moment.

2. Where to ask?

This is a question that I hear a lot when I am talking to people about asking for the first time. The key is to ask wherever the individual being asked feels most comfortable— generally in their home or at their office. Restaurants are not a good place to ask for a donation for a variety of reasons, including the fact that they are noisy. You want to make sure everyone at the table can hear the conversation, and would not want to be in the middle of asking for a gift only to have the waiter interrupt!

3. Who should ask?

Ideally, you want a board member or other volunteer who knows the prospect well to be the one to ask for a gift. Peer to peer solicitation always works best. One important caveat is that the asker must have already made a personal gift to the organization themselves.

When you do not have a board member who is able or willing to ask, then it is fine for the executive director to ask. A third choice would be to have a development staff member do the asking. The most important thing to remember is that asks are getting made. Do not get stuck if your board members won't help with asking!

4. How much to ask for?

This is always a tricky subject and is something that should be discussed in the cultivation stage. If possible, do some basic research to try to determine the assets and giving capacity of the individual. You can do this with a quick Google search, asking other people who know them, and asking the individual themselves about their vacations, kids in college, donations they make to other charities, etc. If they have a history of donating to your organization, you will want to consider their past giving in determining an ask amount.

One of the best ways to determine a gift level is to give them some "hypothetical" choices in the cultivation stage. Show them a list of your needs, with dollar amounts. For example, supplies for clients—$100, a new computer—$800, a new van —$20,000, and staff member's salary—$50,000. Ask them where they could see their giving to your organization and what they would like to contribute towards and at what level.

When you feel you know the answers to most of the following questions, it is time to ask:

1. Do they care about your organization?

2. Are they interested in supporting the organization?

3. What is their favorite aspect of your program, and what are they are interested in supporting?

4. Who do they know at the organization (board members, executive director)? Who is the right person to ask?

5. How much should you ask for?

Whenever you make an ask, it is important to ask for a specific amount and for a specific thing. For example, "we hope you will consider supporting the after school program with a gift of $2,000 this year."

Do not make the person guess how much you are asking for. Also, do not give a range, for example, "we would like a gift of $100 to $500." They will always give the lowest amount in that scenario.

After you ask the person for a gift, be quiet! That's right. If you speak first, you lose the asking game. As uncomfortable as the silence after "the ask" is made can be, you need to give the person a moment to think. If you speak before allowing them to speak first, you are likely to back pedal and say something like, "I know it's a lot, how about less." Already, without them even giving you an answer, you have just lowered the ask.

If the person says yes, congratulations! Say thank you! Next, find out how they would like to make the payment. Should you send them an envelope?

If you get a no, you will need to determine if it is a "soft no" or a "hard no." A "hard no" is generally a "not now, not ever" kind of no. If you get this type of no, you probably were not listening well during the cultivation process.

A "soft no" is a not a "not ever," but a "not now". If you get a "soft no", ask what you would need to do to help the no become a yes. Does the person need more information? Need to get more involved? Is the timing bad? Do whatever you can to turn the no into a yes!

Keeping Loyal Donors: Stewardship

Stewardship is the follow-up or "thank you" stage of the fundraising process and is frequently overlooked and shortchanged by organization staff. They feel such a sense of relief from receiving the gift and are in a rush to get to the next task, that the thank you is often neglected.

You might already know that it is much more expensive to acquire a new donor than it is to retain a current donor. Therefore, it is very important to keep your current donors happy. Thank them often and in multiple ways, including:

- ◆ Thank you letter

- ◆ Thank you email

- ◆ Thank you phone call

- ◆ Thank in person

- ◆ Thank in public (when appropriate) at your events or in publications

As part of the stewardship process, get several people involved. The thanks above can come from multiple people, including board members, executive director and development staff. Be sure to let donors know how their gifts are being used to benefit your clients and your organization.

 Connect with Amy at http://charitychannel.com/cc/amy-eisenstein

Major Gift Prospecting and Prioritization

By Norman Olshansky

One of the most important activities a nonprofit needs to undertake prior to initiating a major gifts campaign is the identification and prioritization of prospects. Some organizations spend a lot of money, time and human resources on prospect mining and research. Others try to identify pockets of wealth in their community and then determine the best way to contact and solicit those individuals.

I recommend the following simple and inexpensive technique to identify and prioritize your major gift prospects.

The Task Group

The first step is to put together a group of individuals who are already committed to your organization and who have good relationships in the community. When recruited they are told that they are being asked to attend a single meeting to identify names of individuals in the community who could be helpful to your nonprofit. The group can be composed of your organization's board, donors, volunteers, members, or a combination of individuals from all of these groups. In addition, if a fundraising committee or major gifts committee has already been established, they should also be encouraged to participate. I prefer to have no less than eight people or more than thirty participate in the focus group meeting, which typically takes about one to one in a half hours. It is helpful to have a diverse group from the various geographic areas served by the nonprofit. You should also try to include individuals who have good connections to high net worth individuals through their volunteer, business and/or social relationships.

Brainstorming

At the meeting, participants are asked to identify any individual they know who is charitable and is capable of making a major gift of $25,000 (or whatever level is established by your organization as a major gift) The goal of brainstorming is to identify major donors so the larger the threshold the better. If too low, you will end up with so many names that it will be hard to prioritize. The emphasis of this exercise is to identify individuals (not corporations) who have major gift potential and will be cultivated and solicited face to face. This includes individuals who utilize private foundations or donor advised funds for their charitable giving. This exercise should not be used for identification of prospects to be solicited by direct mail or for targeting donors who can be solicited by phone or contribute by attending events

The facilitator then encourages people to call out names which are written on flip charts or on a large white board that can easily be read by all.

Once everyone has shared names that came to mind during the brainstorming (hopefully, at least fifty names), the facilitator hands out paper and pencils to all participants.

The Nominal Group Technique

Next the facilitator gives the following instructions.

> *Take a few minutes to look at all of the names on the brainstorming list and write down on your paper the three to five names which best meet the following criteria:*
>
> *A. They have a history of being philanthropic.*
>
> *B. They have a history of making gifts at your major gifts level.*
>
> *C. They are likely to have an interest in your mission.*
>
> *D. They are accessible. You or others you know in your organization can get a meeting with them or invite them to visit with you.*

Nominal Group Technique and Brainstorming

The nominal group technique can also be used to help with prioritization of any other type of brainstorming activity. The beauty of the process is that it involves all of the participants and provides a way to quickly measure and prioritize responses.

 practical tip

---

After adequate time is given for participants to write down their three names, the facilitator goes around the room and asks each person to say aloud the three names. The facilitator puts a hash mark next to those names on the master brainstorming list. When a name is mentioned by more than one participant, additional hash marks are made each time that name is mentioned. Once everyone has announced their three names, the facilitator counts the cumulative hash marks for each name on the master list and circles the top ten names that were mentioned the most. If it is difficult to narrow it down to ten names, circle more than ten and initiate another round where participants now write down two of the circled names which they feel best meet the priority characteristics. Then continue the process of narrowing down the names based upon number of times mentioned. Ultimately, the facilitator's goal is to narrow it down to no more than ten names.

Fact Finding

The last stage of the process is to ask for input from participants on each of the top ten prospects identified. The facilitator or someone else should take copious notes from the comments shared by the group on each of the ten prospects in response to the following questions.

◆ Who in our organization knows this person and could be our key contact to invite the individual to learn more about what we do?

◆ What other organizations is this person involved with and what are her major philanthropic interests?

◆ Do you know how much the prospect has given to other charities?

◆ Does the prospect make philanthropic gifts directly, through a foundation, donor advised fund, etc.?

◆ Is there anything you know about this prospect that could help our staff or fundraising committee to engage the prospect with us?

◆ Do you personally know, have a relationship with, and have access to anyone who knows the individual and has a close relationship to this prospect?

◆ Is there anything you know that might lower the priority level of this prospect?

Follow up

In addition to thanking participants, the information learned should be conveyed in detail to staff and volunteers involved in major gift fundraising. Hopefully, your fundraising leadership and staff participate as well and use the session to identify additional volunteers, who attended the session, who can assist the committee going forward with prospect research, cultivation, and solicitation. The top ten names should be among the first prospects targeted as part of the major gifts initiative. After the initial priority names have been assigned and solicited, other names on the brainstorming list should also be approached in the order of the priority established, taking into consideration your ability to access and engage each prospect.

A similar process can be used to identify and prioritize corporate prospects. However, the type of individuals you will want in the task group may be different from those you select to focus on individual donor prospects.

 Link with Norman at http://charitychannel.com/cc/norman-olshansky

Screening Sessions for Major Donors

By Linda Lysakowski, ACFRE

Many times in smaller organizations, executive directors and development directors will bemoan the fact that they do not have the "movers and shakers" on their board and therefore, cannot consider a major gift program or a capital campaign that relies heavily on leadership level gifts. Before writing off your board members, consider doing some brainstorming on major donor prospects. You might be surprised at the connections your board has in this regard.

Brainstorming is best done in the form of screening and rating session. There are basically three ways in which to conduct screening for major donor prospects. For all three methods the screening committee could include:

◆ board members;

◆ staff;

◆ development committee members;

◆ members of a leadership gifts committee; and

◆ volunteers with broad community connections.

Select your committee members very carefully and make them aware that the information shared in these meetings is *very confidential*. If your board or committee volunteers have never done screening before, explain to them that this method is used routinely in most organizations and is the best way to determine the key ingredients of a major gift—Linkage, Ability and Interest (the LAI Principle). If you are working with a consultant, they will generally lead the screening meeting. If you do not work with a consultant, be sure that the meeting is led by an experienced group facilitator. It will be very important to keep the group on task and explain the methodology and reasons behind the screening meeting to those who are not familiar with the process.

It is also crucial to start with a preliminary list. It is often hard to get a brainstorming session started with a blank slate. Prepare a list of the top 10 percent of donors to your organization or other prospects that you feel might have the potential to make a major gift. List the giving history of these people, with their largest gift and most recent gift. Provide a column for each of the key ingredients—Linkages, Ability and Interest. Be sure to mark the sheets "Highly Confidential." You will not want to list gifts that have been made anonymously. You might feel more comfortable listing previous gifts by category rather than by the amount of the gift.

Now to the three methods:

1. *The Open Screening Session*—Invite the group to assemble in a quiet room and open the discussion with brief explanation of the process, its importance to your organization and why they were selected to help with this task. Then distribute the lists and discuss each name on the list, attempting to determine the *best* linkage—who knows this person best or would be the best person to make the "ask." Often there will be several linkages and the task of this group is to determine the best solicitation team. Next, try to determine ability—what *could* this person give to the organization if so motivated. Without revealing confidential information, the screening committee members often can "guesstimate" the person's net worth and/or income. Then try to determine interest—does this person have knowledge of your organization, is this a cause they are known to support? Is there a specific program of your organization or part of your project that you think would interest them? As each name is discussed, complete the form with the linkages, ability and interest named. The advantage of this method is that there is discussion and consensus; the disadvantage is that some people feel uncomfortable discussing prospects.

2. *The Closed Session*—this method is very similar to the first, except that instead of discussing each prospect among the group, participants in the session are asked to complete the answers to the Linkage, Ability and Interest sections to the best of their own knowledge. Each person works independently without discussion among the group. Lists are then collected and the person in charge reviews the lists and determines the consensus of opinion. The advantage of this method is that people might feel freer to comment on prospects if they are doing it confidentially; the disadvantage is that once the lists are collected (each screener should mark their name on their list before turning it in) there is a lot of guesswork and perhaps follow up to clarify what a screener has written. Without the open discussion it is sometimes difficult to figure out why one person thought this prospect had the ability to give $1 million and another suggested $10,000.

3. *The Private Screening Session*—this method is similar to the first except that it is held one on one with a staff member and a screening committee member. The list is reviewed with screening committee members one at a time in the privacy of their office or home. The advantages of this method are that it is easier to schedule people at their convenience than getting them all together in one room and the open discussion takes place at least between the staff and the screening committee member; the disadvantages are that it take a lot more staff time to meet with screening committee members individually and again the lack of open discussion might mean follow up to clarify major differences of opinion.

In all three methods, you will want to make sure to encourage screeners to add their own names to the list. Often seeing the list will jog people to think of other potential donors for your organization.

Whichever method you use, you will most likely uncover some hidden "stars" among your current donors and uncover new prospects along the way. Good luck and happy prospecting.

 Link with Linda at http://charitychannel.com/cc/linda-lysakowski

Ten Tips for Soliciting Major Gifts

By Norman Olshansky

I f your nonprofit organization needs significant financial support for a capital campaign or other special project, beyond memberships, broad based campaigns and operating revenues, it is time to develop and implement a major gifts campaign.

This article shares tips that can be utilized to train and support leadership, staff, and volunteers to become better solicitors of major gifts.

1. Do Your Homework

Make sure you are familiar with the needs, programs, and importance of the project. Review your organization's "points of pride" (major accomplishments), and, if possible, be prepared to share a personal experience that impressed you about the special programs and services your organization provides to the community.

Gather important information about your prospect. To the best of your ability, together with other leadership and staff, develop a profile of the prospect:

◆ What are the donor's interests?

◆ What has been the donor's history within the organization?

◆ To what has this donor contributed previously?

◆ What is the largest gift the donor has ever given?

◆ Does this donor give individually or through their company or family foundation?

◆ Does this donor have a donor advised fund with a local community foundation? If so, how large is the fund?

◆ Is the donor a candidate for estate planning and/or deferred gift discussions?

◆ Who are the donor's key financial advisors?

◆ Has this donor recently sold a business or inherited significant resources?

◆ If the donor is a business owner, how is the business doing?

◆ Does this donor have a loved one who might be appropriate for memorializing or honoring with a gift?

◆ Are there other people who can be supportive with the solicitation who have special relationships with the prospect?

◆ What are the likely concerns the prospects might raise in the solicitation?

◆ Determine in advance what would be the best setting to conduct the initial meeting.

◆ Would it be helpful to have staff, a board member or others participate in the solicitation?

◆ What materials, handouts, or visuals would be helpful to have for the solicitation?

◆ Finally, establish a "rating" for the individual. How much should you ask them to consider as a gift?

2. Leaders Lead

As a leader of the campaign and organization, it is important that you make your own gift prior to soliciting others. It will be easier to obtain a quality gift from your prospects if you are comfortable that your gift is also credible and a quality one, based on your own personal circumstances. The ability to share the fact that you made your gift, when you are soliciting, will give the prospect more confidence in your support and leadership.

Prospects will take into consideration what leadership has given in determining their own gifts. Initial gifts will be "yardsticks" for giving by those who follow. Remember that you are representing the organization, and, therefore, you need to be a good role model in your relationships, communications, and giving.

3. Personalize the Solicitation

Major gift solicitations should not be conducted over the phone. Large gifts are often not closed with one visit. Family members, financial advisors, and/or business partners might need to be involved prior to a decision. Obviously, if you know who the key decision-makers are (if they are not your prospect), they should be included in the solicitation meeting.

A major part of the success of a solicitation is the chemistry of the relationship between the solicitor(s) and prospect, as well as how one is asked. If at all possible, at least two solicitors should participate in the solicitation. It demonstrates to the prospect the importance you have put on their gift, it shows that there are others equally committed to the success of the campaign, and it provides for different perspectives to be heard.

The old saying that two heads are better than one also applies to solicitations. While one person is answering questions or explaining the need, the other person can better observe responses, body language, etc. Evaluating the solicitation and together determining best approaches for follow-up are enhanced with multiple solicitors.

4. The Appointment

The most critical aspect of major gift solicitations is getting the appointment. Be enthusiastic and let the prospect know that you want to share with them some exciting information about the organization. Note that the project is near and dear to you and that you would like to solicit their advice, involvement, and support. Make sure that you make the appointment at a time and place that is convenient for both the prospect and solicitors.

Also, try to schedule at least thirty to forty-five minutes for the initial meeting. Try to avoid an environment where others might overhear conversation or where there will be distractions. If the prospect asks if you are looking for money from them, be candid and enthusiastic, such as, "Absolutely. I would like to tell you about what's happening with our organization and have you join me as a supporter this year. But, just as important, we would like to get your input on additional ways we can succeed in our efforts on behalf of our nonprofit organization, which is doing such amazing things." Make it clear that you will be asking for their support.

5. Engage the Prospect

Do not try to close the gift too quickly. Share the mission, services, potential outcomes, points of pride, and needs of the project and organization. While informing the prospect of the needs, you are also demonstrating the commitment of leadership. Donors want to be confident that the organization and the project are being led by knowledgeable and committed leadership. Enthusiasm is contagious, and so is negativity. It's your choice.

6. The Meeting

Take a few minutes to break the ice and to establish a comfortable environment. Introduce yourself and those with you, through your involvement and commitment to the organization. In a concise manner, share with the prospect what the organization has accomplished. Refer to the points of pride. Emphasize the opportunities for the future based on the new vision and strategic plan for expansion or further development of the organization. Discuss the importance of their participation, in addition to their financial support. The organization needs their advice, expertise, identification of new leadership, and introduction to other prospective donors. Once you have shared your enthusiasm about the project and demonstrated the need, it is time to request the gift.

7. The Ask

Using the number that was agreed upon during the rating session (see item #1), the request can be introduced as follows: "We would appreciate if you would consider a gift of $ _____ to the campaign." (If there are significant projects/or programs that need to be funded at the level of the request, mention the one or two that you think would appeal to the prospective donor.)

Once you have asked for the gift, it is time to be silent and let the prospect respond with questions or other comments. There is no need ever to apologize for asking for a gift. The individuals you are approaching expect you to ask, have likely been asked before by many other charitable organizations, and have, at times, been solicitors themselves.

8. Questions, Objections, and Dialogue

Answer the questions as best you can, but do not get into a debate. If you are unsure as to how to properly answer a specific question, tell the prospect you will find out the answer and get back to them or have one of the other leaders or staff provide them with the details. (Make sure you or someone on staff follows up promptly.)

If the donor offers a gift significantly lower than what was requested, you can supportively ask if, by spreading the gift over time, could it be more significant, or if it is structured as a deferred gift, with certain tax benefits, would she consider a larger amount? Do not press if he indicates that what he had offered is the limit to what they want to do. Thank her as enthusiastically as possible and ask them to complete the pledge card you have developed for the campaign.

If he indicates that he want some time to think about it and discuss it with others, thank him for his consideration and request a specific time when you can get back to him for a response. Think of yourself as an enthusiastic and committed supporter; you are not "begging." Make sure that you are a good listener as well as a good presenter.

Let all your prospects know how important this support is to your organization and ask them if they can help you to engage others who might also be interested and have financial capacity.

Once the gift is closed, stress the importance of your organization's need for cash by the end of the year. Thank the donor and have her complete the pledge card, which should also have information on how and when she will be able to make payments.

9. Follow Up

Make sure that appropriate staff and leadership are briefed on your solicitation results, any new leads, and that there are follow-up communications thanking the prospect, even if a gift was not made. A handwritten thank-you note, from the individual who initially set up the appointment and/or was the solicitor, in addition to whatever is sent officially by the organization, is always appreciated. Solicitations should be a positive experience for the prospect. A successful solicitation can set the stage for future involvement. An unsuccessful solicitation can turn off a donor to the campaign, as well as to future potential for support of the organization.

10. Remember the Basics

There are several axioms that are basic to major gift fundraising: See article, "Ten Basic Fundraising Axioms Simplified," page 207.

Keep in mind that people are more likely to contribute to make dreams happen than to solve problems. The more you can connect the donor to your organization and project mission in their hearts and minds, the more you are likely to connect through their wallets.

Connect with Norman at http://charitychannel.com/cc/norman-olshansky

Marketing Planned Gifts

By Norman Olshansky

Nonprofits are facing increased competition for and more challenges related to annual fundraising for operations. Organizations that have strong endowments have been able to weather the storm. Today, almost every nonprofit organization is looking to develop an endowment fund. Those who have had the most success have demonstrated that endowment fundraising is more about long term relationships and stewardship than advertising and print marketing.

Prime prospects for planned gifts, bequests and legacy giving are not necessarily the "major annual donors." The best prospects for endowment gifts are those donors who have a long history with your organization, are more than fifty-five years old and who have reasonable net worth. Many of these prospects are living off unearned income, have concerns about their ability to provide for themselves long term and or other family members. Their net worth might primarily be in property or assets which do not produce income. They are usually individuals who have been small or moderate long term contributors to your organization.

Many organizations are not in a position to have full time professional planned giving staff. However, volunteers can be very effective in opening doors for planned giving which can be followed up by financial advisors or others. Many small organizations are collaborating with community foundations or other nonprofits to share professional resources related to planned giving. With or without professional staff, the following marketing strategy has proven very successful and can be modified for organizations depending on size and scope of service.

Create a giving club for long term donors. It can be called Organization ABC Heroes, Golden Givers, Organization ABC Angels, etc. Note that club members will be invited to a recognition event each year (regardless of how much they give each year). A donor of twenty-five dollars each year will be recognized as much as a donor of twenty-five thousand dollars each year. The most honored donors will be those who have given the longest. A special program that highlights the history and current involvement of the organization can be part of each event.

Identify those donors to your organization who have been contributors for more than twenty years (or fewer years if your organization has not been in operation that long). If you do not have good records of historical giving, let all donors self identify for membership in the club. To be a member, they must meet the threshold (number of years) of giving.

Promote the club in your newsletter and annual reports. In each edition of your newsletter show a photo of a club member or couple with a brief caption/quote as to why they have supported your organization for so long.

To obtain the photo and quote, have a planned giving staff person or volunteer solicitor be the one who interviews the individual(s) for the newsletter. Get the prospects to tell you their unique story of involvement and caring for the organization, how they got involved and why they have been such committed long term-supporters. At the conclusion of the interview, comment on how impressed you are with their commitment and caring. Either have them give you a photo to use or have one taken.

Ask if they have ever considered making a legacy gift to the organization that will serve as a gift in perpetuity. Typically, they will respond that they are not wealthy and don't have the ability to make such a gift.

The staff person should respond as follows: "If you were in a position to make a legacy gift, and had the resources, would you want to make a legacy gift in perpetuity to the ABC Organization?"

In most cases (not all) the answer would be that they would if they could, but they can't. That opens the door for the interviewer to respond as follows.

"If we could show you a way that would enable you to make a legacy gift, without any cash out of your pocket and the possibility to receive income for the rest of your life greater than you are earning from some of your investments, would you be interested in learning more?"

In most cases, long term supporters will be curious as to what you are suggesting and will be willing to learn more.

If the interviewer is a planned giving professional they can continue the conversation. If it's a volunteer, they should ask if it's okay to have one of the organization's advisors to set up a time to share with the prospect some of the ways they can make a legacy gift and also receive income and significant tax advantages.

The next step would be to determine the primary assets of the prospect: (residence, collectibles, life insurance, other appreciated assets, etc). In addition, a determination should be made regarding investments in low performing instruments. (Money market funds, CD's, bonds, etc.) With that information, the professional/advisor can suggest some of the techniques that would best fit for that individual (gift annuities, trusts, life insurance, bequests, etc.).

It is important to encourage prospects to engage their own financial advisors to make sure what is being discussed is appropriate based on more detailed knowledge of their unique financial situation and needs.

The professional/advisor should offer to contact the prospects' financial advisor once the prospects have had a chance to initiate the discussion with them.

Follow up is important. The photo and caption should be used regardless of response from the prospect regarding legacy giving. Timely follow up to provide information and initiate discussions with advisors is critical.

My experience working with organizations that have used this strategy has indicated that at least two out of ten prospect contacts/interviews of club members result in some type of planned gift.

Recognition and ongoing stewardship of all gifts is an important component of any planned giving program. Relationships make the difference.

 Connect with Norman at http://charitychannel.com/cc/norman-olshansky

Planned Giving and Major Gifts: Realizing the Legacy

By Charles R. Reynolds

Are you surprised that I put planned gifts first in the title? It is a bit unusual, however, there is very good reason for it. You see, if done properly, planned giving will evolve naturally from the excellent work done as part of your major gifts development. They are not mutually exclusive and independent. Think of it this way: Securing those major gifts for your organization is the first step toward the realization of a planned gift.

Put yourself at ease because you will not be expected to know the technical aspects of planned gifts. Unfortunately, the fear of not knowing the technicalities often prevents professionals from pursuing planned gifts. The complexities and intricacies of the gifting instruments and the legalities to execute them are not your responsibility. I will show you how to avoid these pitfalls and reduce your stress. Early in my career, I spent too much of my time on the technical aspects for gift instruments such as gift annuities. Instead of running software calculations, my time could have been devoted to cultivating donors.

Finding a Champion

Very early in your journey, identify a volunteer who has passion for your organization and the good work you do. Recruit this champion. You need a philanthropic champion. You might have an individual in your organization that is already a donor and is waiting for the opportunity to become engaged at a higher leadership level. I cannot emphasize enough the value such leadership will bring your giving program. You will experience a level of excellence you did not think possible for your organization. These individuals want to invest their time, talents and treasures into an organization that requires their leadership. If your organization is doing good work and has a compelling case, your leadership will respond. It might just be a matter of asking.

A few guidelines that I think will help you:

1. Contributions should be referred to as investments for your organization's good works and deeds.

2. Never misjudge worth of donors by, what I call "lifestyle appearances." Some of the most significant philanthropic gifts have come from the most unexpected donors.

3. Volunteers in major gifts and planned giving should not be called solicitors, rather *ambassadors for your mission.*

Where are the Bucks?

It is important to remind ourselves that approximately seventy five percent of American philanthropic giving comes from individuals (this figure jumps to nearly eighty-five percent if you count bequests, which always come from individuals). This is a tremendous tribute to the generosity that exists in this country. You, as the professionals and your volunteers make this overwhelming response to need a reality! Have you ever asked yourself the question, "Where would we be as a society without this generosity?"

 **practical tip**

---

4. A call on a donor or potential donor is a visit; this term signifies a relationship process.

5. "The ask" for an investment is the end result of the process, not the beginning.

6. Cultivation involves conversations with and listening to the donor. Listening is an art.

7. Planned giving involves the donors' assets and engages a higher level of consideration, timing and planning.

8. Do not consider yourself a financial advisor or a legal resource for the donor; this immediately makes your journey easier. This will avoid potential conflicts and unrealistic expectations. This confusion of roles is a stressful reality for development professionals moving into planned giving.

9. The journey requires sensitive cultivation and you will find yourself invited into different parts of the donors' lives and possibly a sharing of confidential information; this shows you are trusted and respected. It is a beautiful aspect of the philanthropic journey when donors want your guidance on how to be charitable for your organization. This is an aspect not appreciated fully by some of us that are privileged to partner

---

Seek Legal Counsel

I continuously requested that legal counsel be budgeted for our planned giving department. It was never given priority status. It affected our productivity and donor relations.

 warning!

with such generous people. Remember...never violate the donor's trust.

10. Timing "the ask" is knowing when the donor is ready. "The ask" might not be necessary if the cultivation has been sensitive and effective. Untimely asks are a disaster and lead to lost investments, sometimes forever! I have seen this happen. Volunteers who get overeager for the gift need to be guided by the professional.

It is the cultivation that produces profitable results. I would suggest if you have a conference or some type of function where other volunteers will be in attendance, invite the individual(s) you are cultivating to such an event. Exposure to peers outside your own organization creates an interest and renewed vigor for the work you are doing. Peer influence can be a powerful motivator.

While I will not address the development of a here, it is a key component for your fundraising plan. It is an excellent way to train volunteers, develop a comfort range for them to make visits and puts in place quality control for consistent and productive visits to donors and making the ask. There is some confusion among professionals as to what exactly is a case for support so be sure to get help with this if you don't feel you have the skills to develop a strong case for support. I have seen some poorly developed cases for support and some that spent too much on the publication design with weak content.

Train volunteers to be ambassadors for your organization. Do not make them run for the hills when they

---

Polite Persistence Pays Off!

A volunteer whom I was hoping would make the first leadership gift for a new giving society for our organization agreed to attend a volunteers' conference sponsored by our national office. Attending this conference was seen as another step in a long cultivation process to make sure this individual remained connected to our institution. He was the one we needed for philanthropic leadership. As we were returning home and discussing the need for a leadership giving society, he asked me as we were flying thousands of feet in the air, "What is the leadership society gift amount?" After I told him the amount, he gave it on the spot!! We are not done. He then told me that he would be the chair of this new giving society and recruit other colleagues to join. "The ask" was not needed here. *Why?* The prospect was sufficiently cultivated to "ask himself" for the gift!

Five Percent Rule

If you spend your time cultivating, you will discover the ask comes last and often is only a small part (5 percent) of the process. Unfortunately, all too often, professional and volunteers reverse this process and put most of the time (95 percent) into getting to a premature ask.

hear you want them to ask for money. How many times have you heard, "I cannot ask for money; please do not ask me to do it! Ask me to do anything else." Few of us are comfortable asking for money. If you get your volunteers passionate about your mission, raising the dollars will follow. Some of my most effective fundraisers were first and foremost ambassadors for our organization.

The value of a personal encounter with the person/need, not a cold statistic, but a real human being, is priceless! The statistic hides the human face we must all see in order to be compassionate.

Training and Orientation Are Critical—For Everyone

I took my campaign volunteer leadership team on a tour of the institution's programs and services. There was, in our organization, an expectation that all volunteers working for a campaign will get to see, first-hand, what the organization is doing to address the needs of the community. The chair of the campaign was a part of this team. With the reputation this individual had gained for raising funds, some people felt that there was no need for this person to go on a tour—*wrong!* Regardless of reputation or experience, training and orientation are critical. As the team was gathered around a program station observing the work being done, a client turned and looked my campaign chairman right in the eye and said, "You are a nice man!" Later, the chair wanted to know why he was singled out of the group. I knew that this leader, so touched by this moment, would and did become a tremendous campaign leader.

 practical tip

It is not the amount of the gift that is important as much as the mindset when undertaking this journey. We are talking about making "visits" and facing a donor eyeball to eyeball; in these visits you will have serious conversations about the prospect's philanthropic responsibility within the context of making a difference. These individuals, who are candidates for major gifts and a future planned gift, are interested in how their investment with your organization can do some good and begin building a lasting legacy.

Remember to find many ways to thank your donors. You might have heard that you should thank a donor seven times before asking for the next gift. I have used this as a guide. It challenged me to remain in contact in creative ways throughout the year. The prerequisite, however, is that the thank you must be meaningful to the donor; it must not be a manufactured gesture. A simple call to the donor and an invite to lunch is a thank you. Sincerity and honesty are requirements for a trusting relationship. Volunteers who are participating in a meaningful relationship other than giving money are more likely to become significant givers.

Let me talk to you about visits and how sensitive you must be to the particular circumstances surrounding the donors' lives during each visit. I had the unfortunate responsibility to be the contact person to a family of a young woman connected to our institution who had been murdered.

What evolved for me was an incredible journey in which from tragedy came blessings. The family and community were devastated by this senseless murder. Over the course of time I tried to listen through the terrible grief; there was a message of searching coming out of the terrible loss. The parents and a younger brother accepted me, over time, as a trusted friend of the family. I am convinced to this day it was due to my sincere effort and struggle to listen to their grieving. What emerged was the desire of the parents to create a lasting legacy to their daughter. They looked to me for help. What a difficult place to be. After sensitive listening to the family, we decided that a scholarship in their daughter's name would bring them comfort while assisting others in need. There were many conversations, some with tears, over the kitchen table. There was never an "ask" in this journey! They knew I could be trusted as they shared their grief. The scholarship became a way in which the community could also participate in this philanthropic tribute to the daughter of a neighbor. Be prepared to participate in a process to help, perhaps, to bring some comfort and healing; this is the beautiful gift of our profession. In this case my spouse, who is a hospice nurse and an excellent listener, got involved too. As a volunteer, her involvement was an asset as we teamed to support this family in their grief. The family welcomed her participation.

> **The Right Fit**
>
> Find ways to determine the best utilization between your volunteers' interest and your needs. Often fundraisers do not take the time to learn the skills and talents of volunteers before trying to fit them into organizational needs. A misfit volunteer is not happy, is not productive and is frustrated with the way your organization functions. Make sure your volunteers are doing something they feel is meaningful. Keep your volunteers busy!
>
> At the right time, have your volunteer prepared to make "the ask" for that significant investment. I have seen first-hand that the lack of an effective "ask" ends up missing a golden opportunity. If the volunteer is passionate about your organization and the work it is doing, the donor will be moved. Treat a "no" as a first opportunity to return for another visit.

In another instance, I found that the information on the contact report and data base did not reference that the family I was visiting was reeling from being offended by the organization. I was able to again, through the art of listening, sense that something was not right. The initial meeting was a forced courtesy. Over time this family, who were past leadership level supporters, informed me that our organization was left out of a very significant estate consideration. They had justifiable reason to be hurting.

Once I was privileged to learn this information, my only focus was to *right a wrong*. Only over time and many visits was the hurt resolved. It was beautiful to see how our organization became, once again, the love of this family's life. It was moving to see the way we were able to restore a loss to these individuals. The journey included attending the funeral of one of the offended siblings. I knew the day I was invited to the funeral was a special message that our organization was regaining credibility. Again, "the ask" evolved from the cultivation. The family offered their generous investment when it was right for them to do so! Making the transition to planned giving is not as difficult as some professionals make it.

How to Get Started

The following scenario shows you some steps you can take to undertake a planned giving program. The professional advisory team noted in this scenario was involved to help our organization with the technical aspects. This is why I stated earlier that the technical areas need not be a concern for you. It gives the experts on an advisory team the opportunity to participate. These experts like to be asked to share their knowledge for a charitable effort. Now let's move to some practical steps for you to make planned giving a reality.

◆ Publish a semi-annual newsletter with one issue devoted to year-end giving. Include service and giving testimonials to bring home the message that your business is meeting the needs of people and community. There are workshops and seminars available if you are interested in learning how to design an effective newsletter. It does not have to be an expensive and slick publication. The content should be clear and appealing to your audience.

◆ Maintain donor contact reports and make it as detailed as you desire. A word of caution, however, the more information you collect the less likelihood you will use it. As soon as you leave the visit, find a comfortable place to record your visit and the particular details for a follow up visit. I find a one page well designed report is all that is needed. I immediately begin reviewing the details of the meeting. I am constantly amazed at tidbits of information that would have been lost if I delayed completing the report.

◆ The magic is in the passion and energy you and your volunteer(s) bring to the visits especially when "the ask" is made. It is the passion and belief in the need that will resonate with the donor. During your visit you are inviting this donor to be your partner in addressing a need. The tools and materials you bring to the meeting are helpful, but remember that it is your passion for the mission that

---

Cool Your Heels

The visit gives you invaluable information for continued cultivation. The time you take to review and record your visit requires discipline! Our tendency is to let it wait. Sometimes I would sit in the car or go to a nearby restaurant and complete the report with special notations (illness, special occasions, birthday etc.) regarding the next steps. You might feel that you need to get on to the next visit or back to the office. Don't delay completing the contact report—do it while it is fresh in your mind.

warning!

is the strongest tool. The materials serve to enhance the flow of your visit including the case for support. Be relaxed during your visit; remember it is a conversation. As my son reminded me one day, there is too much stress in today's world. We are so busy doing things when all we really need to be are human beings, caring for each other. I have seen professionals get lost in the materials and trying desperately to "sell" their agency when they should have been focusing on the donor.

At the time of the visit when "the ask" is going to be made, have an agenda for you and your volunteer. Your case for support is the primary material used for the visit. I have found two organizational representatives, the volunteer and the executive, are most productive. Another volunteer is fine if there is a purpose and reason for that individual to be present. One of the volunteers is the door opener (the person responsible for arranging the visit). The executive represents the institution's community visibility, credibility and integrity. The *volunteer* makes "the ask" at the appropriate time. It should be done with conviction, passion and a firm belief this donor's support is needed. There is probably no time in the process that the ball is dropped with more damage than when it is time to make "the ask"! A quality "ask" is critical. It is important to make sure the spouse is included in the visit especially, when "the ask" is to be made. A spouse's participation is imperative for a successful and rewarding conclusion to the gift cultivation process. Cultivation is a life-long process. Do not forget the donor(s) after the gift is secured. Continue follow up visits and explore ways to keep the donor involved and connected to your institution.

◆ The best place for the visit is often the source of much discussion. This is a no brainer! The selection should be where your donor feels most comfortable. Out of your office is the best choice, in order to avoid interruptions. The donor's home, a restaurant, membership club are some of the options. One of my visits was an invitation to a CEO's home to cut fire wood on a beautiful fall Saturday. It was a relaxing exercise for this CEO and, I realized my wood cutting participation was a great way to build a relationship. When you are invited to one's home it is a sign you are accepted and the work you do is respected. One of my visits was to a person I had never met and she suggested we meet in a public mall. She wanted security in a public place until she had a chance to size me up and make sure I was legitimate. It was a delightful lunch and one of many visits to follow. I have found that the donor's choice of place has value-added benefits. You meet the spouse, other acquaintances and have the opportunity to profile your organization with interested parties including community leadership. Just keep in mind, the community is your office, not your desk!

Finally, I ask you to believe in the value of the work you are doing. Never forget the human equation we are engaged in as we live our lives. Reflecting back on the family who lost their beautiful daughter to a tragedy, it might be appropriate to end with this quote from James Barrie: "Remember those who bring sunshine to the lives of others cannot keep it from themselves." You and your volunteers live the sunshine every day.

 Connect with Charles at http://charitychannel.com/cc/charles-reynolds

Capital Campaigns—the Ingredients for Success

By Linda Lysakowski, ACFRE

If a capital campaign is in your organization's future, you will want to do everything you can to assure success. There are several key ingredients to every successful campaign and three of these ingredients, when analyzing successful campaigns, surface as the most crucial.

The following items will help assure success:

◆ a strong annual fund history;

◆ a realistic goal;

◆ a sufficient pool of qualified prospects;

◆ strong staff support;

◆ campaign policies;

◆ campaign organizational structure; and

◆ an adequate donor software system.

And the three *key* ingredients:

◆ a compelling case for support;

◆ a committed board of directors; and

◆ strong volunteer leadership.

Annual Fund History

When preparing for a campaign, many organizations strive to find new donors, seeking to solicit major gifts from foundations and corporations from which they have previously been unsuccessful in raising money. Most donors (whether individuals, companies or foundations) are reluctant to support an organization with a major gift unless they already have a track record with this organization. Although you might not have a cadre of major donors, it is always best to start with those who have a relationship with your organization. Look at the top 10 percent of your annual donors to see if there might be some prospective lead donors for your campaign. Another group to review is your list of "loyal donors," those people who support your organization year after year. Even if their gifts have been small, it is possible that among them there might be a few major donor prospects, who were simply *never asked* for a large gift before.

Realistic Goal

To determine the goal of a capital campaign, first start with the architectural study. The architect initially works with the organization to determine usage and function needs in order to determine initial cost of construction and FF&E (furniture, fixtures and equipment), total square footage needs to be established. With that information, the architect can then determine cost per square foot and estimate total cost of the project. This does not include soft costs, fundraising, reserves, etc. An architect will develop renderings and a preliminary budget for the project which you will then use in presenting your case for support to potential donors. Donors will be motivated to give if the vision is inspiring. A building that looks too extravagant might turn off donors to a human service agency if they feel money is being spent on buildings that could be better spent on program. On the other hand, however, the building should inspire people to see how the clients of your organization and the community will be better served by this building. Once these plans are in place, they need to be tested in the community, usually by means of a planning study. The planning study will also determine the interviewee's thoughts regarding the proposed goal. It is important to realize that the case that will be presented as a preliminary case for support, and that the feedback from interviewees might alter the plans in order to arrive at a realistic, attainable campaign goal.

Qualified Prospects

The difference between a prospect and a *qualified* prospect is that adequate research has been done in order to determine the linkage, ability and interest (the LAI Principle) of the prospect in order to have them qualify as viable prospective donors for this campaign. Without the three qualifications listed above, it is unlikely a major gift will be forthcoming from any prospect. Screening sessions during the early phase of the campaign can help you determine the ability of a prospect to give, and at what level; who is the best team to make the ask; and which possible named giving opportunities might appeal to this prospect.

Some questions you should answer in your campaign policies include:

◆ Are there certain types of gifts you will not accept?

◆ Are there funders from whom you will not accept gifts?

◆ Who will manage the campaign funds and how will they be invested?

◆ How will donors be recognized?

◆ How will in kind gifts be recognized?

◆ How will you dispose of gifts in kind that cannot be used directly in this campaign?

◆ How long will the campaign run?

◆ How long will pledge payment period be?

◆ Will the project be financed and if so, what portion?

◆ At what point in the campaign will construction begin?

◆ How will existing operations be impacted?

◆ Is there a business plan in place that demonstrates sustainability?

◆ Will the project be built to allow for future expansion or only what is needed in the next few years?

◆ Is there an endowment portion of the campaign?

◆ Will annual giving be included in the campaign or will there be a separate annual fund conducted during the campaign?

◆ How will the campaign affect annual giving?

◆ How will contractors and vendors be selected?

◆ What are the policies on named gifts?

practical
tip

Staff Support

A capital campaign tends to disrupt the overall operations of the development office. The campaign, because it is running on a tight timeline, will require intensive periods of concentration on developing prospect lists, working with volunteers, developing campaign material, and scheduling solicitation visits. The CEO of your organization will need to be involved in identifying, cultivating and soliciting donors. Fifty percent or more of your CEO's time might need to be devoted to the campaign. Support staff is also crucial during a campaign. There will be a lot of paperwork generated during the campaign, volunteer training packets, letters of solicitation and acknowledgement, recording of gifts and pledges, grant proposals. Often, additional staff support is hired for the duration of the campaign.

Campaign Policies

Before launching a campaign, you will need to have clear polices in place regarding what type of gifts you will accept, how those gifts will be disposed of, how they will recognized and other important issues affecting the acceptance, recognition, reporting, distribution and disposal of gifts. It is important that volunteers and staff are aware of policies before they are assigned to solicit prospective donors.

Campaign Organizational Structure

A campaign plan should be developed before recruiting the campaign cabinet. This plan will include position descriptions for all members of the campaign cabinet, timelines, campaign budget, and a scale of gifts, along with suggested goals for each division of the campaign. An organizational chart showing how many volunteers will be needed in each division is crucial before recruiting volunteers to head up each campaign division. If you do not plan to hire a consultant to manage your campaign, you would do well to consider engaging the services of a consultant to develop the campaign plan and show you how to implement the plan.

Donor Software

An adequate donor software system needs to be in place during a campaign. For many organizations, the capital campaign might be the first time an organization needs to record pledges. Most campaigns will have a three-year to five year pledge period, and often donors will want to make quarterly or semi-annual payments on their pledges. Therefore it is important to have software system that can manage all this, in addition to being able to record which solicitors are assigned to which prospects so that tracking results of each solicitor can be done. If you are financing the building project during the pledge payment period, it will also be crucial to have as system that can generate a cash-flow projection report in order to show the bank when pledges are expected to be paid.

The Three Key Ingredients

While most of the qualifications discussed above can be developed during the early phase of your campaign, there are three key ingredients that should be in place before a decision is made to go forward with your campaign.

Case for Support

There must be a clear, compelling case for support which inspires and motivates your donors. The case is often referred to as being "bigger than the organization." The case talks about the people who will be served by this building, the importance of this project to your community, and the difference the donor can make in the lives of people by supporting this campaign. Once the preliminary case is tested during the planning study, it should be reviewed again in light of the input received by community leaders. If it is found that the case is not strong enough, it might not be the right time for the organization to run a campaign, at least not for this project. The case forms the basis from which all campaign materials will be developed; therefore, it needs to be written early on in the campaign. It will be used to inspire volunteers and donors.

The case needs to include:

- your mission;

- your vision;

- a brief history of your organization;

- plans and the budget for the project;

- a campaign goal;

- organization and campaign leadership;

- a gift pyramid showing the number and size of gifts it will take to succeed;

- information about recognition and named gift opportunities;

- sustainability of the project;

- the impact this project will have on your community/consumers; and

- reasons the donor should support this project (what's in it for me?).

practical tip

Board Commitment

Board commitment must be present before making a decision to proceed with a campaign. Your board should pass a resolution approving the campaign once the planning study report is received and discussed. Board commitment means that the board is committed to this campaign in every respect—emotionally, mentally, spiritually and financially. At last five or six board members should be willing to serve on the campaign cabinet. One hundred percent of your board must make their financial commitment before any other gifts are solicited for the campaign. It is will be crucial to show other funders that the "family" of your organization has made its commitment first, and at the highest level possible for each board member. This is the time to ask board members to stretch their giving to a truly visionary level.

Volunteer Leadership

Good leadership can make or break a campaign. It is essential to select a campaign chair or chairs that can inspire others to become involved and to support this campaign. The selection of the campaign chair might take several months in order to identify, cultivate and recruit the right person(s). Prepare a recruitment package that includes the case for support, the campaign timeline, and position descriptions for each member of the campaign cabinet along with an organizational chart. Whenever possible, the campaign chair should be someone who has been involved with your organization. The chair should always be someone who believes in your organization's mission and supports it wholeheartedly. The campaign chair should also be someone who is known and respected in the community and has the ability to both give a leadership gift themselves, and solicit leadership gifts from others. Once the campaign chair is in place, others key positions should be filled on the cabinet. These volunteers will, in turn, recruit others to serve on the campaign as needed.

With effective volunteer leadership, full board commitment and a compelling case for support, good planning, staff support, attention to detail, and realistic expectations most campaigns will succeed.

 Connect with Linda at http://charitychannel.com/cc/linda-lysakowski

They Said They Would Raise Money; Now What? Twelve Tips to Help Board Members Hold Each Other Accountable

By Andy Robinson

If—as the saying goes—the road to Hell is paved with good intentions, then I've met a lot of board members walking down that road. "Sure, I'll help raise money," they say—and then life gets in the way. Given the competition for our board members' time and attention—family, work, and so on—their commitment to raise money might feel like a lower priority.

While it's important to honor the intentions of our volunteer leaders, it's even more important to support them and help them to follow through on those intentions. Here are a dozen ideas that can assist you in creating a culture a fundraising on your board and—even better—a culture of accountability. Not every idea is relevant to every organization, so treat this list as a menu and choose the items that best fit your needs and circumstances.

1. Identify a sparkplug or a team of sparkplugs—then empower them to lead

If you're striving to build a culture of fundraising on your board, somebody needs to say to the other board members—peer to peer—"Yes, this *is* our job. Let's figure out how we can support each other to better follow through on own commitments." If the word, "sparkplug" doesn't work for you, how about coach? Or cheerleader? Or enforcer? Without assertive board leadership, the ideas that follow will be much less effective.

2. Develop a board agreement or job description that includes fundraising

Be explicit and detailed. The best of these documents are reciprocal: they itemize both what you expect of the board members, but also what they can expect in return. For example, if you want them to raise money, it's only fair for board members to receive relevant training, materials, and list of fundraising activities from which to choose.

3. At each board meeting, everyone self-reports

Take ten minutes for a go-around so every board member can say, "This is what I've done since the last meeting to support fundraising." There's no shaming or blaming, just self-reporting. However, the expectation of having to speak might provide enough incentive to get those wavering souls to follow through in advance of the meeting.

4. Create a line item in the budget for board giving

When the annual budget is prepared, trustees must ask themselves, "How much can we collectively give? Are we a $2,000 board? A $5,000 board? Is $10,000 a good goal?" Debate the number, set a target, then hand out pledge cards. At board meetings, each budget review serves as an indirect reminder to those who have not yet fulfilled their pledges.

5. Create a line item for board fundraising

This is money that board members raise above and beyond their own personal giving. Once again, the board debates a goal, sets a dollar target, and reviews progress at each meeting. If board and staff do something together—for example, they team up to meet with a major donor— then credit the gift to the board. Since our overall goal is promote follow-through, it helps to reinforce positive behavior.

6. Solicit challenge gifts based on board behavior—not necessarily tied to dollars raised

For example, approach a major donor or foundation with the following request: "To inspire our board, we'd like a challenge gift of $_____ contingent on board involvement in major donor outreach. We've set a benchmark of twenty asks—if board members participate in twenty donor meetings, can we count on your support with a gift of $_____?" The beauty of this approach is that it's tied to behavior, not results; you can approach twenty prospects, get turned down twenty times, and still receive the challenge grant.

7. Provide regular fundraising training to your board

This could be a full-day workshop at an annual retreat or twenty minutes at every other board meeting for a quick practice session.

8. Invite a group of your donors to talk about why they give

Once a year, dedicate time to hear from your supporters: why they care about your work, how they liked to be approached, etc. Include Q&A. Demystify fundraising by having a conversation with actual donors.

9. Offer rewards to those who make an effort

Approach local restaurants for free meals. Ask local shops for gift certificates. Encourage a bed-and-breakfast or local hotel to provide a free night during their slow season. As appropriate, reward prizes to those who meet their individual goals, show courage, and inspire others. It's important to understand that even small gifts to board members might present an ethical issue—for example, if your board includes government representatives, they are forbidden from accepting any compensation. So while this idea might work with some boards, it could be hazardous for others.

10. Make it competitive

This won't work with every organization, but I've seen boards that respond well to competition. Divide the board into two teams—Greens vs. Blues, Hummingbirds vs. Woodpeckers, whatever—and see which team can meet with the greatest number of donors, generate the largest turnout for the annual event, raise the most money, etc. Once again, prizes may be used as incentives, as long as you follow the advisory outlined in the previous item.

11. Define real consequences for not meeting commitments—then apply them

What happens when board members don't meet their goals? More pointedly, what do you do if they flat-out refuse to participate? Are they asked to take on other responsibilities to free up the willing fundraisers? Are they encouraged to leave the board or take a different role within the organization? These consequences can't be mandated from above, but they need to be discussed openly: "With the knowledge that we're all volunteers, how do we set expectations for each other? How do we hold each other accountable? If people can't meet our shared expectations, is it appropriate to transition them off the board? If so, how can we do this in a transparent and humane way?"

12. Bring in new blood

New people often bring a fresh perspective. If they're recruited with the understanding that fundraising is a shared responsibility, they are much less likely to say, "That's not my job," or "I didn't join this board to raise money." When recruiting, remember to let them know that board fundraisers receive training, support, and appreciation.

Finally, remember that culture change is long-term process. Your investment in creating a culture of fundraising will pay off slowly at first, but with persistence and patience it can transform your board and, by extension, your entire organization. The sooner you begin, the sooner you win...so get started.

This article was previously published in Grassroots Fundraising Journal.

 Connect with Andy at http://charitychannel.com/cc/andy-robinson

Time, Talent & Treasure: What Your Organization Needs to Know About Getting People to Give All Three

By Linda Lysakowski, ACFRE

In recent years, we have seen the very best and, at times, the worst face of philanthropy. This second face has made our country more aware than ever of financial abuse, misuse and fraud on the part of charities and nonprofit organizations. Many people are more reluctant than ever to donate time, talent and treasure to the many nonprofit organizations that truly need and deserve help. It becomes increasingly difficult for donors and volunteers to decide which organizations deserve their support and which ones will use their gifts wisely.

How can your organization distinguish itself from among the many charities that ask for money? How can you ensure that when people are deciding which organizations deserve and need their money and their time, your organization will rise to the top? How can you assure donors that their money is being used wisely?

You can encourage your donors to follow this rule of thumb when evaluating a charitable request: Ask if the organization adheres to the Donor Bill of Rights. The Association of Fundraising Professionals (AFP), the Council for the Advancement and Support of Education (CASE), the Association for Healthcare Philanthropy (AHP), the Giving Institute, and others formulated this document. Numerous other associations representing the nonprofit sector have adopted it. By encouraging your donors to be aware of the Donor Bill of Rights, you will show them that your top priority is their best interest, not your organization's interests.

Here are some key points that can help you help your donors make educated decisions about their philanthropic giving.

Mission

Does your organization have a clear mission statement that is articulated to the public? Is this mission one that the donor supports? Is it clear what your organization does to carry out the mission? Many organizations have similar names and some, unfortunately, purposely choose a name similar to a well-established, reputable charity in order to defraud the public. You need to make sure your donors understand your organization's purpose and mission and what it does before asking them to get out their checkbook.

Leadership

Article II of the Donor Bill of Rights states that your donors have a right to be informed about the people who provide leadership and governance to your organization. Questions to ask yourself include, "Is our board of directors comprised of community leaders who are known and respected?" "Is the board qualified to govern our organization and assure that it fulfills its mission?" "Do the members of the board have term limits, and how long have they served on the board?" "Who are the leaders of our organization; do they have the credentials required in the field in which we operate?"

Savvy donors will look for a list of the board and executive staff on the letterhead, annual report, or other written materials of the organizations. Many donors also feel more comfortable knowing that the board has made a financial commitment to the organization and might ask to see copies of the annual report to see if the board members are listed as donors.

Fundraisers who are members of AFP also subscribe to a code of ethics that, among other things, prohibits them from receiving a percentage-based compensation. Many statewide associations of nonprofits also have *Standards of Excellence* programs, which grant a "seal of approval" to nonprofit organizations who have met rigid criteria covering financial, fundraising, personnel, ethics and program areas. Looking for the Standards of Excellence approval on charities is one more way donors can assure they are contributing to a well run charity.

Financial Information

In a majority of states nonprofits are required to register with a state regulator of charitable organizations before they can raise money from that state's citizens. This registration requirement is true for any charity soliciting residents of the state, regardless of where the charity is based. Solicitations from all organizations that are required to register must generally contain certain information; this might include a written disclaimer that directs potential donors to the state regulator for more information about the charity, such as copies of the charity's financial statements. If donors wish, they may contact their state regulators and ask for the additional information.

Most 990 forms (the informational return required to be completed by most nonprofit organizations and filed with the IRS - this includes Forms 990-EZ and 990-PF as well as the more extensive Form 990) are available on the Internet through the Guidestar website—*www. guidestar.org*. The 990 forms will list income and expenses of the charity including fundraising expenses.

In addition to registration of the charity itself, fundraising counsel usually must be registered as well. Another category of companies and individuals who are often required to be registered are professional solicitors that make phone calls on behalf of charities. When donors receive phone solicitations in some states, they are encouraged to ask if the caller is a volunteer or a paid solicitor and, if they are paid solicitors, what percentage of the money raised actually goes to the charity and what percentage goes to the paid solicitors. Some telephone fundraising firms work on a flat fee basis, which is the ethical way of being compensated, according to the Association of Fundraising Professionals.

Acknowledgment and Recognition

The Donor Bill of Rights also states that donors are entitled to proper acknowledgment and recognition for gifts to charities and that they have a right to remain anonymous if they choose to do so. Donors can have their name removed from any lists that the charity may sell or give to another organization. Charities are also required by the IRS to tell the donor the fair market value of any substantial goods or services received in exchange for a donation. For instance, most purchases at charity auctions are not tax deductible because the donor has received goods equal to the value of their "contribution" to the charity. This is just one on the areas in which the IRS holds nonprofits accountable. You might want to check with your accountant, tax attorney or the IRS to assure that you are following all tax guidelines and laws.

How Do Donors Decide to Share their Time, Talent and Treasure?

First of all, a significant number of donors are more informed than ever—they follow news stories about local and national charities, they might ask your organization's leadership to provide information about the charity before making gift. Savvy donors read the materials your organization publishes, such as annual reports, brochures, website, etc. They might talk to board members of your organization or to others who donate to your organization.

They might even test the organization. Many people give small gifts to an organization first and track how the organization acknowledges and recognizes their gift before making a more substantial gift. Or, they might want to get involved as a volunteer for your organization, sharing talents and time, before making a gift, as a good way to discover if your organization is one for which they feels a real passion.

Ultimately, your organization should strive to have its donors focus on the positive aspects of philanthropy—assuring that their gift to your organization can make a real difference in the life of a child, a family, or a community. This will result in a longer and more fulfilling relationship between the donor and the organization.

 Connect with Linda at http://charitychannel.com/cc/linda-lysakowski

Is It Time for a Development Audit?

By Linda Lysakowski, ACFRE

A development audit is an internal assessment of your fundraising program and your readiness to embark on new development ventures. The development audit looks at involvement of board, staff and volunteers in the fundraising process and offers recommendations on how to best use the human resources available to the organization. It further evaluates the strengths and weaknesses of your development systems, including fundraising software. The audit also offers suggestions to help improve donor communications and stewardship.

Many organizations consider a development audit when they are:

- preparing to embark on a major gifts, capital or endowment campaign;

- not satisfied with the results of their annual giving program;

- seeking to increase board participation in fundraising efforts;

- attempting to compare their results with similar organizations;

- looking for an objective evaluation of their development program;

- trying to diversify their funding streams;

- engaged in the strategic planning process;

- looking at restructuring their development office; or

- seeking to take their program to a higher level of professionalism.

In most cases, the audit is done by a consultant in order to gain both objectivity and utilize the knowledge and years of experience the consultant will bring to the table. The staff, while not involved directly in the evaluation process, will need to devote time to the audit process. Typical staff roles include:

◆ completion of development audit questionnaires;

◆ providing supporting documentation; and

◆ meeting with the consultant to clarify information and set goals for the audit.

The board is also involved with the process, usually completing questionnaires and participating in interviews with the consultant. Typically the board chair, chair of the development committee and other selected board members will be involved in interviews. The consultant generally makes several visits to the organization to meet with key staff, board and other volunteers.

These are the typical areas addressed in the audit:

1. The Organization's Readiness for Fundraising

◆ Legal structure—does the organization have 501(c)(3) status?

◆ Organizational structure—to whom does the development office report?

◆ Strategic planning—does the organization have a long range plan?

◆ Fundraising guidelines—are there gift acceptance policies in place?

◆ Case for support—is there a written organizational case for support and case statements to support various fundraising needs?

2. The Board's Role in Fundraising

◆ Board composition—is the board diverse, and does it have the appropriate mix of skills and talents?

◆ Board performance—is the board actively involved in fundraising and do board members support the organization financially?

◆ The development committee—is there a development committee or other volunteers involved in the fundraising program?

3. The Role of Staff

- Departmental Structure—is there adequate staff, doing the right jobs with the right tools?

- Functions of the Development Office—does the development staff have the time and skills to perform all development functions?

- Training & Educating Staff—is there a commitment to professionalism in the development office?

- Role of the CEO in Fundraising—is the CEO involved in fundraising and does he/she communicate regularly with the development office?

4. Systems and Procedures

- Donor database software—is there an adequate donor software program in place and is staff trained to use the program?

- Integrated accounting software for proper accounting of gifts

- Procedure manual—are procedures in place to receive, record and acknowledge gifts?

- Hardware—is there adequate hardware to support development systems and programs?

- Internet usage and website—does staff use technology to improve donor relations?

5. Cultivation and Stewardship

- Are regular cultivation events and activities being held?

- Does the organization adhere to the Donor Bill of Rights?

- Are donor acknowledgements sent in a timely manner?

- Is there a donor recognition program in place?

- Does the organization follow all IRS and other legal guidelines for fundraising?

6. The Integrated Development Program—does the organization rely too heavily on one source of funding or is there a plan in place to develop funding from various sources including:

- Grants
- Special events

◆ Direct mail

◆ Internet fundraising

◆ Telephone fundraising

◆ Major gifts program

◆ Corporate appeals

◆ Planned giving program

◆ Membership

◆ Social enterprise

Once the development audit is complete, a report will be prepared by the consultant and shared with development staff and executive leadership. The recommendations in the report can be used to develop a strategic plan for development, addressing the areas raised as issues needing improvement in the audit, as well as integrated in the organization's strategic plan. A comprehensive development audit can help your organization build on its strengths, overcome its weaknesses and address opportunities for future growth.

 Connect with Linda at http://charitychannel.com/cc/linda-lysakowski

Writing a Sustainability Plan that Sings!

By Jane Hexter

Some lucky proposal writers have the good fortune to be able to write "Organization XYZ has sufficient resources to sustain this program, once developed, as part of its core programming. Our board passed a resolution on April 1st to commit itself to sustaining this project in full once grant funding expires, see Appendix." If this applies to you, please stop reading now and use your time more profitably.

The rest of us need to be a little more creative.

Most public RFP's and many foundations ask respondents to 'demonstrate how you plan to sustain the proposed activities after the grant period.' Typically, proposal writers address this question with cursory comments such as 'we intend to investigate alternative funding from public agency Y, corporation X and foundation Z.' However, by taking a little time to brainstorm with your grant proposal team you can devise a sustainability strategy that will stand above the rest.

A good sustainability strategy will show the reviewer that your organization is so well managed that not only have you conceived this imaginative, responsive and visionary project plan but you also have the ability to conceive its long-term future.

During the program planning phase it is helpful to decide how you will create a long term sustainability plan once funding begins and then show the funding agency that you are well-prepared by including as much detail as possible in the proposal. Several organizations such as the National Center for Community Educators, the After School Alliance, the Finance Project, and the Center for Civic Partnerships have created tools and recommendations for sustainability planning. The following is a brief synopsis of their recommendations to give you a flavor of the information that is available.

When to Start Planning for Sustainability

Sustainability planning should start during the proposal planning phases and be implemented as soon as the project begins. Your first board meeting should include sustainability on the agenda. That three-year, $5 million grant is going to expire sooner than you know. Get the sustainability team in place and start on contact building and creating a thorough sustainability plan.

Who Should be Involved in Creating a Sustainability Plan?

Consider who will conduct your sustainability activities. Do not assign the project director the sole responsibility of sustaining the project. Since the community benefits by continuance of successful projects, then the community should be involved in addressing long-term sustainability from the beginning. Ask whether your entire governing board should be involved in sustainability planning or just a subcommittee. If you choose a subcommittee, make sure that it includes all the key stakeholders and reports directly back to your full board. Don't forget to put sustainability planning into your project timeline. Strong management is *essential* to create and sustain outstanding programs. Make sure that you have high caliber internal administrative and management systems in place to provide program efficiency and stability; without them no sustainability plan will succeed.

Create a Positive Climate in Which to Advocate for Program Sustainability

Most programs can only be sustained with a broad base of community support. You can build on the trusting relationships built during the program planning stage and nurture them during program implementation. Consider the following.

Leaders and Champions

Your program will need a committed leadership and several champions. Ask your champions to keep key stakeholders, elected officials and policymakers informed. For example, if your project prevents youth violence there should be a measurable drop in pressure on the police and court systems. If representatives from the juvenile justice system are not involved in project implementation, let them know how the project is going and what results you have achieved to date.

The Media

If it is not already in place, develop a plan for creating a strong relationship with the local media. This will enable you to keep the general public and your communities of interest informed about the program's impact.

Community of Interest

Successful programs often result in cost-savings for some group in your community and benefit several constituencies. Create a strategy for identifying organizations and people who appreciate, need, or want your program. Keep these groups informed and ask them to advocate for your program in appropriate ways.

SWOT Analysis

Identify internal and external threats and opportunities to give the program the ability to adapt to changing conditions.

Determine What to Sustain

Before creating a sustainability plan first define a clear programmatic vision and decide how to set sustainability goals. In the *Community Toolbox*, Jenette Nagy recommends this simple rule of thumb, "If it helps keep your organization or its work going, and if it's something you would have had to pay for if it hadn't been a donation, then developing it fully will be part of your financial sustainability plan."

The sustainability team should determine how to set sustainability goals based on the evaluation data. They might choose to sustain all components at 100 percent, all components at a lower rate, only some successful components, or expand on some or all components. They will need to decide what the evaluation parameters will be and decide when you will have enough sound evaluation data to make decisions.

Creating Your Plan

Identify Resource Gaps

Once the team has determined what it wants to sustain it can then determine what resources are available and where gaps exist. Use this information as the basis for funding research to identify untapped funding sources.

Funding research

Plan to conduct research on grant funding options. Your sustainability team will need to look at existing community funding, such as formula grants, as well as discretionary grant funding sources. This funding research should result in a list of funding sources to sustain your project.

Sustainability plan

Create a plan that identifies who will seek what from whom, when and how. This plan will help to clarify thinking and provide common goals and objectives and clearly show how much effort will need to be expended to sustain the program. Get feedback on the sustainability plan from key stakeholders and partners. Implement the plan and celebrate successes.

Once your program planning team has thought through how your organization/collaboration will approach sustainability planning you will be able to lay out a clear, focused strategy in your proposal that will stand out in the crowd.

A presenter recently said at a bidders' conference "We know you're making it up. Just make up something good." By investing a little proposal planning time into thinking about your long-term sustainability strategy you can create something that is realistic and will benefit your team during program implementation. It will also give you the opportunity to put the icing on the cake and flourish on the proposal script.

 Connect with Jane at http://charitychannel.com/cc/jane-hexter

How Volunteers Can Transform the Grants Process

By Lynne T. Dean, CFRE

Successful development means building relationships with a variety of constituencies, including foundations. Many nonprofit organizations have no development staff or have one person handling development as well as marketing and public relations. These organizations often address the challenge of limited staff with a variety of strategies ranging from outsourcing to recruiting volunteers to involving more staff members in the grants process. Those organizations opting to work with volunteers often establish a grants committee and recruit individuals to work on grant research and writing. If the organization is conducting a special project or even a capital campaign, the nonprofit will seek well-connected, influential committee members to "open doors" to foundations by talking with trustees or program staff or to participate in a site visit. We've worked with both groups and share these two examples of organizations building successful grants teams with volunteers.

Two women, both retired school teachers, served as the grants committee for a rural library. Mary Jo and Sue, both volunteers and passionate about libraries and their community, had virtually single-handedly developed project ideas, found prospective funders and wrote and submitted proposals for library funding for more than two years. And, they wrote the thank-you letters and prepared reports. When they weren't working on grants, they were attending workshops on foundations, grant writing and any other related topics.

On a capital campaign for a new women's shelter, we facilitated the organization's recruitment of an energetic, community volunteer as chair of the Foundations Division of the campaign. Elizabeth serves on the school board and is active in several school, community and church organizations. She knows almost everyone in her community and in the towns nearby. As part of her work in this campaign, she has personally contacted members of the board of trustees of several area foundations on behalf of the shelter and the campaign, signed cover letters to accompany campaign proposals and hand-delivered proposals to foundation representatives with whom she is acquainted.

Important Contributors to the Overall Development Program

These two different examples illustrate the variety of ways that volunteers can have an impact on the grants process—everything from the initial research to the writing of the grant as Mary Jo and Sue did to making contacts with potential funding organizations as Elizabeth enjoyed doing. These foundation and grants volunteers can provide valuable assistance in your overall grants process and become important contributors to your overall development program.

Grant volunteers frequently form a grants committee for an organization and their roles and responsibilities can range from help in identifying potential funding sources, giving feedback on grant proposals, and writing grant proposals. "Outside" volunteers often serve on an organization's board of directors, a capital campaign leadership committee or a resource development group. They have community connections, are passionate about the mission of the nonprofit they serve and actively seek ways they can help.

Key positions on a grants committee often include a grant researcher and a grant writer, although in many cases, each person on the committee can accomplish both tasks. What qualifications should you look for as you recruit members for a grants committee?

Seek Those Familiar with the Internet to Assist in Research

For grant research, seek individuals with a background in online research who are self-motivated to peruse the Internet and other sources in search of donors whose philanthropic interests and funding criteria fit well with your organization and its programs. Internet proficiency should be a required skill.

Research volunteers should be able to assess the alignment between the prospect's interest and the mission of the organization so that they can recommend next steps for that prospect. They must also be able to overcome "hurdles" through follow-up communication such as emails or phone calls. These hurdles can range from technical ones (a website link might not work) or clarification of the grant process (what are the funding priorities or who is the correct contact).

Volunteer grant writers should have a writing background and enjoy and value a team environment in which other team members provide feedback. Writers with an almost uncanny ability to utilize a variety of styles, wording and content to align grants with a donor's philanthropic interests, needs and funding priorities are best suited for this work. Seek dedicated, tenacious individuals with an "as soon as possible" mindset, because you will want someone who can complete proposals and applications by due dates with little or no follow-up from a staff member.

Volunteers Can Also 'Open the Door' to Foundations

Well-connected community volunteers can tell the story of the organization to prospects, in many cases, members of a foundation's board of trustees. Their tasks might range from calling, visiting or writing an acquaintance who also serves on a foundation board or "opening the door" for the submission of a proposal to a foundation whose guidelines stipulate that "unsolicited proposals not accepted" or "contributes only to pre-selected organizations." When a foundation makes a site visit, these volunteers can be particularly helpful by sharing why they are involved with the organization.

Are there any great secrets to success in working with volunteers in your grants program? The bottom line is that your organization can make the program work with the right volunteers and the right leadership. Here are a few ideas to keep in mind.

1. Develop job descriptions

Whether you're forming a grants committee or the foundation division of a campaign, you should clearly outline the roles and responsibilities of the position.

2. Maintain regular contact

Remember that saying, "out of sight, out of mind?" Keep in touch with volunteers, establish deadlines and don't waver from them and have meetings as needed. Communicate in person, by phone or by email frequently.

3. Assign a staff member to oversee the committee and follow up on assignments

Having a staff liaison to work with volunteers will help ensure that tasks and action items are completed by the necessary deadlines.

4. Celebrate success

When you get the news that your project will be funded and you recall that two grant writers stayed up late three nights in a row to complete the proposal, make sure those two grant writers know that their efforts were successful. Share the news with everyone, call or email them, invite them for coffee or lunch or grab some noisemakers from the local discount store and have a celebration band at your next meeting.

5. Thank them

Acknowledge and recognize the time and efforts of your grants volunteers. Let them know you appreciate the work they do for your organization in conversations with them or in a note or email.

Lastly, the grants team, staff members and volunteers, need to have an overall understanding of your organization's work including projects and programs happening now and those planned for the future. Those with a general knowledge about fundraising and a dedication to following up and completing the grants process will be effective and successful in winning grants for your nonprofit.

 Connect with Lynne at http://charitychannel.com/cc/lynne-dean

Discovery Visits with Foundations

By Lynne T. Dean, CFRE

C onsider this scenario.

Scott J. serves on the ABC Advocacy Center board of directors with Susan M., who holds a position on the XYZ Regional Foundation board of trustees. Scott J. is also involved in the local hospital capital campaign. When the hospital decides to approach the regional foundation, foundation representatives ask whether any campaign committee members have friends, colleagues or acquaintances on the foundation's board of trustees. Scott J. shares with fellow board members that he and Susan M. have sons on the same soccer team and he would be pleased to speak to her on behalf of the hospital.

Scott J. contacts Susan M. and requests time for himself and Karl B., president of the hospital, to meet. At the agreed upon time, Scott J. and Karl B. arrive at the foundation's offices. Scott J. introduces the president of the hospital to Susan M. and they discuss the growth of the hospital, the need for new facilities, the impact the planned facilities can have on the community and the region, and the opportunities for involvement and investment.

They talk about the foundation, how it began, its purpose, important milestones in its history and the values of the donors and the trustees. They explore the foundation's leadership in community philanthropy and how the hospital might fit into the vision and goals of the foundation. They share stories about the impact of philanthropy on the lives of individuals, neighborhoods and communities. They agree that the hospital's new addition fits within the guidelines of the foundation and discuss how best to approach the foundation.

Establishing a Connection, Identifying Mutual Interests

Often, larger development offices utilize similar visits, called discovery visits, to get acquainted with potential individual donors. These initial visits provide critical information that often results in the establishment of a connection between the prospect and the organization, identifying mutual interests and determining the possibility of future involvement and investment. More and more organizations and their development staff are finding that discovery visits such as the fictitious one described above can often be the starting point for building a long-term relationship with a foundation just as they often do with potential individual donors.

Before making the phone call to schedule a date and time for a discovery visit, however, you and your organization have to "do your homework" on the foundation. Just as you found it necessary to complete your science homework so that you could pass your fifth grade science test, you and your organization need to devote time to homework, in this case thorough research, before approaching a foundation. Your research should uncover the answers to two important questions: is there a match between the mission of your organization and the funding priorities of the foundation and how does the foundation specify that potential grantees should contact and approach them.

What happens if you see that dreaded phrase "contributes only to pre-selected organizations" in the foundation's description? Discovery visits can sometimes provide a point of entry to an otherwise closed-door foundation and offer another opportunity for board members to utilize their links and relationships in the community. You should circulate the list of the foundation's board of trustees among board members, volunteers and staff members. Ask them to look for anyone with whom they might have a connection and are willing to approach on the organization's behalf.

Consider Approaching Past Grantees

None of your organization's board members have those connections? Consider approaching past grantees of the foundation. Informal discovery visits with organizations who have won funds from a "closed door" funder might often provide important insights and a better understanding of the foundation. Additionally, these grantees might also recommend your organization to the funder. Choose a grantee with whom you have a good relationship and one providing different services from yours (elderly services vs. the environment) to alleviate the concern of the grantee viewing you as a competitor. The grantee might gain even more by winning points from the funder for finding them a good-fit applicant.

Now that you've arranged the appointment and are sitting across the desk from a foundation program officer or trustee or even a grantee, what questions should you ask in a discovery visit? Questions will generally reflect the personalities of the board and staff members involved in the visit, however, as you gain experience, you will learn the best ways to get the information you need while remaining conversational.

Ask about the foundation's first grant or perhaps the grant which has had the most impact.

◆ Are there particular projects funded that have captured the foundation's attention more than others? What types of projects inspire the most support?

◆ Are there programs or funding priorities that will be emphasized more this year or in the future?

◆ Ask about the foundation's position on a current topic or issue such as emergency relief and how that fits into funding decisions.

◆ Determine what outcome measurements are most important to the foundation. How does the foundation want to make a difference in the lives of individuals and communities?

Answers to these questions can lead the discussion to your organization and provide you the opportunity to discuss your projects and ask which might be of interest to the foundation. Ask about appropriate grant request ranges and suggestions on how to follow up in submitting a letter or proposal. And, remember, large foundations differ from smaller family-led foundations.

Only 23 percent of family foundations fund unsolicited requests, according to a 2009 survey by *Foundation Source*, and a large percentage of grantees have relationships with the foundation. Comments from respondents indicated that organizations should deploy their own board members effectively and provide opportunities for family funders to get to know the nonprofit in low-pressure environments. Fifty-eight percent of respondents affirmed the importance of "someone I know and respect being closely involved or asking me to support the project."

When making a discovery visit to a foundation receptive to face-to-face meetings, you'll be implementing a strategy that in the best of circumstances can significantly impact your organization's bottom line. The rationale is simple—competition for foundation funding is increasing and that is not expected to change in the near future. If you have the opportunity to show a foundation in a discovery visit how your mission and vision matches their interests and values, you stand a better chance of having your proposal placed at the top of their pile. Get noticed, build loyalty, get funded!

 Connect with Lynne at http://charitychannel.com/cc/lynne-dean

Is Your Organization Grant-Ready?

By Linda Butler

During times of economic uncertainty, grants become critical to nonprofits. Fundraisers, proposal writers and/or consultants are hired by many organizations to generate support and fill budgetary gaps. Increased competition and savvy funders force organizations and grant professionals to help the organization assess its grant-readiness before churning out proposals.

In order to position your organization as grant-ready, I offer two core ideas. First, I will identify criteria that a grant professional can use to assess an organization's capacity for grant seeking and readiness to obtain funding for project implementation. Second, I will discuss steps to identify methods to implement organizational practices that enhance grant-readiness. These core ideas are reflected in the Grant Professionals Association's Grant Professionals Certification Institute that identify "*Knowledge of organizational development as it pertains to grant seeking*" as a validated, measurable competency and skill for a grant professional.

Assess Organizational Capacity

Grant seeking is often misunderstood as the limited activity of writing a proposal to secure funds for the organization or a project. While proposal submission is a key step in the process of grant seeking, the grant professional's role includes educating staff about the "3 Rs of Grant Seeking" in priority order:

◆ **R**elationships (i.e., contacts and opportunities);

◆ **R**esearch (i.e., geography and fit with funder); and

◆ w**R**iting the proposal (i.e., writing skills).

It is crucial for the grant professional to assess the organization's capacity to seek, write, implement and manage grants as well as to encourage the "culture of fundraising" (i.e., philosophy supporting the values, ethics and principles of raising dollars) before starting the proposal development process. Grant seeking, writing, implementing and managing is a *targeted* process that involves planning, researching, cultivating relationships, fundraising principles and monitoring. To facilitate this, I have developed a *Checklist for Success* as an important component of the toolkit for assessing the organization's grant-readiness. Several of the items on the checklist are requested attachments by many funders in order to meet the guidelines and/or application requirements. When an organization doesn't have the items listed, the checklist becomes an organizational "to do list" in order to build capacity and address necessary infrastructure issues.

Checklist for Success

Collect the following documents and keep multiple hard and electronic copies available to ensure grant-readiness!

- ◆ 501(c)(3) determination letter from the IRS (plus renewals and updates)

- ◆ Annual report and organizational materials (e.g., brochures, newsletters, articles)

- ◆ Employer Identification Number (EIN)/ tax ID #

- ◆ Data Universal Numbering System (DUNS) # and National Information Management System (NIMS) registration

- ◆ Evaluation, outcomes, performance measures

- ◆ Future funding statement for continued funding/sustainability (including list of pending proposals and/or awarded grants)

- ◆ History of organization including year established, staff data, programs, mission, vision, values/ philosophy, awards, stories/testimonials, accreditations/certifications

- ◆ Calendar of events

- ◆ List of board of directors/ trustee members and officers, titles, affiliations, contact info

- ◆ Volunteer data

- ◆ List of management staff and contact information

- ◆ Map of target area and demographics of those served

◆ Minutes of board meetings and resolutions for past year

◆ Most recent audit

◆ Most recent financial statement, state and federal filings

◆ Current fund development plan that includes *targeted* grants and proposals

◆ Current strategic plan/business plan

◆ Table of organization/organizational flow-chart

◆ Current project and organizational budgets with budget narratives

◆ Recent newspaper clippings, evaluations or reviews

◆ Resumes and/or job descriptions of current and/or proposed staff

◆ Sample letters of support/commitment

◆ Target population, demographics & needs ("best-practice models" or "evidence-based programs")

◆ Mission and vision statements

◆ Certificate of Incorporation and bylaws

◆ Logic models for programs

◆ New 990 Form with required information re: governance and fundraising (effective 5-09; www.IRS.gov/eo)

◆ www.GRANTS.gov Central Contractor Registration for all federal grants (This registration needs to be renewed annually.)

Each funder's application will have application guidelines. Be sure to note the format and content required.

Remember the Golden Rule: *Whoever has the gold makes the rules.*

Identify Methods that Enhance Grant-readiness

In order to maximize this *Checklist for Success*, the grant professional can advance the grant-readiness of the organization by implementing strategies that enhance, support and strengthen the organization's ability to apply for and secure grant funds.

Educate the staff, especially the administration, about the grants process

A common, erroneous assumption made by many grant professionals is that the staff understands the grants world and process. Although some staff might have experience with grants, most do not fully understand the process, ethics and/or context within fundraising. To assume that a clinician or a faculty member understands what grants involve is comparable to assuming that the grant professional has the expertise of the clinician's or the faculty's work.

The grants professional must teach the staff about the importance of the team approach in the proposal development process and about the importance of assessing each project's grant-readiness. To facilitate this education, I suggest several strategies such as providing:

- ◆ presentations about the grants process;
- ◆ regular newsletters/ e-newsletters from the grants office that can highlight funded projects, funding opportunities and/or prioritized projects that align with the strategic plan;
- ◆ reviews of successful and challenging grant-funded projects;
- ◆ creation of a clearinghouse/foundation for all organizational grants and fundraising (that can require completion of a project development form);
- ◆ team input into the annual fundraising plan that includes targeted grants and proposals;
- ◆ a grants team that is created for each project; and
- ◆ grant trainings for the staff that focus on the specific organizational needs.

Cultivate and Maintain Relationships with Funders

The first and most important "R" in the "3 Rs of Grant Seeking" is *Relationships*. Cultivating professional relationships with the grantors and maintaining consistent, open communication are keys to advancing organizational grant-readiness. Past and prospective funders have interest in the project's progress and success. Keep funders informed with regular progress reports, newspaper clippings, newsletters and invitations to events. The organization's board members are responsible for financial stability that includes fundraising. Therefore, board members have the responsibility to cultivate and maintain relationships with funders in coordination with administrators.

Conduct Research and Fund Development in a Systematic, Organized, Timely Manner

The second "R" in the "3 Rs of Grant Seeking" is *Research.* In order to prepare for funding opportunities as they arise, the grant professional must establish an organized, structured and timely way to research funders that align with the organization's strategic plan, priorities and projects. As a consultant, I create "grant plans" with my clients that detail funders, contact information, alignment of the organization's mission with the funder's priorities, funding cycles and deadlines, the submission process and action steps. The grant plans are updated monthly and reviewed by the grants team in order to align funding opportunities with targeted projects based on receipt of completed project development forms.

By practicing these two core ideas and using the *Checklist For Success*, you can help your organization become grant-ready and ready to tackle the third R—w**R**iting!

 Connect with Linda at http://charitychannel.com/cc/linda-butler

Developing a Convincing Needs Statement

By Lynne T. Dean, CFRE

What makes the needs statement such a crucial and interesting part of a grants proposal? This is the section of a proposal that provides the grant writer the chance to not only spark the grant maker's interest but also to prove without a shadow of doubt that you've identified a critical need and that your organization has the programmatic response that seems to be a natural solution.

If you are uncertain of the importance of a convincing needs statement, think about the difference between getting your proposal seriously considered, or quietly put aside. Yes, the needs statement is *that* important. This section of the grant proposal might represent the pivotal part of your case for grant funding.

Call me crazy, but researching, organizing and writing the needs section of a grant proposal ranks among my favorite grant writing tasks. I've often compared it to developing the case for support in a capital campaign, another high-ranking fundraising pastime of mine.

What makes the needs statement such a crucial and interesting part of a grants proposal is that this section gives you the chance not only to spark the grant maker's interest but also to prove without a shadow of doubt that you've identified a critical need and your organization has the programmatic response that seems like a natural solution. Your goal in writing the needs statement is to define the problem, its causes and systems while at the same time convincing the funding source that these issues are important to your organization and to them.

Usually, grant writers follow a six-step process to ensure that their organization's proposals will not be one of those tossed aside.

1. Define the problem or need, its causes, and symptoms

The need you address should be clearly related to the mission and purpose of your organization. It should focus on the people you serve, rather than the needs of your nonprofit. Be specific in identifying the problem or need as it exists in the targeted community. Focus on the geographic area the project will serve. Clarify whether the problem is local, regional, statewide or national.

2. Research, research, research

Gather all relevant statistics, studies, evaluations, and other information that will help define the problem and support your organization's proposed solution. In addition to online research, remember to check other sources such as copies of annual reports, meeting minutes from board and committee meetings, previous grant applications, speeches made by executive directors and board members, and program evaluations.

Be certain that all statistics are up-to-date and relevant to your issue. This will ensure that you'll avoid the embarrassment of having a funder tell you that your information is outdated or incorrect.

3. Organize your data

After you complete your research, organize your findings into three piles (for hard copies) and three documents (for online sources). The first should be reserved for information which documents the need or problem; the second should contain information that provides a compelling and accurate assessment of the impact of the need; and, a third should be reserved for information that provides a clear picture of the desired "state of affairs" that should or could exist.

If you're like most proposal writers, you will accumulate much more information than you can possibly use. Therefore, you'll need to select statistics and other results from your research that best support your argument.

Comparative statistics and research are particularly effective for needs statements. Two additional ways you can make an even stronger case for your organization's proposed actions are: (1) Describing a community that did something similar to what you are proposing and the program's beneficial results; and, (2) Quoting authorities or experts on your topic. Include names and sources of information when utilizing expert quotes so that the information can be verified.

4. Make it personal

Use touching anecdotes about the impact that the program has had individual participants and remember to ensure that these stories support and are related to the hard data you have provided. A well-supported needs statement that also includes effective stories is a winner.

Another way to personalize the needs statement is to utilize the supporting data acquired by using a professionally designed participant survey. These can be handout out to participants and tallied results report to funders.

You might also want to assemble a focus group of current participants and other individuals in your target market to gather information and to help show grant reviewers what impact your project is expected to produce.

5. Write in sections

After you have condensed and edited the mounds of information you've compiled, you are ready to write. I generally write needs statements in four sections similar to those described in the book *Proposal Writing: Effective Grantsmanship* by Coley and Scheinberg.

In the first section, you will need to define the program need and explain who is experiencing that need. You will provide an overview of the number of people who have the need and specific information on their ethnicity, gender, and educational level. The next section, you will focus on factors contributing to the need or problem. In the third section, you will look at the impact of the need on the individual and the community at large. This section will also include potential benefits derived through the intervention, treatment, or prevention of the specific problem or need. In these three sections, you will lay the groundwork for how your project can address the need you have defined.

In the fourth section, you will begin talking about your proposed project by focusing on promising approaches that indicate improved results. You can point out successful approaches used in other geographical areas and perhaps mention barriers to improving the problem or successfully addressing the need. You can also reference particular theoretical and practical program components that will be effective in addressing the need or problem. You can include pros and cons of particular strategies and consider the unique needs of your participants. Note that the section of the proposal which outlines your methods will build upon the rationale you have already described in the needs statement.

And while we're talking about rationale, I want to caution you about a very common mistake know as "circular reasoning" (sometimes mistakenly included in needs statements). Circular reasoning can occur when you contend that the problem is a lack of the service that you are proposing.

For example, your problem statement might express your agency's need for a new senior center. However, funders want to hear what problems your senior clients are experiencing (rather than your agency's funding challenges). Your need statement must address how the center will help address client needs.

6. Ask someone else to read it

Does the need identified relate to the purpose and goals of your organization? Was documented evidence included to support the existence of the need or problem? Was compelling case made for the need for your project or program?

After you ask yourself these questions, give your need statement to a non-technical person or someone not associated with the proposed project. Ask them to rate the needs statement on each of these three questions.

Remember that a convincing needs statement will motivate the reader to act. Persons reading your statement should feel compelled to make a personal donation to your cause.

Lastly before finalizing a need statement, most grant writers separate it from the other sections of the proposal. It should read as a stand-alone piece and should feature compelling language and be written in a logical sequence.

Edit, edit, and edit again. The goal is to have each paragraph build upon the previous one to create a persuasive case for the issue and proposed solution. As part of the editing process, experienced grant writers look for places to insert subheads and bold or italicized phrases which might strengthen the document.

When you provide foundation program officers with convincing needs statement, you are giving them an important tool on which they can make a positive funding recommendation. Developing compelling needs statement with strong facts to back up your organization's claims can help ensure that your proposals are among those strongly considered for funding rather than one that is quietly put aside.

 Connect with Lynne at http://charitychannel.com/cc/lynne-dean

A Grant Writing Primer

By Joyce Luhrs

Every time I set out to read an application for a grant, I remember the first words the teachers told me in elementary school: Read the directions first! These helpful words are still true today.

A proposal requesting a specific grant can be the most complicated or the easiest document to complete. The key is to understand the funder's requirements thoroughly before sitting down to write the proposal.

Before you decide to forge ahead and submit a proposal to a specific funder, get copies of the request for proposal and the application. Many funders (foundation and government) post their applications online in a downloadable format. Other agencies might accept telephone or email requests, while some funding agencies still require that a written request be mailed on an organization's letterhead.

Read the Application

First, review the application quickly to get an overview of its sections, eligibility, points of contact, the deadline date and other requirements. You don't want to spend time reviewing a lengthy document if the deadline is past or your organization is ineligible.

Then, go back and read the entire application carefully from beginning to end. Check that all the pages are included. Occasionally, application booklets might be missing a few pages or are printed incorrectly.

Be sure that you have the most current version. As more funders place their guidelines on their websites, check that the information is up to date. Information posted on websites might not be updated frequently. An application might state that it might be used only for a specific time period or a date might be found on the front cover, indicating when it was modified or updated.

Eligibility requirements

Before responding to the request for proposal, you need to make sure you meet the eligibility requirements. Some common requirements are stipulated according to the type of organization—nonprofit, Internal Revenue Service designation as a not-for-profit 501(c) (3) organization, community-based nonprofit groups, government agency, local educational agency, private school, higher education institutions, consortia, partners, among others.

These are other eligibility requirements to check:

◆ the purpose of the grant;

◆ stipulations about how grant funds may be used;

◆ targeting organizations that meet a specific need;

◆ identifying groups or individuals that work with a particular niche in the community;

◆ matching funds requirements;

◆ specific geographical locations are identified; and

◆ qualification requirements.

Compatibility

Decide if your organization's needs and the funder's interests are compatible. The funders' mission and interests should be found and understood. Specific eligibility requirements should be identified. These might include awarding grants to only a particular geographical area, the income levels of the people to be serviced by a project, how funds may be used, or specific racial/ethnic groups that should be assisted in a project. Sometimes funders require matching funds, specific qualifications for personnel, or provide other stipulations not required in past RFPs.

Contact the funder's program officer about your organization's proposed project concept before submitting an application. Some funders might agree to speak with you by phone or in a meeting. Unless an application states that the funder does not accept unsolicited applications or does not take inquiries, this step might help your organization clarify the appropriate approach to use in the application, while saving you the time and expense involved to prepare and submit a proposal that might be declined if the project idea does not meet the funder's requirements.

Watch out for these "gotchas"

- page limits;

- specific font size;

- margin requirements;

- the type of paper to be used, including recyclable, printing on the front and back of the paper;

- line spacing requirements of single or double;

- bound or unbound;

- printed or electronic copies;

- number of copies;

- submitting applications only online;

- conflicting instructions found in different sections of the RFP;

- the number of copies to submit;

- pre-proposal notification requirements and dates;

- partner requirements;

- stipulations about attachments; and

- deadline phrases such as "postmarked by" or "due on."

Read the fine print. Don't ignore it. Look out for asterisks, as additional information is sometimes noted or found in another part of the application. Note any exceptions or waivers, such as how a document may be submitted or what to do if technological glitches occur when uploading a proposal.

warning!

Deadline date

Deadlines vary from rolling, once a year, several times a year, or even every few years. During an economic downturn, some funders scale back their deadlines to only one a year. Others might decide not to accept any applications this year, while some might limit the application process to organizations that are past recipients.

Amount available and number of awards

Look for the minimum and maximum award amounts, the average size of a grant and the number of awards that will be made. Some funders might stipulate distinct award amounts for different purposes.

Signature requirements

Identify any signature requirements throughout the application. Original signatures might be required on a cover letter, a form, on attachments, and in other parts of the application. Know in advance who has the authority to sign-off on the application and give that person advanced notice to be available to review and sign the final copy.

The appendix

If an appendix is included, don't overlook it. Occasionally, funders, especially government agencies, will insert legislation that provides additional details and requirements to complete the application.

Develop a checklist

Prepare a list of all information that is requested and check that everything has been completed before the application is submitted.

Make a copy

Accidents happen. On the day the applicant inserts the original version of the forms into the printer, it jams, and the paper pops out torn. Tea or coffee stains on the forms will surely not reflect well upon the applicant. Either request an extra copy of the application or make another copy to be available if Murphy's Law should strike.

Follow the Directions

Read the application's directions very carefully word for word. Directions pertinent to one part of an application might not always be found in the same section. They might be continued in another part of the application.

If a guideline is unclear in the application, call the designated contact person listed in the RFP. Do not assume anything. Write down your question(s) before picking up the telephone or sending an email. Program officers are willing to help, but they do not want their time wasted.

Deadlines might be posted as rolling (ongoing), one per year, several times a year, or even every few years. Try to complete everything one to two weeks before the due date. While this might be a dream and an inconceivable reality for some, the current push by government agencies and more and more foundations and corporations requiring that applications be submitted electronically, means that organizations and individuals are now at the mercy of several entities working properly such as the applicant's computer system, the recipient's technology, and the Internet service provider of everyone involved.

Look for exceptions or waivers that might be discussed. For example, if your organization is located in an area where Internet access is extremely limited, you might be allowed to submit a proposal through the post office or a commercial delivery service. The directions might stipulate that an applicant planning to do this must notify the funder by a specific date.

Tell a Good Story

Keep the funder's reviewers engaged by telling a good, compelling story in the narrative. Provide the facts and the case that presents why the proposal should be considered and funded. Don't leave the reviewer with unanswered questions or points that do not make sense. Each point in an application should be logical and connect from the beginning to end. Information provided in the narrative should be reflected in the budget and vice-versa.

Don't use slang terms, jargon, or language that leaves the reviewer with a negative impression. Sentences and ideas should be clear and concise.

Provide only the information requested in the directions. Give only what is requested, no more, no less. Answer all questions completely and honestly. If a form must be completed, provide only the information required. Sometimes the form may be scanned or completed using word processing software.

Some funders list very specific guidelines about how an application must be organized. On occasion, funders, especially government agencies, state very clearly in their applications that a proposal will not even be reviewed if those guidelines aren't followed.

Make the Right First Impression

The application is often the only thing that a prospective funder has about your organization. Preferably, prepare the application and all attachments on a computer. Although the typewriter has become somewhat of a dinosaur, forms that cannot be scanned easily will need to be completed using this older technology. If a typewriter is unavailable, you may hand print the information neatly with block. Narratives should be typed.

Read the entire application and check for spelling and grammatical errors. Ask other people to read first and final drafts of the completed application.

Reaching the Finish Line

Try to complete everything one to two weeks before the due date. Leave time to rectify any last minute hiccups and be sure to submit the application to any review panels within your organization with advance notice. Make sure that anyone who is required to provide an original signature on the application is still available to sign the final document.

If you submit the application through postal mail or a commercial carrier, get a dated receipt as proof of the mailing. Funders that require applications be submitted electronically might send a postcard indicating that the application has been received or they might send an email with that message. Always save these messages as proof that the application was submitted on time.

Back-up the entire document. Always make electronic and hard copies of the entire application.

 Connect with Joyce at http://charitychannel.com/cc/joyce-luhrs

Tips for New Grantwriters

By Shelley Uva

I became a grant writer almost totally by accident. I needed a job. I lived within walking distance of New York University. One day, I looked through their book of employment opportunities and saw a listing for "development writer." At that time, I had never heard of development, but I knew what writing was, and, in fact, I was a writer. I applied for the job, and today, more than thirty years later, I am still at it.

As it turned out, many of the skills I had developed from working in college and community journalism translated well to grant writing. In those days, fundraising was a newly developing profession, and many people came to it from public relations, journalism, advertising and other fields in which writing played a key role. Today, development is an established profession, and many grant writers come from college programs. Of course, people still come to development in less formal ways. If you are new to grant writing, if you have taken a course or two, or if you are one of the many people who have some other job at a nonprofit, and grant writing has just been handed over to you, these tips are for you.

1. Think about what a grant proposal is

A grant proposal is not a work of art, but it can be so well written and crafted that it is a thing of beauty. And it always is much more than a collection of sentences. A grant proposal forms the bridge between a nonprofit organization and its funding sources. It represents the culmination of many ideas that identify a specific problem, describe a program or project to address that need, and demonstrate why funding is needed and how it will be used. One way to look at a grant application is as the middle part of a timeline that begins with conception and ends with implementation. The grant application is how your organization gets from the former to the latter, and your words and sentences are the engine that drives it.

2. Learn about your prospective funder

Most grant proposals are written for foundations. The best resource to learn about foundations is *The Foundation Directory,* which includes listings for most foundations with information about how to apply. Foundations have varying requirements: some provide a short answer form; some ask you to send a short letter; some will accept a full proposal right away but ask you to follow a particular format or use a common application format; others require no particular format. Some foundations are much more available than others. By this I mean that there are foundations that will accept telephone inquiries from development offices and help you shape a proposal. Most often, this occurs when there already is a funding relationship in place and you are preparing a renewal request. In my experience, while many foundations say their doors are always open, the reality is somewhat different. It is often very difficult to get someone at a foundation to speak with you about your proposal. Many simply don't have the on-site personnel to handle lots of inquiries. You can look at a foundation's listing to see what types of funding it has provided in the past. You also can do a search by specific funding areas to see who funds each one. In addition, you can look at 990 forms and other documents to see what a particular foundation has funded in the past. Of course, it is always helpful to have personal contact with a foundation, but it is not always possible. Lack of personal contact should not automatically eliminate a foundation from your plan. I know that some people will say that submitting proposals cold doesn't work, but I have seen it work often in my career.

3. Read all instructions and follow them!

Do not improvise when writing a proposal. If your funder asks for specific information, do not substitute some variation. For example, most funders will ask for your current and last year's budget. Do not just provide one or the other. If your funder asks for information in a specific, numbered order with each item numbered, provide the information in that format even if you think it reads better some other way.

4. Create and use templates for proposals

I always create proposal templates for general operating support and for each program my organization maintains. Because so many of the foundations to which I have applied through the years accept the New York/New Jersey Common Application Form, this is the template I use most often. There are several regional organizations and other groups that have created common application forms that are accepted by various foundations. Most foundation websites and listings for foundations in the *Foundation Directory* indicate what, if any, common application form they accept. If this information is not clear to you, call the foundation and ask if they require a particular application form. If a foundation requires a particular form and you are not sure where to get a copy, you can Google the name of the form and this will, in most cases, lead you to it.

Using these forms works well because even foundations that use their own formats tend to ask many of the same questions. By preparing a template, I have most of the information I will need on hand. Of course, using a template does not mean that I just send the same proposal to everyone. A template easily can be tailored to a specific donor. Working from a template will save you lots of time and eliminate endless duplication of effort.

5. Learn about the subject matter

In order to know the subject matter of your proposal, you have to ask questions. Most often, you will need to interview the program people in your organization and/or some clients. Make sure you check your organization's files for past proposals on a particular program. These kinds of files can be very helpful in showing you how a program has evolved through the years. Sometimes you might want to place your program in a larger context so you might need to do some library or online research. Make sure, however, that you don't get lost in research. If you work with a community-based organization, it is logical to put your program in the context of the larger county or city, but maybe not so logical to try and relate to national issues. While we're on the subject of knowledge, make sure you also know the giving history of any particular funder you approach and acknowledge it in the "ask" portion of your proposal and/or the cover letter. One thing most donors really dislike is not being acknowledged for what they have contributed already.

6. Be totally honest

Do not make claims that are exaggerated or, even worse, untrue. Two of the most overused words in proposal writing are "unique" and "innovative." Lots of programs are well-run, economically sound and worthwhile without being especially innovative or unique. I know that many funders say they are interested in innovation and many ask why your program is unique, but I think it is best to use these words with caution.

7. Be straightforward and stick to the point

A grant proposal needs to tell a story. You want to communicate the importance of the work you do and the ways in which it affects the lives of your program participants. It is easy to fall into the "hearts and flowers" trap. Try to use less flowery language, rather than more, and don't intentionally pull at the heartstrings. At the same time, don't be afraid of being eloquent. I know this sounds contradictory, but this kind of writing is a real balancing act. One great way to tell your story is to use short profiles of the people you help and quotes from them. Let them tell their stories. And remember, a good proposal should have heart, but not give heartburn.

8. Watch those outcomes!

Many funders will ask you to predict outcomes for a particular program. Be very careful what you predict—it will come back to haunt you in reports and renewal requests. Do not inflate your outcomes to grab the attention of a prospective funder.

9. Admit your mistakes

Every organization has had programs that didn't work and outcomes that were never achieved. Don't try to cover these up or sweep them under a rug. Instead, try to explain what happened and what steps you have taken or will take to correct the situation. Try to make mistakes a learning experience that helps you create better programs in the future.

10. Do not miss deadlines

This is a pretty obvious tip, but worth repeating. Do not miss deadlines. Your funder does not care if the dog ate your homework.

A few other things to remember:

◆ Keep copies of everything

You might end up doing ten versions of one proposal. Keep them all and use the track changes feature available on your computer so you can see how and when things get changed. You can ask each "editor" to track changes in a different color so it is totally clear who suggested what.

◆ Write up notes from all of your meetings and phone conversations

It is very common for people to develop selective amnesia about things they said or didn't say. The point of this kind of record-keeping is not to play "gotcha" but to know whose idea it was to change something long after no one really remembers.

◆ Make sure you know your basic grammar

Don't begin a sentence with a number—write it out. Don't use the percent sign (%)—write out the word percent. Know the difference between which and that (I won't tell you— you find out). Don't confuse directions with quantities. Over is a direction; more than is a quantity. Don't split infinitives. An infinitive is a compound verb made up of the preposition "to" and the basic form of the verb. One example would be to learn. A split infinitive occurs when you place a descriptive word in between the "to" and the verb. An example would be to fully develop. What you want to say is to develop fully. Here it is in a sentence. Split infinitive: The program's goal is to fully develop the town's water system. Better version: The program's goal is to develop fully the town's water system. Even better version: The program's goal is to develop the town's water system fully. Don't use semi-colons when you should be using commas, and don't use commas when you need semi-colons. Find out if your organization uses a particular style book and if your organization doesn't have one, either find on you can all agree to use or develop your own.

11. Work hard on budgets

If you have worked in development for more than a week or so, you already know that gathering budget information can be really difficult. Sometimes, the information exists, but not in the format you require. In other instances, there might be multiple, contradictory budgets. It is your job to find the people in your organization who really know budgets and work with them to put logical budgets together for your funders. Don't leave the budget for the last minute. It can take more time than writing the entire proposal!

12. Neatness counts

Neatness does count. Make sure you check your spelling and page numbering. Make sure budgets are legible. Do not use little tiny type in an effort to squeeze in more information. Do not spill beverages on your proposal. Make sure you follow all instructions about numbering pages, the order in which to present attachments and labeling attachments. Do not send material, such as video tapes, unless it is specifically requested.

 Connect with Shelley at http://charitychannel.com/cc/shelley-uva

To Importune or Not to Importune

By Shelly Uva

Good writing skills are essential in many occupations, including fundraising. While the best-written solicitation letter or proposal might not be the deciding factor involved in obtaining a grant, few things will turn off a foundation officer or individual donor more quickly than materials that are poorly written, sloppy or just plain boring. Fiction writing is an art, which might or might not be possible to teach, but development writing is a craft, and it can be learned.

Good development writing should always be conversational and matter-of-fact. By conversational, I do not mean that you should employ slang or street talk. No one is going to take seriously a solicitation letter that opens with "Yo dog" as opposed to "Dear Mr. Jones." By the same token, proposals written in the style of an 18th century fop asking his king for a land grant can be equally irritating.

Here are a few points that you might want to consider:

1. Who is your audience?

Before you begin to write, think about whom your audience is and what your audience knows. If you are writing a proposal about a specific program, such as supportive housing for people coping with mental illness, and the foundation you are approaching specializes in funding housing programs, mental illness, or both, you don't have to explain what supportive housing is or why, in general, it is important. You only need to make the case that your program serves the targeted population and does it well. If, on the other hand, you are sending your proposal to a foundation that is not focused as specifically, you might need to explain the terminology you use and put in more information about why your program is needed and important.

2. Get organized

Organize your thoughts before you begin to write. Some funders have a very specific format they want you to follow. This makes your organization easy. Follow their format. Other funders, however, don't provide a specific format so you have to organize yourself. This is a very typical format for program proposals:

◆ a half to one-page summary that begins with "the ask";

◆ a page or two about your organization, including such information as when you were founded, your mission statement, where you are located, how many people and what population groups you serve and what relationships you have with other nonprofits;

◆ a funding request including information about your specific program—what it does, why it is important, who it serves—the finances of the program— what it costs to run, how it is funded currently, what you will use this new funding to accomplish—and how you will evaluate the program and sustain it after the grant ends; and

◆ a conclusion that sums up the importance of the gift and outlines any recognition opportunities available.

The question of how you sustain a program can be really difficult because we all know that lots of programs, especially in social services, will never be self-sustaining and the only way they can go on is with continuing support. This might not be what a funder wants to hear, but it is always better to tell the truth. Think about this question as an opportunity to educate people who might not realize that a program that can't pay for itself can still be critically important and effective.

3. Choose your words carefully

Language is important. Don't abuse it. Don't use such words as utilize or prioritize. I know everyone does it, but to me, these words scream management jargon. You don't need to utilize; you can make use of something instead. And you don't need to prioritize; you can set priorities.

4. Be wary of claiming too much

Don't call everything you do "unique." If you call something unique, you better be sure that it is actually one-of-a-kind. Do not call everything you do innovative, either. I know that these are buzzwords often used by funders, but the fact is that there are many programs that are "tried and true" that work and that is why they deserve funding. This is a hard case to make, I will concede, but you can do it!

5. Over vs. more than

Try to remember the difference between directions and quantities. Do not say your program serves over 500 clients. Over is a direction. Instead, say your program serves more than 500 clients. More than is a quantity. This is a really difficult one, I know, because usage has made "over" acceptable to a lot of people, but it still drives me nuts.

6. Methinks you doth . . . etc., etc.

Don't use antiquated words because you think they sound "classy." Some examples of these kinds of words are amongst, amidst, betwixt, and behooves. These are real words and they might have their place in some writing, but not in proposals and solicitation letters.

7. Which vs. that

Learn the difference between which and that, and do not use which all the time because you think it sounds classier.

8. Try not to enrich and enhance

Beware of enriching and enhancing. We all like to think that our programs enrich and enhance people's lives but these two words are seriously overused. My rule is that when you find yourself using words like enrich and enhance in your everyday conversation, it's time to drop them from your proposal writing.

9. Stay active

Don't use more words than you need and try to keep your sentences in the active, present tense. Instead of saying that "The Program to Rid the World of Pretentiousness was implemented by the Committee for the Good in July 2010," say "The Committee for the Good initiated the Program to Rid the World of Pretentiousness in July 2010."

10. Try to avoid jargon of all kinds

I don't know how the rest of you feel, but I really hate the words "paradigm" and "modality" and I don't think either should ever be seen or heard again.

11. Get to the point!

I used to really dislike funders who asked me to describe a program is three sentences or 500 words, but I am beginning to appreciate the discipline it requires to weed out the extraneous and get to the heart of the matter quickly. Even if there is no word limit on what you are writing, it can be a good idea to set your own limit. Always remember that the people reading your proposal have to wade through hundreds of these requests. If your funder remembers your proposal because it is the longest one he or she has ever read, that is not necessarily a plus.

12. On the other hand, don't be too brief

If you are asking a foundation or an individual for a large grant, for example, $1 million, you need to provide a sufficient amount of information to justify that level of commitment. You need to explain who you are, what your program hopes to accomplish, what your past experience has been and what you intend to use the grant to accomplish. If you are writing about complex subjects, this will require more than one or two pages. There is no real ideal length for a proposal. Some funders will tell you not to go beyond five pages or ten pages and, if a funder gives you that kind of guidelines, be sure you follow it. If no guidelines about length are provided, use your common sense.

13. Avoid excessive emotional appeals

Don't whine. Don't plead. Don't beg. Use the facts to make your case and let your case speak for itself.

14. Avoid excessive emotional appeals, part two

Don't clutter up your proposal with hearts and flowers and violin music. I'm not talking about case histories because these can help sell a proposal and they are totally appropriate. Case histories can and should be very moving. I'm talking about adding lots of adjectives and descriptions meant to tug at the heartstrings. You have to remember always that you are competing with other nonprofits that also bring help and hope to those in need. Proposal writing should not be a contest to see who can be more emotional.

15. On the other hand, don't be too dry

A proposal is meant to tell a story about what you do and why it is worth doing. It should never be just about numbers, although numbers do play a role. A proposal should be about people and how, with your funder's support, your organization can help those people achieve a worthy goal.

16. Commas vs. semi-colons

Don't, go, comma, crazy, but on the other hand do not be afraid to insert commas where they are needed and don't confuse commas with semi-colons.

17. Watch those capital letters

Be careful about how you use capital letters. If you are writing about the Tai Chi Program for Seniors (capitalized because that is its formal name), you can then capitalize the word Program when you refer to this specific program later on in your proposal. However, you don't want to capitalize words to make them seem more important. For example: the Joe Smith Mental Health Clinic (capitalized because it is the name of the clinic) treats adults and children with a variety of Mental Illnesses, including Depression. Mental illnesses and depression should not be capitalized in that sentence.

18. A final word

The title of this essay is "To Importune or Not to Importune." Never importune. Just ask.

 Connect with Shelley at http://charitychannel.com/cc/shelley-uva

Grant Agreements: Read the Fine Print

By Teri S. Blandon, CFRE

The first thing any of us do when receiving a letter from a funder is to scan it quickly to see if our proposal was funded. But after the initial yelp of glee and happy dance of celebration, it is time to carefully review the document to determine the rules and regulations stipulated by the funder.

Grant agreements come in all sizes. Sometimes it is a simple one-page letter from the funder indicating the grant amount, time period and reporting requirements. Other times, it is a multi-page document with much detail. No matter the length, it is a legal contract between the funder and your agency, and it must be reviewed carefully. A lack of attention to this critical document can mean headaches months down the road.

In this article, I'll provide a checklist of the basic elements often found in a grant agreement, and explain what you are looking for and why.

Where it all begins

Actually, the grant agreement is only half of the contract with the funder—the other half is the proposal you submitted. In the proposal, you are making a commitment to the funder that if awarded a grant, your agency will carry out a specific program within a specific time period and spend a specific amount of money doing it.

The Proposal

The proposal is a promise to the funder to carry out certain activities in exchange for funding. The proposal should reflect the reality of what can and will be done. Your proposal is part of the contract, either by reference ("In accordance with your proposal dated…") or by inclusion ("In accordance with the work plan contained in Appendix A of this agreement…")

Therefore, the first step in reviewing a grant agreement is to re-read the proposal you submitted. Funders sometimes take six months to a year to make a decision on a proposal, and projects can change during that time. Don't rely on your memory—make sure you review what your agency promised it would do with the money.

You and the project manager should ask the following questions:

◆ Is the project still fundamentally the same now as when we wrote the proposal?

◆ Have the timeframe or milestones changed?

◆ Have there been any changes in the project staff?

◆ Is the budget projected to be the same?

If possible, it is also important to have legal counsel review the grant agreement before your chief staff officer signs it. After all, the agreement is a legal document, and your counsel might find issues that you and the project manager wouldn't find.

If there have been any changes in the project, staff or budget, you must talk to the funder before the agreement is signed. The funder has the right to withdraw the offer of support if he or she believes that the project is no longer what had been originally promised. The funder also has the right to accept the changes and proceed with the support. Remember—a grant is a partnership, and for the partnership to be successful, both sides must be open and upfront with each other.

Document the Grant

While it can be fun to just receive a check for a project, your accounting staff (and auditors) won't appreciate having such little information. At the very least, a cover letter should be sent with the check, indicating the amount of the grant, the purpose (for example, for general support or for a particular project), the name and address of the donor and the time period that the grant is to cover.

Items in an Agreement

I have received grant agreements that are barely a page in length, and others that are fifteen pages long. The simplest agreements are one-page letters that reference the proposal, state the amount awarded and indicate whether any reports are committed. The longer ones are more complicated and provide a great amount of detail on rights (usually the funder's) and responsibilities (definitely yours).

When reading the agreement, here are the elements to keep track of:

Grant period

The grant period tells you the beginning and end dates of the grant. This is critical information, as only expenses incurred during this period can be charged to the particular grant. (In some federal programs, you can charge related expenses to the grant up to three months prior to the official start date, but only if the agreement allows it.)

Look to see if the grant period makes sense for the length of the project and the size of the grant. If it appears that your agency will need to spend too much money in too short of a time, you might need to negotiate a longer grant period with the funder. I once reviewed a grant agreement that required a project to spend high six-figures in only a few months. Because I had not worked on the proposal that led to the grant, I double-checked with the project director that this grant period made sense. Once she explained why it was so compressed, the shortened timeframe made sense.

Payments

For cash flow purposes, you must know how the grant will be paid. Will it be paid up front? Will it be paid as a reimbursement, after the funds have been spent? Is it paid in installments? Do progress reports have to be filed in order for the installments to be paid?

It is also important to know the method of payment. It has become more common for grants to be paid by Electronic Funds Transfer (EFT), although many funders still pay by check. If the funder (and your organization) prefers EFT, be sure to check to see if you need to do anything to set up the transfer process.

> ### Challenge or Matching Grants
>
> Grants are sometimes structured as challenge or matching grants, meaning that funds from other sources must be raised in order for the original grant terms to be satisfied. If this is the case, you need to check to see whether the additional funds need to be raised before or after the grant will be disbursed, and what information must be provided to the funder to confirm that the challenge or match has been met.
>
>

Reports and due dates

Reporting is a critical part of the grant process—funders like to be kept informed about the project's progress. Obviously, you need to keep track of what reports are due and when, but the reporting requirements need to be reasonable. If interim and final reports are required, the grant agreement should spell out what is due and when. Look to see if the reporting dates are reasonable. For example, it takes most accounting offices ten business days to close the preceding month. A financial report that is due one week after month's end is not going to get done on time. Check with your accounting department and the project manager about the due dates—if they are not reasonable, negotiate the changes before anything is signed.

Many funders have specific guidelines for interim and final reports, including whether the reports are to be submitted online or in hard copy. If the grant agreement does not provide reporting instructions, check for them on the funder's website or with the program officer.

Deliverables

Deliverables are those things you must do or provide to fulfill the terms of the grant. Interim and final reports are deliverables, as are evaluations. Other examples of deliverables are workshops, films, performances, conferences, websites, etc.

Does the funder's list of deliverables match what was promised in the proposal? Have any deliverables been added by the funder? For example, the funder might want you to include additional data points in your evaluation. If your program cannot meet any of the deliverables, then you need to inform the funder and negotiate a change in the requirements.

Publicity and acknowledgements

Check to see what is required in terms of public information about the grant. Does the funder require pre-approval of press releases or other public acknowledgements of the grant? Are there specific requirements for the use of the funder's name, logo, web address or other identifying language? Does the funder require anonymity—and is there any problem complying with this request? For example, I have secured funds for PBS documentaries, and the FCC requires that all funders of the productions be identified, either on screen or on a list that is available to the public. In this case, anonymity is not allowed.

Regulations

Government grants—federal, state and local—often come with a wealth of regulations that must be followed. If the grant agreement refers to a specific agency publication (for example, "Department of Commerce Financial Assistance Standard Terms and Conditions"), find it online and read it, as these are your guidebooks for what you can and cannot do with government money.

Rights

Sometimes a funder requests certain rights. For example, if the funder is supporting research, does it have any rights to the results? Or, is the funder requesting a percentage of the sales of the publications, CDs or DVDs that your organization will produce with the grant? It is very common for government funders to want a portion of any income derived from the grant, as this is a return on the taxpayers' investment and can be used to fund other programs in the future.

Sometimes, the funder requires approval of any change in project personnel, since the awarding of the grant was based in part on the expertise and capability of the staff. Is your agency comfortable with this provision?

As I have mentioned several times, you should talk with the funder if your organization is uncomfortable with or confused about something. Grant agreements—particularly those which cover multiple years—can outlive funder and grantee staff. It is critical that the document is clear and accurate so any subsequent staff can easily understand what is required. If there are provisions in the grant agreement that your organization cannot commit to in good faith, do not sign the document. Contact the funder and see if you can negotiate changes—especially with foundations, which can be more flexible in making adjustments than government agencies can.

Finally

After everything has been approved and the agreement has been executed, share copies of the agreement and proposal with anyone who has a hand in carrying out the provisions. This includes program staff, accounting, communications, legal, etc.

Since not everyone on the team has necessarily read the agreement before it was finalized, it can be helpful to draw their attention to specific provisions. Sometimes it can be enough to simply share copies, since you know the team will read the grant agreement themselves and understand the deliverables. Other times, it can be helpful to include a cover memo that details the various deliverables and timelines. Another technique is to have a meeting with everyone involved in the project to go over the provisions of the grant and address any questions.

Make sure someone—perhaps you—is keeping track of the grant timeline. Grant period and reporting due dates need to be noted. There are grants and donor management software packages that can be helpful, or you can use a simple spreadsheet. Sometimes, the old-fashioned method can work—keep a calendar with sticky notes to warn you when reports are due.

The bottom line is this: When your organization accepts a grant, it takes on certain responsibilities to carry out the project as negotiated and account for the funds used. Set whatever systems in place you need to make sure these responsibilities are fulfilled.

 Connect with Teri at http://charitychannel.com/cc/teri-blandon

How to Use a Freelance Development Writer

By Shelley Uva

My first job in fundraising was with a very large university. The development office employed three grant proposal writers and an editor. Later on, I worked as a freelance grant proposal writer for eighteen years, and I was pleased to discover that many nonprofits did not employ in-house writers. These organizations relied upon freelance writers to get out their proposals, newsletters, brochures, etc.

During my years as a freelancer, I discovered quite quickly that some organizations really knew how to use a freelance writer while others were totally clueless. So, this advice is for you if your organization has decided to go the freelance route.

1. Hire the right writer

Development writing is not an art form; it is a craft, but it does require some understanding of how fundraising works and doesn't work. There are many types of freelance writers at large in the world. Try to find one who is a development specialist as opposed to someone whose experience is all in writing advertising copy or poetry or book reviews. Even within development, there are specialties. Some freelance writers are generalists (as I was) but others have perfected expertise in a particular area, such as government grants. During my freelance career, I made a sub-specialty out of writing Kresge Challenge Grant applications. Most often, when you hire a freelance writer it's because you need a job done and you don't have the staff or time to do it. If you have a tight deadline, you really don't want to be involved in on the job training.

2. Remember a freelance person is different than a staff member

Please remember that a freelance writer is an outside person. No one who works with you on a consulting basis is going to know as much about your organization as you do. This might sound pretty obvious, but for some strange reason, organizations often seem not to grasp this fact.

Another thing to consider is that, in the United States, the Internal Revenue Service has guidelines about whether an individual is considered an employee or an outside contractor. You should be aware of these differences in order to determine if you need an outside contractor or an employee.

3. Share information

When you hire a freelance writer, remember that he or she will know only as much about your nonprofit as you choose to share. It is absolutely essential that you provide the writer with the tools needed to do the job. Those tools should include sample past proposals, newsletters, brochures, annual reports and access to staff and, in some cases, board members.

4. Think about what *you* want

Now that you've hired someone and you've provided them with some background materials, you have to think about what exactly you want. Do you want a general support template proposal? Do you want a proposal prepared for a specific funder with detailed guidelines? Do you want your proposal to include quotes from clients? Do you want to put charts and statistical information in your proposal? Do you want a brochure that is very fact-driven or do you prefer one with a lot of human interest in it? A good professional writer should be able to deliver whatever you want *but* you have to articulate what that is. A freelance writer is not a mind reader. Don't expect your writer to guess what you want.

5. Set job parameters

You also need to set some parameters for what the job is going to include. In general, it is better if writing assignments are not treated as multiple choice type activities. Asking your writer to provide you with three or four different versions of one proposal or brochure or newsletter so that you can then read them all and pick the one you like is, in most cases, a real waste of both time and money. Of course, you might not know exactly what you want, but it is good to think about it and talk it through before the writing actually begins. Not only will you save time and money, but knowing what you want can help you decide which writer to hire because some writers are better at some things than others.

6. Two ways to talk things through

I just mentioned talking things through. That includes two types of talk—one with your development officers and one with your freelance writer. You can have everyone meet and cover all of your bases at one time, but often it is difficult to get everyone in the room together. The important point here is whether you meet once or ten times, you need to establish not only the guidelines for the material, but also the tone you want it to have. Sometimes the tone is dictated by the guidelines. If you are dealing with a foundation that allows you only 500 words to explain your program, you don't have a lot of space for quotes or examples or descriptive language. On the other hand, if you are talking about doing a newsletter, you have many choices to make. Make sure you consult with everyone who is involved (including your freelance writer) at the start.

7. Include your freelancer in relevant meetings

If you are hiring a freelance writer to prepare a proposal, include the writer in the meetings you have about the proposal, including, if possible, your meeting with a foundation officer. It is much better to let the writer be present than to have the writer get the information second or third hand. Something always gets lost in translation. Also, your writer might ask questions of the foundation officer which development officers who don't write proposals might not ask. Of course, if you do have your freelance writer participate in a meeting with a foundation officer, you will need to provide the writer with all necessary background information.

8. Be very clear about billing

Some freelance writers charge by the hour so if you want to go through ten drafts of your proposal or publication, your writer is not likely to object. After all, the clock is running and it's your money. Other freelancers work on a fee per project basis, and when you work with these writers, it is important to know exactly what the fee will cover. For example, when I wrote freelance proposals on a fee per project basis, my general rule was that the fee I charged covered meetings, interviews, research, a first draft, one rewrite and one polishing. Other writers might not use an all-inclusive fee. If my client wanted to keep rewriting, that time became part of an hourly fee in addition to the agreed-upon set fee. To avoid extra charges, try to decide what you want before you begin.

9. Use written contracts

Do you need a written contract? When I began freelancing, I rarely used written contracts, but later on, I did use them more often, mostly because at the request of the nonprofits that hired me. A contract not only protects both parties, but also often meets an organization's financial requirements or state registration requirements.

10. What constitutes a contract?

What kind of contract do you need? It can be very simple. If your organization doesn't have a standard contract it uses with freelancers, you can create one easily. The bare essential is a document that states it is serving as a contract between you and the writer and outlines the scope of work to be done, includes any deadlines and lists all fees and when they will be paid. Then you and your writer sign it and date it and each retain a copy. If the job you are contemplating is lengthy and complex, you might want to break it down into a series of deadlines and payments. You also should be aware that in some states, development writers are considered to be "advising on fundraising" and might be required to register as fundraising counsel in that state. This means that the state regulatory authorities might have stipulations about what needs to be included in the contract.

11. Include a kill clause

You also might want to include a "kill" clause and/or fee. A "kill" clause generally means that either one of you can terminate the contract before all of its terms have been met. It is worthwhile to have a "kill" clause because unforeseen events happen all the time. Your budget might change or the foundation you are approaching might suddenly change its mind. You can begin a job in all good faith and then discover you don't really need to finish it. A "kill" clause is a way for you to protect yourself from having to pay unnecessary fees, but you will be responsible for the fees incurred up until that time. If your job is one that will take some time and several drafts and revisions, you usually set a payment schedule. If you "kill" the job, the kill fee will be based on what has been completed, according to the schedule you set.

12. Have realistic expectations

Expect you might need to do a little rewriting yourself. Even when you have provided information, decided what you wanted and articulated it to your writer, you still might find that you need to do some small amount of rewriting. This is just part of the job. Sometimes at the very end of a job, you might discover that one or two sentences are not quite accurate or you might decide you need to add in one additional item. You can, of course, have your writer do this, but often it is easier, faster and certainly more economical to just do it yourself. However, if you hired a freelance writer, you should *not* be writing whole sections of the proposal or newsletter or brochure. The rewriting you do should be very limited.

13. When do you have the right to complain?

If your writer hands in a proposal or copy for a publication that is filled with factual inaccuracies (after you have provided the factual information needed), spelling mistakes and/or grammatical errors, you have a right to complain. If you have asked your writer to prepare a proposal that follows a particular format and your writer has ignored these instructions, then you have a right to complain. If your piece is supposed to be 500 words and your writer gives you 6,000 words, you have a right to complain.

14. When do you have a right to reduce or refuse payment?

As a writer, my experience has been that the nonprofit's right to complain is most often accompanied by an attempt on the part of the organization to reduce the writer's fee. Since fees often are paid in installments, some organizations, in these circumstances, will refuse to pay the last installment. If you truly believe your writer has not met his or her obligations, then you can try to reduce the fee you agreed to pay. What you cannot do is blame the writer for your mistakes and then try to reduce the fee. For example, if you tell me you want one thing and I do it and then you realize you want something else, you cannot ask me to redo the project for free and you cannot refuse to pay me the fee we agreed to at the start. You also cannot try to reduce your fee because you make minor changes in the writing. If you change a comma to a semi-colon or rearrange two paragraphs or prefer to use the words "at present" instead of "currently," you really do not have a right to try to reduce a fee. I would suggest that when there is a problem, you speak to your writer about it. Give your writer a chance to correct the mistake before you simply pull the project away, redo it yourself and then refuse to pay part of the fee.

15. Things to avoid

There are a few things you really should not do when you hire a freelance writer. The first has to do with reducing or refusing to pay fees. Never, never, never, try to tell your freelance writer to forego a fee you both have accepted because the work you do is so important and such a good cause and so many people work for your organization pro bono. You have to understand that when a person works as a freelance writer in fundraising, all of that person's clients do important work and represent worthy causes. Development writing is this person's livelihood. Just as you, as a staff person, are paid for your work, the freelancer also deserves to be paid. And you cannot turn a person you have hired into a volunteer after the fact. Volunteering is, by its very nature, voluntary. You can't impose it on someone you have hired and agreed to pay.

After trying to change fees, probably the thing freelance writers dislike the most is an employer who ignores the job parameters that have been agreed upon and tries to get the writer to do other things. We all know that fundraising events are incredibly labor intensive and can easily take over everybody's job in an office, no matter what it is they are actually supposed to do. It's one thing to ask staff to pitch in and do things that are not in their job descriptions. Depending on your organization, you might or might not be able to do that. But you absolutely cannot do it with a freelance writer. So, don't ask your writer to stuff envelopes or create mailing lists or make follow-up telephone calls. This is not a practice that will serve either of you very well.

16. Have your writer and designer work together

For the most part, I have been talking mainly about writing grant proposals here. Let's say your freelance job is a newsletter that will be published at regular intervals. One thing that is really helpful to a writer is to meet with the designer. There is no reason to keep writing and design totally separate and encouraging collaboration between a writer and designer can really help produce a better publication. Most writers are not designers, but anyone who has done freelance work writing publications has probably worked with many designers and might have some interesting insights into the process.

17. Deadlines count

Speaking of publications, pay attention to deadlines. Make sure you allow enough time for the entire process from planning to gathering material to writing to editing to designing to approvals. Generally speaking, it takes about six weeks to produce a brochure. A printed (as opposed to electronic) newsletter might take a little less time or a little more, depending on access to material and your approval process. Annual reports usually take longer. A common schedule for an annual report that you want to come out in April is to begin preparing it the previous November or December. Don't forget that an annual report is going to have financial information that has to be vetted and charts and other graphics that have to be created.

18. What kind of job works best with a freelance writer?

What is the best type of project for a freelance writer? If you have a writer or two on your staff, but there is just too much writing to be done, are you better off hiring a freelancer to do the big, unusual job (such as a Kresge challenge grant or the case statement for a capital campaign) or the regular, repeating job (such as a monthly newsletter)? There really is no single answer to this question. It depends very much on your staff writers and the capability of the freelance person you hire. When I worked as a freelancer, I was hired by organizations to serve in both capacities, and I found that either one worked for me and the organizations that hired me. It probably is a good idea to keep some kind of separation between staff writers and freelance writers so that you don't end up with a situation in which either everyone does everything or no one does anything. I also think it's a good idea to make sure your staff writer and freelance writer know one another in case they do need to share information and also to defuse any potential situations that might arise. Writers can be very territorial and jealous of one another. Work to make your various writers feel like colleagues and not competitors.

A Final Word

Last, but never least, listen to your writer. A competent professional writer's advice might be more valuable than the fee you're paying. Just as you want others to respect your professional abilities, you should respect the professional abilities of the writer you hire.

 Connect with Shelley at http://charitychannel.com/cc/shelley-uva

The Importance of Branding for Nonprofits

By Stacy Lewis

Branding is all the rage in our consumer-based, emotionally-driven society. From cars to computers, clothing to food, everything in our society, and in life for that matter, has a 'brand.' In recent years nonprofit organizations have learned that branding can serve as a strategic tool to build relationships with key supporters, strengthen organizational focus and build capacity by attracting the resources and relationships needed to support their mission and cause. From larger national nonprofit brands like United Way, Red Cross and Habitat for Humanity to smaller, local direct service providers in markets across the country, nonprofits are seeing branding as more than simply 'marketing' and instead have come to view it as an operational strategy to achieve organizational success.

So, What Is a Brand?

Most people are familiar with the word branding but fewer people have a clear understanding of what a brand actually is or more importantly how to build one. Your organization's brand image is essentially how others think, feel and perceive your organization. If you ask people what comes to mind when they think of your own organization, those initial impressions comprise your current brand image. A brand is comprised of two aspects: 1) what you do and 2) 'how you feel', or your brand personality. For example, when you think of the brand Disney, you most likely associate what the company does with its 'entertainment' offerings, i.e., amusement parks, movies, etc. When it comes to its personality, you most likely think of *family fun*. When you think of a brand like the Red Cross, you most likely associate it with disaster relief. But in terms of their brand personality, you might think of words like safety, security, hope and life. These brand traits give the organization emotional meaning, and are critical to positioning the organization in the minds and hearts of stakeholders. So, in addition to reinforcing what an organization does, brands serve to demonstrate important *emotional values or attributes* such as trust, credibility, hope, freedom and empowerment.

What a Brand Is Not

It is important to know what a brand is not. A brand is not a logo mark, advertisement, brochure, website or slogan. Eventually all of these things serve to *reflect* and reinforce your brand. An organizational brand is a succinct concept or 'reference' about your organization that *clearly* reinforces three key things:

1. what your organization does;

2. what makes it unique and different from other organizations; and

3. your key value proposition—i.e., what 'valuable benefit' or 'need' you fulfill for those who engage with your organization.

Position and Brand vs. Vision and Mission

For nonprofits that tend to be mission-driven, the concept of positioning and branding can be confusing. Branding should be seen as a means to achieve your vision and mission as opposed to a replacement of these things. In addition, it is important to know the difference between a *position* and a *brand*. Both are distinct from each other but inherently work together to comprise your total brand strategy. Your *position* is *that unique place you own in the marketplace that is clearly different from your competition. It clearly states 'what you do.'* Your brand, on the other hand, reflects the personality, tone and feeling of your organization and is reflected through the intentional use of imagery, words and colors and the culture you project about your brand. Brand is less about 'what you do' and more about 'how you feel.' Together your position and your brand work to establish the unique place you own in the *hearts and minds of your community and supporters.*

Before we continue, take a moment to ask yourself two important questions:

◆ **Mission:** your organization's purpose; its reason for being

◆ **Vision:** a shared image of what impact you envision in the future

◆ **Values:** your unique beliefs and intentions that direct culture and behavior

◆ **Positioning:** what your organization does in and for the community that addresses a specific need and is different from other options; your value proposition

◆ **Brand:** how you act and feel to the marketplace; your organization's character and personality

◆ **Marketing:** the process or technique of promoting, selling, and distributing your product/service/brand

1. *Why would anyone want to donate time, services or money to your organization?* As you formulate your answer, list three tangible and compelling benefits that someone will personally *receive* from donating their time, services or money to your specific organization.

2. *Now ask, what makes your organization different from other nonprofit organizations they could be supporting?*

If it is taking you a long time to answer these questions, chances are your organization could use a little branding. If you were able to quickly *and compellingly* list the reasons and benefits, chances are your organization has gone through a branding process.

Why Brand Now?

The need for efficient and compelling communication is becoming critical in today's growing nonprofit sector as more organizations face the challenge of cutting through the clutter to engage and build relationships with supporters. In marketing, there is a common theory called the 'AIDA' model. As the figure below demonstrates, branding supports your efforts to efficiently move potential supporters from having *no awareness of you* to gaining enough understanding and interest *to support you.* Whether this appeal is for funding or collaboration, branding allows you to consistently and efficiently highlight *what you do for the community that serves a specific need and is different from all other options.*

Having an organizational brand helps someone quickly understand what makes you different from all of the other options that exist in the community.

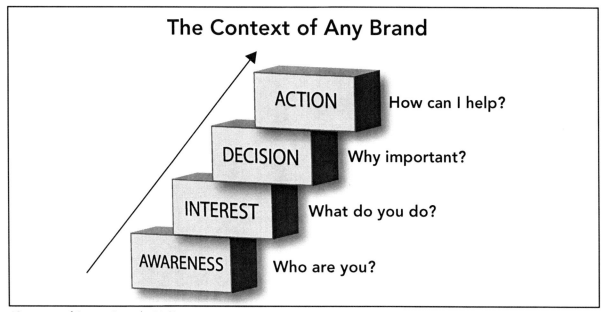

(Courtesy of Sector Brands, LLC)

Brands Set You Apart and Build Share of Heart

Brands serve two key purposes for nonprofits. One, they work to differentiate your organization's mission and 'cause' from the multitude of others that exist in the community. Secondly, they build an authentic emotional connection with key supporters so that they have an easy way to support a cause that they care about.

Beyond the many 'external' benefits of a branding effort, I have witnessed over and over the transformative impact a branding effort has on an organization internally. The process of branding becomes an opportunity for any organization to stop, take a fresh look at itself and most importantly, rediscover and redefine its own greatness.

Brand-Building Takes Discipline, Focus and Guts

Brand-building is a highly strategic process that happens from the inside-out and requires a collective and courageous assessment of your organization, your market, your target audience and key trends. Brands are not haphazard. They are intentional and self-created and, not unlike the wording in your mission, your brand comes down to a strategic choice among many possible options.

One of the most important things to understand about brands is that a brand represents *one idea*, not many. Remember the stair-step chart earlier? If you are too many things to too many people, getting people to quickly grasp why you matter and why they should engage with you can take forever. For nonprofits, who historically try to be all things to all people to attract as many resources as possible, brand-building requires taking a fresh look at the organization from all angles in order to identify that one compelling concept that makes it stand out. That one idea emerges from a carefully led, thoroughly conducted assessment that begins internally and strategically blends insights gathered from outside research and assessment.

How to Build a Brand: A Blend of Art and Science

So, how does one go about building this mysterious thing called a brand? In brief, branding is a unique blend of art and science. The science comes from using qualitative and quantitative research to gain a thorough understanding of your own organization and your key community stakeholders. It is also

---

Why Brand?

Branding achieves three key things for staff, board and volunteers:

◆ Branding re-ignites passion and purpose.

◆ Branding reinforces what you are best at.

◆ Branding builds your resource engine.

critical that you understand other key factors like your competition, industry trends and other political, environmental, societal and technological influences. The art of branding comes from analyzing and creatively synthesizing all of these insights into a clear, unique and differentiating brand platform that captures the heart and soul of an organization.

Plan Before You Brand

To maximize your time and investment in a branding process, we like to recommend that organizations go through a formal strategic planning process prior to beginning a brand development process. A brand is no replacement for good planning.

Building a brand requires a thorough examination and assessment of these three areas. With these insights in hand, you can begin to identify your unique brand position.

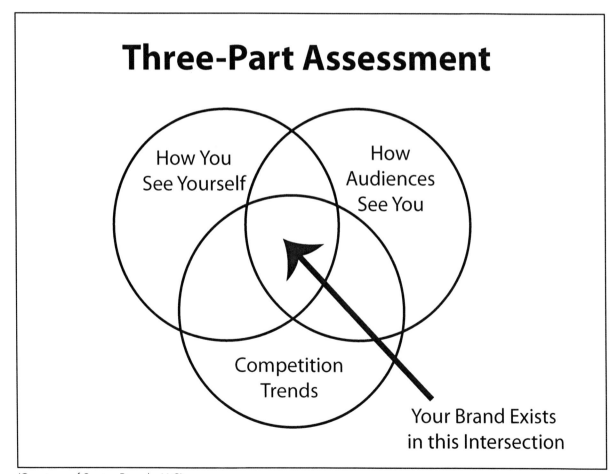

Three-Part Assessment

How You See Yourself

How Audiences See You

Competition Trends

Your Brand Exists in this Intersection

(Courtesy of Sector Brands, LLC)

Three Key Steps to Building a Brand

Step one: Look inside

The first step in building your brand involves getting to the 'essence' of why your organization exists and what genuine purpose it serves in meeting critical needs in society. Therefore you need to dive deeply into assessing everything from your mission, history and culture, to your service offerings and tangible community impact. All of this information is evaluated and synthesized into what ultimately becomes your organization's position—or that unique place you hold in the marketplace.

What about your brand personality? How does your organization see itself *emotionally?* This is important because your organizational personality, like your own personality, has a huge role in how you 'attract' or 'draw' people to you. Identifying the emotional traits of your organization requires tapping into the more emotional sides of your brain. We often take organizations through a series of exercises that force them to think about their organization metaphorically. It's not uncommon for us to ask folks question like: *If you were a car, what type of car would you be and why? If your organization was a color, what color would you be and why?* While these types of questions might seem superfluous, the patterns and descriptions that emerge result are very rich and important concepts that serve to support the creative translation of the brand.

Go Deep With Your Self Assessment

Ask yourself:

- What is your purpose? Why do you exist?

- Where is your deepest organizational passion?

- What is the powerful market need you uniquely meet?

- What would happen if your organization was not there?

- What five words describe the unique personality of your brand?

Step two: Look outside

Knowing how you see yourself is only *half* of the branding equation. The key factor in any brand is your understanding of how the market sees you, so you can accurately marry your own organizational offerings with what the marketplace needs and wants from you. Research is a critical component to branding. Research reveals your current brand equity and awareness, as well as certain brand 'gaps' that exist between how your market sees you and how you see yourself as an organization. Closing these 'gaps' is what successful branding is all about. While research can be expensive, as a starting place, we suggest conducting an electronic survey with key stakeholders to assess your image in a similar fashion that you assessed yourselves. Ask key stakeholders:

- ◆ How do they see you?

- ◆ How do they *feel* about the cause, problem, or need you fill?

- ◆ What five words would they use to describe your organization?

- ◆ If your organization was a car, what type of car do they see you as and why?

- ◆ What would happen if you went away?

> ### It's *Not* About You
>
> The mistake many organizations make is that their brand is exclusively how 'they' see themselves, when in fact a brand exists solely in the mind of the target audience. It is how the client or prospect sees you, your category, your issue and your cause that is most critical.

Step three: Pull it all together

So what happens with all of these insights? Brand strategists are trained to not only collect the information in such a way that it leads to some clear conclusions, but more importantly, they are trained at synthesizing all of the information to uncover your unique brand value. This is exactly the first step in finalizing your brand. A brand practitioner, like a good therapist, will see things in you that you can't see in yourself. The brand expert will organize these insights into a number of differentiating positioning platforms (what you do) and brand personality traits (how you feel) for your organization to then review and discuss. It is critical that you actively participate in creating and choosing your own brand with the consultant. After all, you'll have to live the brand everyday as you use your brand to achieve your mission.

Traditionally, a brand practitioner will present you with a number of key deliverables, including a formal statement of differentiation (or, your positioning statement), your brand personality traits, a range of key messages to support your brand positioning statement as well as some rationale as to how your services, culture and mission all support your brand. The process of building your core brand strategy, not including any creative elements such as your new logo, website, etc. is traditionally sixteen to twenty weeks.

Bringing Your Brand to Life

Once you have chosen your unique positioning and brand platform, your brand platform then becomes the foundation of everything you do, from how you talk about your organization and reinforce it with cultural behavior and language to how you present yourself through communications graphics, pictures and words. There are degrees of outcomes from a branding effort, including but not limited to, a new organizational name that better reflects your brand; a new organizational logo, or brand visual identity' to reflect and symbolize what you stand for; new visuals, images, collateral materials; and a new website. Suffice to say that once you know who you are, the process of translating that into how you present yourself at every level becomes the next stage of work.

Yes, building a brand does take work. But in many ways, it is one of the most important and rewarding journeys an organization can embark on. The work pays off by re-igniting your organization passion and commitment, enhancing your organization's esteem, and attracting additional resources to support and expand services.

 Connect with Stacy at http://charitychannel.com/cc/stacy-lewis

Get Your Strategic Plan and Website Working Together— And Then Take It Up a Notch!

By Marion Conway

Your strategic plan and your website are both important. They both become more effective and powerful when they work together. This article discusses integrating your strategic goals into the *design* of your website...and then taking the next step. Your strategic plan and website working together is about more than just having a page on your website with a summary of your strategic plan.

If your strategic plan has goals in these categories here are some ideas on how to use your website to support those goals.

Fundraising

I've never worked on a strategic plan where there weren't fundraising goals, but they are different for each organization. If you want to increase individual giving adding a donate button to every page of your website is one basic strategy. Donor Digital has teamed with Amnesty International and completed an excellent research project on this subject. Read the article http://www.fundraising123.org/files/donordigital_donation_page_optimization_research.pdf for advice on the details of planning a "donate now" plan for your website. Paying attention to the fine details such as size, placement and color of the "donate now" button can improve your results! If you want to take it up a notch then it is time to commit some real time to developing a social media strategy—using venues such as Facebook, Twitter and YouTube to build relationships and eventually drive friends and fans to your website.

If you want to increase grants, figure out how your website can help you with your funders. *Funders do check out your website.* Some ideas are:

◆ List your grantors with an optional link to their websites.

◆ Clearly state your mission on the home page—this is basic but important.

◆ Provide a page outlining your strategic plan and update it with current strategies *and* accomplishments. (Funders love accomplishments!)

◆ Include current information, pictures and maybe even video on the website for specific programs you will be making grant requests for. If you know the hot buttons for particular funders try to address them on your website not just in the grant application. It might be evaluation or serving a particular community or addressing accountability. Make sure your website addresses what you think funders will think is important.

Advocacy

Design advocacy into your *navigation* and have strong tools to support it. Provide brief position papers that your supporters can understand without having to be familiar with all the nuances of the issues. Provide a list of who you want supporters to write or call. Even better, provide email links so that a message can be sent straight from your website.

Blogs work especially well to support advocacy programs so you might want to add a blog to your website with a specific goal of promoting advocacy. To take it up a notch, become active on Twitter and post links to your blog when you have new posts.

Program Marketing

Many nonprofits fail to use their website for marketing effectively. Build your navigation so that visitors can clearly see the opportunities. Show the schedule, fees, who to contact for more information, event dates, etc. Consider applying for a Google ad word grant. You might be eligible for local ads on a Google search even if you are a small 501(c)(3). Do some Google Analytic keyword analysis to be more effective—it's worth a try.

Facebook and Twitter can be very effective at promoting events—especially if you are trying to attract a younger crowd.

Education

Include a resource section in the navigation. This can include information papers, videos, publications for sale and links to other websites. Blogs are also an excellent vehicle for advancing education goals.

Relationship Building

Your website isn't just about providing information and collecting donations. It is an important tool in relationship building. If this is one of your strategic goals, keep your website fresh and updated. It is important to coordinate your email campaigns with your website too. If you are having a campaign to raise funds to send children to summer camp get rid of the Christmas party pictures on the home page and have pictures of kids at camp last summer.

As donors are becoming more sophisticated, consider including more about your financials, strategic plans, and planned giving. If you are rated "four-star" by *Charity Navigator*—say so.

If you are updating your website often then you are probably ready to make use of social media. Being active on social media sites such as Facebook, Twitter, YouTube and LinkedIn is a perfect complement to work with your frequently updated website. And working together is definitely the way to go for relationship building with the under fifty generations.

Volunteers

If developing your volunteer program is part of your plan, feature volunteers on your website. Keep it updated and upbeat. Highlight a brief bio of featured volunteers and mention what they do when they volunteer and get quotes from them about how they value their volunteer experience. If they work for a corporate sponsor—or a potential corporate sponsor—include their employment information.

Take it up a Notch

Now, take it up a notch—integrate real time strategic planning and social media.

If you are a strategic planning veteran pro and have a great website then you are ready to take it up a notch. Here are two suggestions:

Real-time strategic planning

Many organizations who have been through more than one thorough strategic planning cycles feel the need to do some serious planning but are not interested in the whole strategic planning "McGillah" from soup to nuts. David LaPiana's book, *The Nonprofit Strategy Revolution—Real Time Strategic Planning in a Rapid Response World* provides an excellent alternative. It provides a straightforward model that can be used to address a "big question" facing your organization and doesn't require going through a traditional strategic planning analysis. David defines strategy as "a coordinated set of *actions* designed to create and sustain a competitive advantage in achieving a nonprofit's mission." This understanding of strategy as *action* rather than as a goal is central to the real time strategic planning model. Planning using this model can be a matter of weeks rather than a matter of months it usually takes to complete a traditional strategic plan and it provides for focusing on a single issue rather than a comprehensive plan.

Social media

Before you get involved with social media for nonprofits it is important to get your web 1.0—your website—in order first. A lot of social media strategy is about driving traffic back to your website—so getting your website in shape is the first order of business. Sorry folks but it really is true.

Once you have dusted off that website and updated it to be synchronized with your strategic plan, you are ready to take it up a notch and get involved with social media. There are five basic steps for getting involved with social media: listen, participate, generate "buzz," share content and community building. Web 2.0 tools such as blogging, Facebook, Twitter, YouTube, and Flickr, are the next frontier for communicating with and building relationship with donors, volunteers, funders, customers, supporters and friends. But discussion on social media and nonprofits is a whole other chapter.

Get your basics in order first but don't sit on your hands when you get there—take it up a notch!

 Connect with Marion at http://charitychannel.com/cc/marion-conway

How to Write a Truly Helpful Web Development RFP

By Monique Cuvelier

Requests for Proposal (RFPs) for new websites rarely fill me with joy. Usually, they don't exist at all, and if they do, they're in the form of a jargon-y request for proposal. Those can be a source of confusion, business-speak and unfinished thoughts. Nonprofits tend to be the worst, often because whoever wrote the brief is juggling the desires of committee members who aren't always in agreement or conforming to confusing document requirements. If I decide it's worth responding to—a big if—I have to spend hours making sense of it so my company can send a reasonable bid to the requesting organization. Wary web development consultants are exactly the opposite of what a charity looking for a new website wants.

Once in a while, I'm happily surprised. Sometimes I'll receive an RFP that's so concise and detailed I might have written it. These RFPs fill me with delight to see so at early stage of a project, because I know they will make the project run smoothly. It tells me that the client has been planning, and that's the secret to a winning web project.

There's no single way to create a project brief because every website is unique. However, there are a few considerations you should take when writing any brief to help your project move smoothly from inception to completion.

Think it through

The clearest RFPs benefit from discussion and planning beforehand. Make sure you talk with your team to form clear ideas of what you want your website to contain and what it should look like. We hand out a client questionnaire at the beginning of every project that helps clarify your wishes.

Write clearly

Some people look at official documents like a brief as a reason to pull out their cryptic "business-ese" thesaurus so they can load it with fancy words nobody really understands. Some people are intimidated by the process of writing technical requirements when they aren't technical experts. That's okay. Write what you can and do it clearly. Pretend you're explaining what you want to an idiot. Trust me, web developers get more out of it that way.

Write a succinct profile

Put into a paragraph who you are and what your organization does. This will help you focus your needs with the website, and it will help any developer better understand how you work. It's also useful if you include ways you differ from others in your industry. It goes without saying to leave out the jargon, right?

Include demographics

Next, provide a profile of the people who you serve. These are the people who visit your website—or who you wish would visit your website. Note their age, location, gender, website connection speed—whatever you can do flesh out who will be using your website. People who fit the sixty to eighty age range use websites differently than those in the fifteen to twenty-five age range.

Plan your objectives

You cannot hope for a site that reaches your goals unless you know what they are before you begin. Think what you want the results to be, and then plan backwards. If you want to be the go-to guide for volunteering opportunities, make sure that every decision you make from that point forward feeds back into that goal.

Order your objectives

Some objectives are "must-haves," others are "nice-to-haves." Rank yours.

List your favorites (and non-favorites)

You've seen sites you love, whether they are your competition or a mega-commercial site like Amazon.com. Any time you see a site you like, add it to your bookmarks so you can pass this information on to the web developer. Make notes on what you like about them, such as the color palette or layout or some kind of functionality. This holds true for print materials too. Look for inspiration in a photograph with beautiful colors or a brochure whose photography you like. Similarly, make a list of the sites you don't like. This can give a web developer valuable insight into your preferences as well.

Know your branding

Unless you're new to the concept of marketing, you've probably gone through some kind of branding exercise in the past, where colors, logos and other standards were developed. If you're not aware of what these standards are, start asking around. We just had to redesign a website whose colors and logo were completely wrong in an earlier version, because no one checked. Translation: an expensive mistake.

Name your widgets

If you want any special functionality, like slideshows, animations, photo galleries—anything—write it down. These technical items affect cost. It's also helpful to know the outcome of functionality you've seen, because a web developer might be able to help you explore alternatives that work best for you.

List primary tasks

Note how you'll be using the site on a daily, weekly and monthly basis. This can help you budget your own time when it comes to managing the website, and it also helps prioritize the information there. The tasks you do on the website will be different from what your visitors do. Put yourself into your audience's shoes, and make a prioritized list of the things you want them to do when they're at your site. This might be registering to volunteer, donating money, or attend an event. You don't need to guess. Ask your audience what they think is helpful. Pull together an informal focus group and get people brainstorming. Write a survey and distribute it to your lists.

List technical needs

If you're bound to maintain your website in a particular format, you like a content management system like Drupal, or you don't have the staff bandwidth to do updates, cite these constraints. Also note if you need web hosting.

Name your budget

I know, I know. You don't want to come right out and say how much you want to spend, but your web developer really needs at least a ballpark. We receive calls from clients who have four hundred dollars to spend, and those who have forty thousand dollars to spend. We can't help everyone, but it saves everybody a lot of time if I can tell them up front whether we can or not.

Mark deadlines

If you absolutely must launch a website in time for a big event, to fulfill a grant requirement or for some other reason, write it down. Look a year into the future and plan for any deadlines, vacations or other scheduling requirements that might affect development.

List Contact information

It sounds elementary, but make sure your prospects know how to reach you if they have questions. We received a bizarre system-generated RFP a couple weeks ago that had no personal contact information so we couldn't even consider responding.

Laying this groundwork is incredibly useful for web development companies like ours, but your staff will also thank you if you take the time to plan. Bonus: Your funders will love you for eliminating money-wasting mistakes early on.

 Connect with Monique at http://charitychannel.com/cc/monique-cuvelier

Seven Best Homepage Updates You Should Make to Your Website

By Monique Cuvelier

The people who visit your website want to help you. Maybe they want to volunteer, give money, pledge their support, or tell their friends and colleagues about what you do. You'd be crazy not to take advantage of what those people are offering. That's why you should do everything you can to make your nonprofit website easy for well-meaning individuals to support you.

I see websites every day that are loaded with missed opportunities. No donate button. No calls for volunteers. No way to sign petitions. Instead, I see self-serving items like a lengthy mission statement or a navigation menu modeled on an organizational chart. Remember, you want to *eliminate* barriers for support, not create them.

Speaking with a professional web strategist and developer will help you align your website's goals with your organization's goals. There are still many updates you can make to the most visible page on your website—the homepage—that will increase participation and make it easier for people to find the information they want.

The following are seven relatively straightforward changes you can make to help your audience members help you.

1. Add a big, bold button for donations

The more dependent you are on donations, the bolder it should be. Snag your reader's attention, and make sure that once they click your donate button it's absolutely easy to give you their money. These design elements make buttons eye-catching:

◆ *Color:* Pick a color that contrasts with the rest of your color scheme, e.g., orange pops against purple; yellow stands out against blue.

◆ *Size:* Make that button too big to miss. Make it a bit bigger than the other buttons on the page.

◆ *Position:* Most website users look at the upper left-hand part of the page first. Place your button here to catch the most eyes.

◆ *Shape:* Buttons are often square because squares fit nicely in a grid. However, eyes are drawn to circles, so think of something round rather than rectangular.

◆ *Use "Give" or "Support":* I also like to use "Give" or "Support" for wording more than "Donate." Those are evocative, clear words that cover monetary donations as well as donations of time or skills through volunteering.

2. Create a menu that guides visitors

Navigation menus are meant to be a road map to your site and the single most important element in web design. They tell people how to move around the site, they should not be a reflection of who sits where in the office. Most people don't care who your staff members are, but what kind of work you're doing and how they can be involved.

Navigation menus are also not the place to be creative. They should be clear, intuitive and conventional. Think about the most important tasks you want your visitors to complete (give money, read about a new construction project, sign up for an event), and transfer those tasks to your navigation menu. Do this in order, from the most important to the least important.

3. Make it easy for volunteers to sign up

I know many organizations that rely heavily on volunteers—sometimes nearly exclusively on volunteers—but you'd never know it from the website. There's no mention of their importance or where to sign up.

If you need volunteers, announce it on your homepage—it's the first place people go. Also link to your open volunteer opportunities from your employment page, from your "Give" page and pepper the site with stories and examples of satisfied volunteers. Don't forget to make it very easy for potential volunteers to sign up. Provide many ways for them to contact you, including an email address, an email form, a phone number, and links to your social media accounts.

4. Keep visitors abreast of news updates

Websites should reflect the progress and activity your organization makes, so deliver the news. This might be anything from volunteer listings to training events to new initiatives. The important thing is to carve out a dedicated spot for updates on your homepage that you keep up to date. People will learn to keep coming back to your site to pick up the latest.

Blogs are great vehicles for this. You can start using one of the myriad free tools out there, or a blog can be built into your website. They're useful because they give your visitors a reason to keep coming back to your site and collect news. If they're handy with RSS feeds, they can also receive your news updates as soon as you release them. Blogs are also easy to quote elsewhere, which increases promotion.

If a blog is too much of a commitment, at least provide a dedicated section for news. It should be a simple list of newsworthy items accompanied by a date.

5. Provide a way to connect

Encouraging word of mouth is vitally important for nonprofits—it's how you start people talking about your cause and enlist more support. A reliable way to encourage discussion is to give your website visitors as many different ways for them to connect with you and each other as possible. A few ideas:

◆ *Newsletter sign-up:* Put a sign-up box on every page so they'll always see it.

◆ *A tell-a-friend feature:* Allow visitors to forward articles or your website to their friends directly from your site.

◆ *Comments:* Create a way for visitors to leave comments on articles or blog entries.

◆ *RSS feeds:* These can be generated by blog postings, news updates, or calendar entries and let people receive updates instantly from their computer.

6. Tell compelling stories

Fundraisers already know that the best way to reach potential supporters is through engaging stories. The same goes for websites. People connect on an emotional level through stories, which leads them to act. When it comes to the Web, you can take advantage of multimedia to tell your story. It can be a written profile on someone whose life you affected—either a beneficiary of your program or a volunteer who made a difference. (Hint: This is a great topic for the news updates feature I mentioned in number four.) A story can also be a video that you added to a service like Vimeo or YouTube and then embed on your website. Also consider capturing speakers with a digital recorder, and then turn that recording into a podcast. Or think of telling your volunteers to snap pictures at the next event and put those images together into a slideshow.

7. Make it easy to find what's not on the homepage

The homepage can only do so much. It should never become so cluttered that a visitor feels overwhelmed and doesn't know what to do next. It should be a way of showcasing the most important information and then be the launch pad for the rest of your website. Rather than cram everything onto one page, include a search box. If someone needs information they can't find at first glance, let them search through all your pages and archives with a search tool. Provide multiple entries to deeper pages on your website that encourage visitors to educate themselves.

These seven ideas are just the beginning. Always evaluate how people are using your website and think about how to make it even easier to use. Monitor analytics software, such as Google Analytics or Clicky, and watch how people use your site. Paying attention will cue you in to deficiencies and also reveal where you're succeeding.

 Connect with Monique at http://charitychannel.com/cc/monique-cuvelier

Required: State Registration of Charitable Organizations

By Helen Arnold, CFRE

While governmental oversight of charities dates from 1955, there is a new awareness by nonprofit organizations regarding state registration requirements. With the implementation of the updated IRS Form 990, charities are now required to affirm, under penalty of perjury, that they are complying with all applicable laws. (IRS Form 990 Part VI, Question 17; 990-EZ Part V, Question 41; Schedule G, Part I, Question 3) This means your nonprofit must comply with the charitable solicitation and registration laws in each and every state where your charity solicits, or receives, donations. These states must be listed individually in your organization's annual IRS Form 990.

Why must charitable organizations register? Quite simply, it is the law. In addition, it demonstrates transparency, as well as ethical and responsible business practices. Solicitation laws focus on the solicitation of charitable contributions from the public and require comprehensive reporting by the nonprofit. Registration requires nonprofits to provide specific information about the organization and its operations. Grantors and auditors, and of course the IRS, will want to see this information. Penalties for non-compliance can and have been levied including

---

Unified Registration Statement

State registration for nonprofit organizations is required under law. For ease of registration, the Unified Registration Statement has been developed and is now accepted by thirty-seven states. Three states do not accept the URS. The form can be found at http://www.multistatefiling.org. This site also lists detailed requirements by all states at http://www.multistatefiling.org/n_appendix.htm. Six additional states require specialized registrations (such as for foundations only).

practical tip

Why Register? Here's an Example...

A charity based in Iowa does a substantial amount of business (solicitation) in California. The charity finds that many of its most generous contributors have retired to the warmer climate offered by California. Many of these contributors have long since retired and are in the autumn of their lives. The charity is informed that they are the beneficiary of a substantial portion of the contributor's estate. Following the death of the contributor several of the family members feel slighted by the amount bequeathed to them. A will contest ensues and the family members allege that the charity exerted undue influence on the aged contributors. The charity prepares to defend itself and, indirectly, the integrity of the contributor's will. During the Discovery process the family members' attorney learns the charity had never properly registered with the State of California as is required by statute. The attorney files a motion to have the charity struck from the case. The judge grants the motion.

warning!

fines and suspension or loss of ability to solicit in the state. And, if not appropriately registered, the organization might put itself in the position of jeopardizing large gifts.

The National Association of State Charity Officials (NASCO) is the association of state offices charged with oversight of charitable organizations and charitable solicitation in the United States. Individual state oversight offices can be found at: http://www.nasconet. org. Individual states exercise regulatory authority over nonprofits when the nonprofit is physically located in the state and/or when the nonprofit solicits funds in the state. States are constantly initiating new or updating current registration requirements. At this time, four states (DE, MT, ID, and NV) have no registration requirements; forty-six states and Washington, DC require some kind of registration, some more comprehensive than others. In addition to registration requirements for nonprofit organizations, fundraising consultants and professional solicitors might be required to register.

What is registration? It begins with the initial registration, normally including more substantial documentation and a higher fee. After the initial registration, most states require the second step of an annual financial report with a customarily lower fee. There is little consistency among states, with each state devising its own registration approach. Some states have one-time registration. Others require the annual renewal of registration. Some require governance and financial documents, while others accept just the IRS Form 990. Documentation, fees, registration dates, annual renewal requirements and fees, plus miscellaneous filing requirements can vary quite a bit from state to state.

Which nonprofits must register? Generally, any nonprofit [(501(c)(3) and (c)(4) organizations] conducting a solicitation within the border of any state must register in that state. The state might pose a question such as "Has an organization purposefully directed a request for a charitable solicitation to a resident of our state?" The solicitation can be by any means: face to face, phone call, letter, advertisement, newspapers and magazines, direct mail, radio, TV and website.

The option to donate via website is a somewhat unique. To address this, in 2001, NASCO, with the National Association of Attorneys General (NAAG) published "The Charleston Principles: Guidelines on Charitable Solicitations Using the Internet." National Association of State Charities Officials "The Charleston Principles: Guidelines on Charitable Solicitations Using the Internet." http://www.nasconet.org/Charleston%20Principles%2C%20Final.pdf.

In summary "An entity that is domiciled within a state and uses the Internet to conduct charitable solicitations in that state must register in that state." If an organization *actively* solicits via an Internet website to residents of a certain state, or if the organization receives contributions within the state "on a repeated and ongoing basis," then it must register within that state. State charity officials must quantify for themselves what they will consider "repeated and ongoing" in terms of the actual number of contributors and the total dollar amount of contributions received in a fiscal year. Furthermore, e-mail solicitations will be treated the same as mail or telephone solicitations, and registration will be required when a state's residents are solicited via e-mail. Also, organizations that invite further "offline" activity to residents of a certain state via a website must register within that state. (Usry, Jamie). "Charitable Solicitation Regulation for the Nonprofit Sector: Paving the Regulatory Landscape for Future Success." http://www.imakenews. com/cppa/e_article001162331.cfm?x=b6Gdd3k,b30DNQvw,w.

For some states (NY, FL, NJ), simply having a "Donate Now" button on a website, allowing donations by residents of that state, triggers the registration requirement whether or not any other kind of solicitation has happened in that state.

As a way to manage online donations and minimize the number of states in which you must register, your nonprofit might elect to restrict online donations to your home state or selected states through specific donor software programs; or it might choose to accept online contributions solely through a web based nonprofit which is already registered in all states, such as Network for Good.

There are exemptions from registration in most states which can include religious organizations, political organizations, hospitals, educational institutions (higher education), and organizations that raise less than twenty-five thousand dollars a year, organizations for which solicitations are limited to membership fee, bona fide employees or volunteers, or appeals by volunteers on behalf of a named individual. However, check with each state to make sure of the regulations. For instance, the definition of 'religious institution' can vary from state to state.

Professional fundraisers or fundraising firms are defined as having direct solicitation contact with donors, and might have custody or control over funds solicited. Currently 45 states require professional fundraisers/professional solicitors to register. These entities are closely regulated with comprehensive reporting requirements, to protect against any kind of fraud. Generally a bond is required of professional solicitors.

Fundraising consultants assist, advise, and/or manage initiatives for nonprofit organizations, but do not directly solicit from donors. While they are required to register in many states (currently twenty-eight), the reporting requirements are not generally as stringent as for professional solicitors.

Both classes must submit copies of contracts or Agreements for Services. Both fundraising firms and fundraising consultants must register prior to the commencement of services. The fundraising firms should make sure to renew its license prior to the expiration date. Commercial co-venturers are entities that do a sales promotion using the charity's name to sell its products or services, *and* make a gift based on the sales. Registration is required in four states (ME, MA, AL, and HI). Twenty other states regulate the activity but do not require registration.

When must a charity register? Legally and ideally, the organization must register before the first solicitation. While it is a violation of the law to not register in advance of solicitations, states generally support good faith efforts to bring a nonprofit into compliance. If the charity chooses not to register, penalties can vary from a letter of reprimand, to loss of right to solicit in the state, to civil penalties, to fines, to criminal penalties/felony charges, to potential jail time.

The process to register is time consuming. Depending on the state, it can also be complicated. It is currently estimated that registration and annual report processes will take at least four to five weeks of full-time staff. In an effort to streamline the process over so many participating states, NASCO and NAAG developed the Unified Registration Statement as part of the Multi-State Filing Project. The website http://www.multistatefiling.org/c_statement.htm also includes a list of additional documentation required by each state that accepts the URS. However, while many states (not all) accept the URS, they also might require a state-specific form. In many cases, this state form is less complex, and the URS might be unnecessary. Current total registration fees will vary depending on the states where registration is required. Some states are zero; some states are several hundred dollars. Renewal fees tend to be lower. There are firms that can handle the registration process for you.

The first step is to assess the donor database by state. List the states from which donations are being solicited. How many prospects are being solicited? How (direct mail, online)? What is the total return (level of gifts) from each state?

Using http://www.multistatefiling.org as a source, access the specific documents for each state on your solicitation list through the appropriate state agency of the states that accept the URS. Forms from the states that do not use the URS can be accessed through the state attorney general or secretary of state websites.

List the registration documents required and the initial registration fees. List the annual report documentation and fees required. If the organization is not receiving sufficient contributions to make registration in that state make sense, the organization might want to consider ceasing solicitations in that state. Register effectively, and make sure there is a return on the investment.

Collect all of the documentation that will be required for various states. (Might include but might not be limited to: articles of incorporation; current bylaws; board of directors; IRS Form 990; IRS letter of determination; most recent audit; state forms if required in addition to URS; fundraising contracts; certificate of incorporation; completed URS.)

Note the applications that require notarized signatures. Note the dates required for initial submission as well as annual reports. Make sure get these dates on a calendar, and follow the calendar. There is a lot of photocopying involved. Submit your original registration on time, with a complete set of required documents. Some states accept submissions online, some require surface mail. Colorado will only accept submissions online. Your organization must issue checks for each fee.

Register in your organization's home state first. After the initial submission for registration, you will often be asked for more information, clarification, or additional fees. Some states communicate by email, most by surface mail. As a caveat, the requirements are generally not appealable.

Depending on the number of states involved, you might or might not want to handle the registration and renewal processes in-house. There are third party providers of these services. The registration fees will be the same, and the checks for fees to states will be issued by the nonprofit. Get an estimate from the third party providers for their services and assess if it is cost

Some Resources to Help:
Affinity Fundraising Registration: http://fundraisingregistration.com
Clearly Compliant: http://www.clearlycompliant.com
Copilevitz & Cantor, LLP: http://www.copilevitz-canter.com
Labyrinth, Inc.: http://www.labyrinthinc.com
Montgomery, McCracken, Walker & Rhoads, LLP: http://www.mmwr.com
Perlman & Perlman, LLP: http://www.perlmanandperlman.com
Webster, Chamberlain & Bean, LLP: http://www.wc-b.com

practical tip

effective to retain outside services or if it would be more cost effective to commit internal staff time. If you are using internal staff, remember to factor in the time to learn the system and keep up with changes in requirements, staff turnover, and internal ability to meet annual deadlines on a timely basis. Whether you handle registration internally or externally, you will have to collect and submit the updated documents required by states for annual reports on a timely basis to ensure compliance with filing dates. Filing late can incur fines, in some cases up to $1,000 a day. Most states are willing to grant reasonable extensions on deadlines.

According to The Giving Institute, charitable giving totaled $303.75 billion in 2009. Your Nonprofit is responsible for not just 'doing good,' but 'doing good well' with your donors' investments. Compliance with state registration laws helps you ensure that actuality. State charitable registration is also the unavoidable reality.

 Connect with Helen at http://charitychannel.com/cc/helen-arnold

No More Playing Superman

By Terrie Temkin, Ph.D.

Too many organizations seem to think they have to play Superman and single-handedly take on the responsibility for saving the world—at least their little corner of it as defined by their mission. Folks, Superman was a comic strip character! Jerry Siegel, his creator endowed him with powers that don't exist in real life. We are setting ourselves and our communities up for failure if we think we can cure the world's problems on our own. However, that doesn't mean that Superman's accomplishments aren't achievable if we work together, making liberal use of the intellectual capital, resources and skills that exist outside our own four walls.

The biggest challenge I believe we face to doing this successfully is our deeply-ingrained belief in the value of competition. It is the value that causes the number of nonprofits in the U.S. to grow by 175 each business day or one every two to three minutes. Such a number signifies that a lot of people believe they can solve our community's problems more effectively than those that have come before them. Yet, how many programs geared to mentoring children do we really need in a community?

The result is an "us against them" attitude that is magnified by the belief that resources are limited—e.g., there are only so many major donors, so many big names to attract to the board or so many column inches the local paper will devote to nonprofits in the community. Therefore, these limited resources must be claimed first. This only deepens the feelings of competition.

I believe our future lies in learning to work together, rather than as siloed, competitive entities. There is no single or easy way to accomplish such a seismic culture shift, especially if people dig in their heels, intent on protecting their turf. But, if your board is committed to the concept of true collaboration, its directives can facilitate important change. Here are some techniques that can speed the process.

Start with Vision

Begin with affirming the organization's vision for the community. Note that I said "community." The general public is not interested that your organization strives to be the biggest, best funded or most visible. It is essential that everyone have a similar picture in their mind of how the community will be different—better, stronger, healthier—as a result of your organization's efforts. Without this, it is difficult to determine who and how others can best help you achieve your goals, or even how you will prioritize your goals.

If your organization does not currently have a community-focused vision, one simple way to accomplish this is to ask board members and staff to complete the phrase, "As a result of our work, the _____ in our community will _____." Have them fill in the blanks as many times as they can, considering the effect on clients, families, politicians, businesses, funders, police, educators, media, and so on. A limited number of significant outcomes will pop up repeatedly, providing the desired picture for the community. Then it's merely a matter of distilling the ideas into a statement.

Turn Vision into Reality

Ask the board and each department to consider its role in turning the vision into reality. The following questions will guide this process:

- ◆ For what steps must each be responsible if the vision is to be actualized?

- ◆ How will they prioritize these steps?

- ◆ What resources—monetary, human, physical, etc.—will they require to accomplish each step?

- ◆ Which of these assets are already on hand?

- ◆ Which must be obtained elsewhere?

- ◆ How will they know they've achieved each step?

- ◆ What conditions will the board and each department have to meet as they move through the process?

- ◆ What obstacles will require a workaround?

- ◆ What strengths can be built upon?

◆ What assets exist within the organization that can be shared with others outside the organization? After all, the intent of this article is to generate more collaboration and that means everything can't just be about benefiting your organization, but rather must embrace the idea of benefiting the community as a whole.

Once these questions are answered, everyone within the organization will have a better idea of what realistically can be done internally with the current resources. Such an exercise also clarifies what is still needed from the greater community in order for each of the organizations to accomplish their goals.

Determine who/what organizations share your vision and might be able to help you move the community forward. Consider other nonprofit organizations, for-profit organizations, government agencies, educational institutions, religious institutions, researchers, capacity builders, donors, clients, entrepreneurs, people of all ages, and so on. One of the easiest ways to do this is to plug the strategic intents from your vision statement into a search engine along with the type of organizations you've identified above and see what specific names come up.

Don't forget to consider virtual partnerships. They will become increasingly valuable as our communities continue to expand globally and the technology allows us to do even more. Already, the availability of the following types of services provides no-cost or reasonably-priced access to people all over the world. (Note: These are merely some of the more well-known services and are not offered as either a complete or endorsed list.)

◆ Conference calling—e.g., FreeConference.com; InstantConference.com

◆ Video calling—e.g., Skype; ooVoo

◆ Web-conferencing—e.g., GotoMeetings; SharePlus (available through many of the conference calling services for a small fee)

◆ E-governance—e.g., BoardEffect; Huddle

◆ Document sharing—e.g., Google Docs; Microsoft Office Live

◆ Shared calendars—e.g., Google Calendar; Huddle

◆ Email—e.g., gmail; hotmail

◆ Schedule meetings—whenisgood.net; needtomeet.com

Techniques to Work Synergistically

Establish how you can work synergistically with those you've identified so that everyone's needs are met while each is positively impacting the community. You might start by bringing the different groups together and using a technique designed for large groups to get at key issues and the means for dealing with those issues. Some of these include:

◆ World Café

◆ Open Space

◆ Future Search

◆ Appreciative Inquiry

◆ Mind Mapping

◆ Whole Scale Change

You could also use Community Puzzle, a product available through Trainers Warehouse or www.CommunityPuzzle.com that helps people see the interlocking relationships that exist. One way of using this is to have each individual or organization draw what it brings to the table on a puzzle piece. The pieces can be then be put together in any order to represent the process the group will take to achieve the vision

Encourage questions. Expect to share the power for decision-making. Especially important is being transparent in all you do.

Conclusion

The relationships you form might be a short or very long-lived depending on the environment and community expectations. Essential in each case, though, is rapid response and fluidity. You can't afford to get caught up maintaining what constitutes your organization today, because tomorrow its boundaries might necessarily look very different. In fact, there are some who project that nonprofit organizations as we know them will not even exist in as soon as ten years. While your organization might not be faster than a speeding bullet or able to leap tall buildings in a single bound, by working collaboratively and flexibly with all possible entities, it will be able to successfully meet the challenges of the future.

 Connect with Terrie at http://charitychannel.com/cc/terrie-temkin

Appendices

Appendix A—Editorial Advisory Panel

Leo Arnoult, CFRE, M.A.

Leo Arnoult established Arnoult & Associates Inc. to help nonprofit organizations strengthen their development programs. He was the founding President of the Memphis chapter of the Association of Fundraising Professionals (AFP), and has served on its national board of directors. He currently serves on the board of the Giving Institute, formerly the American Association of Fund Raising Counsel (AAFRC) and is past Chair of the Giving USA Foundation, which publishes Giving USA, the annual report on charitable giving and philanthropic trends.

 Connect with Leo at http://charitychannel.com/cc/leo-arnoult

Bob Carter, CFRE

Bob is Principal at at the firm Of Counsel Philanthropy and serves as Senior Advisor to Omnicom NPG and Changing Our World. Previously he enjoyed a twenty-six year career with Ketchum Fundraising and served for fifteen years as president of the company. He has significant expertise in national and international fundraising with a broad range of services provided to such clients. His volunteer service as board member and chair of numerous not for profit boards lends firsthand experience to his governance counsel. Bob served a three-year term as an Educational Partner on the Industry Advisory Council for the Council for Advancement and Support of Education (CASE). Additionally, he was appointed to the Association of Fundraising Professionals (AFP) International Board of Directors Executive Committee, Vice Chairman External affairs and also served as first chair of their Industry Partners Council. He is board Chair-Elect of AFP International, the National Aquarium and now chairs the Mote Marine

Laboratory board. He is a current board member of The Center for Philanthropy at Indiana University and past trustee of numerous charitable and educational organizations. He is a frequent lecturer and presenter throughout the nonprofit sector. Bob is a graduate of the Johns Hopkins University.

 Connect with Bob at http://charitychannel.com/cc/bob-carter

Alice Collier Cochran, M.Ed.

Alice is the author of *Roberta's Rules of Order* and principal of Fast Forward Facilitation. She is an experienced nonprofit governance consultant, facilitator and workshop leader. She is a Faculty Fellow in the Institute for Leadership Studies and adjunct faculty of the School of Business and Leadership at Dominican University in San Rafael, California. She is also affiliated with the Center for Volunteer and Nonprofit Leadership in Marin County, CA and the Interaction Institute for Social Change in Boston, MA.

 Connect with Alice at http://charitychannel.com/cc/alice-cochran

Nathan Garber

Nathan Garber has distinguished himself for thirty years as an innovative leader in the nonprofit sector, serving as executive director, board member, and fundraiser for a number of internationally recognized organizations. In recent years, he has been a national consultant and trainer. He also served as the founding editor of CharityChannel's *Nonprofit Boards and Governance Review.* Visit his website at http://garberconsulting.com.

 Connect with Nathan at http://charitychannel.com/cc/nathan-garber

Jane Garthson

Jane has provides governance, ethics, and strategic planning consulting services through the Garthson Leadership Centre. She is past co-editor of *Nonprofit Boards and Governance Review* for CharityChannel; Contributing Editor, Governance, of *Canadian Fundraiser and Philanthropy*; author of the monthly ethics column for Charity Village; past chair, founder and board member of the Ethics Practitioners Association of Canada; secretary of the Prix Aurora awards; and board member for an all-volunteer annual music festival. She has had a distinguished career in nonprofit leadership and has received extensive recognition for her work throughout Canada and the U.S. Jane also consults to businesses and governments on ethics and social responsibility.

 Connect with Jane at http://charitychannel.com/cc/jane-garthson

William C. McGinly, Ph.D.

Bill is president, CEO of the Association for Healthcare Philanthropy (AHP). He also heads the AHP Foundation and the Hospital Development and Educational Fund of Canada, which conduct annual giving programs and major capital campaigns. He is past chair of the Greater Washington Society of Association Executives (GWSAE), a former member of the boards of directors for Center on Philanthropy at Indiana University Indianapolis and eTapestry, a web-based fundraising software company; and he is an active member of the American Society of Association Executives (ASAE), an I/D/E/A/ Fellow, a Certified Association Executive (CAE).

 Connect with Bill at http://charitychannel.com/cc/bill-mcginley

Andrea McManus, CFRE

Andrea is President of The Development Group, a nonprofit and fund development consultancy, in Calgary, Alberta, Canada. She is a recognized leader in the nonprofit sector throughout Canada and internationally and is currently Chair of the international board of the Association of Fundraising Professionals (AFP). She is the first international chair to hold this position. Andrea is a contributing author to *Management of Nonprofit and Charitable Organizations in Canada,* the first book published on this topic specifically targeted to Canadian nonprofit organizations, and also to *Nonprofit Management 101: A Complete and Practical Guide for Leaders and Professionals.* Andrea is a member of the Imagine Canada Ethical Code Advisory Committee and Technical Issues Working Group for the Canada Revenue Agency. A Master Trainer, Andrea speaks frequently at conferences and workshops in Canada and in 2007 Andrea was the recipient of the Calgary Chapter's Outstanding Fundraising Professional Award.

 Connect with Andrea at http://charitychannel.com/cc/andrea-mcmanus

Michael R. Pender, Jr. CPA, PFS, CFF, CFE

Michael is a partner in the firm Cavanaugh & Co LLP, Certified Public Accountants. He holds the CPA designation in the states of Florida and North Carolina. In addition to the CPA he holds an ACFE designation of a Certified Fraud Examiner (CFE) and AICPA specialty designations as a Personal Financial Specialist (PFS), Certified in Financial Forensics (CFF) and is a member of the AICPA Tax Section. In addition he has served as treasurer of national, state and local charitable organizations for many years. He has been a featured speaker at the FICPA Not-For-Profit Conference on the topics of "Private Foundations" and "Non Profit Governance." He serves as the 2010-11 President of the Florida Institute of CPA's.

 Connect with Michael at http://charitychannel.com/cc/michael-pender

Lisa A. Runquist

Lisa A. Runquist is a principal in the law firm of Runquist & Associates. She has over thirty years of experience representing nonprofit organizations. She is rated AV Preeminent (highest rating given by *Martindale-Hubbell*) and is the first winner of the Outstanding Lawyer Award, a nonprofit lawyers' award presented by ABA Business Law Section, and in 2010 became the first person to win both the Outstanding Lawyer Award, and the Vanguard Award for lifetime achievement. She has authored and edited numerous publications on nonprofit and religious organizations. She is a member and leader on several professional and state Bar committees and organizations.

 Connect with Lisa at http://charitychannel.com/cc/lisa-runquist

Nancy E. Schwartz

Nancy serves as president of Nancy Schwartz & Company (NS&C), designs and implements marketing and communications programs to help nonprofit and foundation clients nationwide. Ms. Schwartz shares her expertise in nonprofit marketing and communications by writing and publishing *Getting Attention* (free, bi-monthly e-newsletter designed to help nonprofits succeed through effective marketing) and the Getting Attention blog. Earlier in her career she served as director of marketing at the Foundation Center. She is a frequent conference speaker and lives in the New York metropolitan area.

 Connect with Nancy http://charitychannel.com/cc/nancy-schwartz

Terrie Temkin, Ph.D.

Dr. Temkin is a thought leader in the areas of governance, board development and planning. She is an award-winning speaker and a sought-after group facilitator who, as one meeting planner said, "serves steak with her sizzle." Terrie authors the biweekly "On Nonprofits" column, which appeared in the *Miami Herald* for five years and is now published by *Philanthropy Journal.* She has written four books, has chapters in three others and her articles are found in nonprofit publications around the world. She is past co-editor of CharityChannel's *Nonprofit Boards and Governance Review,* teaches governance at Florida Atlantic University and is a Principal with Core Strategies for Nonprofits Inc.

 Connect with Terrie at http://charitychannel.com/cc/terrie-temkin

Gail Vertz

Gail Vertz has over twenty years experience in the grants industry. She is the Chief Executive Officer of Grant Professionals Association (GPA, formerly AAGP). GPA is a national organization that specializes in enhancing the role of individuals in the grants profession. Currently, over

4,600 persons have joined and they have forty-four active chapters. She has served as the executive director of a consulting firm, director of grants for a local United Way, business manager of a local health department and as a grants manager for the Area Agency on Aging.

 Connect with Gail at http://charitychannel.com/cc/gail-vertz

Mark B. Weinberg

Mark founded and manages the Tax Exempt Organizations Practice Group, and co-manages the Estate Planning and Administration Practice Group within the firm Weinberg & Jacobs, LLC. He served for over six years with the Chief Counsel's Office of the Internal Revenue Service. There he was responsible for matters concerning nonprofit organizations, charitable giving and estate and gift tax issues. Mr. Weinberg represents a wide variety of clients including public charities, private foundations, advocacy groups, national trade and professional associations, and social clubs.

 Connect with Mark at http://charitychannel.com/cc/mark-weinberg

Michael Wells, GPC, CFRE

Michael is owner of the grantwriting firm Grants Northwest (www.grantsnorthwest.com), and has been consulting since 1987 helping dozens of nonprofit organizations to raise over $100 million. Michael has a Masters degree in Humanities and teaches Grantwriting at Portland State University. He is a past editor of the *Grants and Foundation Review,* a past board member of the Grant Professionals Association (GPA) and the Grant Professionals Certification Institute (GPCI), and author of the *Grantwriting Beyond the Basics* series: *Proven Strategies Professionals Use to Make Their Proposals Work; Understanding Nonprofit Finances; and Successful Program Evaluation.*

 Connect with Michael at http://charitychannel.com/cc/michael-wells

Barnaby W. Zall

Barnaby is Of Counsel to the firm Weinberg & Jacobs, LLC. He practices tax-exempt organization law, constitutional and statutory litigation (including drafting and defending ballot initiatives), and commercial law. He is rated "AV" by the *Martindale-Hubbell* legal rating service—the highest possible rating. Mr. Zall had been chief executive officer and principal government relations professional for a variety of nonprofit organizations involved in community development and legislative action. He was a consultant to the National Commission on Neighborhoods.

 Connect with Barnaby at http://charitychannel.com/cc/barnaby-zall

Appendix B—Contributors

Helen B. Arnold, CFRE

Helen is President of Arnold Olson Associates, a firm that provides fund development consulting services for nonprofit organizations. Helen has received the Outstanding Professional Fundraiser award from the Eastern Iowa Chapter of the Association of Fundraising Professionals. She currently serves on several national AFP committees. She is also a principal at Clearly Compliant, a company that offers state registration services for nonprofit organizations.

 Connect with Helen at http://charitychannel.com/cc/helen-arnold

Ken Berger

Ken joined Charity Navigator in 2008 after almost thirty years experience working in the charitable nonprofit sector. He has held leadership positions at a variety of human service and health care agencies, both large and small, and has operated programs serving the homeless and the disabled, among many others.

 Connect with Ken at http://charitychannel.com/cc/ken-berger

Teri S. Blandon, CFRE

Teri S. Blandon, CFRE holds a masters degree from the Johns Hopkins University and a bachelor's degree from LeMoyne College. She works for WETA TV/FM where she secures grants, online services and capital needs. She is a member of the Association of Fundraising Professionals and the Grant Professionals Association, and serves on GPA's national board of directors.

 Connect with Teri at http://charitychannel.com/cc/teri-blandon

Jesse Bowen

Jesse is a trainer, speaker and is currently co-owner of JAZ Training and Facilitation. She has over twenty years experience working with and developing people as a counselor, trainer, and volunteer resource manager. She has authored articles on training and development, grief and loss, volunteers, and building a training coalition. Jesse can be contacted through www.jaztraining.ca.

 Connect with Jesse at http://charitychannel.com/cc/jesse-bowen

Steven Bowman

Steven is a director of Conscious-Governance.com online resources, based in Melbourne, Australia. He is sought after by nonprofits globally as an expert adviser on conscious leadership, governance, strategic innovation, and awakening the power of strategic awareness within nonprofit organizations. Steven may be contacted at www.conscious-governance.com, steven@conscious-governance.com.

 Connect with Steven at http://charitychannel.com/cc/steven-bowman

Jana Braswell

Jana has managed initiatives for governmental as well as non-profit organizations. She is currently employed with the Virginia Department of Behavioral Health and Developmental Services coordinating Cross Systems Mapping workshops across Virginia. Previously she worked for the Virginia Department of Criminal Justice Services implementing Evidence-Based Practices. She holds a Masters Degree from Virginia Commonwealth University and an Undergraduate Degree from Antioch College.

 Connect with Jana at http://charitychannel.com/cc/jana-braswell

Heather Burton

Heather Burton, product marketing director for Sage North America's Nonprofit Solutions business, has been involved in the nonprofit sector for more than a decade. Burton currently serves as past board president for the BookSpring organization in Austin, Texas. In her five-year board tenure, Burton has helped manage through a merger, re-branding, and the building of a highly functional and engaged board.

 Connect with Heather at http://charitychannel.com/cc/heather-burton

Linda Gatten Butler, MSW, ACSW, LISW-S

Linda is President of Butler Consulting, serving nonprofits primarily in the Miami Valley of Ohio. She is the founding President of the Miami Valley Ohio Chapter of the Grant Professionals Association and serves on the national board. Her article, "Getting Your Organization Grant Ready," appeared in the *Grant Professionals Association Journal.*

 Connect with Linda at http://charitychannel.com/cc/linda-butler

George Colabella

For more than thirty years, George has worked closely with a number of charitable organizations, both as a development and nonprofit management professional. With graduate degrees in both Psychology and Business Administration, he combines analytic skills with an insight into the special nature of the philanthropic community. He is the author of numerous articles, frequent guest lecturer, and workshop leader. He continues to provide pro bono assistance to select groups and sits on several boards.

 Connect with George at http://charitychannel.com/cc/george-colabella

Marion Conway

Marion's experience includes strategic planning, board development and technology/social media. She is a popular speaker, facilitator and workshop presenter. Marion holds bachelors and masters degrees from New Jersey Institute of Technology. She is an active member of two nonprofit boards. Visit Marion's blog at http://marionconwaynonprofitconsultant.blogspot. com.

 Connect with Marion at http://charitychannel.com/cc/marion-conway

Monique Cuvelier

Monique started building websites back in 1994. She's now CEO of Boston-based e-learning and web development company Talance, Inc. (www.talance.com). Monique frequently talks and writes about the web and technology. Her articles have appeared in Wired News and NTEN. She's the author of a book on Internet research, and has contributed to many other book projects. Monique has also been quoted in *Fast Company* and *The Wall Street Journal.*

 Connect with Monique at http://charitychannel.com/cc/monique-cuvelier

Pamela E. Davis

Pamela is the founder, president and CEO of the member companies of the Nonprofits Insurance Alliance Group. Together these 501(c)(3)tax-exempt insurers provide property/casualty insurance for more than 10,000 nonprofits in twenty-six states and DC. For more information, visit www.insurancefornonprofits.org.

 Connect with Pamela at http://charitychannel.com/cc/pamela-davis

Lynne T. Dean, CFRE

Lynne is Managing Associate of Dean and Associates, a Texas full-service nonprofit consulting company. A graduate of the University of Texas at Austin, she has more than twenty years of experience in nonprofit management, fundraising, and marketing. She has worked with a wide range of local and national nonprofits in Texas and beyond. You can reach her by email at lynne@deanofdevelopment.com.

 Connect with Lynne at http://charitychannel.com/cc/lynne-dean

Amy Eisenstein, MPA, CFRE

Amy is the owner of Tri Point Fundraising a full-service consulting firm for nonprofit organizations. She is the author of *50 Asks in 50 Weeks: A Guide to Better Fundraising for Your Small Development Shop,* a book in the *In the Trenches Series* published by CharityChannel Press. She has a master's degree in public administration and nonprofit management from the NYU and her bachelor's degree from Rutgers University. Amy can be reached through her website at www.tripointfundraising.com.

 Connect with Amy at http://charitychannel.com/cc/amy-eisenstein

Jill Friedman Fixler

Jill Friedman Fixler has over thirty years of experience and is a nationally known leader recognized for her innovative approaches to re-inventing, re-engineering, and re-vitalizing nonprofit and public sector organizations. She is a trainer, facilitator, public speaker, and coach with nonprofits throughout the United States and Canada. Jill has authored two books on volunteer engagement and can be reached through her website at www.JFFixler.com.

 Connect with Jill at http://charitychannel.com/cc/jill-friedman-fixler

John R. Frank, CFRE

John is Founder/President of The Frank Group, a consulting firm that presents a holistic and relational approach to serving non-profit organizations. He has a Doctor of Ministry degree in Leadership in the Emerging Culture and a MA in Philanthropy and Development. He has authored articles on stewardship, development and leadership. He has also authored two books, *The Monthly Partner* and *The Ministry of Development.*

 Connect with Frank http://charitychannel.com/cc/john-frank

Nathan Garber

Nathan Garber has distinguished himself for thirty years as an innovative leader in the nonprofit sector, serving as executive director, board member, and fundraiser for a number of internationally recognized organizations. In recent years, he has been a national consultant and trainer. He also served as the founding editor of CharityChannel's *Nonprofit Boards and Governance Review.* Visit his website at http://garberconsulting.com.

 Connect with Nathan at http://charitychannel.com/cc/nathan-garber

Jane Garthson

Jane provides governance, ethics, social responsibility, strategic planning and community building consulting services through the Garthson Leadership Centre. She is a past editor of *Nonprofit Boards and Governance Review* for CharityChannel. She is author of the monthly ethics column for CharityVillage; and is active with several professional associations. She has been recognized for her work throughout Canada and the U.S.

 Connect with Jane at http://charitychannel.com/cc/jane-garthson

Gayle L. Gifford, ACFRE

President of Cause & Effect Inc., Gayle is a nationally known speaker, columnist and consultant advising nonprofits on organization development, strategy and governance. She is author of many articles and two books, including *How am I doing?* a popular guide to evaluating the nonprofit board. She shares her tools, provocative articles and lessons learned at www.ceffect.com and Twitter @gaylegifford.

 Connect with Gayle at http://charitychannel.com/cc/gayle-gifford

Ernie Ginsler, M.S.W.

Ernie brings over twenty-five years' experience in community development, human services planning, and community capacity building to bear on today's most challenging community issues. He works with community organizations, donors, and governments in such areas as homelessness, hunger, community research, and multi-sector coordination and collaboration, to help bring out the best in community service agencies, local businesses, and government programs.

 Connect with Ernie at http://charitychannel.com/cc/ernie-ginsler

Margaret Guellich, CFRE

Margaret has thirty years of fundraising experience and has been Director, Annual Giving for RFB&D. Previously Margaret led Catholic Relief Services direct marketing $55 million program and its selection as Non-Profit of the Year. She is Executive of the Year 2000 for DC's AFP Chapter In 2001 she was named the Women's Direct Response Group's Woman of the Year and selected as one of the twelve "Most Powerful Women in Direct Marketing." Margaret is an internationally known speaker.

 Connect with Margaret at http://charitychannel.com/cc/margaret-guellich

Ted Hart, ACFRE

Ted is an expert in both online and traditional fundraising. His consulting and speaking skills are sought after internationally on topics related to nonprofit strategy and board/volunteer development both online and offline. He serves as CEO of Hart Philanthropic Services. He was Founder of the ePhilanthropy Foundation and is an author and editor of many articles and books including, *People to People Fundraising: Social Networking* and *Web 2.0 for Charities.* His two new books are: *Internet Management for Nonprofits* and *The Nonprofit Guide to Going Green.*

 Connect with Ted at http://charitychannel.com/cc/ted-hart

Jane Hexter

Jane, President of GrantsChampion, has written more than sixty successful proposals and has raised over $28 million for education institutions and human service agencies throughout the U.S. She served on the National Board of the Grant Professionals Association, was a Subject Matter Expert for the Grant Professionals Certification Institute and has served on peer review panels for New York State and the U.S. Department of Education.

 Connect with Jane at http://charitychannel.com/cc/jane-hexter

Mary Hiland, Ph.D.

Mary Hiland, Ph.D. is an independent nonprofit governance consultant with over thirty-five years experience in the sector, including executive and board service. Mary is a researcher and published author with a Ph.D. focused on nonprofit leadership and governance. She has extensive experience working with boards and executives to build their partnership and maximize the board's value. Contact her at mary@hiland-assoc.com.

 Connect with Mary at http://charitychannel.com/cc/mary-hiland

Tammy Holland

Tammy holds a masters degree in public affairs from the University of Texas and an undergraduate degree in social work. She works at the Texas Youth Commission administering its volunteer services department. She is frequently asked to speak at conferences and share her experience of engaging the community and mobilizing volunteers to achieve organizational success. Contact Tammy at tammyvega1165@gmail.com.

 Connect with Tammy at http://charitychannel.com/cc/tammy-holland

Bonnie Koenig

Bonnie is president of the consulting practice Going International which works with organizations on developing or expanding their international engagement. She is the author of the book *Going Global for the Greater Good: Succeeding as Nonprofit in the International Community*. She can be reached by e-mail at bonnie@goinginternational.com.

 Connect with Bonnie at http://charitychannel.com/cc/bonnie-koenig

Stacy Lewis

Stacy is a partner in Sector Brands, a Denver-based social purpose branding firm that helps organizations leverage the power of branding and marketing to become dynamic forces for social good. She is a twenty-year veteran in the world of marketing, strategic planning, branding and creative program development. Stacy can be reached at stacy@sectorbrands.com.

 Connect with Stacy at http://charitychannel.com/cc/stacy-lewis

Joyce Luhrs

Joyce is president of Luhrs & Associates. She works with nonprofits and businesses to increase their visibility and revenues through creative marketing, targeted public relations campaigns, grants research, proposal development, and written products. She received degrees from Oberlin College and Columbia University. She can be reached at info@luhrsandassociates.com.

 Connect with Joyce at http://charitychannel.com/cc/joyce-luhrs

Linda Lysakowski, ACFRE

Linda, president/CEO of Capital Venture, a fundraising consulting firm, is one of fewer than 100 people world-wide to hold the Advanced Certified Fund Raising Executive distinction. She is an internationally recognized presenter who has trained more than 18,000 professionals in all aspects of development. Among her books are: *The Development Plan, Recruiting and Training*

Fundraising Volunteers, Fundraising as a Career: What, Are You Crazy?, Capital Campaigns: Everything You Need to Know and others. Contact her at www.cvfundraising.com.

 Connect with Linda at http://charitychannel.com/cc/linda-lysakowski

Stephen C. Nill, J.D., GPC

Stephen is the founder and CEO of CharityChannel, established in 1992 as a community of nonprofit sector professionals who work together to advance philanthropy. He also founded CharityChannel Press, the publishing arm of CharityChannel and the publisher of the *In the Trenches*™ series of books, of which this book is a part. He is a practicing attorney with thirty years experience advising nonprofit organizations and educational institutions. He has also served as chief development officer of a large west coast university, as CEO of a large healthcare foundation, as senior vice president of a west coast nonprofit hospital chain, and as the co-founder and development director of a thriving parachial school.

 Connect with Stephen at http://charitychannel.com/cc/stephen-nill

Michael J. Nizankiewicz, Ph.D., CAE

Mike has over thirty-eight years of association executive leadership and organization development experience. He is a principal of Association Transition Management and an affiliated consultant with Transition Management Consulting. He received his Ph.D. in business management from LaSalle University, his Master of Arts degree in voluntary agency management from Central Michigan University, and his Bachelor of Arts degree from Assumption College.

 Connect with Mike at http://charitychannel.com/cc/mike-nizankiewicz

Caroline Oliver

Caroline has over thirty years experience working with boards and is a highly trained specialists in the Policy Governance approach to purposeful, effective and ethical board work. She is Managing Editor of the Jossey Bass journal *Board Leadership* as well as author of three books and founder and Chair of the International Policy Governance Association. Further background information about Caroline and Policy Governance can be found at www.goodtogovern.com.

 Connect with Caroline at http://charitychannel.com/cc/caroline-oliver

Norman Olshansky

Norman is president and CEO of the Van Wezel Foundation. He has over forty years experience as a leader, executive and consultant with nonprofit organizations throughout the United States, Canada and Israel. He owned and was the President of NFP Consulting Resources for sixteen years and is an author, lecturer and workshop presenter on topics of interest to the nonprofit sector. Earlier in his career he was a VISTA Volunteer, directed social service agencies and was a Jewish communal professional. Additional articles by Norman can be found at http://nfpconsulting.blogspot.com.

 Connect with Norman at http://charitychannel.com/cc/norman-olshansky

Robert M. Penna

Robert holds a Ph.D. from Boston University. After serving on the staff of the New York State Senate, he joined the Rensselaerville Institute as a senior consultant. He designed the prototype for the United Nations' results reporting system, and has written numerous articles on local government and nonprofit performance. He is the author of *Outcome Frameworks,* and of *The Nonprofit Outcomes Toolbox.* He also serves on the advisory board of Charity Navigator.

 Connect with Robert at http://charitychannel.com/cc/robert-penna

Charles J. Reynolds

Charles J. Reynolds, A.B., M.A., has been responsible for raising millions of dollars, serving as President of a United Way and Director of Planned Giving and Major Gifts at Marywood University. He was recognized as "Outstanding Fundraising Executive of the Year" and completed the National AFP Faculty Training Academy. He has additional training at the Executive Management Program, Harvard University, and the Kellogg Graduate School of Management Program, Northwestern University.

 Connect with Charles at http://charitychannel.com/cc/charles-reynolds

Andy Robinson

Andy Robinson (www.andyrobinsononline.com) has provided training and consulting to nonprofits in forty-seven states and across Canada. He specializes in the needs of grassroots organizations working for human rights, social justice, environmental conservation, and community development. Andy is the author of four books, including *Big Gifts for Small Groups.*

 Connect with Andy at http://charitychannel.com/cc/andy-robinson

Lisa Kay Schweyer

Lisa Kay earned her Bachelor's degree in Political Science from Indiana University of Pennsylvania and Master of Public Management degree from Carnegie Mellon University. With over twenty years of experience, her career includes starting/revitalizing programs and fundraising. Lisa Kay consults and teaches nonprofit management, governance, volunteerism and marketing. She also volunteers with the Pennsylvania Association of NonProfit Organizations. Contact: LKSchweyer@gmail.com.

 Connect with Lisa Kay at http://charitychannel.com/cc/lisa-kay-schweyer

Patricia A. Smith

Patricia is president of Management Strategies. She has a Masters Degree in Community Services Administration from Alfred University. In her consulting capacity, she has served as interim director of six different nonprofit organizations, helping them through the transition and facilitating the hiring of a new director. She has extensive voluntary board service with both local and state organizations. She provides board training, strategic planning facilitation and organizational development consulting. Visit Pat's blog at www.management-strategies.net.

 Connect with Patricia at http://charitychannel.com/cc/patricia-smith

Beth Steinhorn

Beth has twenty-five years' experience as a consultant, lecturer, executive, marketing director, trainer, evaluator, and program director. Beth has also edited and published many articles and books, including co-authoring *Boomer Volunteer Engagement: Facilitator's Tool Kit.* As a Senior Strategist with JFFixler Group, Beth specializes in training, volunteer engagement, marketing, communications, and research and can be reached through her website at www.JFFixler.com.

 Connect with Beth at http://charitychannel.com/cc/beth-steinhorn

Terrie Temkin, Ph.D.

Dr. Temkin is a thought leader in the areas of governance, board development and planning. he is an award-winning speaker and a sought-after group facilitator who, as one meeting planner said, "serves steak with her sizzle." Terrie authors the biweekly "On Nonprofits" column, which appeared in the *Miami Herald* for five years and is now published by *Philanthropy Journal.* She has written four books, has chapters in three others and her articles are found in nonprofit publications around the world. She is a past co-editor of CharityChannel's *Nonprofit Boards and Governance Review,* teaches governance at Florida Atlantic University and is a Principal with Core Strategies for Nonprofits Inc.

 Connect with Terrie at http://charitychannel.com/cc/terrie-temkin

Andrew Urban

Andrew has spent more than eleven years working directly with nonprofit organizations. Andrew currently works as Head of Sales and Business Development for FirstGiving. Additionally, he ran his own private nonprofit consultancy, Your Mission, and worked for Serenic Software, Kintera and Convio. His first book was published in May 2010 entitled *The Nonprofit Buyer: Strategies for Success from a Nonprofit Technology Sales Veteran.* He has an undergraduate degree from Sewanee: The University of the South.

 Connect with Andrew at http://charitychannel.com/cc/andrew-urban

Shelley Uva

Shelley has more than thirty years experience in development and communications. She is a contributor to CharityChannel's *Grants and Foundations Review* since 2002, co-author of *The United States in the Making,* and author of two short story collections: *At the Lost and Found* and *Time Flies.* She is a graduate of Boston University (B.A.) and New York University (M.A.).

 Connect with Shelley at http://charitychannel.com/cc/shelley-uva

Reid A. Zimmerman, Ph.D., CFRE

Reid has thirty years of nonprofit experience as an executive director, fundraiser, board member, strategist, coach and evaluator. He teaches Nonprofit Leadership/Management in the graduate schools of Hamline, Capella and St. Thomas Universities. Since 1987 RAZimmerman Consulting has worked with thousands of nonprofit leaders and organizations. Dr. Zimmerman's research focuses on nonprofit organizational effectiveness. Contact Reid at zimmerm@ecenet.com or 320-358-3583.

 Connect with Reid at http://charitychannel.com/cc/reid-zimmerman

Appendix C—About CharityChannel

Y*OU and Your Nonprofit* was conceived, written and edited by leading third-sector experts whose collaboration was sparked through CharityChannel. If you aren't yet familiar with CharityChannel, we invite you to visit http://charitychannel.com.

Now in its twentieth year, CharityChannel is the world's oldest and largest online nonprofit sector professional community, and is a leading force for advancing philanthropy by promoting the professional competency of, and fostering a professional network to support, tens of thousands of nonprofit practitioners.

This book is just one example of CharityChannel colleagues working together to advance philanthropy. Over the years, CharityChannel members have contributed thousands of peer-reviewed articles, posted tens of thousands of messages to its professional forums, taught nearly two hundred online webinars, attended the annual conference (the CharityChannel Summit), and collaborated with each other in countless other ways.

Perhaps most gratifying is watching as "newbies" are brought along over the years by their more experienced colleagues, eventually becoming the seasoned professionals who are now giving back by writing articles, writing books for CharityChannel Press, teaching CharityUniversity webinars, leading CharityChannel Summit sessions, and being active with CharityChannel Professional Groups.

In celebration of its twentieth year, CharityChannel has just rolled out its new state-of-the-art website, which incorporates the technologies found in LinkedIn, Facebook, Twitter, and YouTube—and adds some things not found even on these sites.

Through CharityChannel, you may connect to thousands of nonprofit colleagues who face the same challenges you do. Here are just some of the ways:

◆ Invite or accept invitations from colleagues to connect with each other's Profile pages. Once connected, a world of possibilities open up as it becomes easy to engage in professional discussions, collaboration, document sharing, video sharing, event scheduling and notifications, blogging, and much more.

◆ Join a CharityChannel Professional Group to advance your professional competence or even just to receive help and support from your colleagues on the state-of-the-art discussion forums. Professional Groups are the centerpiece of participation on CharityChannel, enabling you to connect with colleagues who share a professional interest in the subject matter of the Group.

◆ Create and oversee a professional group of your own, whether it's for any CharityChannel Member or Associate, or just for those you invite.

◆ Search out colleagues in your local area, or who work in your particular professional niche, and send a private message.

◆ Start a professional blog.

◆ Attend a CharityChannel Summit™, our annual conference.

◆ Teach a CharityUniversity 90-minute webinar.

◆ Write an article.

◆ Write a book for CharityChannel Press.

Index

Just Released!

FUNDRAI$ING
as a Career

What, Are You Crazy?

www.charitychannel.com

Just Released!

50 A$KS
in 50 Weeks

A Guide to Better Fundraising for Your Small Development Shop

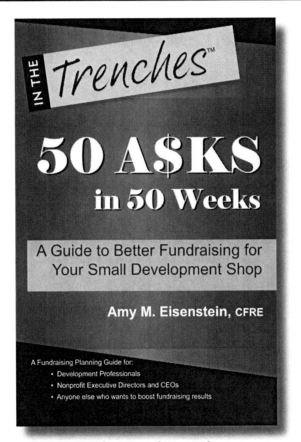

www.charitychannel.com

CharityChannel
P R E S S

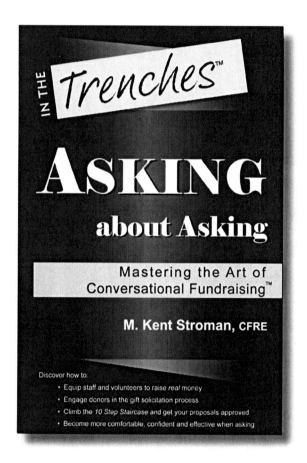

CPSIA information can be obtained at www.ICGtesting.com
Printed in the USA
BVOW022057110213
312991BV00005B/73/P